Operation Phoenix

Tony Stuckless
Many thanks for all your help

Allen Bennie,

Operation Phoenix

Acknowledgements

I have always been annoyed by those authors who listed pages and pages of names in their acknowledgements until I tried my own. I have been working on this novel for nearly 20 years. During that learning process there were so many who appeared at just the right time to answer a critical question that was blocking further progress. I am sure I would miss some very important ones, and the list would make a book unto itself.

How much can be attributed to my parents and neighbours of the dirty '30s and the experience of living this type of adversity? That type of experience is not available to most people today. How about my economics/money and banking professors at University? The various brilliant CEOs I worked under and with? How should I credit the two English language Soviet newspapers I was subscribing to when the USSR went down in 1990? While I had studied how societies went down going back to the Roman Empire, the question of how modern technology would affect the downfall of a society was very much on my mind.

Then the senior and exotic bankers who contributed to my knowledge as I went about my work as a consultant to these leading edge banks. Not to mention the many librarians, websites, and many others who assisted mostly for free in the research process.

Now we come to the "learning to write" process itself and that list is also a very long one. The numbers of editors and friends who read early versions and commented thoughtfully will be appreciated forever. I am sure that nearly 200 percent of the positive things about the manuscript were plagiarized from their comments. Then there was the writers club I joined briefly – awesome people.

Now the people who are giving me marketing ideas are another critical link in the chain.

Lastly are the people who I bumped into in the real and

Operation Phoenix

historical world. Nearly every scene has some relationship with the real world. For instance Patti, was modelled on a KGB Special Ops woman who was killed in January 2008 in a freak accident. (SEALs don't or didn't have female ops.) The kidnapping was based on a Brazilian kidnapping. The dog eating on a dead human came from war torn Africa.

I must specifically mention to two people; Joerg Schroeder who provided many details and Linda Traynham who had so many wonderful ideas. Without ALL of the above people I would be still stuck on some sidetrack. Thank you all humbly.

Allen Currie

Operation Phoenix

For
Kim and Marc – The best things to ever happen to me.

Operation Phoenix

Chapter one
Tuesday 14th February -- Day one

The voice on the phone was unusually abrupt.

"Gary, it's Nils."

Nils was Nils Jenson, SVP, Treasurer, and number four man at Foremost American Bank, a bank with a reputation as being the most advanced bank on the street. One reason was their uncanny ability to forecast major upcoming events and to position themselves to be in the right place at the right time, equipped to take advantage of events as they occurred. Very good readers of chicken entrails was the summation on the street.

"Oh hi. What's up?"

"Can you make a meeting here at 2:30?"

"Yes I suppose so. What's it about?"

"I don't want to discuss it on the phone."

Gary tried to elicit a bit more information so he wouldn't look totally stupid walking into a meeting blind. "Who's going to be there? Just you?"

"We'll talk about that when you get down here."

"Okay, see you at 2:30."

Nils was always cautious, almost paranoid, about discussing confidential information on the phone. That was reasonable with billions of dollars and possibly the future of the bank at stake. Gary's blood began to get electric. New and difficult problems in pretty much any field fascinated him almost to the point of obsession until he controlled them. He viewed new information, situations and much of life as an adventure to be approached with excitement.

Why do mountaineers climb ever more difficult mountains? There isn't usually a lot of gold at the end of that particular rainbow. How much fame did the fifth person to climb Mount Everest gain? Yet every person starting that climb knew there was better than a 50/50 chance that a small miscalculation or an act of God would send them a long way down. There was an excitement of danger and anticipation that stirred his blood.

Methinks thou hast sacrificed another chicken. Looks like a strategy session and marching orders for a big change. They need a very special person to do whatever they are going to do. And I think I may have an idea of the direction you are marching in.

Gary ran a one man 'head hunting' agency, specializing in finding and recruiting one of a kind executives. The kind where maybe half a dozen people in the world had the qualifications to do the job. About half his business was with the world's most advanced financial institutions. The other half was extremely varied. He had just deposited a fat check from a typical 'other' search.

A new, rich beryllium deposit had been discovered, now one of six in the world. Lighter than aluminum, six times stronger than steel, with extremely good electrical and metal fatigue properties, it was a wonder metal, darling of the defence and aerospace industries. Beryllium was very benign in its finished form, but a brief exposure to its dust during the refining

Operation Phoenix

process lowered life expectancy significantly.

With only five producing mines in the world there were probably about ten or twenty people in a world population of six billion with experience in designing a safe production line. How do you find this person among six billion people? Never mind how do you entice a valuable, highly remunerated and comfortable candidate to even look at a new opportunity? Not that he thought he knew everything there was to know about beryllium mining, but he did know enough to recognize someone who did and not be taken in by a con job.

But, if you passed him on the street you might give him no more than a glance. Six foot, mid 40s, with blond silvery hair, fair complexion and an average build, he would not have impressed you any more than most men his age. It was his eyes that riveted you. Deep blue, they scrutinized, sized up and dissected all in one look.

At 2:15 as Gary turned into Foremost's foyer of the glass and marble monolith representing a banker's view of the latest and coolest in architectural art, a lead gray sky dripped wet snow on to already gray sloppy New York Streets. A worsening recession hung like a pall over the land. Citizens darted for cabs, dived into subway entrances, or simply slogged along in the grey slop in resignation.

Foremost's trading floor was on the 32nd floor. He took the elevator up, all the while trying to brush the wet clots of melting snow from his topcoat and hair. It wouldn't do to meet senior bankers looking like a drowning rat. The elevator deposited him in a hallway facing a wall of thick bullet-proof security glass. Beyond lay the trading reception area.

Shannon, the receptionist, seemed unusually busy. Gary walked over to the security door and waited patiently for her to notice him rather than interrupt the huge volume of calls she

Operation Phoenix

was handling by buzzing her. After an unusually long wait she finally noticed him and released the security lock on the door. The reception area was very properly decorated in banker's muted abstract modern, and the clock on the wall behind her fit. "I'm a few minutes early for a 2:30 with Nils," he told her. Flying fingers doing battle with rows of blinking telephone lights, she still confirmed with a nod and a smile.

As he turned to remove his overshoes and hang his well cut gray tweed topcoat in the courtesy closet Gary thought *That gal sure is good at her job. I've never seen her so busy but she is still on top of it. To generate this number of calls something important must have happened while I was on my way down here. Maybe another big bank has gone under. That would get Foremost's attention fast.* Happiness to a banker is feeding on choice cuts of a competitor's carcass at a deep discount. But you had to move really fast before the other sharks came. He glanced left down the hall towards executive country and Nils' office. Someone shot out of one office and into another in a flash.

Crossing back in front of the reception desk, Gary walked to the bank of floor to ceiling glass windows overlooking the trading floor. The second Tuesday of each month was always an important US Treasury bond auction day. For the bond crew it was the day they put a few dollars sure profit in the pot, buying direct from the treasury and reselling immediately to their clients at a slightly higher price. Tomorrow was too late as prices might move against them overnight. From shortly after 2:00 when the auction results came out they would be focused on selling the inventory they had. Most bond people would be hunched over their phones concentrating on their sales pitch, or if that were their personality and style of selling, leaning back in their chairs joking and cajoling their customers into buying. Tense and important work but they were in control.

Operation Phoenix

Today the body language was all wrong. Today everyone was tense but didn't seem to have a direction. About half were on the phone, a few were just standing staring at the screens, and the rest were moving aimlessly.

On the foreign exchange side of the room normally at this time of day the bulk of the commercial transactions for the day would have been finalized and the trading day would be winding down. The activity would slow to more relaxed kidding around complete with crude jokes. Today everyone was agitated, standing up, sitting down, waving their arms and fists. While Gary watched as one trader actually stood up, hurled his telephone handset into the bank of computer screens in front of him and stalked out.

Gary was turning to go to the courtesy corner sectional couch to think over what he was seeing when tall, blond Nils actually galloped at high speed around the corner. Seeing Gary he slowed to a rapid walk and nonchalantly put his hand in his pocket. Gary was aghast. He had never even heard of a senior banker running except for exercise. Their image required they always be in dignified control. Running was out of control.

While still approaching Nils started speaking hurriedly emphasizing a slight European accent. "I'm sorry. I tried to call you to cancel our appointment. The treasury auction was a failed auction. There weren't enough bids to cover the bonds offered. Everybody went nuts. The markets are jumping out a window."

Gary felt an electric charge run through his body. His heart rate went up. He tried to keep his voice and manner measured as banker 'in control' demanded. What he had been seeing made sense now. He had recognized and studied this problem for years. The world had just decided that 'the full faith and credit' of the US was worth about as much hot air as it took to say it, and they refused to lend more. Accordingly, the US

Operation Phoenix

dollar was falling off its pedestal. There is nothing quite as despicable as a fallen angel. If a top athlete is caught cheating on his wife his whole reputation will suffer. Yet he is still a top athlete and his moral standards have nothing to do with his athletic ability. Judging from Foremost's track record and his conversations with Nils they might even have been preparing for this eventuality.

"So you were probably a bit late with your forward looking plans this time. How bad is the currency crisis?"

Nils took his hand out of his pocket and gestured, all the while doing a small dance, picking up his foot and taking a very small step in preparation for leaving, again and again.

"Yeah, we were finally coming around to your scenario. No one, you or I or us together as a government can borrow forever without paying back someday. People are lending money, not giving it. Confidence in the dollar is pretty scarce right now. Anyone with dollars or treasuries makes a long face today. Derivatives are killing us. Gold jumped ten percent in as many minutes. The dollar is falling hard against every major currency. The world financial system is at risk." Nils continued his 'gotta leave in a hurry' dance.

"You have to be in a near panic mode. I'll call you in a week or two when we have a better idea how this will shake out."

Nils began to turn. "Yeah, I gotta save what I can." He was at a full run before "See you later" got out

"Yeah, later," Gary mumbled at Nils rapidly disappearing back. While Foremost had not completed their preparations they were further along than most who had not even thought of this possibility. The world and its rules had just changed dramatically. Most would not break free from the world and rules they currently knew and understood. At least Foremost

Operation Phoenix

should be reacting to the new rules and conditions rather than the old order which didn't apply any more. Whether this would save them was very much in question because a big bank is not something you turn around on a dime.

The world is well into the Age of Aquarius and Aquarius is all about change. Not that all change is viewed as beneficial. With the advent of the computer chip change can take place at the click of a mouse. Change has also become very impersonal. In WWI one man shooting at another was very personal. Today we drop smart bombs from ten miles up, or nukes from space, and we can drop them down a stovepipe. In the 60 seconds after the auction failure was announced, billions and trillions of dollars whooshed around the globe at the speed of light as traders tried to get out of losing positions.

As he hurried over to borrow a phone book from Shannon, Gary recalled a luncheon he'd had with Nils. Gary liked Nils and lunched with him about once a month. Invariably the conversation turned to the long and short term forces driving the markets. They often lunched at Bob's Steak House because the steaks were excellent and the plush booths muted conversation making it easier to discuss matters which bordered on confidential. The rosewood walls were decorated with shelf after shelf of old books encouraging quiet and serious conversation.

This particular day the discussion had turned to a newspaper article about federal finances. The annual federal deficit was approaching two trillion dollars, and growing rapidly. The Feds were admitting to a debt of $19.5 trillion, but the auditors were refusing to certify the government financial statements because the statements were entirely misleading. The auditors estimated that the federal government was responsible for debt approaching $50 trillion, which did not include another $40 or many more trillion in other, uncounted obligations, such as pensions, social security, Brady bond guarantees, and so on.

Nils dismissed the whole subject as 'just numbers'.

"Not so," argued Gary. "It is true that people in government, and traders like you, think of dollars as just numbers because you've had to learn how to move billions around unemotionally. The average Joe who actually owns those same dollars gets pretty emotional about them. They may have worked a lifetime for those dollars. People still count emotionally, one, two, three, many. A billion or a trillion is totally incomprehensible to the human mind. Tell me, how many zeros in a trillion?"

"Uh, nine." Nils paused. "No, that is a billion. A trillion has 12 zeros."

Gary shrugged. "See what I mean? A trillion is simply 'many'. Let's see if we can make it more understandable." Gary dug out his credit card sized calculator. Multiplying 60 seconds times 60 minutes an hour, times 24 hours per day, times 365 ¼ days per year, he got just under 31.5 million seconds per year. "If we were to pay off that debt at one dollar a second, we would divide $19.5 trillion by the number of seconds in a year to get how many years it would take to pay it off." Gary pushed equal, and said, "Over six hundred and nineteen thousand years." Even Gary wasn't sure he had got his decimal point right.

"My God. Have human beings even been a species that long?"

"I don't know, but I doubt it." Gary's face was grim. He worked his calculator some more. "That ignores the $136,679 per second interest on the Federal debt. It also ignores state and city debt, corporate debt, and personal debt, each of which runs in the seven to nine trillion range. We've mortgaged our souls financially, environmentally; more ways than I care to count. We are the most indebted nation in human history."

Operation Phoenix

"Twenty trillion dollars here, nine trillion there, pretty soon you're talking serious money," Nils grinned. "Then there's the world oil and other trade based only in dollars, but we won't even go there. And about one and one half quadrillion of highly leveraged and totally artificial derivative products which are actually loans in disguise. Nobody knows for sure. Twenty trillion is only a very small fraction of the total debt outstanding." He paused. "Now that's why I like spending time with you. You know where the mainstream is, but mostly you choose not to be there. You make me think."

"And to save by spending money you don't got ain't so smart either. A trillion here and a trillion there for things like armament to expand the empire or on social security as a political giveaway and pretty soon you're bankrupt too."

Now, with the whole world financial system ready to implode, split seconds mattered. Gary swung into emergency mode to try to survive the events likely to follow. The situation reminded him of an iceberg. Salt water melts the under-water part of an iceberg faster than the air, which might still be freezing. Soon even a breath of breeze or a single wave can inexorably turn the iceberg upside down in a matter of seconds. Now a huge financial 'debtburg' had started rolling. Governments would surely do anything they could to save their power by saving the treasury.

St. Valentine's Day Massacre may no longer mean Al Capone's boys slaughtering the opposition in 1929. Gary made a face and shrugged.

He looked up Premet National Bank, considered the city's premiere bullion dealer, and went back to the corner courtesy phone. Working his way through to Jan Kerr, special accounts officer, he demanded and got an urgent appointment for 3:30. He'd met Jan over a year ago when he'd opened an account for this very circumstance. It helped to have them in a position where, on the books, he had an established relationship. They would have 'known' him for some time, whether they had checked him out or not.

With the appointment secure, he grabbed his topcoat and overshoes and strode quickly to the elevator, which took forever to arrive, and then frustratingly, seemed stop at nearly every one of the 31 floors on its way to the lobby. At Premet, as he threaded his way through the crowd on the main floor, between the circular island for normal deposit and withdrawal banking activities on his left, and the foreign exchange and precious metals counter and offices on his right, he wondered suddenly why bank buildings needed to have such high ceilings. "I suppose it's a money temple, like the old churches. Make the patrons feel insignificant so it's easier to take their money." Gary muttered heretically to himself. It even smelled like money, although he wasn't exactly sure what money smelled like.

The back half of the main floor rotunda was largely occupied by the special accounts department containing reception and secretarial pool, conference rooms and a myriad of smallish dark wood paneled executive offices decorated to cater to high rollers, special customers who didn't even have to wait for an elevator.

It was not yet 2:40 when he arrived at the receptionist's desk. He told the receptionist that he was in the building, should Jan Kerr be available before 3:30. On an impulse that he would come to regret much later, he added that he would be at the gold counter across the way.

He joined a line of four people. It turned out that two were buying and two were selling. Gary had to restrain himself from asking the sellers not to sell, at least right now. The sellers both

Operation Phoenix

looked to be among the newly unemployed. Dejected looking, their coats were designer labels, but a bit tatty. By the time he got to the counter, there were eight people behind him in line. They were all dressed well. Probably all were buyers.

A bright young man served him. He made Gary feel very mature. *Old would be a more accurate word.* Gary told himself wryly. The kid was short, maybe five foot six. It appeared he might still have some growing to do. Gary looked closely to make sure he actually needed to shave. It didn't look like it. Obviously a recent college grad on the fast track, being given a week or two's experience in each department before going on to better things. Even Gary's children looked more mature than this boy.

"Hi," said the young man. "How can I help you?"

"Can I use a credit card to buy gold?" Gary leaned against the counter.

"Certainly, Sir. We treat it like a cash advance. How many ounces would you like, Sir?"

"Six bars, one ounce each. What is your price?" Gary straightened up.

"I have to phone the trading room for that, Sir. The price has been changing a lot in the last hour or so. It was $2,567.50 plus applicable charges."

"What's your spread?" Gary demanded.

"I beg your pardon Sir?" The young man frowned.

"Your spread. The difference between the price you will buy for, and the price you will sell for. It's called a spread. That's how you make a profit. You bought from the guys ahead of me, and even if the price had been the same, you would have sold to me at a higher price." Gary disliked bankers who knew less about their profession than he did.

"Oh. Uh, Four dollars Sir. I'll just go and get a price now,

Operation Phoenix

Sir," and he scurried over to the direct phone line to the trader, because only the gold trader was allowed to set prices. He returned shortly. "$2,579.90, Sir." He raised his eyebrows at Gary in enquiry.

Gary nodded and began to mentally calculate. *$2,579.90, to be safe say $2,600 to include bar and service charges, times ten is $15,600. I can afford more than that.* "Are there any taxes?"

"Not on purchases over $1,000."

"I think I'll take another three ounces," Gary decided. "Three more one ounce bars please."

"I'll have to book it, and get another price Sir," said the clerk as he finished the purchase order, time stamped it, and passed it to Gary to sign, and fill in his personal details including name and address. Gary started filling in the form, and handed over two credit cards. "One card for each purchase," he said.

The teller went back to the phone. He returned looking a bit uncertain. "The price is now $2,584.10, Sir. I'm sorry. The trader says the market has gone up. I double checked for you Sir." The young man chewed on his lip.

Gary's eyes narrowed as the price movement, and its speed provided more confirmation of the conditions in the market. "Fine," he snapped. "Do it."

They finished the paperwork and the clerk handed over the bullion. Gary slipped the bars into his suit coat pocket and then quickly shifted them to various pockets. Half a pound of metal was making his suit look as if he had Billy the Kid's Colt .45 in his pocket. Such a thought might make bankers nervous. He hurried back to the special accounts section. Jan Kerr was just bidding goodbye to her previous client.

As she walked toward him the male in Gary looked her up

Operation Phoenix

and down approvingly, as he had the first time he'd met her. He had seen her again later at the Stamford Centre shopping mall, but she didn't seem to recognize him so he didn't press it. About five foot five, with beautiful medium length auburn hair, she was slim without a hint of being skinny. Probably in her early or mid 30s. Her very appropriate banker's dark business suit hinted at the figure beneath. She walked in a self-confident, but distinctly female manner. *No rings,* Gary noted. *But that doesn't mean much these days. Not stunning in banker's blue, but one very attractive lady.* Gary was divorced, and while he still liked women he had no urgent interest in remarriage. His thoughts returned to the business at hand.

"Hello Mr. Alden." Jan said pleasantly with a smile, as she put out her hand. "Please come in."

Gary noticed the flecks of green in her brown eyes and the light scent of her perfume. Her handshake, smile, and perfume returned his mind to her as a female. *Women have never understood that the handshake was a ritual developed by early men to gauge a potential opponent's physical strength, and to check that he was unarmed,* thought Gary, momentarily annoyed. *Women use it as a touching -- a bonding – which has sexual implications in the male mind.* He shook his head slightly as he followed her into her small mahogany wood-paneled office.

"How may I help you?" Jan began professionally after they were seated.

"During our last meeting, when I opened an account with you, I indicated I was opening it in anticipation of a specific set of market circumstances that now appear to be in progress. I have a substantial position in options to buy gold. I took these positions when gold was $2,100-$2,200 an ounce. A few minutes ago, I purchased a few ounces of bullion at $2,579, and

Operation Phoenix

a few more at $2,584. Gold seems to be running up rather quickly because of today's bond auction failure."

"We don't make speculative loans here Mr. Alden," Jan interrupted him. This was a standard bankers position but Gary had to get her off this train of thought quickly.

"No. No. Please hear me out," Gary leaned forward. "I am not interested in a speculative loan. I intend to convert my market holdings into bullion should gold go over $3,000. Should gold actually run up and should I sell my market holdings, the fastest I can get my funds from the broker is the following day at the earliest. Assuming gold rises rapidly as it is now, if I sell my market holdings today and can only buy tomorrow at a higher price, I'll lose a great deal."

"What precisely are you suggesting?" Jan was willing to listen, but wasn't yet persuaded.

"I'm interested in some sort of an overnight bridge loan. I would like to arrange an agreement whereby my broker, Wilkinson Brothers, will transfer directly to you the day following the sale, the money resulting from the sale of my gold options. Using the bridge loan I would immediately purchase gold bullion, through your gold department, for delivery after you receive the money from Wilkinson. So you see you will be covered twice, once because Wilkinson is committed to send you the money and again because you are holding the gold until you actually get the money. For shuffling a few pieces of paper you get a good rate of interest and all those bar charges and commissions," Gary sat back.

"The bar charges go to another department." Jan frowned slightly and looked down at her notes.

Gary had been a head-hunter to banks for long enough to know the internal politics she was thinking about. Individual bankers asked themselves, how many 'Merit Points' will I

Operation Phoenix

receive towards my bonus for this deal? But whoever initiated the order would receive a good deal of credit for these same charges.

"Ah, but I would be ordering through you and therefore you initiate the order. The charges will probably run between five and ten percent of the total, I would guess between eight and nine percent, not to mention your spread."

"Well," she paused, looked up, and then said slowly, "I have a credit committee meeting shortly and I will present your case. How much are you looking for?"

"I can't give you a specific figure now but it would be several million dollars." Gary said evasively. Then he decided to up the ante a bit.

"You don't seem very positive, Ms. Kerr. Under the circumstances, I will have to approach my regular corporate banker as back-up finance. Of course, that would make it more complex for me, but on the other hand, it will give me more bargaining power as to whom I actually dealt with in the purchase of bullion." That was not as much of a confrontation as it appeared since backup was a normal, common sense business practice, but the threat was real. One banks dollar was the same as any other bank's dollar.

"If you have a problem with time, that long wait through the line at the gold window with all the other people could be very difficult," Jan bargained.

Unlike most folk, who thought the bank had all the power, Gary understood that he was the customer, and in control. Since she could not possibly know how important time was to him he exerted his control, "Yes, that's why the bargaining power I have, in being able to deal with several firms on a large order is important. Besides, if I ordered a large quantity through you personally, would you not handle the order?" Whether she had

Operation Phoenix

consciously thought of it or not, his words and manner had identified him as a 'part of the banking world' person, and while she would likely try some of the usual tricks, she would back off quickly.

"I suppose it would depend on how busy I was," she sniffed.

"Fine. I'll phone you tomorrow morning. Would you advise your secretary to put me through? I won't be able to leave a number. Here's my broker's business card, Vance Paul at Wilkinson, so you can check details with him. Perhaps we should set up a tentative appointment now to be confirmed in our morning call. Depending on the situation we can cover whatever else you might need. I'll call you around ten."

"Okay. I might be able to squeeze you in for a couple of minutes around 1:00."

"Great. We'll pencil that in then. Thank you for seeing me on such short notice. I'll talk to you tomorrow morning," Gary stood, and left.

He came out of the bank into the dreary February day, still in emergency mode, and looked around for a pay phone. *Ah, a hotel – a quieter phone.*

As he hurried over to the hotel, he wondered how hard she would fight for the loan in credit committee. *Some of these bankers seem afraid to go to the bathroom alone.* The deal should easily stand on its own merit, but not if she presented it negatively. She seemed pretty sharp. Maybe this cautious, non-committal façade was her way of coping in the still very macho financial industry. *Still, she gave me an appointment, and if the answer were definitely 'No,' she would have stalled.* He mused

As he entered the hotel he suddenly thought, *you could lead me in here blindfolded, and I would know it was not a bank. Carpeted floors, not hard stone so it sounds different.*

Operation Phoenix

People actually laugh and enjoy themselves in hotels. And hotels definitely have a different smell.

He looked around for the phones. In the centre of the lobby, pacing up and down in a very serious self-conscious manner was a flashily dressed young man with a cell phone. *OK, I see you ordering your pizza.* Gary thought. Then he spotted the pay phones. Off in that corner sat a man in a trench coat and with a battered briefcase. He was hunched over a sheaf of papers he held in his hand. His cell phone was barely visible. *Guess which cell guy is making more money.* Gary thought cynically.

When Gary was away from the office, he refused to be pestered by every Tom, Dick, and Harry, who thought he had something earth shattering to sell. Nor was he interested in talking to somebody who had just found a pimple on his ass. Gary would be damned if he would carry any of the latest show toys. He did keep both a cell phone and a satellite phone in the car, which he seldom used, and then only for outgoing calls.

Gary called his daughter Lynn, who lived in White Plains, and his son Eric who lived in Rye, to arrange a family conference at Lynn's apartment for later that evening. He called his regular commercial banker, Gordon Symes at North Midland Bank in Stamford, arranging for an early breakfast meeting the next day.

Then he rang his broker.

"Vance Paul, Wilkinson."

Gary was never sure why he had selected Vance as a broker. Vance was a small man, and certainly not as knowledgeable as some, but he was so earnest and tried so hard that Gary thought he would rather deal with someone who was definitely on his side rather than 'maybe' being on his side, and had gone with him.

Operation Phoenix

"Vance, it's Gary. I understand, to use the ancient Chinese curse, that the market has become quite exciting." In ancient China an exciting life meant war, and the peasants always suffered during war.

"You can say that again." Vance laughed. "Despite the exchange's safety features, the Dow closed down nearly 1200 points. Bonds, which usually go the other way from the stock market, are down too, way down. Currencies are wild. The dollar is down eight to ten percent across the board. It would be a lot worse except that nobody can figure out where to put their money. Even the Euro is burning. Gold is up. It closed the day here at $2,622.30. It is still rocketing up in the after hours trading."

"Whew." Gary exhaled almost a whistle between his teeth. "I bought a few ounces near what I thought to be the close, and I paid $2,584. Those last seconds before the close must have been brutal for it to go up that fast."

"You said it would. Gold opened this morning at $2,229.80." Gary could hear Vance clicking his computer keys. "That most recent bunch of out of the money gold options you bought a couple of weeks ago for 30 cents?"

"Yeah?"

"They closed at $38.60. That's more than a hundred times your investment right there, and you stand to make more."

Of course Gary was interested in how the market was doing, but he had called primarily to set up the details of his overnight financing. He warned Vance that Jan Kerr and Gordon Symes might be calling, asked him to treat them nicely, and then asked, "Do you foresee any problems or need anything to make this go smoother?" a

"No, It's pretty straightforward. Exactly how many ounces do you control, Gary? It would take me all day to add up

Operation Phoenix

your position."

"514 contracts." Gary said promptly.

"That's 51,400 ounces. Now that gold is over $2,400, you'll be making $51,400 every time gold goes up a dollar," Vance's voice radiated admiration. "That's a home run in anybody's league."

"Yeah, that's about right, and I will also lose $51,400 every time it goes down a dollar." Gary said laconically.

Gary ran for his Metro North train to Stamford Connecticut, up the coast from New York City. The car was half full and the wet slop on people's cuffs smelled of salt and wet cloth. During the 43 minute train ride, Gary relaxed a bit and dropped into his usual way of thinking. *Patience,* he counselled himself. *You've studied the currents and eddies in the river of life and enjoyed the sunshine while waiting for this opportunity to drift by. You have watched quietly from the sidelines long enough. Now is the time for the one intensive effort to pull the opportunity in. This is the key log in the logjam we have to move to make all the rest of the logs flow without more effort. Review your plans to survive and prosper during the downfall of an empire and the social disruption that follows. Empires rise and fall. That's the way the world works.*

Gary thought of calculating where an opportunity was sure to appear as being the lazy way of solving problems, but he was anything but lazy. His insatiable curiosity filled his days with activity and led him into the oddest corners of the intellectual and physical universe.

Over 20 years ago Gary became disturbed about the number of potential crises brewing on the horizon. The world's hydrocarbon supply was huge, but finite. Peak oil was real. Super diseases were beginning to appear. The world population was growing at rates that would ultimately leave standing room

Operation Phoenix

only, with no space for food or commodity production. The world was in the midst of a war on terror, with nuclear events always a possibility. Books were being published that commented that particularly the US, could not dispose of their substance by borrowing forever, but would have to pay back someday. International lenders were beginning to notice that the US had no intention of paying back with full value dollars, only dollars depreciated to half or less their previous value, if they paid at all. A financial day of reckoning beckoned.

These were but some of the potential problems Gary could foresee. The world was at a major 'tipping point', and massive, abrupt change was likely. Accidents could surely happen easily. Natural disasters such as earthquake or solar flares knocking out electrical distribution systems were certain but not predictable as to when. After giving the future of mankind and the US some thought, he recruited his son Eric and they spent many long hours on an in depth study of similar conditions throughout history, all the way back to the fall of the Roman Empire. They found astounding numbers of parallels.

One problem had bothered them. There had been massive technological advances since the Roman Empire or even since 1930. Surely modern knowledge would change how a crash unfolded. They were lucky to be able to observe in real time what happened to the USSR, another technologically advanced nation when it went down in 1990. The details differed but the pattern remained the same, just as it had in every other collapse they studied. Social disruption killed very many people and the standard of living deteriorated dramatically.

Confucius had once defined disaster two ways. One was "catastrophe," the other was "opportunity." When the giant stumbled the laws of gravity would take over and the ultimate result was predictable. Crash. What one could not predict was when, and in which direction he would fall. One did not know from where the final blow would come nor the efforts the giant would make to keep himself upright. It does not help to predict he would fall and then be standing directly under where he fell. The only goal that could be worked on was 'don't be standing where he was going to fall.' Be prepared to move quickly out of the way.

He heard a woman in the seat ahead describing to her friend, in rather graphic, loud, and crude terms, the details of her date the night before. It sounded as if they were a part of the threesomes or moresomes sex scene. He'd been there, tried that once, and no thanks. It seemed to be more of an exercise in acrobatics than making love. To him, making love was not as superficial as simply getting your jollies. Gary frowned, and went back to his review.

It would seem reasonable that Gary had made more preparations earlier, but with no way to tell 'when', 'how', or even 'if' with certainty, a collapse would occur, preparations such as he was doing now, for every eventuality, would have been foolish as late as yesterday. The US was not only falling apart financially, it was sitting on a powder keg with about 50 burning fuses leading to it.

If a nuclear bomb exploded radiation patterns would determine many of their actions but the populace would likely pull together against a common enemy. If the collapse were financial the social deterioration would likely be quite different as people fought each other to save their own small slice of the pie. If the trigger were a super disease the object would be to move fast and light to a non-populated area where becoming infected was less likely. To a large extent all the problems and opportunities were intertwined, and each would affect all the others like dominoes collapsing in a row. A bomb or disease killing millions of people would reduce the tax base income to the point where the debt burden would not be serviceable, leading to financial bankruptcy.

As time had gone on, all the dangers had grown but none nearly so fast as the financial risk. Gary and Eric had altered their thinking and preparations to acknowledge this fact, and to include new factors such as the possibility of cyber attack on the heavily technologically reliant armed forces, something that China, the predominant world manufacturer of computer chips, seemed to be exploring. Russia too, had developed an extremely sophisticated hacker community.

The problem at hand was to get away with enough resources to allow them to survive and prosper. Destination was not yet a concern. One location would not fit all scenarios. The first goal was simply to get away from the major population centres where social disruption would likely hit hardest. In the present financial collapse, the first tool needed was a medium of exchange, a store of value in one form or another to acquire the remaining tools they needed for longer term survival. During a bank holiday, cash in hand would be king - for a time at least.

Another part of the 'getting away' problem was to estimate what survival skills, food, clothing, shelter, heath care, motive power or energy, self defence, and other things would be needed to set up a self sufficient community, and then keep it running on a daily basis. Ultimately, no one person could have all the skills needed, so a small community of one to three hundred people would be necessary to act as a beacon of light for humanity. It was entirely possible that precious metals would not become a medium of exchange, but for centuries and millennia, in turmoil people had run to them. It seemed probable they eventually would again. Gold was not even the most important of many tools they thought might be useful, albeit one

Operation Phoenix

that had to be acted on immediately if they were to secure it at all, lest government make it unavailable. It was simply one part of the funding that would be required to acquire other tools such as food, which would be vital.

Not that he knew exactly what was going to happen, but he knew the safest place to watch was from a distance, usually away from the heavily populated areas.

The 'park and ride' lot was still quite full as Gary hurried over to his nondescript older model gray Toyota. That nondescript look was deceptive though. Whether it had recently been washed or not, mechanically it was always in mint condition. The tires, suspension, steering and braking systems were the best available. The oversized motor purred. The car could lay down rubber with the best of them even if Gary only did so in emergencies.

Out on Broad Street he stopped at Mooney's Guns and Sports, a privately owned gun shop. Mooney himself was not fat, but was getting on the wrong side of fat and old to be galloping around the bush hunting. However, he sure knew his guns and gun-smithing. Gary had purchased a .357 magnum from him recently and the reports were on file so Mooney winked at the background check waiting period.

Not that Gary liked the idea of gunfights but if the other guy has a gun and you don't it gets one sided fast. He purchased three Glock 40-caliber pistols, ammo, and shoulder holsters and two 12-gauge shotguns, affectionately known as street sweepers. A full 16-inch barrel, with semi automatic six shot capacity; they were mounted on a pistol grip stock. Mostly they were only good for scaring their victims to death, because they were so difficult to aim properly. Their only practical use was in cramped quarters, such as a car, where their shorter overall length was a distinct advantage. He left a deposit for 22 more

Operation Phoenix

Glock 40 cals, holsters, body armour, and a large quantity of ammo for pick up Saturday.

At the Stamford Centre Mall next, Gary cleaned out a luggage store of all its available large square black rigid leather accountant or lawyer's briefcases, then nipped next door to a dollar store and purchased three dozen each plastic containers in two sizes. The smaller plastic container would comfortably fit inside the larger with about one quarter of an inch to spare all around. To top things off, he purchased a number of large cans of spaghetti sauce and headed for home.

The Springdale district of Stamford was an older, down to earth neighbourhood of mixed houses common in the 1950's. Cape Cod and Raised Ranch style homes mingled with small apartment blocks and corner stores. Gary's yellowish-red brick Raised Ranch style home was situated on a spacious corner lot and faced south. On the east side a wide driveway led to an attached double garage. The front door with its small, three step cement porch and wrought iron railings was located about the middle of the house.

In common with most ranch style designs the interior was pretty much open concept. Originally three bedrooms and two bathrooms had formed an 'L' shape running from the front door to the northwest corner. Gary had converted the second largest bedroom, the one near the front door, to an office. The master bedroom with its ensuite bath was at the northwest.

Completing the 'U' shape, a space leading to the back patio doors, a four person wooden breakfast table, a short six foot wall with fridge and stove against it, and an 'island' counter. Across from the short wall, under the windows was a counter and sink with cupboard space along side. Against the garage wall a laundry room, stairs down, and a door into the garage.

Gary dumped his load of purchases on one side of the

Operation Phoenix

garage, threw the gold bars into his desk drawer, and started for Lynn's apartment in White Plains.

Operation Phoenix

Chapter Two

As he drove to Lynn's, Gary thought proudly and fondly of his two children who were now in their early 20s. Eric, who worked as a technician, was probably the most modest and reserved in manner. Some people would call him introverted, but that description was inaccurate. He was exceptionally quiet, did his own thinking, and unless information was needed, tended to keep his thoughts to himself. Then he would quietly go off and do his own thing. He would happily, regardless of the outcome, lean against the wall at a party under his mop of corn blonde hair, to see if he was noticed. If someone did approach him, the conversation invariably was long because he was intelligent and interesting to talk to.

Lynn was more extroverted. She worked for a pharmaceutical company where she'd been quickly climbing toward a senior management position. She'd participated in several mergers as the company acquired promising new drugs. Her reputation as a whiz at merger/acquisition transition was growing because of her talent for integrating people into a cohesive group. She was quicker to gather people around her, but for the same reason Eric often became the centre of a group. Their ideas were just enough different, but logical and intelligent, that people were intrigued.

Tall, buxom, dark blonde Lynn opened her fourth floor, one bedroom apartment door for Gary and, knowing her father, asked whether he'd like a sandwich or a drink almost before the door closed. Suddenly realizing he was famished because he'd forgotten to eat, he accepted gratefully. He said "Hi" Eric who

Operation Phoenix

was seated on the couch at the end of the living room to the left. Lynn had taught English in Japan for 18 months, and her living room was festooned with kimonos, shrines, and other memorabilia. The brightly coloured Japanese kimonos hanging on wooden rods with stylized Phoenix birds woven into them in gold thread seemed especially prophetic to Gary tonight.

Lynn led the way straight ahead to her neat pocket-sized kitchen. Gary sat at the two-person kitchen table. As she got out the makings for a sandwich, Eric joined them, leaning his slim, six foot two frame against the entrance archway.

As usual, their teasing and horseplay commenced while Gary was still in the hall. He announced; "Your munificent benefactor is here to spread wisdom and largess among the natives."

"The only wisdoms he has came from the walls of the public toilets. I already know who to call for a good time," Eric taunted with a boyish grin.

Lynn added, "The largess is in large bills I presume? All of them unpaid."

After more bantering Eric turned serious, "I guess I'm not sure what the situation is. What happened today?"

"Gold closed the day at $2,622.20, up by about $400 on the day. Most of the action came in the minutes after the Treasury auction failed. This thing is running much faster than our worst-case scenario." Gary drew a deep breath. "Frankly, despite our being more prepared than most, what lies ahead scares the hell out of me."

"Why?" Lynn asked. "There are three things that are over-rated in this country - hot chicken soup, sex, and the power of money."

Gary studied the apartment block next door through the kitchen window. Most people don't even want to understand

Operation Phoenix

banking and the financial system. They take it for granted without explanation and think of it as being boring or complex. Yet banking is very simple. You use a bank to keep your money safe. The banks have strong vaults and security systems. You trust them to give your money back when you ask for it. Every thing else is greedy bankers trying to scam more profit.

Bankers since the beginning have suffered from greed and larceny. It is what goes on with your money behind the counter that can be complex. The first bankers secretly stole depositors money and lent it to someone else as if it were their own. Of course they kept the profit. If a depositor wanted their money, they stole someone else's money and gave that to them, or simply replaced it when the loan was repaid. As time went on they worked this theft into the contracts for opening an account and lobbied governments till it was passed into law. Then their behind the counter shenanigans got really complex. *Way back in 1850 Frederic Bastait really pegged it. "When plunder becomes a way of life for a group of men... they create for themselves, in the course of time, a legal system that authorizes it, and a moral code that glorifies it."*

Gary said; "Anything acting as a medium of exchange, be that dollars, precious metals, coloured shells, or stone wheels, must be acceptable to everyone in the community as a currency. People must have confidence that everyone else will accept it in exchange for goods and services. In fact, the dollar is confidence at its extreme. If you'd accept a $10 or $20 bill for an hour's work, would you accept an equal weight and size of toilet tissue? There is nothing very special about either piece of paper except confidence and green ink. The US has enjoyed extreme confidence in its dollar for so long that nearly every currency in the world rests on a reserve base of US dollars. But, confidence is a very fragile and fickle thing. If you catch a trusted employee stealing, how long will it take for your confidence to evaporate? Would you ever trust him to the same extent again?"

Lynn cut the ham and cheese sandwich in two and poured Gary a glass of milk.

"Aren't you guys being a bit paranoid? You've been running around screaming 'the sky is falling' for ages. Some auction failed. So how does that affect me? I work for a pharmaceutical company. People will still get sick and need drugs."

Lynn's thinking was not unexpected. Gary had seen some pictures, taken by a security camera that survived in 2004 and overlooked the seawall in Thailand as the tsunami wave came in. A large Indonesian island had jumped 33 feet south earlier due to an earthquake, so a massive water displacement was entirely predictable.

The early pictures showed the tsunami as a thin dark line on the horizon. People went about the business of having a holiday. A later frame showed the people beginning to notice and stare at the dark line which was actually coming in at jet plane speeds. At this time, if someone had recognized what it was, and screamed "Tsunami, run for your life," the chances of survival for many people would have gone up exponentially. Since they had no experience, they simply stared at it in confusion. It was only when the 100-foot wall of water was about 100 yards away that people began to recognize the danger, and run for higher ground. Too late.

Like most intelligent people, Lynn was unable to envision a dramatic change in the fortunes of humanity. She'd never experienced a major social or economic reverse in her life. She couldn't imagine the magnitude of what could happen. If Gary couldn't convince his daughter, how many potential members of a new community could he convince? He had to wait until events made them ready for his solution. Then they would be eager to participate. Experience is a liability when one is faced with something new.

Gary blew out his breath. "The fact that there weren't enough people willing or able to lend the US more money was perceived by many as a lack of confidence in the US and its dollar. They sold US assets, such as stocks, and the dollar. They bought precious metals, which is the only currency not based on credit, or ultimately, the US dollar. The dollar and the stock market plunged, and gold rocketed. Enough people around the world are worried that you now have to be concerned that if you take your dollars down to the grocers, he may not exchange them for food." Gary took a drink of milk, which he habitually drank huge amounts of, a holdover from his farm boyhood.

"Sell me a bridge in Brooklyn. America is the strongest country in the world." Lynn said as she sat down on the other chair across from Gary.

"Russia was a superpower until the world suddenly noticed that they were bankrupt, and look at them now. The country broke apart, and they are fighting all over. I saw a picture in the paper in the early 90's, shortly after Russia's economy collapsed. A retired couple was ploughing the back yard so they could grow some potatoes in order to be able to eat the following winter. What made it noteworthy and showed how desperate people were was that the old wife was hitched to the plough, pulling it. The whole system broke down."

"That's different. Russia was not a free country." Lynn persisted.

Gary threw up his hands. "Despite all the propaganda, Russia was an advanced country. They put a man in space before we did. Maybe their financial system was not as good as ours, and they went broke before we did. We're only pointing to

Operation Phoenix

Russia as an example of what can happen to a technologically advanced country. Our problem is that the US is now bankrupt. We can look at the USSR for examples of how bad it might get in another advanced country, that's all. It won't be exactly the same. The world is already changing at the fastest rate in history. Unfortunately, there is no guarantee that all change will be to your liking."

Gary paused to take a bite, then said. "We are expecting bank holidays, so what I want you to do soon, tonight even, is go to a bank machine and start drawing out your maximum allowable cash from every account and credit card you own. Cash-cash. Not numbers in some account. Don't pay any more bills this week. If you have a 401K-retirement plan, or mutual funds, or anything, collapse them tomorrow as quickly as possible. Try to have the cash in your hands by Friday the latest, even if you're charged a penalty. Tell them you need the money desperately. Tell them any story – like I had a heart attack and you need the money for the treatment – anything at all, but get the cash."

"My creditors will have a heart attack if I stop paying. Besides, on holidays you can use a bank machine," Lynn turned away slightly.

"Not on this kind of holiday. The object of this kind of holiday is to stop money from being moved, regardless of the consequences to the people. It's a bank holiday. On orders from the government, everything is shut. Tight. Credit cards. Bank machines. Thrifts. Credit unions. Stock markets. All financial institutions. Closed. Tight."

Eric, who had typically been silent all this time added. "Something I read during that power blackout across the Northeastern US. A guy who lived in Detroit got stranded more than a tank of gas away from Detroit. He had about two dollars cash in his pocket, lots of credit cards, and about a quarter tank of gas. Clearly, he got pretty cold and hungry before the power came back on and he could use his plastic. He couldn't even buy food. If the power went off right now, how much cash do you have? How much food could you buy? It seems to make some sense that people with extra cash could buy all sorts of things for pennies on the dollar from people who needed cash for food."

"I know it's hard to believe," Gary tried to be as gentle as possible. "Right now we have to plan for the worst, and hope for the best. It's almost inconceivable that gold ran up by twenty percent in the last hour of trading. It could even be worse than we anticipated. That's why, until now, Eric has been buying a few ounces of gold here and there so it won't be noticed, while I've been making other preparations. That way, we as a family could probably survive if one part of the plan didn't work." Gary drew a deep breath. "I put my money into highly leveraged gold futures options, hoping I could act faster than the government, and get out with mega-bucks, some of it in gold. If it doesn't work, we are going to need your cash. If it does work, we won't have to worry about money for the rest of our lives, although the government may be pretty annoyed, particularly with me."

"What exactly are 'gold futures options'?" Lynn's brow furrowed.

"Gold futures options are one of those derivative products you keep hearing about. To spare you all the technicals, you can think of it like house insurance. The insurance company has a formula that tells them that, on average, out of every 1,000 homes they insure, one or two or three will burn down or be destroyed during the term of the policy. So they total up the cost of the houses that they estimate will be destroyed, add a little for profit and more for a safety margin, and divide by the 1,000

Operation Phoenix

insured houses to get the premium that every house owner must pay. The term doesn't have to be for a year. It can be only until April, or June, or December. Over a five or ten year period, some years no houses will be destroyed, and some years double the usual number of houses will be destroyed. But because of the low average, everyone pays a small premium.

Lynn shrugged. "So how does that affect us?"

Gary waved the remains of his sandwich in emphasis.

"Insurance companies get into trouble when something unusual occurs, like a forest fire or a hurricane destroying all of the 1,000 houses they insure in one small town, rather than the one, two or three they expected by their formula." Gary stopped to take the last bite of his snack, and talked around it. "Futures options are like that. You can take insurance that the price will go up, or down, in a wide range of commodities; grains, gold, orange juice, whatever. They use a formula that tells them on average how much they are going to have to pay out. They can then set a premium for their particular insurance. On average they will make a nice profit. Technically, in North America, the main point about options is the ability, but not the obligation, to buy gold at a specific price throughout the life of the contract. If you expect the price to go down, you buy a put option."

"So some speculator will suffer. I still don't understand how that affects us."

Gary took another deep breath. "The problem is that a huge financial tsunami wave has started racing around the world, destroying the entire world financial system. So we have to get the money out and into something we think will survive before the financial industry realizes it is bankrupt." He swallowed and changed the subject. "By the way – You both have passports don't you?"

Both Eric and Lynn nodded.

Operation Phoenix

"Good. About two business days after gold goes over $3,000, we have to go to Switzerland. All of us. As well, we have to take a day off to hide the gold that we will keep here in the US before we go overseas. Can you get three or four days off on short notice?"

"Whatever for?" Lynn demanded, "And why would we all need to go?"

Gary studied the brightly coloured fridge magnets for a second.

"We're expecting the government to retroactively make gold ownership illegal, and to seize it. It's not fair that just because they are greedy, that they steal what we have. Of course we don't want all our wealth in one place. If someone finds it, we will be penniless. We made plans to hide it in several places. If we lose one stash, then we still have enough to survive on. It makes sense to have a part outside the jurisdiction of our government, even if it might be hard for us to get to."

"What this means Lynn, is that we're afraid our way of life is changing entirely," Eric said seriously. "Clearly, what is popping up will make living deteriorate beyond what is known by most people alive today. I assume that the public and the government will try to bring back the good old days of just a couple of weeks ago. They will certainly be wasting their energy on the wrong thing, and actually blocking beneficial efforts. I haven't a clue how this is going to unfold, but if we get into a tight situation, and it becomes necessary to get at this stash, then each of us must know where it is and have access to it."

Lynn stared into the distance, then said; "I suppose I could take a day off to help you with your gold, but I can't go flitting off to Switzerland. I still have to have a job, and I am up for a promotion."

It was still too early to recruit Lynn. Gary wasn't happy,

Operation Phoenix

but saw little reason to waste effort trying to browbeat her. She'd come around as events convinced her. "We have what we have. The important thing is that we get our valuables out of the system quickly, and we've just arranged for that. One problem at a time." Gary abruptly changed the subject. "Also, I asked you about a year or so ago to get a weapons carry permit. Did you get it?"

Eric nodded, but Lynn scowled. "Guns are not an answer to anything. They're just a phallic symbol."

"Really? I heard they were selling a lot of pistols with two inch barrels."

Eric cocked his head to one side. "Some guy armed with a gun held up the Best Food Market in Houston. A fast talking employee persuaded the thief to sell his gun to the employee for cash. The tabloids had a field day. 'Hold-up victim tricks-flea brained bandit into selling his gun – and forces bandit to flee empty handed.' Clearly, most things, including the almighty dollar, are always hostage to the power of a gun. Yeppers, sometimes the only way to stay alive is to have your gun out first. It would be nice to be legal if we need it."

"Well, I am up for a promotion, and I can't afford to take the time off to go flitting off to Switzerland," she repeated. "Things can't change that much."

They arranged for situational updates on the morrow, and Gary left.

He was in bed before midnight, unusually early, because he suspected tomorrow would be difficult, and he would need his wits about him. Amazingly he fell asleep almost instantly because he was exhausted from the emotional tenseness of the day.

Chapter Three
Wednesday February 15th. Day Two;

The 6 AM news lacked many of the specifics Gary might have preferred, but the talking heads did confirm at breathless and inane length that the market crash had accelerated around the world as he slept. That was all that he really needed to know. He kept one ear on the news as he hurriedly completed his morning ablutions.

On his way out to his breakfast meeting with Gord Symes, he took care to set all his security system alarms, since things were going to get worse before they got better. As often happens after a storm, a warming trend had caused a slow drizzle overnight, so the slush of yesterday was gone. The drizzle was stopping, but the streets were still wet.

When Gary had first purchased his spacious corner lot home in Stamford, there was a sturdy, six-foot high wooden fence separating him from his neighbour at the rear with hedges on the property's other three sides. Much to his annoyance, both children and adults 'short cut' through his property by stepping through the hedge border ruining the lawn that he was diligently working on. He put an end to the trespassing by tearing out the hedges and erecting a four-foot stone wall on the other three sides of the property. The driveway leading to the double garage now sported a sturdy decorative, but lockable, wrought iron gate. Aside from the patio at the back, and two ornamental fruit trees, the grounds were given over to verdant grass.

As part of the awareness of the possible problems facing

Operation Phoenix

the US and the rest of the world, he had increased the security precautions at home. He installed alarms, night vision cameras and floodlights capable of covering every foot of the grounds. Where there was wall, he had planted climbing roses with particularly nasty thorns. The house windows were bullet-proof glass with tasteful wrought iron working shutters.

His breakfast meeting with Gord Symes, at a restaurant just down the street from Gords Stamford bank office, was pretty much a rerun of yesterday's meeting with Jan Kerr. Gordon extracted a $5,000 fee for processing the loan application, and warned of another 'arrangement fee' if Gary got serious. He mentioned that the bank was getting a bit hesitant about making new loans in view of economic conditions. Gary's antennae went straight up at this information. He had expected the banks to pull back, but not this fast. Financing anywhere could soon become impossible. It wasn't until breakfast was over and they were about to leave, that Gary asked casually whether Gord expected any problems processing the loan.

"The big problem is going to be getting a quorum of the credit committee together on short notice. If I can do that in time, I don't expect any problems. You're a long-time client, and this is a very short-term loan. I should have an answer by 10:30 or 11."

Somewhat relieved, Gary raced for the train to New York. Arriving at 9:30, he grabbed a cab to the broker's offices. An assistant ushered him to Vance's double cubicle. Vance was frantically responding to the phone, with all lines lit up. Vance waved and smiled, but stayed on the phone, "It's really a no man's land. The Dow has a lead balloon tied to it. It gapped down on the open 653 points, and is now down over 1300. There's all sorts of offer but nobody is bidding when they think they can bid later at a lower price. The computer cease trading ban is already in effect and it appears we will have a total 'cooling off' shutdown very soon."

"What's up?" Vance continued with his customer. "Well some currencies are up, particularly the Euro and the Yen, but not as much as you might think. Precious metals are way up, particularly gold. It opened here in New York at $2,763, and now – uh – it last traded at $2,872.40." Vance glanced pointedly at Gary, and turned the screen a bit so Gary could see it. "Yesterday it closed at $2,622. It has been rocketing up all night, overseas.

"Okay, I have an order to buy as many June gold futures at the market as possible with your available funds. I probably won't be able to get back to you quickly. The market is such a zoo that it sometimes takes a while for the confirmation of a trade to get back to me."

Listening to all this, Gary's adrenalin meter was heading up toward the red line although he was trying to maintain a calm exterior.

"Okay, I'll talk to you later." Vance gave the orders to the floor trader and hung up. "What can I do for you, Gary?" he said with one hand still on the phone.

"I have heard all I need to. I want to borrow one of those client cubby-hole front offices with screens and a phone if I may." Vance's assistant, Cheryl, found him an empty cubicle, and as Gary hung up his topcoat, she turned on the computer. She showed Gary how to look up codes in the codebook, and enter them to call up screens of various markets. He asked Cheryl to run off several copies of his account, and to fax a copy to Gordon Symes.

After a bit of fumbling, Gary punched up gold on the screen, then picked up the phone and dialled Jan Kerr. After some argument with the secretary, he got through to Jan, who

Operation Phoenix

was in a meeting.

"Yes Mr. Alden. I'm not really in a position to discuss this fully at the moment, but in principle we are in favour of going ahead. Can you call me at 10:55? I'll try to squeeze in five minutes to cover."

Obviously her 'dumb, helpless' façade of yesterday was an act.

"I may be able to do better than that. I'm at Wilkinson now. I'm getting a printout of my position as of last night, so we can make a closer estimate of the numbers. It's 10:10 now. I can have that over to you by 10:55. At the same time, if you have any paperwork, I can pick it up."

"Yes, a printout would be helpful. Fine, 10:55."

He stood up to go and find Cheryl, and bumped into her at the door as she walked in with his account copies. "Hey, we have to stop meeting like this. People will talk," he joked lamely.

Cheryl smiled. "Here are your copies, Mr. Alden. Vance stamped and signed them. Is there anything else?"

"Tell Vance the bridge loan at Premet is approved in principle. I'm on my way over there now."

Gary turned back to the computer screen, and punched up in turn, April expiry gold call options, then June, August and December. For each he quickly copied the last trade price for his holdings. He returned to the gold screen, and entered the last trade price of gold, now $2,899.70 in his notebook. As he watched, the price of gold broke $2,900, and traded at $2,901.50.

He grabbed his papers and notebook, and at a walk that was nearly a run, broke for the elevators. Again the elevator took forever to come, and again it stopped at nearly every one of the 22 floors on the way to the lobby.

Operation Phoenix

He sprinted out to the street and tried to hail a cab. "Cabs and cops – never there when you need them," he muttered. "It's only four or five blocks. I can walk." Off he went at a high-speed lope, dodging through the crowds.

About half way to Premet he suddenly stopped. *Hold on. Hold on. Calm down,* he thought. *It's only two blocks, and I've got at least twenty minutes. Take three deep breaths.* After breathing deeply, he slowed to a normal walk, and arrived cheerful and unflustered, except for his hair, which was unruly as usual. As he walked up to the front of the building, he paused and blinked.

"'Ello, 'Ello, Wot 'ave we got 'ere?" he said to himself. Two security guards were shouting, "Gold line forms here," pointing to a line of shivering people stretching down the block. Suddenly Gary remembered his topcoat, back in the Wilkinson offices. Three of New York's finest in blue had a couple of people up against the wall, probably for fighting for a position in line.

It wasn't just himself, or the professionals like Nils in the market who were stressed, the tension was on the streets too. The public had to be buying to raise the price of gold this quickly. Still, the size of that line, and the presence of cops indicated more public fear, spreading faster than he had predicted. He wondered what the Federal Treasury was thinking about all of this.

Subdued, Gary gained entrance to the bank by telling the guard controlling the doors he had an appointment with special accounts. After telling the receptionist he was early for an appointment with Jan Kerr, he sat down, and flipped open his binder. He started writing down the current value of his holdings, using the prices he had picked off the screens at Wilkinson. Assuming he sold at $3,000, as he planned to do, he

Operation Phoenix

simply added $100 to the price of his holdings, and calculated the expected amount he would realize. He added the total dollars to be realized, and it was only when he was inserting the commas in the final number that he fully realized its magnitude. $33,767,800.

For a guy who didn't care all that much for money, on paper he sure had a lot. A small grin of pride lit his face briefly. *Not bad for an initial investment of less than $50,000. Those out of the money options really only work well as insurance against violent price moves, otherwise they are pretty useless Now to convert those paper profits to reality.*

How many ounces would that work out to? If say, 15 percent were eaten up by bar charges and suchlike, that would leave about $28 million. Say the price went up to $3,200 before the purchase could be completed, then $28 million divided by $3,200 would equal over 8,500 ounces, about 600 pounds, or over one quarter of a ton. Luckily some was going out of the country so he would not have to deal with all that weight personally.

"Mr. Alden!" The receptionist sounded exasperated, as if she had called him before.

"Huh – oh – yes?"

"Jan Kerr will see you now."

"Oh – Right." Gary gathered up his things quickly and followed the receptionist to Jan's small but opulent office.

"Gareth." Jan extended her hand. "We don't have a great deal of time so I'll get right to it. In principle, the bank is prepared to make you the loan. Did you bring the printout?"

"Yes," as he fished the original printout sheets out of his binder. He handed one to Jan, and kept the other for himself. "And call me Gary. Most people do. It's easier."

He breathed her light perfume and asked, "What terms

Operation Phoenix

were you thinking of?"

"Interest at 25% per annum, plus an arrangement fee of $100,000."

Overnight loans such as he was seeking, would usually attract a high interest rate because the total dollars returned in interest would be very small for a one day loan. Arrangement fees were common when the bank had to do a lot of work to line up a number of borrowers to take part in a large 'syndicated' loan. Now, they were simply gouging, albeit as usual because arrangement fees were so common. Gary decided not to appear too eager because there might be more bargaining.

Fixing his eyes on her, he exploded, "Hold on a minute. You're talking mega bucks in bar charges and commissions, plus a huge amount in spreads, and you want to whack me with a $100,000 arrangement fee? Not to mention 25% per annum for shuffling some paper?"

"Exactly how much money are we talking about here Mr. Alden?"

"Well, I was able to put some numbers together quickly while I was waiting for you, and I must admit they came out to more than I had anticipated." Gary said as he ripped the page out of his binder. "But they look right. The first column is the printout I just gave you. The second is the prices I picked off the screens while I was waiting for the printout. At that time, for all intents and purposes, spot gold was trading at $2,900 per ounce. If I sell at $3,000, then I just add $100 to get the estimated selling price. I then multiply by the ounce position total to get dollars realized."

Jan studied the page briefly before looking at Gary from under her eyebrows, one of which was slightly raised. "Nearly 34 million dollars is a rather large 'few' million," she said, head cocked slightly.

Operation Phoenix

"I think I said several, but I agree. Nevertheless the money is not leaving this bank, and the process is exactly the same, except you add a zero. You're probably talking a couple of million profit in spread and bar charges here."

"Gary, how many ounces do you estimate you will be buying?"

"Probably 8,500 ounces, plus or minus."

Jan pursed her lips, picked up the phone and dialled. "Dick Menach, please."

"Dick, it's Jan Kerr from special accounts. I have a customer here who is planning a substantial purchase of physical bullion, probably about 8,500 ounces, to be delivered tomorrow. Can you deliver?

"No he doesn't want certificates he wants physical bullion.

"Various sizes as I recall," Jan said into the phone while looking at Gary with one eyebrow raised.

Gary nodded and said, "If that is the gold department manager may I speak with him?"

"Hold on. I'll turn you over to Gary Alden, the customer. He can describe his needs." She handed the phone to Gary.

"Gary Alden here."

"Dick Menach. I understand you would like 8,500 ounces of physical gold bullion. Do you know how much weight that is?"

"Yes, I'm prepared for that. I'm looking for a range of sizes, with a preponderance of small sizes. How is your stock of small bars and coins?"

"It's pretty good Mr. Alden, although I'm not sure offhand if I can cover all the sizes until I see the order."

"I do have a bit of flexibility. I could drop off a tentative list in 15 minutes or so, since I'm here in the bank. There is one other thing. The order is to be split into four lots for shipping. I

Operation Phoenix

expect that Willis Armoured Cars will pick up. Can you do this?"

"No problem. Bring me the breakdown and we can talk then."

Jan glanced at Gary in a slightly speculative way, dug out her phone book, looked up a phone number and dialled.

Aha, thought Gary. *Security check. She's calling Vance and wants to look up the number herself, no relying on something that I gave her because it might be part of a scam. You are one smart lady. You have definitely become a candidate for head hunting, my beautiful banker.* Aloud he said, "His name is Vance Paul. P.A.U.L. His assistant's name is Cheryl. They are expecting your call. Don't let anyone put you off."

Jan smiled, nodded, and worked her way through the system till she was talking to Vance. She confirmed a number of details and arranged for the paperwork flow. She hung up and turned to Gary.

"Gary regarding your loan. I am prepared to reduce our arrangement fee to $10,000. The best I can do as far as interest is concerned is 22% on this kind of loan. We will process your order for gold at our normal posted fees for bullion. Is that satisfactory?"

Gary grinned. "Well I've got to grumble a little bit. You're making a fortune on that arrangement. Providing you can substantially deliver on my order, and size requirements, that is agreeable. I take it your bid/offer spread is now eight dollars?"

"Yes, I believe eight dollars. I assume you are expecting to do this transaction today. What time do you expect to sell?"

"If gold is over $3,000, since we had a one o'clock appointment I thought we could do the paperwork and sell immediately. That way we could be complete here by market close."

Operation Phoenix

"Yes, that would be good." Jan glanced at her watch. "My goodness, its 11:15. I'm way behind."

Operation Phoenix

Chapter Four

Gary took a seat in the reception area to draw up his charts for Menach. While 400-ounce bars were readily available he wanted smaller sizes, despite the premium he would pay for them. His best guess was that one ounce of gold would ultimately purchase goods currently valued at $16,000-$32,000. If one had only a ten ounce bar, and wanted to buy bread, $160,000-$320,000 would buy too much bread to be practical, even if food was so scarce that bread was $50 a loaf then.

He decided on a mix of for every 100 ounces of gold; one kilo bar which was just over 30 ounces, and 40 ounces of smaller bars from ten to one ounce. The balance, of just less than 30 ounces, would be in coins ranging from one twentieth of an ounce to one ounce. A one-twentieth ounce coin with a purchasing power of $800 was still a lot of bread, but it was more manageable.

The receptionist provided someone to escort him over to Menach's area, since security was tightly controlling everything around the retail gold and foreign exchange department.

Dick Menach, in contrast to his Scottish derived name, turned out to be a slim, dark skinned, dark haired man with an oozing, unctuous manner. He was able to flag a reserve on almost all the sizes Gary wanted. All the while he complained that Gary was wiping out his supply of small sizes of gold for sale to his retail customers. He wanted Gary to take only large bars, which Gary didn't want any of. Final details would await a determination of exact quantities, which in turn would depend

Operation Phoenix

on exactly how much money Gary had to spend.

Seeing it was close to noon, Gary borrowed a phone and called Vance to advise him the signing would be at one o'clock. "What's happening in the markets?" Gary asked.

"The latest rumour is that the IMF and 17 countries, including Finland for Christ's sake, have been supporting the US dollar overnight. The US had only about 50 billion in foreign exchange to contribute to the effort because they have been supporting the dollar previously as it slid lower. If we can't survive without Helsinki….. Well, I don't know. China alone has over a trillion they want to dump. Japan too. Gold is currently trading at $3,283, but that is more because of dollar weakness than intrinsic value. Happy?"

"Seventeen countries and the IMF supporting the dollar? With things moving this fast, I'll bet even the central bankers' bowels are moving. However, I'll be much happier when I get this transaction completed. I'm really beginning to like this new math," Gary grinned, although Vance couldn't see that

Gary found a deli nearby where he was able to get a sandwich. The big question was; when would the government get around to intervening with gold running up so fast. With gold moving so violently he expected the authorities were already mumbling to each other about controls or other options. With the tension so high, he was getting emotionally exhausted and slightly irritable. However, the storm had broken up this morning and the sun was out sporadically, so the atmosphere was not so glum. The temperature was probably about 40 degrees by now.

At 12:40, Gary was back at the special accounts reception at Premet. The gold line was longer, now disappearing around the corner of the block. Half a dozen cops were patrolling up and down the line. This just added to people's tension, as the

Operation Phoenix

display sign in the window showed the current price of gold rocketing up.

Gary idly asked the receptionist whether Jan had eaten lunch. The receptionist didn't think so, so Gary hurried back to the deli and grabbed a coffee and Danish. Gary would have done so anyway, but he was also aware that during negotiations whether they trusted you depended partly on whether they liked you. He was back in time to meet Jan as she was coming out of her office to greet him. As he watched her walk his loins began to tingle.

"Here's a coffee and Danish," he said, holding out the bag. "The receptionist didn't think you'd had time for lunch. I guess that was my fault for holding you up at 11."

"Is that for me? You are very sweet." Jan took the bag. "You're right, I haven't had time to eat. I could use that."

They returned to Jan's office. Jan opened the coffee and took a sip, then pulled out a file. "If you would sign the note here, the document allowing us to sell out your position if you do not perform, and the document directing Wilkinson to transfer the results of your sale directly to your account here, our delivery person will deliver it to Wilkinson."

Gary signed with a flourish and said, "Phew, another step done. I'll have Wilkinson fax you the dollar amount as soon as we are done, and I'll phone as well. Then I'll come over and deal with Menach."

"That's fine. Thanks for the coffee and Danish, and thank you for dealing with us." Jan smiled with her whole face including her eyes. Gary thought it made her look very beautiful.

Gary strode out and walked back to Wilkinson, quite quickly, since his topcoat was still in the cubby-hole office there, and the weather was still cool and damp. It was 1:30. The

Operation Phoenix

screen was still on and showed spot gold trading. $3,361.00.

Gary frowned, and picked up the phone to dial Vance. "I'm back at the cubby-hole in your offices. I'm not sure I am working this screen properly. Is gold really – uh - $3,372.50 now?"

"Yeah, my screen shows the same." Vance said. "And another thing. In the last couple of minutes the market has gone eerily quiet. Lots of phone calls, but hardly any trades crossing the screen. It's the same all over. Currencies, the Dow, bonds, everything. Strange, like the whole market is holding its breath."

"Okay, go ahead and start selling my options. Quietly work the price as much as possible without disturbing the market. If the market starts moving either way, dump everything. Get out as quickly as possible at any price. At this level I am afraid the Fed will intervene." Gary instructed.

"Yes, I agree. I don't like the feel of this market. It's so quiet it's eerie. I'll start selling you out."

Gary punched up the screen for options. As he watched, a trade went by for the 2,320 strike price option, April expiry. *That's got to be mine,* he thought. Then a June 2,290-strike price reduced the last trade price by $1.00. *Also mine.* Then another June 410 reduced its last trade price by a $1.00. *Jesus, I hope those are all mine.*

Suddenly December expiry options dropped by five dollars. Then across the Reuters split screen, an announcement scrolled, "US treasury announces release of gold to the market."

Gary dialled Vance. Cheryl answered. "Cheryl, it's Gary. Give me Vance urgently."

"He's on the line with the floor trader finishing your gold options."

"Tell him to dump everything at the market. The Fed is intervening in gold." Gary hung up and looked back at the

Operation Phoenix

screen. December options were down $20. He checked the time: 1:48 – 12 minutes to 2. *God I hope I'm out.* He walked unannounced into the broker offices and headed for Vance's desk. Vance was on the phone with a client.

"Maybe you want to hold off a bit on selling. The Fed announced it was intervening in gold, and the market may have turned around.

"I can't accept an order like that. It has to be specific. Buy or sell. Maybe you could call me back in a few minutes?

"Okay, I'll talk to you later." Vance turned to Gary. "It's sure hard to keep customers in this market. They keep wanting their money. I suppose you're going to skip out on me too?"

"Well, not totally. When you report to Jan Kerr, hold back $200,000 in case of errors. Besides, I have something else I want to do. Am I out?"

"I don't know." Vance shrugged. "I don't have all the tickets back yet. I would assume so." He pulled out a notepad. "Let's see." He looked up at Cheryl, who was signalling for the phone. "Take a number." He started separating Gary's tickets from the pile on his desk. "You got $1,113.50 an ounce for 24 of the April 2,270 contracts, and $1,080.90 for 80 of the April 2,320's," he mumbled as he continued through the tickets. "We're still missing tickets for seven contracts of June 350, two August entries, and one large December entry." Vance glanced at Cheryl. "I'll take that call."

As Vance dealt with the customer, Gary grabbed the pad, ripped a blank sheet out of the middle, and copied down the list of completed contracts. Pulling out his calculator, he began extending the amounts to determine the total dollars received.

Gary hadn't noticed Cheryl move, but she handed Vance several tickets. Vance sorted Gary's tickets out of the pile while he talked to his other customer. Gary rapidly copied down the

Operation Phoenix

prices from the tickets, and continued extending them. As Vance got off the phone from giving his latest sell order to the floor trader, Gary completed adding the totals, and entered the grand total. Vance raised an eyebrow, and held out his hand for the sheet. Gary drew back and clutched it to his chest, and said. "How much are the commissions?"

"$100 per contract. 514 contracts wasn't it?"

"Yep, and your percentage should make you a happier puppy," as he subtracted $51,400 from his previous total, and then handed the sheet to Vance. Gary kept staring at his calculator, which displayed the final total: $53,704,420.

Vance whistled, turned to his screen and punched something up. "You know," he said, "I've never known anyone who actually sold at the top before," and he turned the screen to Gary. Gold was trading at $3,110. "Are you actually going ahead with your purchase of gold at Premet Gary?"

"Oh yes. Firstly, I got unbelievably lucky, but I think this is a false rally. They had a similar rally in 1929. It was called a fool's rally because it sucked in more fools; the people who believed things had turned around. And, even if gold goes back to $2,200 where it was last week, I'll still have plenty of money to retire on."

Vance shrugged and handed over the paper and a pile of tickets to Cheryl. "Make a photocopy for Gary. Check the numbers are correct. Deduct $200,000 from the total, and prepare a fax to Premet to advise them the total to be transferred." He turned back to his ever-blinking phone lines.

"Wait," said Gary. "Gold is going to continue downwards for a while. I have seen this before. Gold will go down either one third or one half of its advance. Take $100,000 and buy as many gold put options as you can. How much is gold now?"

"3,077.20"

Operation Phoenix

"Okay, buy December 2,800 or less strike price gold put options. If I am not here when spot gold gets to," Gary paused and mentally calculated, "$2,700, sell half. If gold gets to $2,600, sell the other half. How much are long bonds now? 30-year US Treasury bonds?"

"Bonds?" said Vance in bewilderment at the sudden change in thinking. Gary had long ago made his distaste for US Treasuries known.

"Um", he punched up 30-year bonds on the screen. "93 and change, say 94. The eight percent 30-year bonds were $115 and change day before yesterday, for a yield of about six percent."

"Take the other $100,000 and buy bond put options. The price will go down as the yield goes up. Buy the 90-strike price for December if you can. I'll probably be back before it happens, but when bonds reach 60, sell. Work the price, but make sure I'm totally invested in precious metal and bond put options today – even if you have to buy other strike prices and other months. After you have sold according to the orders I just gave you, take all the available funds and buy one year treasury bonds, and register them in my name for delivery."

"Sixty!" yelled Vance. "That's a yield of over 14%. And what do you mean, back?"

Having already said too much, Gary ignored the last question. He didn't want anyone to know that he had gone to Switzerland.

"Actually, I expect bonds to go to 50 or below. As more companies and people rush to borrow money, just to keep themselves afloat, the bond prices will drop as the yield is bid up. Our Government, among others, will try for a while to keep borrowing to cover the amount they are spending, more than they are taking in. That's what our wondrous deficit is. Not only

Operation Phoenix

that, but next week, and the week after that, and the month after that, they have huge amounts of bonds maturing and coming due."

Gary waved his finger in emphasis. "They're so used to the idea that they can just roll them over, they won't expect the world to refuse and demand payment. They're a bunch of kids using their parent's credit cards to spend wildly with no thought at all about paying back. Confidence in the dollar is shot, and no one will lend. Economic conditions are falling like a rock around the world. The money is not there to lend, even if the other countries wanted to with credit contracting around the world. Anyway, I've got to get over to Premet. Put the orders in, and I'll talk to you as soon as I can."

Gary hurried back to the cubby-hole office and dialled Jan Kerr. Her secretary informed him she was in a meeting. Gary left a message saying that his sale done, and giving the total for Jan, and saying he would be over shortly. He asked to be transferred to Dick Menach.

"Dick Menach."

"Mr. Menach, it is Gary Alden here."

"Oh yeah, the guy I never heard of before who may be going to buy megabucks in gold," Menach sneered.

"What is your bid/offer for gold now?" Gary ignored the insult. Because he was dealing with bankers, he maintained bank etiquette, and spoke calmly and unhurriedly.

"3,008 bid, 3,058 offered."

Gary punched up gold on the Wilkinson screen. Last trade $3,011.60. It was a $50 spread, and all in the banks favour. Gary, who had been annoyed at Menachs attitude got more than annoyed at this childish attempt to gouge him.

"What the hell are you playing at? Gold is falling like a rock. The last trade was $3,011.60. I negotiated a spread of eight dollars. I have no intention of just giving you an additional $42 an ounce. I'll tell you what," Gary started punching numbers into his calculator. "How would you like to get rid of some of your inventory, which is now losing value by the second? I'll increase my order to 15,000 ounces, and give you base price of four dollars over the market offer as shown by the screen at the time of the transaction."

"I make more money per ounce if I sell at retail," whined Menach.

"That's bullshit and you know it," Gary snapped. "How much gold are you going to sell at retail in the next hour with prices plunging? In the meantime you are going to lose a hell of a lot more money on all the rest of your gold inventory as the price falls. Moreover, if I have buy tomorrow, not only will the price be a lot lower, but I will shop the order. Do you want to play or not? Otherwise I call another bullion bank now."

"Well okay, Mr. Alden. Four dollars over the market offer." Menach sounded very, very injured.

"I'll be over in a few minutes." Gary hung up.

Gary called Joe Seligman at Willis Armoured Car Services, whom he had also talked to about a year ago. It cost him but he arranged for a pickup of the gold and cash shipments just before 11:00AM the next day. Ordering dedicated trucks would insure the Swiss shipment would make it to the airport for the evening flight. It would clear Swiss customs early Friday, and be held in Willis's Zurich offices till Tuesday. Hopefully the Swiss would not be seizing gold yet. The local shipment would be delivered two hours after pick-up from Premet.

Gary grabbed his coat and ran from the Wilkinson office. Once outside, seeing no available cabs, he galloped to the Premet building, and suddenly stopped. The line of people

Operation Phoenix

waiting to buy gold had vanished. In its place a large crowd, with a liberal sprinkling of security guards and cops, milled aimlessly in front of the building.

"Ah so," Gary murmured. "People now velly confuse. Gold plice going down, but not want to roose prace in rine, just in case."

Gary went to special accounts and asked the receptionist to advise Jan that he was in the building to see Dick Menach, to please provide someone to walk him to Menachs office, and that he would be on the courtesy phone while he waited.

The receptionist gestured at the phone in the corner and picked up her own phone. Gary dialled the number of his lawyer, Ron Thompson in Yonkers. Ron was a specialist in international and constitutional law, but for some reason he liked Gary and tolerated him as a customer. Gary arranged to use Ron's boardroom as a shipping address for the local shipment of gold and cash. It was an unusual address because valuables are usually shipped from less secure sites to more secure sites and would confuse potential robbers. Also, if someone like the government tried to trace the shipment later, the address would be something of a dead end, because of client confidentiality. Not for long of course, but it would buy Gary time. He also requested that Ron have Mary, his secretary, arrange for a couple of armed guards, preferably uniformed off duty cops, to be present from one PM till six.

"Using our boardroom would be agreeable, especially if you have guards here. Let me determine if it's is available." The line hummed as he was put on hold. Ron was back on the line in a few seconds. "I've reserved the boardroom, and Mary is arranging for two guards for tomorrow. Is there anything else?"

"Yes, we discussed using your correspondent lawyer in Zurich for local legal counsel. Would you contact them and

Operation Phoenix

arrange for that. Demand an answer by 10am our time tomorrow. I will need their exact address and other coordinates. I'll call as I get things straightened out, but I'm very rushed right now."

Chapter Five

Jan Kerr walked briskly out of her office to the reception area as Gary hung up. Despite the tension of the moment, the male in Gary resurfaced momentarily.

"Hello Gary," she smiled. "If you'll come this way, I believe everything has been arranged. You are purchasing this afternoon, are you not?"

Gary followed her across the main lobby toward the gold department. "Yes I hope to, although tomorrow is starting to look pretty good with the price of gold going down. Did you receive everything you need from Wilkinson?" he said as nonchalantly as he could, but he still felt as if he were sweating adrenalin from every pore.

"Yes, everything is in order." Jan was silent until they stopped at the thick glass security door, around the corner from the retail counter, where she buzzed and asked for Dick Menach

Menach came to the security area personally, to escort them to his office. Gary noticed that Jan started to leave, and then apparently decided to see the deal through, and followed them into Menach's plate glass office. *Smart lady*, he thought, *She's going to keep an eye on it personally, since I appear a bit uptight. She knows she has better people skills than Menach. I wonder if he realizes that. Probably not.*

"First, I'd like you to show me spot gold on your screen," Gary stalled.

Menach, seated at his desk, punched up spot gold. He

Operation Phoenix

scowled and turned the screen so Gary could see it. Bid $2,950.10, ask $2,952.60, last trade $2,985.90. *Gold is still falling fast,* thought Gary. *I would really like to hold off, but I have to finalize quickly. Who knows what the Fed will come up with next? A few dollars doesn't matter. It's more important that I finalize the deal.* Aloud he said, "Okay, call your trader for their best price."

As Menach dialled, Gary, seated across the desk, picked up the bank forms, which now had everything but the gold price filled in to enable quick extension and completion. As he glanced over the form suddenly his eyes narrowed and his mouth formed a thin straight line. Those bastards were trying to do it to him again. The bar charges and commissions, or premiums over the market price of gold, were way up. He had to do the deal today so maybe he shouldn't notice. Still it made him mad to get ripped off. Not only that but his hand was very strong. Gold was still falling like a rock. It would help to delay. He decided to stay in character. As Gary glanced at the clock on the wall, he felt Jan watching him. It was 2:41 – 19 minutes to 3:00.

Gary flipped open his binder and began copying quantities and bar premiums.

Menach frowned as he saw what Gary was doing. Still holding the phone he said, "Our base asking price is $2,945.00, plus charges of course."

"Your commission for gold coins is four percent, is it not?" Gary asked in deadly quiet tones.

"We had to increase our commissions to six percent since gold is so volatile," Menach said defiantly. Gary glanced at the screen. It now showed bid $2,942.80, ask $2,945.00, last trade $2,950.10. Gary finished copying the last of the quantities and bar charges.

Operation Phoenix

Menach said with some exasperation, and maybe some desperation, "Well, do you want to do the deal or not?"

Gary placed Menach's pre-filled form back on the edge of the desk. Jan, at the side of the desk, immediately picked it up. "Your bar charges and commissions have gone up substantially in the past few minutes, just for me. Bar charges and commissions have nothing to do with volatility. That is what spreads are all about. You can put down the phone." Gary was speaking quietly, flatly.

Gary stood. "Someone in this organization should remember a quote which was I think, attributable to the WWII air force. 'There are old men. There are bold men. There are no old, bold men.' Someone in this organization is beginning to appear very bold." He walked out of the office and turned toward the counter area, rather than toward the entrance.

Through the office glass wall he saw Menach sit blankly for a couple of seconds, and then start up to follow Gary. "Wait, you can't go there." Jan, who had been quiet all this time, shifting her gaze back and forth between Gary and Menach, reached to pick up the phone. She began to dial.

"Mr. Alden," Menach rushed after Gary. "You're not allowed to go out there." Two steps later, Gary stopped at the end of the aisle between the desks leading to the retail area, where he could see a sign listing bar charges. Menach caught up with him.

"Why can't I look at your posted bar charges? Afraid I might find them lower than the ones you're charging me?" Gary opened his binder and began copying the posted bar charges by size.

"We haven't had an opportunity to change our signs," Menach said defensively. "For security purposes, the public's not allowed to go beyond this line. Please return to the office."

Operation Phoenix

"Since I am standing behind the line, and since you are standing here to ensure I am not going any further, it looks as if your effort to get me to return to the office is simply a device to stop me from looking at the posted bar charges," Gary said absently as he continued to copy the few lines on the notice.

Seeing Gary was getting what he wanted anyway, Menach changed tactics. "Of course we aren't trying to stop you from looking at our sign, but if you go out there I could lose my job. Besides the new bar charges are now more realistic as a percentage of the gold price."

Finishing his list, Gary snapped his binder shut. "Well we wouldn't want you to lose your job would we?" he said, and returned to the office.

Jan was listening intently on the phone. "Dick's just returned to his office," she murmured in a low voice to alert the party on the other end of the phone, "I'll follow that line of thinking," and hung up.

Gary said, "Do you mind if I use this chair for a few minutes? I'd like to get a handle on what these bar charges are," and sat down without waiting for an answer. He took out his calculator and rapidly determined total bar charges and commissions for each size of bar using first the prices proposed by Menach, and then the prices listed on the notice board. He added up the columns, and glanced at the clock on the wall. It was 2:46. He looked at the screen. Gold was bid $2,910.50, asked $2,912.50, last trade $2,916.80.

The slide in the price of gold was not slowing. Gary thought rapidly and wished he could take the chance of waiting until the next day. The price would probably be down much more. It was down $450 from what he'd sold just at about an hour ago. But it had to be today. He had to figure a price they would do business at, but still not allow them to gouge him.

Operation Phoenix

Those bar charges were at least partly real, and not simply bank profit. It costs to exactly weigh and stamp those bars and coins. He couldn't get much there. He decided to be content with going back to the posted prices, and a four-dollar premium on the offer price. At least he was pretty sure they'd do business at that level.

He leaned toward Menach and scowled. "I have calculated the cost of purchasing 15,000 ounces under your posted bar charges, versus the suggested bar charges on your pre-filled form that you wanted me to sign. With this cute little trick you thought you would stiff me for over a million dollars. To be exact, $1,044,200. Add that to the $361,000 spread trick, and you are talking a million seven. That looks unbelievably greedy to me. I don't blame a person for trying to make a profit. What I don't like is how you tried to gouge me. Gold is falling like a rock, and the markets close shortly. If I have to wait till tomorrow, not only will I be paying less, but also I am most assuredly going to get competitive quotes. Now the question is not whether I want to do business, rather it is do you want to do business."

Menach blustered, "Of course we want to do business, but at a reasonable return for the risk we are taking in a volatile market."

"Right now," Gary interrupted, "gold is still going down fast, and we don't have a deal. To me your risk looks like you may be selling your inventory of gold a lot cheaper tomorrow, if you sell at all."

Jan cut in smoothly. "Dick, while you were out, I called the head of treasury. He says that since it is a special accounts customer, it is a special accounts problem. So I guess I'm the one who has to sort it out."

Love your wording lady, thought Gary. *Menach is out, cut off at the knees. Kerr is in, all smooth and almost bloodless.*

Operation Phoenix

"Gary, what do you want?" Jan asked.

"Since we have no deal, the price will be at the market, with the spread being the spot market offer at the instant we agree as shown by the screen, plus a four dollar spread charge, with bar and commissions as posted on the board."

"Depending on your other conditions, we can live with that," Jan agreed.

"The gold is to be prepared for shipment, free of charge, in a manner acceptable to Willis in four shipments, broken down as I direct."

"And?"

"I will want very substantial amounts of cash, probably as much foreign currency as you are likely to have on hand. Up to $50,000 US dollars each in Euros, Canadian Dollars, Swiss Francs, and Japanese Yen. And up to $20,000 each in Pounds Sterling, Hong Kong Dollars, and Australian Dollars. Spreads are to be treated the same as we are doing gold, half of last Monday's spread added to the market offer price. I will want the balance in U.S. cash. I will pay a fee of one eighth of one percent handling for the U.S. cash," Gary continued.

"We need one quarter of one percent handling on the U.S. cash." Jan frowned "Exactly how much money are we talking about here?"

Gary decided to let her win one in front of Menach as he said, "I have no idea. It depends on how much we have left after this transaction. It will be several hundred thousand at least. I'll know better after these transactions are complete. Okay, one quarter of one percent handling for the U.S. cash."

"Is this another one of your 'severals', like the total of your order, that will just grow and grow?" Jan cocked an eyebrow at Gary.

"Possibly, but I doubt it. Do you really care? There are

Operation Phoenix

good fees – good normal retail level fees on a wholesale level transaction - to be earned here." Gary shrugged. "My account will probably be empty by tomorrow night."

Jan picked up the direct line to the trader and explained the methodology of the trade to her, and asked if she was willing to trade on this basis. Apparently she would, because Jan turned to Gary with the trader still on the line and said; "If I accept all of your conditions, are you willing to complete the deal now?"

Gary glanced at the clock. It was 2:57. Then at the screen, Bid $2,875.70 Offer $2,877.20. Last trade $2,883.40. "Yes, if you accept those conditions, I offer to buy from you 15,000 ounces of gold at a price of $2,877.20, plus agreed upon bar charges, spreads and commissions," Gary said formally.

"He has offered $2,877.20 plus $4 to total $2,881.20 to buy 15,000 ounces. Do you accept?" Jan said into the phone. Jan turned to Gary. "We accept. We are done." Then into the phone she said, "Thank you Heidi. We are done," and hung up while watching Gary, still in a speculative way.

Gary looked back at the screen. As he watched, gold dropped another $8 and then another $15 as the traders rushed to get their trades through in the final seconds before the bell.

The paperwork took 20 minutes to finish. When the final calculations came in, Wilkinson was transferring $53,704,420. to Premet. Gold purchases to date totalled $52.226,180, leaving a balance of $1,277,240. That balance would go first towards the foreign exchange, and then any remaining funds in U.S. cash. Counting was arranged for 10:15, since the funds from Wilkinson were expected by ten.

Gary requested a private phone, and Jan walked him down the quiet, dark wood-paneled hall where the big money plays to a vacant conference room. As they walked, Jan looked at him out of the corner of her eye and said, "You're some negotiator!

Operation Phoenix

I'm impressed. You must have nerves of steel to deal with only two minutes to market closing." She tilted her head and stared at him. "But why did you keep looking at the clock? Your calls in the market have been so accurate, it makes me wonder why you want to own gold today."

A small, involuntary grin of pride escaped before Gary said nonchalantly,

"I suppose the deal could have been arranged through the after hours market or the orient later, but it would probably have been more difficult. By the way, as a head-hunter - excuse me, 'Executive Search and Recruitment Consultant' - to the investment banking community, I have been watching you too. You have excellent people skills and I'd like to put you on file. Good people are hard to find on short notice. If things return to normal, which I do not expect, or at least for a very long time, I'd like to talk to you. Would you feel comfortable about giving me your home phone number? At the office you can never tell when someone might just walk in."

"Fine by me," Jan smiled briefly. "Do you want my resume as well?"

"No," Gary shook his head. "Resumes are an attempt to judge how well a person can do a job. I've seen that. Before I approached a client, I would need one, but if and when we meet, we can get that formality out of the way with a current resume." He turned to the phone. "Dial nine to get out?"

Jan nodded and left. Gary dialled Eric to advise him they were done, and to have him arrange another meeting that night with Lynn.

Now that the first part of the "getting away" problem looked like it might be solved, Gary started the next phase, securing the results from potential thieves, official or otherwise. He called North Midland Bank in Stamford and cancelled the

Operation Phoenix

standby credit, and made some further banking arrangements. About 25 hours had passed since the crash had begun.

He then called SAFE-tee Corp in Rochester, and ordered a total of ten safes, all with the same combination. One was a large office safe, over five feet high and 30 inches deep, to be delivered later next week to a local address he would specify.

Three were smaller, type 6510 safes. He would have preferred that they be the larger and stronger type 6570 safes that made up the balance of the order, but he doubted the larger safes would fit in the trunk of a car. The 65 part of the number indicated the construction of the safe. The 10 or 70 indicated the size.

Six safes were the larger type 6570s. He directed that each 6570 safe be bolted to pallets one inch larger all around than the footprint of the safe. Then they were to build, attached to the pallet, a heavy plywood box around the safes to disguise them. They were to leave the predrilled front panel of the box off, so the safes might be filled and locked before closing the box. The pallets enabled the safes to be moved by forklift, should that be needed. Three 6570s, along with the 6510s were to be delivered to his home at 8AM Friday. Three 6570s were to be delivered by their Zurich offices Tuesday to an address to be specified. The large safe was to be held because Gary didn't have an address yet.

Gary debated calling Vance to see how the market was going, but then realized he'd talked to Vance less than three hours ago. It seemed like days. It struck him that there was very little that Vance could tell him that would have a large effect on him. As soon as the market transactions he'd set in motion today were completed, both Vance and the financial markets would largely pass out of his life. Preparations for today had occupied a part of his mind pretty well every day for many years. It was

Operation Phoenix

rather like throwing out an old, comfortable pair of shoes. But, if the world changed as Gary thought it might, there would be all sorts of new adventures in getting Phoenix to arise from the ashes. He brightened at that prospect.

On his way out, Jan stopped him and handed him her card. On the back she had written her home phone number. Gary glanced at it as he started to put it away, and then paused and frowned. "You live in Stamford?"

"Yes. How did you know?"

"This is a Stamford phone exchange like mine." Gary answered. "You must live close to me. In fact, I recall seeing you at the Stamford Centre shopping mall last summer."

"Oh, small world, isn't it?" Jan smiled and impulsively put out her hand. "I'll look forward to your call. Thank you for your business."

"Yeah, I imagine I might see you tomorrow morning to complete the foreign exchange transaction. It's possible I might want to purchase an additional quantity of precious metals and cash again soon, although it is highly unlikely, just part of the contingency process. Do you foresee any problems?"

"No. The process we used today seemed to work well. How much were you thinking of?" Jan asked. She still seemed to be very curious about Gary's hidden agenda.

Gary shrugged. "I have no idea. The world seems to have gone berserk. If I'm really lucky, it could be a substantial percentage of today's deal, but I don't expect that, and in fact expect nothing." He looked down and suddenly realized he was still holding her hand gently. "I want to thank you very much for all you've done today." The sun came out from behind a cloud for a few seconds and light flooded through the window. Then the moment was over. Gary smiled. "Gotta hop. See you later." He released her hand, hurried out of the bank, and ran for the

Operation Phoenix

train to Stamford.

The train was quite full, and there was a lot of serious discussion about the markets of the nature that "somebody should do something." Of course one loudmouth was spouting his theories about how the situation should be handled. Gary thought *You couldn't even fix a flat tire but you're going to find the hole in the financial system and fix it when the best minds in America can't? If you're so damned smart, where's your chauffeur-driven limo?* By and large, the city was continuing as it always had. Some numbers had changed on a stock market ticker, which worried those that were invested, but it was still an abstract. It hadn't yet changed their eating habits. With the sun going down it was getting distinctly cooler, but Gary was engrossed in his own thoughts and was only vaguely aware of it.

In Stamford he jumped into his car, and tried to race through heavy traffic to the mid-sized mall near his home to buy a dozen top of the line padlocks, and a couple of heavy-duty moving dollies. While in the mall he scooped up a local paper for the local 'for rent' advertisements, and a copy of the latest '*Auto Trader*', a magazine specializing in ads for used cars. Later, he couldn't remember whether the mall was crowded or not he was so preoccupied.

One thing he did remember. Someone had tried to shoplift something and the store security nabbed him as he hit a nearby woman and her buggy while trying to escape. On his way out, Gary spotted the store security and asked him if theft was up.

"Yep, we're in a recession never mind what the government says. Shoplifting always goes way up in a recession."

By the time he pulled into his driveway, it was later than he expected, almost dark. But then, nightfall comes shortly after five in February. He looked over the '*Auto Trader*' quickly, and

Operation Phoenix

spotted an ad that interested him. He phoned the number given and was told the '57 Studebaker listed was on blocks, with most of the bodywork done, but the transmission and engine were both out on the bench, not having been worked on at all. The asking price was $4,000. Gary made an appointment to see it the following evening, in Darien, a few minutes drive from Stamford.

Operation Phoenix

Chapter Six

"Well as long as nothing major goes wrong, we're out tomorrow." Gary had arrived at Lynn's about 7PM with Eric and Lynn's portions of the supplies he had purchased over the last two days. "We bought 15,000 ounces of gold today. Weight's going to be a problem though. We're talking about half a ton in weight. That is a quarter of a ton above our wildest dreams. We really got lucky. I hope our luck holds." He glanced heavenwards, imploringly.

"We're shipping 40% of it to Switzerland. By the time we split the remainder three ways, we will each have over 250 pounds of gold to deal with. And we will have a real stack of cash, literally. Roughly, a stack of bills about 125 feet high if it is mostly twenties. Take away what we are shipping to Switzerland, and that leaves us with about 90 feet, or 30 feet each. Actually your cash will be a bit less Lynn, because Eric and I will be spending a lot, quite quickly to buy things we need. So say 15 feet for you to store."

"I'll store my cash in the bank. Apartments don't have backyards to bury old mayo jars in." Lynn straightened her shoulders belligerently.

"I don't think you understand," said Eric from the couch in the living room where they were seated. "A whole sequence of events will happen. First the government will freeze gold. Then there'll be a bank holiday. Gold and most of the money in bank accounts will be seized. We'd best stick with cash outside the banks. Gold and cash are really a very small part of what we are concerned about. It is simply what we are working on now, because we don't expect it to be available if we don't move

Operation Phoenix

now."

"Snowball's chance," scoffed Lynn, "this is America."

"It can, and does happen," Gary raised his head slightly and looked directly at Lynn. "Historically, every time a government gets into financial trouble, including the US in the past, they react exactly the same way. They take everything they can get their hands on. We don't want our wealth just sitting there for them to take."

"Yeah, history does not necessarily repeat, but people keep making the same stupid mistakes." Eric grinned his boyish grin. "One good place to hide stuff is in your fridge. It'll survive a fire, something that most office safes don't. One of the problems for a thief is that he needs to be in and out as fast as possible. We'll use the vegetable crisper drawer for most of the cash that we cannot store elsewhere. It will likely hold about 12 feet of cash. The most important part is to keep it secret. The second you tell your best friend or even a boyfriend, it will travel like wildfire, no matter how much they are sworn to secrecy. It always happens."

"Are you planning to use my fridge to store part of your money?" Lynn demanded. "Look at me. Do I look like I have a vault door and combination lock on my fridge?" Lynn wasn't overweight by any measure, but she was constantly watching her diet.

"No, we are suggesting that you use your fridge to store a small part of your valuables," Gary emphasized the 'your'. "As for the gold, I brought some plastic containers. Take the larger container and fill it about one quarter full of spaghetti sauce, which I also have in the car. Fill the smaller container with water and push it into the larger container so the spaghetti sauce is about one quarter of an inch thick all around. Pop it in the freezer and by morning you can pull the smaller container of water out, leaving you with a frozen shell of spaghetti sauce that you can't see through. Put some gold into a plastic freezer bag, seal it, and drop it into the cavity. Pour more spaghetti sauce over the top, and pop it back in the freezer. Reasonably well hidden. We should be able to store about 80 pounds each that way. 80 pounds of gold doesn't take much space."

Lynn looked worried as if she still thought they were using her fridge to store their valuables, a hassle she obviously didn't want. "Do you think I will get the Good Housekeeping seal of approval if people start breaking their teeth on the yellow clams in my spaghetti sauce?"

Gary smiled slightly and continued. "For the balance of about 300 pounds each of gold, and possibly a little bit of cash, we have two strong safes each. We'll weld the smaller safe into the trunk of a clunker car. We will store those cars, and their cargo of valuables at separate private garages we will rent to 'repair' the cars. Nobody will know. The other bigger safes will have heavy plywood boxes built around them, and we will store them at public warehouse storage, or a moving and storage company. The box is about three feet by three feet by four feet. We will pay for a year's storage in advance."

"Storing things in cars and fridges doesn't seem smart to me. I suppose I could store your money in my fridge, but it makes me nervous," Lynn shook her head slightly.

"Let's talk about tomorrow." Eric interrupted, raising a finger.

"I'd like you both at my lawyer's offices in Yonkers well before noon so that you pick a parking spot where you can see the elevators, and where you can see each other." Gary directed, mostly to bring Lynn up to speed. "Get the briefcases and dollies upstairs to the boardroom. Try and save a parking spot for me."

Operation Phoenix

"I've got some of those orange road cones. I'll stick 'em in a spot near my car." Eric shrugged as if it were a slam dunk.

"Are you guys psychic? Just why do you think things are going to get so bad?" Lynn demanded.

"Because they always have," Eric exclaimed. "If you read old newspapers you will find people saying and doing almost exactly the same thing at almost exactly the same point in the cycle. Almost word for word – it's really amazing. Humanity really has not advanced much." He shook his head in wonderment.

"Oh, all right," said Lynn, resigning herself to their plans.

"Okay," Eric said abruptly, "do we need anything else?"

"Not for me." Gary looked at Lynn "Do you see any problems?"

Lynn shook her head. "Forgive me if I'm incredulous. Banks that are closed so you can't get at your account. You've made a lot of money, yet you're skulking around like grave robbers and taking a chance on having it stolen from you. And why gold? I'm sorry, but I have to keep my job. I can't take so much time off."

"You may be right." Eric replied. "All of this may look pretty silly later. But if our greatest fears come to pass, we will look brilliant. Ordinary people, who trust things to go on smoothly will have diddly squat."

"Well, I hope you guys know what you're doing. I'll be there by noon with my briefcases."

"Good. We'll see you tomorrow and please don't talk to anyone about cash, or gold, or bank holidays, or anything remotely connected with this. As vulnerable as we are, it wouldn't take much for someone to catch on to the idea and hurt us badly." Gary instructed.

As they went to the car to distribute Gary's load, Gary said

Operation Phoenix

to Eric in disbelief, and slight hurt that his daughter didn't agree now that events were proving their theories. "She still doesn't believe."

"I think she believes we own gold. It just doesn't have any value to her," Eric shrugged. "She seemed more concerned about the cash. Maybe she doesn't understand how much money is involved. I think she feels that she is doing you a favour because she doesn't think of it as being hers – or ours. It's yours."

Gary nodded in agreement.

Eric continued to philosophize. "She can't make the emotional leap from pay checks to millions of dollars. She doesn't believe that it's going to get worse. I don't think I'd have understood if you hadn't dragged me along for some of your research. Reading those old newspapers, and seeing how politicians and people spouted exactly the same things before the crash of '29: 'This time it is different. We now control things much more scientifically', I can believe they will do the same thing on the next step. Deep down I don't suppose I really understand how bad it will get. But after reading about the '30's depression, Brazil, Russia, Argentina, and all those other places, I can believe it's going to be pretty bad."

"Yeah. - 'Those that don't know their history are condemned to repeat it.' Actually, I suppose I don't fully understand how bad it's going to be, either." Gary looked at the ground. "Maybe we shouldn't volunteer much about our other arrangements to her, until she sees for herself. Not hide it, just don't volunteer anything. What do you think?"

"Mmmm, yes," mused Eric, head also down. "If she gets taken hostage or something before she becomes convinced, it would give us a bit more flexibility in trying to rescue her."

"Agreed. See if you can think along these lines of security

and hostage rescue plans. I'll think on it too." Gary went back to unloading Lynn's part of the load.

"You know it just occurred to me," Eric said suddenly, looking up "she may not understand how much money is involved. I know from our work that it has to be about $40 million. But you haven't even told me how much you got in the end. How much was it?"

"Oh my god, you're right. I got $53,503,420 from the transaction, and spent $52 million and change to buy 15,000 ounces of gold, leaving $1.2 million for operations tomorrow when we buy foreign currencies and US cash. We got out at almost the exact top. I was surprised that the Fed released gold to the market, but in thinking about it, that was a win/win for them. It's a cheap way to defuse a panic, and also give them some cash which they desperately need."

After a moment, Gary added, "I think I may know how to make this more real to her. Tomorrow, when we get the shipment in, one of the first things we are going to do is distribute the cash. One of us will simply dump the largest bag of bills on the table. For someone thinking the way Lynn is, seeing that amount in cash is bound to be shocking. We know it is pretty much worthless but it will be more real for her."

"Yeah, we can try that." Eric hoisted two large tins of spaghetti sauce. "You said the Fed released gold to the market?"

"Yeah - I suspect they dumped gold more because they needed money than anything else, but it was also a cheap way to halt the run. And it signalled to the world that gold might not be an alternative to the US dollar. Smart kids them."

"I think that it might have been an even more brilliant strategy than that," Eric opined. "It still leaves them with all their other options. They can still freeze gold, and then confiscate it, just like they did in the '30s."

Operation Phoenix

"Huh." Gary exhaled abruptly. "Ah yes, the Lord giveth and the Lord taketh away. They sell their gold, get the cash, and then take back their gold. A crude but very effective new tax. And it works on those who have enough resources and foresight to maybe be smart enough, and powerful enough create problems for them later. Those people now have less money to manipulate the world, and no gold. The international financial system must be in even worse condition than we think. We can expect the bank holiday and the other operations soonest. We can't foresee when they will move, just that it will be much sooner than we expected. We're not going to get several months to prepare as we expected. A house of cards doesn't take long to tumble."

Eric mused, head back down. "I think we should get started on our other plans as quickly as possible. Trucks, food, freezers, and stuff." He looked up at Gary.

"Yes. Particularly the fuel tankers. I think we may want more than we expected, maybe half or even a dozen or more tanker trailers. As many as we can get anyway. I sure hope that thing with Lynn works tomorrow. We need more hands to accomplish what we have to do. If she becomes a believer, she could help immensely."

Eric nodded. "If it's going at this speed, maybe we should change some of our plans. I think government might freeze everything as early as the weekend. What about the bonds you were going to use to pay taxes on your gains in the market?" Eric's eyes narrowed. "Looks like our plans may be wrong."

They had forecast that bond prices would fall and the yield would go up. Once the US effectively stopped borrowing, the largest demand for loans in the world would no longer be there. Suddenly a surplus of funds would be trying to make interest income. The yield would come down and the price would go back up. When tax time came, Gary could simply pay with bonds they'd made a profit on, or perhaps even argue that these were US obligations worth 100 cents on the dollar.

"You're probably right. The government may decide to just wipe them out. I think the buying of bonds is largely out. That leaves us with cash, or perhaps silver. But we don't have time, because we'll either be in Switzerland or be so busy tomorrow and Friday that we can't do anything else but finish what we have on our plate. Maybe we can get Willis to pick up silver and only deliver in a week? I'll check on that tomorrow." Gary concentrated on keeping Lynn's load of plastic containers from spilling.

They arrived back at Eric's apartment just before nine. Gary found a couple of garages to rent, phoned them, and on his way home, was able to view a perfect garage in Greenwich. The garage was at the back of a residential property, separate from the house, constructed from cement blocks, with a metal door and a plank and steel workbench along one side. That fit Gary's story of rebuilding an antique car perfectly. He left a cash deposit covering six months rent.

Before going to bed, Gary made up a list of drafts, wire transfers, and payments for the following day. Then he prepared his own freezer containers.

Despite, or because of the tension, he was exhausted and was asleep instantly.

Chapter Seven
Thursday February 16th — Day Three.

During breakfast, Gary studied the ads in the papers carefully and found another garage that sounded good and two more 'mechanic's special' cars, clunkers needing extensive repairs. While preparing his car with briefcases, firearms and trolleys for the gold transfer, he found himself anticipating seeing Jan again. The day looked like it was going to be one of those all gray February days with the temperature producing occasional drizzle rather than snow. Winds were light but slightly gusty.

He spent nearly an hour on the phone, arranging appointments to see the cars and garages that night, getting quotations to warehouse the larger safes, and reserving a welding unit and a step/cube van with a pull out ramp. Eric would be looking for clunker cars too since they needed three cars and three garages.

On his way downtown in normal traffic, Gary called Vance to learn exactly what he had purchased yesterday, and how the markets were doing. Vance gushed information. "Well, the stock market isn't open yet, but Tokyo, Hong Kong, London and Frankfurt have all been very volatile, and down badly. Since Tuesday afternoon, every one of the major stock market indices is down more than 50 percent. Foreign exchange markets are also very volatile, but were trading in a range because of government intervention. In the last half hour, the dollar has been sliding badly, so maybe Finland, and Canada, and everybody else, is running out of money to play with. Governments have poured billions and billions into this black hole. The last estimate I heard was one and a half trillion dollars,

Operation Phoenix

of which the US had less than $50 billion in foreign exchange reserves to contribute."

"Hoo boy, central banks are panicking, aren't they? But they have to slow the wholesale abandonment of the dollar despite their increasing displeasure with the policies of the US."

Vance observed, "The US is the worlds largest debtor. 'Too big to fail.' If the US is in trouble, they are all in trouble. Speaking of which, the IMF, the US treasury, and all sixteen other governments in the cabal have all been actively purchasing US bonds the entire time. This not only helps the dollar, but also supports bonds which they have a lot of. But some of the commercials aren't following their government's lead. Japanese and even our own pension plans have been dumping bonds wholesale. Bonds are down to 82 this morning, and gold is $2,690, so you are in the money on your purchases yesterday."

"That is mainly the reason I called. What did you buy for me yesterday?"

"I had to pay quite a bit for some of your put options, since prices were moving fast. I got 120 of the December $2,700 gold put options with the first $100,000. I had to go to September for 50 of the bond put options at $2031.25 each. That overspent your account by about $1,000, but we are 'in the money' now, so we can ignore that rule. I hope that was okay?"

"God, yes. That was exactly right. By the way, I have changed my mind. I still want to sell the options at the levels I ordered, but instead of buying bonds and registering them in my name, just hold on to the cash. I will likely be forwarding the money to Premet as before."

"Okay, I have an order to hold monies, rather than purchase bonds."

After dropping off the equipment needed for the gold transfer at Ron Thompson's, in Yonkers, he parked his car in the

Operation Phoenix

Premet Bank building's obscenely expensive underground parking lot. *I just want to park my damned car for a couple of hours, not buy the whole damned building.* Upstairs, he left word for Jan with the special accounts receptionist that he was in the building seeing Menach. At Menachs office he waited until an assistant led him into the day vault, where Menach, clipboard in hand, was overseeing two sweating clerks who were shifting and counting gold.

The day vault was obviously arranged to limit the exposure to robbery for the relatively insecure retail counter. From the retail counter side, a large coded security door with a bullet-proof observation window gave entrance to the vault. Directly ahead at the other end of the vault, were two large security doors, obviously leading to the secure loading area, and probably to the main vault area. Both sidewalls were lined with security boxes. Four very visible cameras, one in each corner covered every inch of the relatively small room. At the near end, stood two counter-height tables, armed with a variety of counting machines, time stamps, phones and computer display screens. Two Willis guards lounged on some decrepit chairs at a battered wooden table.

In the centre, near the wooden table, stood two heavy-duty four-wheeled, steel industrial trolleys. On one were stacked four 400-ounce gold bars, as well as boxes containing what Gary presumed was 141 kilo bars of gold. On the other, what appeared to be his smaller bars and coins, all packaged. Next to them, on the floor, bags presumably containing his cash.

Menach acknowledged him; "I'll be with you as soon as I finish this."

"No problem'" Gary said as he made his way over to the guards. "What are you here to pick up?"

"We're the dedicated truck for the airport run. We're

trying to catch an earlier flight this afternoon. The other truck should be here any minute."

Satisfied that matters were progressing at least as well as planned, Gary returned his attention to the counting process. Menach came over, counting complete, and Gary suggested that they split out the 40% shipment first, to get the guards on their way. He wanted to get it through Swiss customs before the Swiss might react and seize it. Gary started counting boxes, opened a couple to spot check, and pronounced himself satisfied with the total. One of the assistants went to get an empty trolley, and the 40% shipment for Zurich was split out onto the empty trolley.

Gary pulled out four $50 bills for the Willis guys. "One for each of you, one for the driver, and one for the guy who gets the shipment on the earlier flight. Don't stop for any coffees along the way." The other truck must have been waiting, because these two guards were immediately replaced with two more Willis guards.

Just then, Jan walked in, her auburn hair looking shiny and silky. She had taken off her suit jacket and was wearing a pale blouse with a contrasting bow. Gary broke out in a huge grin. "Hi, Jan."

"Good morning Gary," Jan smiled brilliantly at him. "You're here earlier than I expected. How far along in the process are we?" Jan stopped a couple of inches closer to Gary than normal.

"The 40% shipment just went out and we are about to start the other three shipments." Gary grinned inanely at her. "By the way do you think you could get me a private phone to use for a few minutes on the way out?"

"Certainly. Now that you're nearly complete perhaps you would like to have lunch on the bank as well?"

Operation Phoenix

"I'd like nothing better but my agenda is packed right now. In fact I will be pretty busy till at least the week after next. Perhaps a rain check?"

"Okay shall I call you or will you call me?"

"Better I call you I guess because I don't know what my itinerary will be."

Menach came over with a sour, disapproving look on his face, probably at the somewhat intimate body language that was going on between Gary and Jan. Gary decided to change the subject. "Can you tell me what gold is trading at right now?"

Menach punched up gold on the screen, and got a mixed look on his face. Last trade at $2,656.80 and still falling. Gary whistled to himself and thought, *I'm out of the $2,700 puts at Wilkinson, and damned near out of the $2,600's. Now to get this gold out of the system, out of reach of the greedy claws of government.* "Damn," he said aloud, "I sure wish I had waited till today to purchase. The price is down nearly $300 per ounce." Looking at Menach he said, "Bet you are happy you offloaded a lot of inventory at such high prices. You must be up over five million just on me alone."

Menachs whole body radiated self-satisfaction at finally having won one at Gary's expense.

Jan said, "If you two want to continue on I'll get one of the secretaries to type up any paperwork you need to have done." Menach handed her a couple of sheets from his clipboard. Jan time stamped them and left. Belatedly Gary returned his attention to his beloved gold, which he'd forgotten in Jan's presence.

As they moved back to the clerks and gold laden trolleys Gary asked Menach casually, "I haven't noticed any mention of silver in your operations. Do you carry silver or have I simply been fixated on gold and missed it?"

Operation Phoenix

"Oh we deal in silver all right. But we don't advertise it as much because the lower price per ounce makes for much more weight to make the same dollar return. The additional handling and storing of that volume is more costly. Much of our business is institutional, 100 and 1,000-ounce bars, along with silver rounds, bags of old silver coins. We don't stock as much of the small sizes as we do gold, but we do have them. Why? Are you interested in silver now?"

"Possibly. I'd want to see how my money worked out. But my main interest is gold. Are all your silver bars under 1,000 ounces encased in plastic?"

"Yes, it prevents tarnishing."

"Oh well if the occasion arises, we'll discuss it, but I'd also want to get competitive quotes. What is your premium on 100 ounce bars?"

"On orders under 20,000 ounces, $0.50 an ounce. On orders over 20,000 ounces, $0.25 an ounce," Menach quoted.

"What is your spread?"

Caught, Menach told him. "But on orders over 20,000 ounces we halve that." Menach obviously knew he was now making a competitive quote.

"Are there any other charges of any kind applicable?"

"Just taxes, applicable on retail level quantities not on institutional orders, and of course bar charges on bars under 100 ounces."

"I assume 100 ounce bars come packed in cartons for larger orders? What sort of inventory would be available on short notice?" Gary asked.

"Yes 100 ounce bars are packed in poly or cardboard containers of approximately 185 cubic inches, containing 1,000 ounces each, or about 68 pounds. On the spot we can normally fill any institutional order. Overnight such as you did with your

Operation Phoenix

gold, and particularly with larger sizes, it is virtually unlimited."

The other three local shipments were split apart, loaded and dispatched. Gary tipped the sweating clerks. When Menach looked a bit envious, Gary tipped him as well because he thought Menach could be vindictive. He admonished them that he didn't want the news of these shipments to go anywhere.

Gary hurried to special accounts where Jan showed him to an empty conference room with a phone, and left. Gary dialled SAFE-tee Corp, the safe company, and got through to his sales rep. The Swiss safes were confirmed but there was a question about the large office safe. The older models available were not nearly as heavy as the newer models, which were also stronger with hi-tech metals and composites. Gary asked if they could make the newer safe look older and used. Yes they could do that by painting it with house paint and using a mechanical buffer to simulate wear on parts. Gary agreed and arranged for delivery of the large office safe to an address to be specified, and a delivery date of next week, along with payment details.

Next he called Joe Seligman at Willis Armoured Cars.

"Hi Gary. I don't know if the shipment to the airport has arrived yet."

"I wasn't calling about that just now. They only left a few minutes ago. What I want to know is, are you a company who falls under the jurisdiction of the Foreign Exchange Stabilization act?"

"No our parent company, Willis Bank is, but we're not."

"So if your parent company were to go bankrupt or be closed by a banking holiday, or something like that, you would still be open and able to service your clients?

"Yes."

"Can you do a pickup of precious metals and cash tomorrow and deliver it to a local address only in a weeks

Operation Phoenix

time?"

"Yes but we charge storage fees."

Gary thought the storage fees were high but he needed this worse than the money. They made a tentative appointment to do a pickup at 10:30AM the following morning at Premet. Next he called Vance at Wilkinson.

"Hi, it's Gary."

"Gary! You sure are a money-making machine. Everyone in the office knows about you."

"Well, I am not too happy about that. I am desperately trying to keep a low profile. Try to keep a lid on it, especially if someone official comes asking questions. No one knows anything about where the money went, or anything except what is officially written down," Gary said in stern tones.

"Oh, it would never leave the office."

"It already has, and you damned well know it. I just hope that my name isn't associated with it. Wives have to tell their husbands and they must brag a little to their friends. Say I am ripping mad and that the account is in jeopardy, - or whatever. Destroy any special notes you personally have on me. I don't want anyone official to have an easy time following up. In this atmosphere it is damned dangerous to be known to have wealth. In any case that is not why I called. There have been some changes to my plan, and come to think of it, they make your story about me being boiling mad look real. Where am I on the gold puts?" Gary asked.

He could hear Vance punching up the gold. "You sold half your puts at $2,700 as expected. Gold has just crossed $2,600 so I expect they too have now been sold." Vance sounded quite cowed.

"OK what are long bonds at now?"

"You're a long way toward your forecast of 50. They are

Operation Phoenix

61 and 57/64ths." Vance said.

"What I want you to do is to sell out my bond puts before closing. Then wire the money to Premet first thing tomorrow morning. Just like you did with the gold option money. All the same conditions apply. I will be getting an overnight loan. Any problems?" Gary asked.

"No, I have an order to sell you out before the close, and wire the money to Premet first thing tomorrow." Vance sounded deflated.

"Oh and hold back $100. I want to keep the account open."

Vance sounded a lot brighter. "You expect to be doing more trades?"

"I have no idea. As you saw, my plans can change pretty fast but that possibility exists. I expect that foodstuffs, and oil, will rocket in price. Maybe, maybe not. We will see how this plays out," Gary said. To himself he thought, *Vance, I don't even expect your company to exist after this is over. But you have been fair and $100 is a cheap price to give you some hope.* Aloud he said, "I gotta hop. Do you need anything else?"

"Nope. Sell you out and wire the money. Keep the account open."

Gary rushed out towards Jan's office. She was alone. He skidded to a halt. "Do you have a few minutes? I want to do another deal."

"Why yes, Gary." she smiled at him. Gary's breath caught when she smiled with her whole face and eyes. He got back to business.

"Okay I am really rushed. I want another overnight loan to take effect from the market opening tomorrow, until the money arrives from Wilkinson."

"How much money are we talking about here, Gary?"

Operation Phoenix

"Probably between four and five million."

"Is this another 'few' that will grow and grow?" she asked with another smile.

"Absolutely not. It could even be a bit less than four, although I doubt it."

"What do you want to do with it? More gold?" Jan cocked her head.

"Nope, Silver. I will be leaving this entirely in your hands," Gary said. "I want you to buy at the open tomorrow morning, 40,000 ounces of silver broken down this way", and he wrote it on a sheet of paper.

80 X 100-ounce bars.
800 X 10-ounce bars.
1600 X 5-ounce bars.
4000 X 2-ounce bars.
8000 X 1-ounce bars or coins.

"All plastic encased standard good delivery bars and packed in cartons for shipping by Willis. No logo bars but fill the order as you have sizes and I prefer small sizes. I don't want any 1,000 ounce bars but I will take bags of silver dimes if you have nothing else. I expect that order will eat up over one million, leaving about four million in US cash. Make that roughly equal numbers $5's, 10's, 20's, 50's, and $100 US dollar bills." Jan scribbled her notes as Gary spoke. "Spread fees like the four dollars we did for gold, but 25 cents over the market offer at the time of the purchase. Bar fees as you posted them last week. The overnight loan at 25%, but no arrangement fee because you will only be financing for an hour or so. Willis will pick up at 10:30. In the event that something happens such as a government order before official delivery is made to me, there will be no purchase. Once the title resides in me delivery to Willis must be made, regardless. If there is some block before

Operation Phoenix

the title passes I want straight cash for the entire amount, with your handling fee for cash as agreed. Is that acceptable to you? "

Jan pursed her lips. "I got a lot of flack about your low fees and moreover we were making money on the foreign exchange spreads, which we won't here. I have to have more. How about one eighth of one percent more handling fee for the cash?"

"Ouch." said Gary. "How about an arrangement fee of $25,000? That way the fees would be credited to your department."

"I suppose I could live with that. Let me do my due diligence." While picking up the phone she dug out the forms for Gary to sign. She talked to Heidi the floor trader, Vance, and Menach, while Gary signed the blank forms. "Yes, I can accept your order."

Gary shook the proffered hand and raced for his car. The weather was still gloomy and drizzling rain, but Gary was imagining the next steps and hardly noticed.

Operation Phoenix

Chapter Eight

At Ron Thompson the lawyer's building, Eric had secured perfect places in the underground parking for parking the cars, near the elevators but in separated spots within easy sight of one another. As they waited for the elevator Gary brought Eric and Lynn up to speed on his activities. They were both were dressed casually, Lynn having taken the day off work and Eric having quit his job. Eric had not been sitting around either. He had found some unused air force hangars on a short-term rental to be used as hidden storage places for tanker trailers. The airfield was fenced with a 24-hour guard service. He had also found eight used tanker trailers with a 10,000-gallon, or more capacity. "They seem in good shape but I don't think I am going to get them cheap."

"Ah, yes," philosophized Gary. "There are three ways you can get something - good, fast, and cheap. But you only get to choose two. If it's good and fast, it ain't gonna be cheap. People aren't desperate enough for prices to start falling yet."

In Ron's dark mahogany reception area, two guards, a male and a female in police uniform were lounging on the couch. Gary asked for Mary, Ron's secretary, and she ushered them into the stately, bookshelf-lined boardroom. Behind closed doors Gary instructed Mary. "Make sure neither the receptionist, nor anyone else, gives those guards the slightest amount of information that could be used to identify or trace us later. Post the guards on either side of the door here. They are primarily a deterrent in case of unexpected problems. Order them sandwiches when we leave and let them go an hour after we leave, but pay them to six o'clock. Here are two $50 bills as a tip. Any questions of any kind by the guards are to be dealt with by Ron only."

Mary went to the phone to privately instruct the receptionist since the guards were sitting within easy earshot of the reception desk. Hanging up she said, "Willis has already been up to scout out the lay of the land. They should be bringing up your shipment momentarily." No sooner were the words out of her mouth than the receptionist phoned to say they'd arrived.

As soon as the room was clear Lynn asked, "Why are we being so secretive about who we are? Those are cops."

"At times like these it is the security forces who are the most dangerous," Gary stated flatly. "Anywhere the rule of law breaks down it's the cops and anyone with authority and guns who steal the most. There is no reason for them to have any information. Treat them as if they were about to steal everything we have, because if they can trace us they will likely try."

"That's rather paranoid don't you think?" his daughter asked with one eyebrow raised.

"No there's good reason to be vigilant," Eric said abruptly. "You're not paranoid if the threat is real."

The second and third shipments came in, along with the bags of cash. Gary tipped the guards with a $50 bill each, along with one for the driver, and they were gone.

"You're being pretty free with the $50 bills aren't you?" Lynn asked. "Why are you tipping the cops and the guards?"

"We want them to feel good about us so maybe if they are questioned they will just answer the questions asked, and not volunteer extra information," Gary was locking the door.

"Well, let's get started," Eric said, heaving a large bag of cash onto the table, unzipping it and dumping the contents on the end of the large conference table. A few packets slid off onto the floor. Eric shook the bag to make sure it was empty and tossed the bag into the corner. He started to pick up the packets of cash on the floor tossing them casually back on the pile of bills on the table.

Lynn's eyes widened. "That's money," she said in a stunned tone, "Wait a minute there's all these bags and boxes here. How much money do you have?"

"Well some got shipped overseas, more is to come later, and the price of gold has gone down since we bought, but we made about $58 million in the stock market yesterday and today, so we have about half of that here," Gary busied himself straightening some of the packets of cash that were threatening to slide off the table again.

"Fifty eight million!" Lynn squeaked.

"Shhh. Keep your voice down," Gary hissed, motioning at the door. "I told you we would never have to work again if we didn't want to. Not only that but what we have will be worth a hell of a lot more in the months ahead. It is not mine it's ours. We will use it to buy whatever we need to survive - food, services, bribes, or whatever is needed. In the meantime, to the authorities, anyone with large amounts of cash is suspicious. They assume it is drug money or something and seize it first. Then it gets tied up for years until you prove yourself innocent."

Lynn continued to stare at the pile of money, awestruck. Gary placed three of the square leather accountant's briefcases on the table and said.

"We have to divvy up this cash. Lynn would you take three or six packets of one denomination, say 20s, and walk down putting the packets equally and neatly into the cases. Eric and I will each take an extra packet and put it in our case. We will spend this all pretty quickly."

"Wait a minute," Lynn sputtered. "I didn't know you

Operation Phoenix

made millions. Fifty-eight million is pretty awesome evidence that you know what you are talking about. I have to get up to speed on this. What's next?"

Eric picked up an armload of bill packets, and started distributing it. "We think it's going to be pretty depressing. What I'm saying is the speed and severity makes us also wonder if our worst-case scenario is 'worst' enough, and maybe by quite a bit. Last week we were not rich, we were just working stiffs. We planned, prepared and used our available resources to take advantage of the situation. Plus we got incredibly lucky because we could move fast. We had hoped to get out with as much as $10 million, but the speed and severity of events got us $58 million. We just won the lottery."

As they distributed the cash, and separated the gold destined for the home fridges, Eric told Lynn about the research he and Gary had done. He covered world events and the likely consequences. "It's like dropping a pebble into a still pond. We can predict there will be ripples. Those ripples will go out to touch everything all the way to the edge of the pond. It is going to happen every time and that makes ripples predictable. But this event is more like a huge meteor falling into the ocean. The ripples are a huge tsunami racing around the world, smashing everything in its way. The overall results are predictable because ripples are predictable."

Seeing a kilo bar of gold for the first time astounded Lynn. "Look how small but heavy it is. And it's beautiful."

"Yes, if it were compressed into a round ball it would be about the size of a golf ball, the whole kilo – 2.2 pounds. And those bars about the size of a brick over there are 400 ounce bars, about 25 pounds. One ounce coins are smaller than a quarter."

"How much is it worth?" Lynn asked holding one of the

Operation Phoenix

kilo bars.

"Well in times to come it will be worth a kilo of gold. But today, depending on exactly what the price of gold is at this minute, probably about $70,000. Later we expect it will buy much more goods than $70,000 will today." Gary picked up a load of eight packets of bills to put in the briefcases.

Lynn was silent for some time. "Dad do you want me to quit my job and go to Switzerland with you?"

"Really we would prefer you did not quit your job at the moment. You are in the drug industry. Prescription drugs are going skyrocket in value if you can get any at all. There won't be medical supplies or equipment where we are going. We may be able to get what we need in other ways but it will be more difficult and time consuming than if we had your contacts." Gary said.

He took a breath. "As far as Switzerland goes we feel there is a higher risk that we will lose part or all of that shipment. If we can keep and use it, we feel it might be invaluable. We hope that each of us would be able to get access to most parts of the shipment in an emergency, even if the other two cannot. Our first priority was to get what we had out of the system so it could not be easily found, seized and tied up, and then get a part of it outside the jurisdiction of the US. It is your choice whether you keep your job or not. Ideally if you could take a few days holiday, we could achieve both objectives."

"Okay I'll try to get next week off."

"That's great," Gary enthused. "By the way, what's his name, your latest boyfriend, are you thinking of having him join our group?"

"No, oh Christ no. He is just a Mr. Right Now. I have no intention of giving him a long term engagement."

"Well, it looks as if we are about ready to start taking this stuff down to the cars. We can probably get all the fridge stuff on one dolly so let's do it. Lynn you stay here and lock the door so no one can stick their nose in here. Eric and I will take this to the cars. We need your car keys please." Gary held out his hand.

Despite the high degree of tension of moving a high value shipment unprotected through a public place, the trips to the cars were anti-climactic. As Gary exited the boardroom the female cop eyed him intensely, but the male was simply bored. In the parking area Eric reconnoitred, got out a street sweeper shotgun and loaded it. They loaded each part of the fridge money and gold into the respective cars. Eric climbed back into his car to caress his shotgun while Gary went for another load.

The second and third loads were strictly gold, and were difficult because of their weight. Three hundred pounds was heavy to push. The carpet formed a small wave in front of the wheels of the trolley so Gary was constantly pushing the heavy load uphill. Each time he exited the boardroom the female cop studied him more intently.

Finally they loaded the last trolley, cleaned up the minimal debris, and called Ron in to let him know they were done. As the Gary and Lynn were exiting the boardroom with the load, the male cop who was now alert and scowling, asked, "Are we finished?"

"Not yet," replied Ron. "There are box lunches coming shortly."

"Just a minute," said the female cop. "As a police officer I cannot be involved in anything illegal. I don't like what I'm seeing. What exactly is going on here?"

"Nothing illegal," Ron said briefly.

"We still want to know what's going on," demanded the male cop.

"As an officer of the court I can't be involved in anything

Operation Phoenix

illegal, any more than you can. Also as an officer of the court, I can assure you that as the laws of the land are presently constituted, there is nothing illegal going on here. Eccentric possibly but not illegal. We wouldn't have specified off duty cops as guards if there were the slightest taint about what is going on here."

The male cop looked as if he was prepared to continue the battle but when his partner subsided darkly, he did too.

At Eric's they threw his fridge cash and gold into a closet, covering them with some dirty laundry. Then they drove to Gary's where they backed Lynn's, and then Eric's car into the garage and offloaded the heavier safe gold into piles along the wall. They threw tarps over them to hide them. Eric left with Lynn to get her fridge gold and money into her apartment. Gary backed his own car into the garage, set his alarms and began dealing with his valuables.

Gary had kept six packets of Swiss Francs and all but one packet of the Canadian Dollars in New York. All the other currencies except one packet of each, in case he needed to go to a country and needed walking around money, along with $20,000 US had gone to Zurich. Eric returned having dealt with his own fridge gold and cash. Then they took turns guarding the garage while the other bought clunker cars and rented garages. Gary returned last. "Well we have three garages and three clunker cars," said Gary, giving Eric a high five. Both of them were grinning like Cheshire cats.

"Okay!!" Eric exclaimed emphatically, flopping down into Gary's favourite leather reclining chair in the living room, while grinning widely. "Now we have the tools we need to solve the problem of getting away if we can just keep it from being stolen. Now the hard work begins, accumulating supplies and equipment to make survival possible."

Operation Phoenix

"Yeah and with Lynn onside we've got a team now. But it will be tough keeping ahead of events that are to come."

Chapter Nine
Friday February 17th — Day Four.

About one o'clock Gary phoned Jan. "Did you complete the silver transaction this morning?" he demanded.

"Yes Gary, the shipment went out at about 11."

"Good. All the cash got included?"

"Yes. And I am beginning to see some of your hidden agenda. There has just been an announcement by the Exchange Stabilization Department of the Treasury. Banks are not allowed to sell gold retail. You are awesome."

"Did they mention silver in their press release?"

"No just gold."

"Ah So," opined Gary, "they have just formally admitted to the world that the US dollar is trash."

"Yes we're having trouble completing any foreign exchange transaction. Letters of credit, anything. Foreign banks are putting us on notice that they will not issue guarantees of any kind until the situation stabilizes. Business people are up in arms but the average citizen is not affected."

"That means no more foreign goods being loaded I suppose, but I gotta hop. Thanks for all the help. Hold all the paperwork there and I'll see you in a week or so. Lots of things to do in the interim," Gary said.

"Okay thank you for calling. I'm looking forward to our business date. We very much appreciate your business." Gary perked at this. If Nils had been saying this would he have called it a business *date?*

Operation Phoenix

Gary and Eric had been up well before 6:00 AM. It had gotten cooler overnight and the occasional drizzle of yesterday had turned into the odd flake of snow that melted on hitting the pavement. Eric drove Gary to the van rental place, and then left to arrange a tow truck to move the first of the clunker cars, Gary's 57 Studebaker. Gary picked up the van and welding equipment and was back at the house in plenty of time to receive the safes he had ordered. The three smaller safes were placed at the rear of the garage and a tarp was thrown over them to hide them. The three larger safes on pallets, with disguising plywood built around them, were placed in the back of the van.

They had planned to deliver the cars one by one, wrestle the safes into the trunk, weld them in place, fill them, lock them and then call a second towing company to haul the filled car to its garage. The hope was to break the paper trail by using two separate companies that didn't know about each other. One person would stay at the garage filling the next safe while the other would accompany the filled car to its final resting place. They had just dropped the empty Studebaker in Gary's garage when Eric said to the driver, who was awaiting further instructions, "Excuse us for a moment. We have something to discuss."

Gary frowned and followed Eric a short distance away. Eric said "I was thinking that we have a problem controlling whether these guys see each other. No point in being so secretive if they all know what is going on. One of us will have to go with the truck doing the pickup to slow him down if necessary. It needs at least two to get that safe in the car, and one of us has to go with the drop off truck to make sure everything is locked and secure."

"Yeah and someone has to load the safe, and should be here to watch the garage." Gary thought for a moment. "This is going to add more time damn it. We might not even get all the warehouse safes placed today."

"Do you think it would be better if we used six towing companies for the six loads, and call them as we need them?"

Gary shook his head.

"Those towing companies often operate under several names. I do like calling them as we need them but towing guys say they will be there right away, and that means today some time. Maybe we could take that chance with the full cars, but use this guy to pick up empty cars to bring here. Just don't give him the pickup address until we are ready"

"Okay I'll handle the pickups and you handle the drop offs so the garage won't be unguarded for long." Eric went over to the driver and said, "We do have another pickup in Norwalk but I can't say exactly when, probably in just over an hour. If we give you 15 to 30 minutes notice can you or one of your buddies be there to meet me and pick up?"

"Probably. Friday morning is usually pretty slow," he shrugged.

"How much do we owe you to date?" Gary asked. When the driver told him, Gary paid in cash requiring no receipt. That seemed to delight the driver. Gary was also delighted because it likely meant there would be no record of the transaction and that the driver would be there waiting for the next shipment. The driver left.

They got the safe welded into the trunk and half full before calling a second tow company to pick up the loaded car. Eric would stay loading the van safes till Gary phoned to say his drop off was complete and he was headed back.

Four and a half hours after the first clunker car was delivered the last clunker car was in the last garage with its smaller safe, filled, and welded into the now locked trunk. The

Operation Phoenix

three larger safes in the van had been filled and their plywood fronts had been screwed into place, disguising them.

Eric left with the last tow truck. Gary returned the welding equipment and stopped by his bank to pick up cash, driving the van. When he cancelled his standby line of credit, he had ordered all his investments to be sold, all personal and corporate accounts to be stripped except for one dollar to keep them open, and the resulting cash to be waiting. Another fair sized bag of cash.

Gary met Eric at the first of the public storage warehouses they had selected. Wrestling the heavy safe on to a trolley and into the private storage cubicle proved so difficult that Eric decided to help Gary at the next public storage warehouse. Finally after the second public warehouse Gary said. "Enough, we are going to get a heart attack this way. I'll find a moving and storage company for Lynn's safe, and they can move the safe with a forklift. You may as well get on with purchasing tanker trailers and a place to hide them."

On his way to Orange, on impulse, Gary stopped at a truck stop partly because he was hungry, and partly because he had an idea. As he came up to the restaurant he saw a trucker ambling up toward the door too.

"Excuse me, sir," Gary smiled slightly, putting on his professional head-hunter face. "Do you have a moment and are you familiar with the area? I would like to ask you a couple of questions."

"I am reasonably familiar with Orange. I deliver here a lot."

"What I am looking for is a small local trucking firm, maybe 15 or 20 tractors, that the owner has a reputation of absolute honesty. Do you know of such a firm?"

After a bit of thought the trucker said, "Probably Alpine

would be your best bet, or maybe Habel over on Marsh Hill road."

"Do you know if either of them does small amounts of storage?" Gary asked.

"Alpine has a pretty small building, but Habel has a larger old building. It is part of a farm that the family has. Habel is growing through word of mouth very fast, but everything is paid for. All their trucks and everything I hear. Pretty closed mouth though. I like them, and I have seen a few things stored there. They have a few racks."

"That's great. Sounds exactly like what I am looking for. Do you know the name of Habels owner?" Gary asked.

"Yeah, Chris Habel."

"Thank you very much. You have helped a lot."

After finishing his hamburger, Gary asked another truck driver the same question and got the same response - Habel or Alpine. He went to the phone to look up Habels phone number and address. Chris himself answered the phone. After some hesitation Chris said, yes, they would have space for that kind of box.

Orange hadn't grown out past Marsh Hill Road yet. Gary turned left on to a dirt driveway that intrigued him. The driveway was not gravelled but it was flat and level. It should have been rutted with trucks going in and out. The truck yard was gravelled and not in quite as good a shape as the road. Obviously they paid attention to details in this business.

As well, Chris was not totally out of the farming business because horses and cows roamed in the field beyond the chain-link truck fence. Gary noticed a tanker trailer sitting in the truck yard. After arranging and paying cash for six months storage he casually asked if they used tankers a lot.

"Yes we have a couple of regular customers who use

Operation Phoenix

tanks." Chris shrugged. He was taciturn but sounded reliable.

"If you were buying a used tank how do you tell whether it is good?"

"The tank should have a certification sticker. It has to be renewed every two years I think. I have a mechanic guy I leave all that to."

"Is your mechanic guy employed by you or is he an independent contractor?" Gary asked.

"Oh we are not large enough to have a whole lot of permanent staff. He has a shop just down the street."

"What's his name Chris? I might need someone who knows tanks."

"His name is Roy Bryant. Don't remember what he calls his company but his phone number is 656-3456." Chris said.

Gary noted the name and number and said, "Trustworthy, I take it."

"Oh absolutely. If he says something about anything you can bet it's going to happen. I've used him for years." For such a taciturn guy, Chris's recommendation seemed very fervent.

Gary thanked Chris profusely, promised that either he or Eric would be in touch soon and left. He called Roy Bryant who assured him he could give him a few minutes.

Just as obviously as Chris' place was a farm and a truck depot, Roy's property had been sectioned off from a farm. What appeared to be his home was out behind the large Quonset hut he used as a garage

Roy turned out to be soft spoken, about five foot eight, slim with a wiry build, originally from Peru. The name Bryant didn't sound Peruvian. As ebony black as he was he didn't look South American either. They discussed tanks. Gary asked about the possibility of hiring Roy to give anything they bought a quick once over.

Operation Phoenix

"Maybe," Roy said." It would depend on how busy I was."

"Fair enough." Gary said. "I wonder if you might know anyone in the area, or more over towards Easton, with a small space to rent that has a truck level dock. I have some office furniture to store while we move. I would only want it for a month or two."

After a moment's thought, Roy said, "Well, I know a guy over by Trambull who has an old building. Last I heard he was repairing it but he might have something to rent. You'll have difficulty getting a trailer into their docks, but a straight truck would be easy, if all you are moving is office furniture."

"That sounds great." Gary enthused. "Do you know his number?"

"I can look it up." Roy got out the phone book and wrote down the name and number.

Gary borrowed Roy's phone, called, got directions and made arrangements to meet at the building in half an hour. He only had time to thank Roy and promise that he or Eric would be in touch soon.

Roy's description of the space in Trambull was apt. It was an old stone fortress of a building with loading docks close to the street so a trailer backing in was partly on the street. It was ground floor with a double loading dock which was a basic requirement for Gary. The place did have a musty smell that wasn't too pleasant but Gary thought he could live with that. The price was about half the rate for industrial malls.

He went back to the old man's office and they drafted a simple letter of agreement for a month-to-month lease. Gary paid him in cash which seemed to delight the old man, and received the keys. *Another tax dodger,* thought Gary, pleased.

On his way home he ordered the Trambull space to be alarmed with motion detectors, key entry point breach detectors,

Operation Phoenix

and an alarm notification system. He made travel arrangements for Zurich, paying cash at a local travel agency.

Chapter Ten
Sunday February 19th. — Day Six

The flight to Zurich touched down punctually at 8:35 PM local time, having left New York at 6AM New York time. In a fit of extravagance and some caution, Gary had booked first class seats. He had arranged through the lawyers in Zurich to reserve a hotel room and a rental van with a pull out ramp. Clearing customs presented no problems but when they went to pick up the reserved van the rental agency demanded a credit card as identification.

"I'm sorry I don't carry credit cards." Gary lied. He wanted no paper trail. "Here is my passport and drivers license."

"Well we can't rent to you then. We need the security of a credit card."

"I would be happy to pay for full insurance, no deductible."

"Sorry we need a security deposit. We swipe the card in advance."

"I presume you know the local law firm that made our reservations?" Gary tossed another chip in the pot. "How about a deposit in cash but I require it be returned in cash. How much would the deposit be?"

"The company will forward you a check in due course. We don't keep cash here. The deposit would be 1,000 Swiss Francs."

"What good would a Swiss Franc check be in the US? It would cost me a fortune to cash it. Can you send it to a bank

Operation Phoenix

account here?" Gary knew that rental agencies everywhere wanted credit cards so he was going to have to bend a lot. Ultimately there was already a paper trail to Switzerland in the bank shipment so he would give in and produce a credit card if he had to because he needed that van.

"Yes we could do that."

Gary gave the clerk the data for an account he had opened some years ago, cash, passport and driver's license and they received their van. When they got outside the weather was a high thin overcast and almost shirtsleeve temperatures. Although the breeze was a bit fresh at this altitude it just helped make it smell like crisp, unpolluted mountain air.

During WWII much of Germany was bombed to smithereens and during the rebuilding attention had been paid to modern transportation needs. No so in Switzerland which had remained neutral. On the other hand the highways were modern and a pleasure to drive on. No expense had been spared tunnelling through mountains where necessary. The roads were well maintained even now, whereas pot holes abounded in the US at this time of year. Unlike England they drove on the right. The city streets were another story. The architecture was largely from a bygone era. Both Eric and Lynn commented on the narrow streets and the scarcity of really tall buildings. Aside from the massive financial buildings, of which there were many, the three to seven story structure was common.

It was late, nearly 11 PM, when they got to the hotel. It was a stately pile of rocks obviously catering to the moneyed crowd with massive old portrait paintings, deep carpets and velvet wall hangings. Again they were met with a demand for a credit card but Gary felt on firmer ground here. At worst he knew that pensions and smaller hotels accepted cash and a passport so he didn't need the hotel. Not only that, but since this

Operation Phoenix

was a better hotel he presumed that lawyers often referred clients who preferred anonymity. "I presume the law firm that made our reservation uses your hotel for guests frequently. We are a customer of theirs. I will pay you cash in advance for three days, and settle any extra charges daily." The hotel clerk agreed, probably because Gary didn't object to their obscene rates.

Despite jet lag the three of them immediately spread out to gather information. Lynn purchased several thick newspapers, rolls of plastic adhesive tape, and a city map, while chatting up the hotel shop clerk. Eric engaged the hotel desk clerk while Gary talked to the concierge. Later they gathered at Eric's room to compare notes.

The main Zurich offices of the three largest Swiss banks were gathered a short cab ride away. Since Gary already had an account in one of the banks Eric and Lynn each chose a different bank to open their account. The plan was to obtain a larger than minimum sized safety deposit box to add to the interest of Swiss bankers, making it easier to open an account. Nobody pays money for a box they won't use. Nor do they use boxes to store non valuables.

Gary briefed Lynn and Eric. "Opening an account at a Swiss bank is a real pain. They are arrogant and might deign to accept your money. You will spend most of the morning cooling your heels waiting to see a clerk who is entitled to take your name. You can avoid most of the rest of the hassle by casually mentioning to that clerk that you work as a head-hunter for my firm, dealing pretty exclusively with the world's foremost international banks in New York."

"Do they speak fluent English?" Eric asked.

"Definitely, most Swiss are fluently tri-lingual or more. If you really want to make him pee his pants, you can mention that the market for private bankers for high net-worth individuals seems to be heating up. Do take a resume if offered, or have it sent to your home address so you can 'be sure it won't get lost among all the other resumes we receive daily.' Just ask lots of interview type questions about what he has done. Be very slightly impressed. You know enough about my business to wing it. Then just be a dumb American who wants to open an account and get a safety deposit box. I don't know how much good this will do us because the total world financial system is likely to collapse."

"Now why would we want to open an account if the banks are going to fail?" Lynn demanded.

Gary, with his elbow on the arm of the chair he was sitting on, leaned his chin into his palm. "It's a long shot but the Swiss have been playing this 'secure centre for world banking' game for centuries, and it seems reasonable to bet they will find a way to do so again. It seems worthwhile to gamble a couple of thousand Swiss Francs to be customers in good standing. We will probably need it for trading purposes later. Another thing, you can offer credit cards as identification, but no swiping. We have enough of a paper trail with the Willis shipment to Zurich. We don't want to make it easy for someone in the US to see we were here by having a credit card paper trail as well. Use your passports instead."

They had also found nearby stores selling heavy moving dollies, as well as information about how to best go about finding short-term commercial space to rent. There appeared to be two largish chains of public 'U store' companies in Zurich.

Monday February 20th, -- Day Seven.

Gary left fairly early with the van to look for some commercial space to rent as a drop-off point in preparation for the gold and safes that would be delivered Tuesday. They planned to store the safes at public storage as they had in New

Operation Phoenix

York. Eventually, he found a small storefront with a loading dock at the rear but the one month rental was astronomical. Probably about six months cost. When he objected he was told "It doesn't make sense to lease for only one month. Too much paperwork to make it worthwhile." He opted for six months rental in case it might be useful later and used Lynn's newspapers and tape to cover the store windows.

Eric and Lynn were off opening their bank accounts and purchasing the moving dollies to complete the gold hiding project. They met back at the hotel to drop their purchases, and left immediately to make a round of the banks and become second signators, so that all three able to access each others accounts and boxes.

At Gary's bank, a huge ancient imposing stone pile of a money temple, as all of them were, on impulse Gary asked the lady serving them if they still sold gold.

Behind her marble counter with its antique metal anti-robbery grillwork, she replied, "Yes, we can deliver certificates of deposit for gold purchased and stored with us today. If you want physical bullion there is now a one-week waiting period before delivery. By the way, I see you are from the US. If you are planning on using credit cards, American credit cards do not work today. The US just declared a bank holiday."

Gary and Eric exchanged significant glances. "What is a bank holiday?" asked Eric.

"The government orders all banks and financial institutions closed and not to do any financial transactions. So neither credit cards nor debit cards will work. We just learned about it a half an hour ago because it was only announced at 7AM New York time, and we are in different time zones."

Gary said, "Oh, we were planning on using our credit cards for a vacation. What are we going to do now? Did they say

Operation Phoenix

how long the bank holiday would last?"

"They said for a week."

"Are you exchanging dollars or travelers checks for Swiss Francs?" Eric asked.

"No, we don't know what exchange rate to use."

Gary said, "Let's finish up here and go have a coffee and discuss what to do."

Outside Lynn said, "Is it just me, or is it poor math? You wanted to see what the Swiss were doing about the dollar."

"Yeppers," Eric said, "If the Swiss are not exchanging dollars it is probable that no one else around the world is either. All international trade is kaput. Anything for the US not now on a ship won't get on a ship."

Lynn said, "High in the mountains of upper Switzerland, guarded for centuries by Norwegian fish herders lies the secret: the Swiss could care less about the American dollar."

Gary shrugged. "It is still an abstract to them. It is happening somewhere else. Recession is when your neighbour loses his job. Depression is when you lose yours. America's credit rating has just gone from triple A to triple Z."

At the hotel Gary sat down. "Do you think this changes our plans at all?"

Eric considered for some time. "The speed this is moving at is dangerous, but I don't think so. One change might be helpful. We talked about using public storage in that little town on a lake about an hour outside Zurich. Rapperswill, I think you said. Looks like we have only two major public warehouse chains in Zurich. Taking one stash outside of Zurich would spread our risk."

"Yes, or Stafa, another town on the way to Rapperswill, which is a bit larger and not quite as touristy. I like the idea. Judging by what the woman at my bank said this is moving at lightning speed and it is becoming very urgent to get our other plans underway. We should try to go back tomorrow rather than Wednesday when we are scheduled. I think there is a flight leaving at 6PM. We won't be able to receive the safes and gold shipment, get it packed, stored, and also drive an hour each way to Rapperswill and make the flight. One of us will have to stay over and do Rapperswill and come back Wednesday as scheduled. But which of us should stay? We both have things in New York that have to go forward urgently."

"So what am I? Chopped liver?" demanded Lynn.

Gary blinked and said, "Oh. Sorry. Of course you are right Lynn. I was thinking of my little girl and the weight to be moved. I guess I view females as fragile things but that's rather dumb. You are as capable as any of us. The truth is that none of us could move that safe alone. We will have to have local help."

Gary paused for a moment, remembering them as babies and how very different they'd been. Lynn had loved being cuddled. From the day he was born Eric stiffened up and screeched if you cuddled him. They were still very different but he was so proud of them. He regretted that the divorce was largely his fault. His wife had been a good woman who had worked hard at the marriage. She had even given him custody so the children would get to know their father, because he had worked so much to provide for them that he'd seldom seen them. *If only I hadn't been so rigid.*

Lynn said "I'll bet the lawyers referred by Ron Thompson can help us find a storage place out of town. They should know Switzerland."

It was a great idea and their luck was in. They saw the lawyer half an hour later. By then the secretary had found a storage place and booked a room at the Movenpick Hotel in Rapperswill for Lynn. The lawyers were able to arrange that

Operation Phoenix

Gary and Eric be second signators at the storage unit using a photocopy of their passports.

There was a flurry of activity as they rushed to get back home to confront the problems there. They were able to change their flight plans before other fliers realized their credit cards didn't work and tried to get seats. Being in first class made changing much easier. While they were at the lawyers, they arranged a number of legal affairs including setting up a number of anonymous companies.

Chapter 11
Tuesday February 21st — Day Eight

Back in New York the customs clearing process seemed to be taking a very long time. Gary and Eric had arrived at 8:30 PM local time. Entering the massive customs clearing room it looked as if ten jumbo jets had just landed, all at once. The room was crowded to overflowing. A number loud of arguments were erupting at the customs gates and invariably the people doing the arguing were pulled aside to a separate area. When the person ahead was being processed the cause became clear. The customs officer took the American passport from the businessman, looked puzzled, and searched the passport with exaggerated care. He announced that the businessman was short of a paper. Gary turned to Eric and said,

"It sure didn't take these guys long to set up a cash rich business with the banks closed. They seem to want a bribe to let us back into our own country. Makes sense though, travellers are likely to have at least a little cash."

The businessman erupted in anger as he realized what was happening. He began to shout that he was an American citizen and this was robbery. He was soon pulled off to a separate room for further investigation. The message was clear. Pay now or suffer bureaucratic delay. The more you argue and shout, the longer the delay. Gary reached for his wallet and inserted a $5 bill in his passport before handing it over. Five dollars wasn't much but it would be better to start small. Eric did the same. The customs officer riffled through his passport and asked

Operation Phoenix

"Anything to declare?" stamped the passport, and waved him through. The fiver had mysteriously disappeared. Strangely no terrorism oriented questions were asked.

In view of the ease and speed with which corruption had infiltrated officialdom Gary and Eric were very wary of mugging as they made their way to the car, which was parked in the distant and poorly-lit, long-term parking lot. The temperature was just at freezing or below. The streets were a bit sloppy so there must have been snow that had largely melted while they were gone. The skies were still cloudy with an occasional flake of snow. They resolved that they would both be there, armed, to meet Lynn when she arrived the following night.

Eric and Gary hadn't spoken much on the plane home, not wanting to be possibly overheard, a common way for secrets to get out. High-powered people often discuss things on planes, and other high-powered and smart people hear, add two and two and get about 73. Since they are high-powered, they have the wherewithal and inclination to act. Gary had been reading the paper and handed it to Eric, pointing out four articles, saying, "Day two of a bank holiday, day eight of a crisis."

The Road To Deposit Insurance

In June 1933, Congress enacted federal deposit insurance. Accounts were covered up to $2,500 per depositor (now $100,000). Other laws were passed regulating bank activities and competition, with the objective of limiting risks to banks and reassuring the public that banks were, and would remain, safe and reliable.

Latest year figures indicate that the Federal Deposit Insurance Corp alone was directly insuring $2.7 trillion in deposits. FDIC total assets are but a small fraction of that, about $50 billion. An unnamed source in the FDIC said, "In the present circumstances, there are some straws we desperately grasp at, and I grasp at them too, but that is just for entertainment. Our fate is not in our hands."

Operation Phoenix

Constitutional Crisis Brewing.

Article I, Section 8, Clause 5 of the constitution states that "the Congress shall have the power to coin money, regulate the value thereof, and of foreign coin, and fix the standard of weights and measures." Yet each of the twelve Federal Reserve Banks is a private corporation. The commercial member banks of the Federal Reserve System hold the shares. Worse, the Federal Reserve Open Market Committee, which sets short-term interest rates and influences the size of the money supply by buying or selling government securities, consists of 12 members including 5 Federal Reserve district presidents who have never been seen by the President or the Congress, but have a vote on setting the credit policy and money supply of the United States.

A challenge has been mounted that the money of the United States is unconstitutional.

According to Senator Herbert Johnson, he has "never seen Congress spend so much time on trivialities in a crisis. Our first job is to fix what is broken, not obfuscate by pointing blame elsewhere."

OPEC Halts Oil Transactions In Dollars

The Organization of Petroleum Exporting Countries (OPEC), joined by prospective members, including Canada, [which ironically is a member of the International Energy Agency, (IEA) OPEC's political opposite] Russia, Mexico, and other exporters, have announced that they have halted all sales in US dollars.

Current OPEC Secretary General, Ashraf sihab-Joukhdar of Kuwait said, "At the moment, selling of oil in dollars has been completely halted. The dollar is an unreliable currency, considering its devaluation and oil exporters' losses."

Because the US has depleted its foreign exchange reserves fighting the dollar collapse, this bodes ill for the US. The problem is not confined to oil, it is affecting all US imports.

Whole industries line up with hands out to Washington

With economic conditions deteriorating rapidly, banks, insurance companies, pension funds, the auto industry and even states, cities and counties are mobilizing their tens of thousands of

Operation Phoenix

> lobbyists for an emergency handout after the bank holiday ends. Highly leveraged hedge funds, money market funds, and even the shadow banking financial companies such as GE capital are all complaining that if they don't get money, the financial system, and America will collapse.
>
> All credit markets have seized up. Meanwhile, Washington also has to wrestle with the 800-pound gorillas of Social Security and Medicare with trillions in unfunded liabilities.

It seemed that government was reacting as humanity normally does when it encounters a distasteful problem. First, deny and ignore the problem in the hope it would just go away, then anger, and finally reluctant management of the problem. In this case they didn't even have time to manage reluctantly. Of course government never had a problem with excessive time so long as their own bellies were full. But there was only so much food and oil in the pipeline in our 'just in time' world.

After dropping Eric off at his apartment and driving home, Gary did not do what he most wanted to do, which was to go to bed. He began with his computer searching his own database, and several he subscribed to on the Internet. He looked for ships' brokers, pilots, fuel suppliers, and other classes of ship suppliers; those people who would normally have dealings or business relationships with captains of ships. He paid special attention to ships chandlers who act as the country store, supplying a very wide range of goods such as food and services to all ships.

Because he could not wait longer he phoned Lynn waking her at 5AM Swiss time, and gave her an update on events in the US, particularly at the airport. He finally went to bed.

Wednesday February 22nd -- Day Nine

Operation Phoenix

Expert head-hunters charge obscene fees. The only way to be worth these fees is to find the right person the first time, every time. Many years previously Gary had perfected this headhunting technique, which in theory went like this: if you wanted the best 'widget' salesperson around, the people best able to judge the qualifications of widget salespeople were 'widget' customers. So, all you had to do was ask the people who knew, exactly how effective the salespeople were. Ask 'widget' customers, 'Who served your needs best in the last couple of years?'

Once a name came up twice, (there are some pretty strange one-on-one relationships) he had a good one, with positive references. Now the only problem remained was to get that person to the bargaining table, because good people are seldom looking. They are already being well compensated, both emotionally and monetarily, if their boss has any smarts at all. Gary had developed some good, subtle techniques to get them to the bargaining table too.

"Wolfgang, my name is Gary Alden. I worked with you on the Panzatta deal. Do you recall it?" It was 8:05AM, and already Gary was on the phone to Wolfgang Perl, a shipping broker he had done business with previously.

"Yah, ah do Mon. How are you Gary?"

Gary would have loved to play poker with Wolfgang. Born of a German father and a Jamaican mother, he tended to unconsciously play the race card when things weren't quite going as he would like. Not that he was black, more a beautiful light brown, but he became 'jusa Poah lill ol black boah' presumably to gain advantage. His normal British accent from down Essex way developed a distinct lilt.

"Just great. I'm working on the early stages of a deal that could be trade related. As yet, I don't see any business for you,

Operation Phoenix

but there may be possibilities. I'd like to pick your brains for a few minutes. When would be a convenient time to talk to you?" Gary asked.

"The way the bloody world is going, now would be as good, or bad a time as any. What are you looking for mon?"

"Well Wolfgang, I suppose this is going to sound pretty strange because not many of the details are yet finalized. I am looking for someone, or perhaps more of a specific personality than anything else. I want to find a captain of ocean vessels who runs a tight ship. Not really a tight ship in an authoritarian sense, but more in the sense of being very innovative or imaginative and getting things done. Probably a grizzled veteran, very honest, but knows exactly when, where and how to cut corners with no fuss or muss. Comfortable in pretty well every port in the world. Knows how avoid the pirates in the Straits of Malacca and Southeast Asia, how to squeeze an extra few miles out of a bunker of fuel, how to create loyalty in a crew, how to trade for whatever is not available through normal channels. Someone who is pretty unflappable no matter what the circumstances. Possibly retired now. So in your experience who is the very best, most versatile captain you have run across in the last few years?"

"Well the guy who comes to mind retired a couple of years ago but I heard he took a short term contract. When he finished that recently he swore 'no more'. I think he is reacting to the death of his wife. He doesn't seem to have a problem with people who have values other than his own, but he's bloody rigid in his own values. Honest almost to a fault but pragmatic. If the society he was dealing with requires bribes, I would think he would but only if there was no other way. Looks after his people and they would die for him although he is pretty strict about some things. But, like I said, he has retired and sworn, 'no

Operation Phoenix

more.' "

"Does he walk on water too?" Gary asked softly. "What's his name?"

"Claude D'Antonio. Born in the Azores. Went to sea when he was 13. Highly intelligent, and considering that he is entirely self-educated, speaks English very well. Lives in Jersey, some small town. What do you want him for?"

"Well the ideas I have are pretty vague right now, initially probably consulting as to what is possible and how to get the job done." Gary said evasively. "If we need someone, or something, I would expect he could point us in the right direction."

"That's for sure," Wolfgang enthused. "That guy has been everywhere and done everything. Knows everybody in the business."

"Thanks, I appreciate that. By the way, while I have you, have you ever seen a sort of a junior version of Claude? Younger, probably not yet Captain, very honourable and resourceful, smart. Going to be a Claude someday but not experienced enough yet?"

Wolfgang pondered, "Well, yeah. Kinda hard to tell since the younger ones have no track record, but there's one that I thought handled himself well, a guy named Bruce Nott. He was off the Corinthian. Notices things and is pretty shrewd. Seemed like a straight shooter."

"Wolfgang, I owe you big time and I expect you to collect. How's business?"

"Bloody confusing mon. Mosly it's de financial situation. Nobody wants to trust nobody else's credit, and de bloody banks aren't doing anything. Everyone's afraid of de foreign exchange risk. Yo can't predict whether yo'all will get paid, or how much yo'all will get paid, even if yo do get paid."

"Everything denominated in US dollars is the problem?"

Operation Phoenix

Gary asked.

"Pretty much, but even if you suggest Euros, nobody moves because the situation is so volatile. Nobody can move anything if de banks won't release the documentation."

"Lots of goods sitting waiting to be shipped?" Gary asked now very interested because of his trade plans.

"Never mind waiting to be shipped, full ships are anchored all up and down the coast. The dockyards are full of goods awaiting document clearance, so there's no place to put the goods, even if they wanted to unload. Those dockyards fill up bloody fast with nothing moving out. Just in time delivery has gone out the widow, closing a lot of businesses because they can't get supplies."

"Same situation around the world?" Gary asked.

"Far as I know. Nobody is moving bloody much anything, anywhere with banks closed around the world," Wolfgang complained. "You heard that the banks in much of Europe closed this morning in a bank holiday?"

"No, I hadn't, and that is damned interesting. In a round about way it might work alongside what I want Claude for. Do you think you and I might be able to set up some counter-trade, international trade of goods for goods, no cash involved?"

"Hmmm, Maybe. Those kinds of deals are bloody tough, but it is a thought. Umm, yes, definitely a thought," mused Wolfgang.

Counter-trade or international barter is difficult because no money is involved. Not only do you have to find someone who can take the quantities of product you have, but he has to have something you want in sufficient quantity to satisfy you. Once you agree on the value of what both you and he have then things usually move quickly.

"Tell you what, see if you can get a handle on what sorts

of goods are sitting in containers now. Nothing very specific, just a good idea of what may be available for trade so we can rough out some preliminary plans. Think we could meet in the next couple of weeks?" Gary asked.

"Yeah, that might be an idea. I might as well be doing that because I'm not bloody doing anything much that's productive now. Just chasing ma tail. Okay, I'll try to get a list of what is sitting in the yards and along the coast. Shouldn't be too difficult."

"Okay," said Gary. "What sort of contacts do you have in other ports offshore? Do you know anyone you would trust to act as a counter party in a trade deal like this?"

"A few," Wolfgang admitted. "I'd have to think about it."

"Great," enthused Gary. "It's still early days. But that's exactly what we need; information to make plans with. Talk to you in the next week or so."

After hanging up, Gary started files on Claude D'Antonio and Bruce Nott, recording as much detail as possible. He continued to farm his database, with the drudgery of phoning each name on the list he had dug up. To each he asked the same question. "Who do you know that fits these qualifications?"

At the end, he had a list of five different names of captains, and three juniors. Claude's name had come up the most often, seven times, and his file was growing thicker. *Ah ha, Claude me boy, you I want – big time. Them as what knows have voted you beauty queen in this contest. I don't have to know another thing about you.*

Nevertheless, he began a detailed check on Claude's (born Claudio) background. By the time he finished he had a thick file containing information on his children, data on such things as his house type, and probable resale value, and a massive confirmation of Wolfgang's first opinion. Honest, trustworthy,

Operation Phoenix

smart and adaptable, he was a leader of men. He had fathered three smart children too. His eldest, a daughter, was a surgeon of merit, and she had married a well-respected doctor. The other daughter was a dentist. Only a younger son had followed him to sea. And that son was on the list of three up-and-coming juniors.

He also discovered that Claude had listed his house for sale in the last few days. Probably triggered by his wife's death. He was definitely in the mood for some kind of move.

Gary phoned Claude and was lucky enough to catch him in.

"Captain Claude D'Antonio? My name is Gary Alden. I understand you are one of the most knowledgeable people in the marine end of shipping, or as related to cargo ships. Given the recent developments in the world, particularly here in the US, I may have something interesting to say, in the form of a job that needs doing."

"Mr. Alden, I'm retired now. Worked longer than I expected. I settle down now. I think I pass."

"I can understand your desire to settle down Claude, but I think my project might be of interest to you, particularly as it regards the recent violent changes in our society, probable greater violence and change, along with possible avenues of escaping the worst effects. But initially there is little travel, only that required for consulting purposes, and it pays cash. If you want to bow out afterwards that's agreeable, but your knowledge is desperately needed now."

"I'll tell you what," Gary continued, starting one of his standard methods of bringing a candidate to the bargaining table. Make a good argument and assume the candidate agrees. "I was planning on being down your way. Would you be able to meet for lunch, or maybe dinner would be even better, if the conversation continues? Talk is cheap. Since I'm not familiar with your area I would prefer you picked the place. Something nice, maybe a nice steak house, where we can converse privately. Do you know of a quiet place nearby? The private conversation is the important part."

"Maybe you're right. Talk is cheap," mused Claude. "The world is changing in bad ways. I might be interested in what you have to say. I'm not promising anything. But I will listen."

"I'd be amazed, and probably somewhat suspicious if you embraced what I have to say with as little information as you now have," Gary responded. "There is a lot of water to go under the bridge yet. Which restaurant are you suggesting?"

"I went out to mall to do some shopping this morning. I was astounded at how many shops were closed. Even grocery stores. Nobody is stopping at cash registers on way out. Maybe we couldn't find a restaurant open. I think nobody has any cash. Why don't you come by here for tea?"

They arranged a 2:30 meeting the following afternoon, and Gary got directions.

He started for Eric's on their way to meet Lynn at the airport. As he left the house, he thought he heard a gunshot, probably a block or two away. He dismissed it as kids, maybe with firecrackers, or a backfire. In light traffic after picking Lynn up at the airport they stopped for a time at Lynn's apartment to prioritize. "We will have the hangar rented tomorrow and I will have it alarmed immediately," Eric reported. "There are two guards on duty 24/7."

Gary gave Eric Roy Bryant's number so he could check out tanker trucks, Eric's next job.

"Exactly what do you want in the way of pharmaceuticals?" Lynn asked. "I have to get started on that job."

Gary answered. "There must be some packaged

Operation Phoenix

recommendations for starting a small hospital, and a pharmacy, both in terms of equipment and the drugs they need. In fact if we could get a now functionally working hospital like a bankruptcy, it would be a godsend. In a worst-case scenario, the army publishes a manual that includes a complete listing of the equipment and drugs for a field hospital. If you happen across a list of drugs that a vet would use, grab it. Many of the drugs used on animals are the same ones used on humans. The important thing is to remember that we expect to be going into isolation and even if the drug companies can continue producing, which I strongly doubt, we won't be able to get our hands on more."

    Later, Gary began the work of assembling a database for his next search for a specialized person, someone to arrange security for the community.

Operation Phoenix

Chapter 12
Thursday February 23rd -- Day 10

After completing his database, Gary began the search for a security officer for the community; someone capable of strategizing positive outcomes using unconventional or often limited resources. His search was rapidly narrowing down to a senior officer of the various Special Forces, US SEALs, British Special Air Services, or the Israeli Army Sayaret Mat'kal.

Later he turned his attention to Claude

Outside the clouds were breaking up, and the temperature was about 40 degrees, so the slop on the streets was largely gone. Gary located Claude's two-story brick house with a wooden veranda, and parked. Picking up his binder, and prepared briefcase, he rang the bell. It was 2:25 PM. He was five minutes early. Claude answered the door, ushered him through the living room to the dining room, which had a combined kitchen and dining room at the far end of the house. Seating Gary at a large, oak kitchen table, he then turned the kettle on for tea. Claude was two or three inches over five feet, slim and trim for his age. He had a full head of snow-white hair, a full white handlebar moustache and an olive complexion. Judging from his exactly trimmed moustache, and the general neatness of the house, he was a bit of a perfectionist. Everything was so shipshape. Despite his diminutive size, his erect posture gave him an aura of command.

Gary started off with a discussion of today's world.

"You can't even go to shopping mall anymore," Claude complained. "The shops that are open have nothing interesting

Operation Phoenix

left on shelves. Robbers are so bold, they accost you in halls." Claude remained standing in the kitchen near the teapot.

Gary leaned forward. "That touches directly on why I'm here. All those closed stores represent two things: unemployed people who were barely employed before and therefore have few resources to fall back on, and no new supplies being delivered to these stores even if people had the money to buy. The financial system around the world is crumbling. Governments are in total disarray. The rule of law is breaking down."

Claude nodded. "People are panicking and becoming paranoid. Panicked, paranoid people can't be reasonable. But they must be, to get to solution."

"Exactly." Gary was becoming more intense. "I think we have to create a small community of hand picked, like minded people. People we can get to know well enough that we can predict their actions to some degree, and therefore know how far we can trust each other for our safety."

"I do have my family here."

"I concur, there is probably nothing superior to immediate family," Gary agreed. "But how many immediate family members are we talking about here? Half a dozen in a place where the locusts bearing down on us number in the millions? Doesn't a remote place where few locusts exist, and a family, or community of one to 300 people sound more attractive? A community picked for its skills to survive; a small town, which despite some upheaval, is closely knit and is pulling all its resources together in order to survive."

Claude cocked his head a bit. "How would you organize community like that?"

Gary drew a deep breath. "It seems to me that we have two choices now; anarchy, or a self-regulating community. That

Operation Phoenix

implies a good deal of true democracy. In our massive democracy, the village idiot's vote is equal in power to the most intelligent and informed. In a smaller group the village idiot still has a vote and a voice, but everyone knows everyone else well enough to compensate for the others in the group. We need a variety of skills moving toward similar goals. We need the tools and supplies to make the community self-sufficient. In the current turmoil, we think we can get much of what we need cheaply."

Claude frowned. "Those are big goals. Can you put it into practical?"

"There's no way we can achieve 100 percent operational success. Even if it were as low as one percent, it looks like it would be a whole lot better than the rule of the jungle facing us now."

Claude's lips thinned and he nodded. "There's some truth in that." He turned, poured the tea into two big mugs, brought them over to the table and sat across from Gary.

Gary was sure that there were more delicate teacups available which would have come out if Claude's wife had been serving. He could even see some in the china cabinet against the wall at the stairway going to the second floor. "By carefully selecting the people we want, we can cover most of the bases, and we can always invite those we need. For instance, medical needs. We need your daughters and their families."

Claude looked at Gary sharply.

"Yes, Captain D'Antonio, I've done considerable research on you. I don't have everything on you, but I do have enough to know that you are exceedingly valuable. I intend to treat you as such." Gary looked directly at Claude. "Since life is not a stable thing, even if we had everything we needed today, by tomorrow we'd need something else. We can possibly get these things by

Operation Phoenix

force of arms, or we can trade for them. I think we have to set up a trading mechanism."

"What's to stop me from getting on boat, and getting off at backwater location?" demanded Claude.

Gary rolled a shoulder. "Not much. It does sound appealing at first glance. But you'd be subject to the vagaries of local conditions, politics and resources. Anyone who is visibly wealthy is going to be a target in poor countries. Sipping pina coladas in your hammock is great for a while, but a steady diet of it gets pretty boring."

Claude nodded. "I've been getting restless with nothing to do. Crime is rising here. I put my house up for sale. What are you proposing?"

"As a first step in setting up a community, we need a ship to transport people and cargo. Later we'll need it to transport things we trade for. We hope to have a bit of time pull together the beginnings of the community, but we must be very careful and ruthless about whom we select. When we decide on the destination, we'll know which skills and items we need to trade for. At the same time, we may be able to trade here, and make enough profit to keep the process going."

Claude nodded. "Then, we sail off into sunset."

Gary leaned back in his chair. "You know ships and shipping. You probably know which company with good bottoms is way over extended financially. We also know that the banks and other financial institutions are, and will be, repossessing all sorts of assets and trying to dispose of them for cash. They'll end up disposing of them for pennies on the dollar. *Voila!* We have our ship at prices we can afford."

Claude chewed on his moustache and looked at the ceiling. "You probably need a 15 to 25,000 ton general cargo vessel."

Operation Phoenix

"Yes, my thoughts run along that line. A ship with container fittings, and self-load capacity I suspect," agreed Gary. "I presume you can rig containers to house people and animals for a five to eight day trip without undue discomfort?"

"Animals?"

"Can you imagine where our social system is going to go from here? We don't see this as a short-term infrastructure disruption, so we are preparing a multigenerational survival plan. We are currently concentrating on those things, like rice, meat and milk, to carry us over till we can become self-sufficient. In essence we must become producers, not consumers as the US is now structured. Aside from that, our world is running out of hydrocarbons. The money for exotic solutions to energy shortages is unlikely to be available under the disorganization we face today. We can't clear shipments of either crude or refined oil products now because of the financial disruption. Animals can provide energy for work when fuels are not readily available. Especially in isolated areas." Gary explained.

"Ummm" Claude agreed. "We can probably keep people and animals fairly comfortable, if weather's good. We could do it. Not much exercise for animals though."

"I have a list of good veterinarians and some indication that some have had experience with seasick animals. I haven't done any recent research on them though, and the list is a bit old."

"You really have done your homework," Claude said, looking astonished. "How long have you been at this?"

"Thank you. I first became aware that the financial system, and the US, was headed for a brick wall in February 1987. I made some preparations, but not many. In the twenty odd years since then I've become aware of many more complicating factors. Particularly during the last few years, my study of the matter has been much more comprehensive."

Gary frowned, looked down and picked at the corner of his binder.

"One big concern I have is that once the ship is secured and fuelled, there will necessarily be an interval of worsening violence and other negative conditions before we sail. We have to collect the people, skills and goods we need. In this atmosphere of negativity and violence anyone such as we are, who is suspected of having something, anything, is going to be a target. That target will not be restricted to rogue bandits. If officialdom reacts as it has in the past, those in power will use the name of the power of the law to steal and pillage. So, we'll have to be extremely careful to remain secretive and not come to anyone's attention. Moreover, when someone eventually, accidentally does notice, we have to have a strategy in place to not be there when they arrive."

Claude heaved a big sigh. "I've seen that in third-world countries where fighting and lawlessness exist. There are things you can do to avoid violence. You can't eliminate it. It's always dangerous."

"Claude, I can't think of any part of the planet that is not going to have some danger. If you find a place you can sip pina coladas, eventually someone is going to covet your relative wealth. In fact, I think your present relative wealth is largely now a dream. All of the pension funds and financial institutions paying pensions had invested in stocks and bonds, and they're both in the crapper. There appears to me a great danger bonds will be repudiated. Where's the tax money coming from to even pay the interest, never mind trying to hold a country together? Where's the stock market today? Let's assume it doubles from here. That would bring us back to half what it was a month ago."

"I'm not financial genius. I've been worrying those things. Now I have shelter, and familiar with our community. One does not give up known for unknown at times like this." Claude spoke slowly.

"Why don't we try this then. You go ahead as a local consultant on the preliminary phases. Spend your time and effort as if you were joining us. Plan what you would do if conditions become as we see them, but stay flexible because for sure there will be major differences between plans and reality as the situation develops. Then if you come up with some ideas, we can discuss them and plan accordingly. Start first by finding an appropriate ship and fuel her with every ounce of fuel you can," Gary said.

"And then?"

Gary leaned forward again, elbows on the table.. "Start recruiting crew, particularly those who have some knowledge of sail since a breakdown in infrastructure may force us to look at sail. Choose people you would want to have at your back in dangerous situations. Pick up as many varied skills as you can, especially cross-trained people, engineers, electricians, seamen, fishermen for food, whatever, so we can be self sufficient. Bear in mind, we have extremely limited resources for the size of game we are playing, but don't stint on quality if it means long life and simplicity. We want to build the community to last."

"What happens if I decide no to join you?"

Gary rubbed his forehead. "If at 'sailing into the sunset' time, you have been presented with a better option at least we'll have had the advantage of your knowledge and experience. If you prefer that you and your family join us, we would welcome your son, daughters, spouses, and their children. Otherwise, it's strictly skills we need, providing that the person is the sort of

Operation Phoenix

person we can trust."

Claude said slowly. "That seems reasonable." He studied his mug of tea for a while. "I don't see better offer on the table. What's next?"

Gary dug in his binder and pulled out a series of sheets, and passed the first one to Claude.

"Here is a list of possible needs for a self-sufficient community. It's neither complete nor necessarily a list of 'must have' requirements. It is simply random thoughts of things that might be useful to get a train of thought going. One thing it doesn't do very well is to consider what might be needed for trading purposes once the community has been established. To some extent, that will depend on where we locate, and what items will likely be in short supply at nearby trading ports. I'll leave that for you to consider in your planning. Add or delete as you see fit. We will discuss the results later. However, you probably know more about such things than we do."

Gary handed over the next sheet. "This is a list of people who might be considered for your position, and the juniors are possible future captains. These people have not yet been investigated and I neither recommend, nor reject them. They may be useful."

Claude glanced over the list and exclaimed, "I know every one of these men. They are all top notch. Your homework is astounding."

"We're very interested in the younger people because the community needs genetic diversity as well as skill diversity and redundancies. Over time us old fogies will die off, but in the short term, our experience is essential."

"I see what you mean. Us old fogies don't have energy to build from nothing. We do have knowledge." Claude waited expectantly for Gary to continue.

"I do have a list of possible destinations which I've not brought. As much as possible we didn't want to influence you or stifle fresh ideas. Generally our thinking has run along the lines of finding an isolated location with favourable weather, good soil and growing conditions, deep water access for this trip but more importantly for future trading, and of course, near potential trading partners. We think that in the world of a month ago, there's likely to be some isolated areas that weren't viable because of their small size, but for us would be ideal. We had thought an abandoned mine with a dock might be suitable, if there were a fertile valley close by. There would likely be abandoned buildings we could use as shelter while we got organized. So far, we've not found anything that's suitable, principally because most mines concern themselves with rocky venues, and therefore, seldom good soil. The same holds true of most islands we might consider. Usually poor soil"

Claude looked at him quizzically. "You say 'we'. Who's 'we'?"

"Primarily my son and myself, although I do have a daughter who is rapidly coming on side as circumstances make the situation more real for her."

"You couldn't have convinced me that this situation was possibility a month ago," Claude chuckled and shook his head. "Events can teach you quick, and your plans make sense now. I think we need Noah's Ark"

"I'd like to leave you in charge of recruiting the transportation group. Use your common sense and experience on everything else. We need recruits to multiply our efforts and reach critical mass quickly. One thing I must emphasize," Gary gestured to add emphasis. "Particularly our ultimate plans must remain absolutely secret, even from your children for now. Nothing is in place, so if the wrong person learns about our

Operation Phoenix

plans, everything could easily blow up in our face and we would lose everything. I believe Washington, or maybe Franklin said, 'The only way something can remain a secret if two people are involved, is if one of them is dead'."

"I recognize seriousness of situation," Claude said frostily, icicles dripping from every hair on his moustache. He was sitting ramrod straight, glaring at Gary.

"I had no intent to offend, but I did have to emphasize it. With that over, there appears to be one major thing to discuss immediately. The resources to do the job if you still want to go ahead?"

Claude eventually nodded, but still appearing miffed.

Gary picked up the briefcase and laid it on the table. Working the combination locks, he turned the case half around, and snapped one lock.

"I'll leave it to you to set your own salary. Incomes have gone down pretty dramatically recently, but this is the most important job for humanity that you've ever done. Personally, I've been drawing what I needed on a daily basis. The rest is for expenses as they arise. I ask only that you use your best efforts, and provide a full accounting. We can probably rake up a million dollars for the ship if needed. However, if it does top a million, something else will suffer." Gary pushed the case across the table toward Claude.

Claude frowned, looked thoughtful, and said significantly, "How much is in there?"

"Two hundred thousand dollars," said Gary briefly.

"Why so much? You brought it with you. You're pretty cocky. Is it legit? What are you playing at?" Claude was very squinty eyed.

"Yes, it's legal. I made it in the stock market betting that recent events would in fact occur. They did. My next bet was to pull it out in cash, because I expected a bank holiday. That occurred as well. We're short of time, and I had to prove I was serious. Moreover, what I've told you tonight could ruin my future, and even possibly endanger my life and the lives of my family. So perhaps you can forgive me for being a bit uptight on the secrecy issue. I believe you to be an intelligent, practical but honest man, a man true to his own values. Once I had reached that conclusion, right or wrong, when you compare what I've risked in simply talking to you, with $200,000, the money is insignificant."

Claude snapped the other lock and revealed a classic movie shot of a briefcase full of cash. He leaned back and studied the high, wall-mounted pedestal with a couple of porcelain angels on it to his right for a few moments. Then he leaned forward and placed his arms on the table. He looked grim. "Okay, I am with you for first phase anyway. You can rest assured on the secrecy question."

Chapter 13
Friday February 24th -- Day 11

Next morning, Gary doggedly continued hunting his security officer. The results were both satisfactory and unsatisfactory. He was getting less responses and there was no clear winner as there had been for Claude. That was not entirely unexpected, given the secrecy surrounding all special operations units and the fact that his targets were spread around the world. It just made his job immeasurably more difficult.

At one point he thought he heard another sound that might have been a gunshot. He went to the window to investigate, but saw nothing. Since he'd never heard of such a thing in this neighbourhood, he again dismissed it as kids playing, or backfires, and went back to his search.

Later he put his search decision on hold and called Safe-tee Corp to enquire about the large office safe he had ordered. They told him it was ready, but delivery with the banks closed would be a problem. He left this in abeyance for the moment, and found a used office furniture company nearby that was miraculously open. He purchased, sight unseen, two old wooden oak desks, several chairs and old file cabinets. Again delivery was the problem.

He called Chris Habel, the trucker in Orange. Due to the bank holiday Chris was happy to oblige because Gary was offering cash payment, and he wanted a few dollars to give to his drivers to tide them over the weekend. He agreed to come to

Operation Phoenix

Gary, pick up the cash to pay for the office furniture, and to pick up both the office safe and the furniture, for delivery early the following morning to the old Trambull building. Gary volunteered an additional $500 cash advance against future deliveries. Chris was so effusive in his thanks that it was very clear that he really cared about his drivers. An honourable man of loyalty, one who would try to do the right thing.

He arranged with Willis to deliver the cash and silver they were holding for Saturday morning at 10AM to the same Trambull address.

Claude checked in routinely. Then Eric phoned late in the afternoon. "The hangar rental is a done deal. I contacted Roy Bryant, and he's a gem, smart, and not talkative. He's slow but very thorough. Are you thinking of recruiting him?" Eric asked.

"Yes, the idea had crossed my mind. He seems to have lots of skills in repairing and maintaining anything, and the way I found him was that a closed mouthed customer raved about him."

Eric responded, "He picked out the one bad tank in the lot instantly, and gave the others a thorough going over. He also knew of two more which I also purchased. How was your day?"

"I was able to locate three senior special service officers names. The Israeli was not as well recommended as the other two, so I effectively eliminated him despite my personal opinion that he was probably better trained in strategy and execution of detailed, odds against plans and operations. The two remaining, a local retired navy SEAL, and an ex-SAS officer from Britain, were something of a horse race. The Brit seemed better suited to the job we foresaw needing to be done, but he had two minuses. He didn't seem to be as brilliant a strategist as the SEAL, and getting him and a fully equipped crew into the country could present major problems.

Operation Phoenix

"Have you decided anything?" Eric asked.

"I decided to put the problem aside until early in the week, so that we could evaluate the world travel situation. If the world travel situation becomes unduly difficult, the local choice might be the only one available. However a mistake in the selection of this person could be very dangerous, and potentially fatal."

"Yeppers. We sure don't want to make a mistake on that one."

Gary continued to bring Eric up to date, "Chris Habel, the trucker who recommended Roy, and another one that's possibly also worth recruiting if we need his skills, stopped and picked up cash for the furniture I bought as a cover for storing the safe."

"I'm going to need some tractors to haul all these trailers I have been buying."

"Claude checked in with the news that one of the ships we discussed was likely available. It has a weak lender with problems covering its own cash flow. Claude thought that possibly he might pick up the ship for as little as half a million dollars, and would need another quarter of a million for minor repairs, provisioning, and fuel."

"Wow, That I gotta see. Half a million? Is that all? Where's he stealing it from?"

"Yep. My reaction exactly." Gary said. "Claude thinks this is as good a deal as he is likely to get. I agreed providing it will meet Lloyd's of London standards. He thinks it has had a recent inspection. I told him cash would be available by Sunday, and that ownership would be through one of the Swiss companies we set up in Zurich. By the way we have got to get you and Lynn to meet Claude. I hate deciding on someone by myself for the community. Claude is pretty much a done deal, and appears to be working out. Still, I think we should meet socially. We both think Roy is likely to be a good addition, and if we can't get a third or fourth opinion then it may be possible to go with only two opinions. But one opinion only is going to create problems for sure. How many marriages end up in divorce? Do you think you might be available, say Sunday afternoon if I can arrange to meet with Claude?"

"I think I could get away Sunday afternoon for a while."

"Okay I'll try to set it up," said Gary. "We need to get as many eyes looking as possible to interview the Special Forces guy, before we take him on board. Will you be at the Trambull space to receive silver and cash tomorrow morning? I'll try to get Lynn to come."

Eric took Chris's number. "I need Chris' tractors right away. I'll be at the Trambull space, but late. I have a couple of stops first."

Almost immediately Lynn called, sounding quite excited. "I found a small hospital in Connecticut has bitten the bullet from its cash flow problems, overbuying new equipment. Both it and its pharmacy are up for sale by a lender that appears to be in trouble themselves, and desperate. The equipment is modern, and quite extensive."

"That's fantastic, exactly what we need. Who is the lender?"

"I haven't got that yet, but it should be easy."

"Good you get that and I should know them, or at least be able confirm that they are in trouble too. By the way, can you be available tomorrow morning to come with me to receive a silver and cash shipment?"

"If you think it's important, yes."

"Same as Switzerland, we should all know details about the assets." Gary then repeated his conversation with Eric.

Because he had been consumed with the purpose at hand,

Operation Phoenix

Gary decided to unwind a bit, and fixed himself a nice meal. Usually he didn't drink alone, but tonight he poured himself a glass of good cognac for sipping as he settled comfortably in his reclining chair in the living room, to read. He hadn't even glanced at the news since that fateful Tuesday, a week and a half ago. He looked at the headlines on the first paper he picked up and blinked.

Food Riots in Los Angeles. Stores looted.

He looked at the date on the paper. Today's date, the paper was on top of the pile. He'd been too preoccupied with his own agenda to notice what was happening in the world around him. Suddenly apprehensive, he got up, checked his doors were locked, and set his garage and perimeter alarms. Back in his chair, he studied the article more closely.

Food Riots in Los Angeles. Stores looted.

A protest over bank closures and a lack of food in stores lead to a riot in which stores were looted. The protest started outside district Federal government offices where an estimated 10,000 protesters gathered. Later, looters battled with police who used water cannons, tear gas and rubber bullets to force the rioters back. This is the third such riot across the nation in the last two days.

Police have expressed apprehension about the coming weekend.

The paper was reporting on something that had happened last night, Thursday, of a bank holiday that started Monday. Not only were people living 'hand to mouth' as a way of life but obviously 'just in time' delivery was contributing to the problem. After only three days food riots were in progress. Not that these people were necessarily out of food but if they were rioting it must be of some concern. Or maybe it was simply that people resisted any change that appeared to be negative.

Gary knew that change often brings civil disruption so he'd studied civil disturbance as part of his research.

Operation Phoenix

Historically, contrary to popular belief, the very poor never riot. It was speculated that there were several reasons for this phenomenon. Truly poor people lived so close to subsistence level that they did not have sufficient excess energy to riot. They were lethargic physically and mentally. It was only after they achieved a more nutritious diet that they lost both the physical and mental lethargy. Secondly, they'd lost their self-image and accepted 'poor' as their station in life. Most importantly, the truly poor did not have much to lose. How much worse could their life get? Since most had never known a better life, they didn't realize or couldn't imagine how good life could be.

Middle class people were at the opposite end of the spectrum. Well fed they had energy to spare. They'd tasted a small slice of the pie, and wanted more – not less. When danger threatened their way of life they knew how much they had to lose, got angry in an unreasonable 'road rage' sort of way, and defended what they had. The only successful organization of the 'poor' known was the Coalition of the Poor in the US, and their marches had included many grossly obese people. Hardly poor in normal world terms.

People in the US had been trained to agitate to achieve their ends. Government had quickly learned to include one draconian measure, over and above what they wanted. People would scream but be distracted from the fact the whole idea was bad. Government would give up that draconian measure, and achieve all the other goals they wanted.

Another headline caught his eye.
Police unable to respond to any but serious crime.
Suddenly the sounds he'd thought might have been gunshots assumed greater importance. This was normally a very quiet residential area. So far as he could recall, no sirens had followed the gunshots. *So serious crimes are limited to murder,*

Operation Phoenix

are they? If they missed you, no harm done, and we don't respond, he thought. *I'll bet the cops are filling out the paperwork only, and waiting for normalcy for any investigation.*
   Another unusual article;
   AFT takes credit for a seventh explosion
   A letter, on letterhead of the gang Americans for Freedom against Tyranny, was dropped off at this newspaper today. It was the seventh letter received taking credit after a series of 15 bombings, targeting bank Automatic Teller Machines.

   Gary thought, *someone obviously has a big, long standing beef against banks. This one has been festering for a long time. You don't get organized enough to get explosives and blow up 15 ATMs in four days. It must be an opportunity thing, someone pushed over the edge that had been prepared, but indecisive. Bunch of stupid nut cases. The bank closures are strictly government ordered. There's no doubt that the banks are joined at the hip with government, and that they're a slimy bunch, but this is one that can't be laid to the doorstep of big banks.*
   Other headlines:
Child dies. No funds for drugs.
And;
Crisis costing $1Billion per hour; Economist
And another;
Child kidnapped from private school. $1 million cash ransom demanded.
   An article;
   Teamsters threaten wildcat strike.
   "The bank closures have shut down most independent truckers because they cannot buy fuel. Teamsters Union members are determined to stand by their independent brothers "by creating slow moving blockades on all major routes across the nation to hinder goods getting to market unless normalcy is restored forthwith," said Teamsters president, Allan Wilson, today. "We

Operation Phoenix

expect to receive our pay checks Friday."

Looking over the previous days paper, the front page was given over to a political debate.

Frightened political parties at odds over solution to crisis

Secretary of the treasury, Tom O'Malley, in a speech today, said that the nation would have to get back to old-fashioned values by living within its means. "We've been paying out one third of every dollar we receive in revenue in the form of interest on loans. That means that if we had no loans, we could increase services by 50% over existing levels, or reduce the tax burden. We must tighten our belts and cut the debt drastically. We are no longer invincible. The dollar is no longer as sound as a dollar."

Majority house leader, James Snow disagreed. In a comment to reporters, he said, "The first thing we have to do is to increase the money supply so people can spend and get the wheels back under the economy. We must lower taxes. If that means borrowing, so be it. We can outgrow our problems.........."

With the president not having a majority in both houses, and frightened legislators galloping off in all directions, it appeared a consensus would not arise immediately.

"My God," Gary muttered to himself. "That Vice President of the Bank of International Settlements who said 'If the US dollar collapses, it will take about five days for the US to collapse, and another five days for the rest of the world to follow suit', was not far off the mark. The only thing that seems to be holding this together is that everyone expects things to magically return to normal when the banks reopen Monday." He shook his head in disbelief and sorrow.

He phoned Lynn, and mercifully she was home. "Have you been reading the papers and noticing the skyrocketing increase in crime?" he demanded.

"Yes it's scary to come into the apartment building, and once you're in, you still don't feel safe. Even in the elevators and hallways it feels like they are all strangers and staring at you. Our door security was good, and it has tightened up, but I still put a big chest up against the door last night before I went to bed. We had an apartment invasion and robbery last night. Distracts me from the challenge of my belly button lint."

"Why didn't you tell me?" Gary demanded. "I was so involved with what I was doing I didn't notice how bad it had gotten. While we did expect most of this, we just didn't expect it so fast. We are going to have to get you and Eric to somewhere safer right away. The only place that comes to mind is here because of the security features I installed in the house. But I want to discuss that with both of you first. Maybe we can talk about that tomorrow while we're waiting for the silver to be delivered. Perhaps you should get some help you know and start packing this weekend so we can get your stuff loaded into a container. We can store it at Eric's hangar."

"Well I'd sure like to get all this cash out of the fridge crisper drawer, anyway. I need space for my lint."

"We're certainly going to need that cash if Claude buys that ship, so pack it in the accountant's briefcase. I'll take it when I pick you up tomorrow morning. Keep a packet or two for your own emergencies." Gary ordered.

"Oh the banks will be open Monday so I can get at my own money anyway."

"I'd doubt that you would be able to get at very much of your money Monday. Probably they'll only allow a small amount to be withdrawn. That's why I wanted you to collapse your 401K, and pull out as much as you could in cash from all of your accounts."

"Oh." Lynn sounded crestfallen. "I didn't have time to do that, what with flitting off to Zurich, and work, and everything. I didn't want no facts interfering with what I wanna believe."

Operation Phoenix

"Oh well. We can get by without it. Forget it." Gary changed the subject. "What about work? Do you feel safe there?"

"Yes, once I get to work I feel safe. It's the getting to and from that scares me."

"Okay, Eric or I will try to be available as armed guards to escort you to and from work, or for groceries, or whatever. Would you like to learn how to use a weapon?" Gary asked.

"I've been thinking about what's happening. It's like emigrating to another country. They have different language and customs and maybe a different religion. Unless you adapt to the new circumstances you can't survive. I think I need to know more about guns," Lynn conceded, immediately becoming a full member of the team.

"Okay, I'd like you to phone NRA affiliated gun clubs till you find one that gives the basic firearms training course and hire the instructor to give private courses for you and whoever needs it." Gary changed the subject. "One other thing. Can you be available to meet our new ship's captain, Claude, on Sunday afternoon?"

"Well that's going to cut into my packing time," Lynn teased.

"Okay, you got me," he grinned back.

Later Eric called to announce he was home safely.

"How did it go?" Gary demanded.

"I met Chris Habel. Hired him for tomorrow. I didn't talk to him long, so I don't have a solid opinion on him. He seems to be a smart businessman and probably trustworthy. What did you do to him? He seems to think you walk on water."

"Nothing, just advanced him $500 cash to help his drivers. I'll bet they return the favour. Says something about him."

"Whatever, you can do no wrong."

Operation Phoenix

"Do you need money for tomorrow?" Gary asked.

Eric was silent for a moment. "I'll need about $200,000 total tomorrow. I could probably use another hundred thou or so. We'll load the first load at six AM. I had to bribe the guy $1,000 per load so he would fiddle the books so that we were an 'approved' customer and he could load us. The load, and the payment will go on somebody else's account."

"Lynn wants that cash out of her crisper so that's available immediately, or tomorrow at the Trambull space."

"Okay I'm on it."

Gary called Claude to set up the Sunday meeting. When Gary asked if there was something he could bring, Claude asked if he had any tea as he was about out. Gary offered to bring a few ounces of Jasmine tea, a favourite of Claude's, and a pound of English tea, Claude's usual fare.

Gary called his local wholesale/retail meat butcher and caught Bill Cave, the owner, still in because the store was open till 9 on Fridays, even on a slow Friday. "Bill, it's Gary Alden. How has business been this last week?"

"Pretty slow. Nobody has any cash to buy expensive meat and they're mad as hell about that. I let the staff go early," Bill groused.

"You have a lot of beef hanging, ready to cut up?"

"Three or four sides hanging, and a dozen aging."

"How many sides of beef can you get into a 25 cubic foot, deep freezer?" Gary asked.

"Depends. Usually one and a half to two."

"How about pork? A lot of sides hanging?"

"Probably six hogs. What are you driving at Gary?"

"I was thinking about buying a considerable amount of meat and freezing it. What sort of discount can you give me on several sides?"

Operation Phoenix

"Four or more sides, 20 percent off," said Bill.
"Is that cut and freezer wrapped or is it flash frozen too?"
"However you want."
"Okay, net, how much a pound for cut, wrapped, and flash frozen beef and pork, large order?"
"$1.89 for grade triple A beef. $1.69 for pork," Bill answered promptly.
"Fine. If I take 16 sides of beef and six hogs, when could you deliver?"
"Wednesday or Thursday. I have to cut it up"
"Can you get 1000 pounds of roasting chicken? And what price would it be?" Gary asked.
"Yes, I can get it. I haven't talked to the poultry people since Wednesday, but around 89 cents a pound. I'll have to see the price tomorrow."
"Okay, add 1000 pounds of chicken to the order," Gary decided. "Chicken giblets outside. Everything freezer wrapped and deep-frozen. If you drop by my house later tonight, with some paperwork that confirms our agreement, I'll give you a cash deposit of $4,000. But I want to stress, if you can't replace your stock, you're sold out."
"I'll have to order the chicken. I don't carry that much frozen stock since I can get it on very short notice. I sell mostly 'never frozen'. That is over 200 chickens, about 22 cases."
"How big are the cases?" Gary was interested because he planned to buy deep freezers and needed to know how many.
"Oh a bit bigger than a computer monitor, maybe the size of a 20 inch TV."
Gary and Eric had originally planned to buy up to 25 large chest type deep freezers, load them into a container, and rig some kind of portable electrical generator to keep them running. That was before they had so much money. After he put the

Operation Phoenix

phone down, Gary thought that was a very awkward way of going about things. He had lots of money to play with given his newfound wealth. He should be looking at refrigerated containers. He got on the net and got an approximate idea of the price of new reefer containers. With this in mind he started reconsidering his meat requirements.

Seeing that 9 o'clock was approaching fast, he pondered for a while, and then pulled out $5,000 from his stash. As well, he began his preparations for tomorrow, pulling out a large old tarpaulin, and a sturdy chain and lock from the storage unit at the end of the garage, and loaded them in the car.

Bill Cave rang the doorbell and Gary let him in. Bill had massive, hairy shoulders and arms. He even had hair peeking out of the back of his collar. Gary had caught him one slow afternoon with a rolled up sheet of newspaper burning the hair off his arms. He produced a quotation with all the specifications Gary had demanded. Gary went to get the cash. As he was counting it out on the dining room table, he said, "I've been thinking about the chickens. I don't know how much space you have, but I'd like to get another 44 cases, or 2,000 pounds of chicken. Since I don't know how exactly which day I will get my refrigeration, can you store them for up to two weeks in your freezer until I get myself organized?"

"What the dickens are you going to do with so much meat?" Bill demanded. "Umm, yes, I guess I could store it."

Gary evaded by saying, "Okay, here is an extra $1,000 deposit on the additional chicken. But please order it tomorrow for delivery Monday."

"Why? We can easily get chicken any time."

Gary said patiently, "I expect the price to go up, and I want my supplies purchased and not subject to price fluctuations and availability, so I want them in your freezer. Humour me, it's important to me."

"You're the customer. But you have to admit this is a bit unusual."

"I know but I have my reasons. I'll try to get it out of your freezer next week."

"Okay, I'll get on these orders first thing tomorrow." Bill said.

Chapter 14
Saturday February 25th -- Day 12

It had snowed overnight and the roads were a bit greasy but traffic on his way to Lynn's was unusually light for a Saturday morning. It might be that either people couldn't buy fuel or go shopping because of the bank holiday, or there weren't as many people working, and therefore didn't need to travel. Either way it had ramifications. Along the streets some areas had lots of garbage piled up, others none. It appeared that manual services such as garbage collection were erratic at best. Obviously the city workers were unable or unwilling to work, perhaps because they were rebelling with no pay, or they didn't have the cash to buy gas to get to work with the banking system closed. *Mental note. Get back to Wolfgang soonest to set up both international counter-trade, and local barter trade. Conditions are getting ripe.*

He picked up Lynn and found that Eric had taken her cash the night before. They arrived at the Trambull space a few minutes before the safe and office furniture arrived. They used the lift truck that Chris had sent along to nestle the safe up against some pipes in one corner. After the truck left, they chained and locked the safe to the pipes. They moved the furniture in front of the safe and draped the tarp over the lot, so it wouldn't be so identifiable to the Willis gang coming next. What has not been noticed cannot be reported on later. Most of the precautions Gary was taking would not be of any use whatever, but if only one was effective in stopping the information flow from reaching undesirable ears, then they would all have been worthwhile.

Operation Phoenix

Willis arrived, dropped their load of silver and cash, and left, tramping through the slop since temperatures had begun to rise.

As they worked putting the boxes of silver into the safe, Lynn complained, "This stuff sure is heavy. Whose idea was this anyway? I'm going to have a broken back."

"Yep, there's a lot of weight here," replied Gary as he hoisted the last box of silver into the safe. "40,000 ounces is over a ton and a quarter of metal. Nobody's going to move this safe easily. And see the safe isn't even half full. There's enough room left for over three million in cash." He held out half a million dollars but placed the rest of the bags of cash in, and closed and locked the door. He slid the file cabinets back on front of the safe, and the furniture along side it, and covered the whole pile with the tarp again.

"What's that silver worth again?" Lynn asked.

"Well it's worth 40,000 ounces of silver, or at least that's what we think it will be worth. In terms you might relate to better, we think it will ultimately purchase what it would take $40 to $80 million dollars to purchase today. Remember that the purchasing power of the dollar has been going down steadily. At the end of WWII a cup of coffee was a nickel everywhere. How much is it today? We think that silver will briefly reach a purchasing power of $1-2,000 dollars an ounce in today's dollars."

"Forty to $80 million," Lynn said, putting her hand on her back and pushing to straighten up. "I feel better already."

There was a banging on the door. Gary peeked out and then opened it to let Eric in. "Running a bit late, are we? Any insurmountable problems?"

"Not really." Eric shrugged. "Problems, but not insurmountable. Sorry I'm late; I broke up a rape right out on

Operation Phoenix

the street. He didn't seem to fear any reprisal, and was really mad I broke it up, as if it was his god given right. Right there in the slop and snow. The rest of the loads should go much faster. We just made it six tractors hauling six trailers. That makes the next run the last pick up. Chris has agreed that only he'll know where the trailers are to be stored, although I think he's mighty curious. The other drivers will drop their trailers in his yard. He'll personally spot them at the hangars, one by one. Did everything go OK here?"

"Yes sir, 40,000 ounces of silver present and accounted for, sir. We also have nearly four million dollars in the safe. I also have half a million here for Claude's ship. I'm going to arrange a 24 hour armed guard watching the premises. By the way, I bought meat and changed the plan from having a Rube Goldberg set-up with large chest type freezers and a generator to having refrigerated containers." Digging a paper out of his wallet, Gary said, "I guess you are in a hurry, here are the alarm codes for this place."

"We're way behind but I think we'll make it up. Are you going to the hangar to check it out?"

"Yes I'd hoped to. Will that be okay with you?" Gary turned to Lynn.

"If you think it's important, yes. I have to do some shopping though."

"I'd rather be with you if you're in a public place," Gary said. "We'll do some shopping on the way home. I need some things we might be able to find."

Turning back to Eric he said. "Have either of you thought of anything better than moving into my place for mutual protection?" Both shook their heads. "Okay, we'll pack your stuff into containers, and store them in the hangar. Pack just enough to get by on in suitcases. We'll probably have move

Operation Phoenix

from my place too, to avoid the taxmen and gold authorities. Not being there when they come is one good way of stalling them."

Eric left.

Lynn finally burst out with something that had been simmering in her. "Whatever do you want with all that meat? Or do we run out of beer and become blood thirsty?"

"We think that foods, particularly protein foods, will be in exceedingly short supply. I recall someone from the USSR I met after it went down. He told me that he had traded a full stereo, TV stand, and bookcase console set for the living room, for a kilo of beef roast. He had two elderly and infirm parents who needed the protein and he had planned on sharing it with them. Well he got to cooking the roast, and it smelled so good, he cut a little slice off to taste it. That tasted so good he couldn't resist and he sliced a bit more off. Pretty soon the roast was gone and he was having guilt trips over doing that to his parents. As well as that, we will have a lot of people to feed if we get the boat thing off the ground, both during the trip and while we get settled. There won't be a grocery store available. We need lots of food."

They locked up, set the alarms, and left for the hangar space. By this time the temperature was above freezing level so much of the overnight snow was disappearing.

The old air force airfield had all its buildings crowded near the gate end of the field. An old three story administrative building and its parking lot were first on the right, followed by a series of massive hangars in a row. At the security gatehouse they entered the guardhouse and asked the guard on duty about the hangar.

"I'm sorry sir, I'm not allowed to let anyone in there."

"That's my son, Eric who rented this place, and I want to

Operation Phoenix

go in there." Gary said.

"I'm sorry sir, my instructions are very clear. I am not to let anyone go in there that I do not have direct authorization for." The guard was polite but adamant.

Gary reached into his pocket and held out a $20 bill. The guard just sat there, and made no motion toward accepting it or opening the chain-link fence sliding gate.

Gary smiled and said, "I really think your attitude is wonderful. Those instructions were exactly what we wanted, and you have followed them superbly. No one, but no one, is allowed to go in under any circumstances, except the four people who will be authorized, or people who directly accompany them. I want you to take this $20 as thanks for refusing to be buffaloed. We'll wait till Eric comes and authorizes us. How many guards do you have servicing this site?"

"We work two per shift, with one patrolling the airfield perimeter and buildings, and one guarding the gate at all times. We take turns patrolling. Ten guards in total for 24/7 coverage." The guard eyed the $20 bill. "Do you really mean that sir? Are you going to wait for your son to authorize you?"

"Yes, I just wanted to know how good the security was. I don't even have the alarm security codes for the building. Take the $20 as thanks for a job well done."

"Thank you sir. I really could use that with the banks closed."

"Among the ten guards are there any who you think might be buffaloed by one tactic or another?"

"No sir. Well, maybe one." The guard said after reflection.

Gary took out another ten, $20 bills. "I want you to contact the other nine guards and give them each $20. Impress on all of them how fanatical we are about security and secrecy,

Operation Phoenix

particularly the marginal guard. I'd like to have you do it as soon as possible, by phone if necessary. I'd imagine they need cash too. The extra $20 is for your trouble and the job well done. Can you do that for me?"

The guard said, "Nobody ever paid us extra for doing our job before."

"I'm paying you for extra quality. The sort of quality one seldom gets. I'm pleased enough to think of it as thanks for a job well done. We'll wait in the car."

"Thank you very much sir. I'll get on to the other guards right away."

Gary turned to the door and then stopped. "Do you have our phone numbers in case of problems?"

"Just your son's phone number. Do you want me to have yours too?"

"Yes, in case you can't get hold of Eric, I want you to call this number at any hour, providing it's a problem you can't handle yourself. I don't want to be woken up just for a report, but I do want to be contacted in case of fire, or any serious problem that you can't handle yourself. And I want the fact that we are renting space here to be strictly confidential. If any guards come in before we leave, I'd like to meet them too, so they know our faces." Gary handed him his card, and he and Lynn went back to the car.

"What is this, some kind of prize show the way you're giving away money?" Lynn asked.

"Not if I think it will buy some loyalty. Guards are pretty much at the bottom of the heap, and everybody treats them like that. They almost never get any praise, so the money is just reinforcement for the praise. It says the job they are doing is important. Nobody ever gives them extra money, so it's really high praise indeed. In any case it gets things done, and that's the

Operation Phoenix

reality of our new world."

A few minutes later, Chris rolled up with his truck. Gary and Lynn climbed into the cab.

"Eric should be along in a few minutes. He was just settling up the bill." Chris said. "We were all loading at once."

"Good," Gary said. "Things are getting so hectic that time is at a premium. Everything needs to be done yesterday. How's business doing?"

"Well we don't usually do much business on the weekend so the drivers were glad to get the cash."

"When do you expect to get the rest of the trailers yanked over here? That's a lot of work for you personally and we really appreciate it," Gary said.

"I'll get most of them over today and the rest tomorrow morning."

Gary frowned. "The crime rate is really getting bad and we think it will get worse. We want all this secrecy because if it's not known there's something to steal, it's less likely that theft and vandalism will occur."

"It's pretty quiet around our neck of the woods but I suppose you're right. What people don't know about they won't think of stealing."

"How did you get into this business?" Lynn changed the subject.

"Oh it was pretty strange. I was a veterinarian out west in cattle country and my father got sick so I came home to run his small firm. Somehow I just stayed after he died. Mother was also sick and died a couple of years later, but I still live on the old farm."

"You're married I take it." Lynn said.

"Yes with three wonderful kids."

Eric drove up, and they all got out to see him and the

guard. The guard doing the patrolling was back, so introductions were made all around.

Eric said to the guards, "We are the only four people with unrestricted access to the site. I'll take them in with me but we can all come in at any time."

Both guards thanked them very profusely and opened the gates. They went to the building, and learned how to turn off and reset the alarm system that Eric had arranged for. Chris drove into the building, backed the trailer into place, and then left to pick up another tanker.

"That's gasoline isn't it?" Lynn said. "Are you thinking of storing our clothes in here with those tanks of gasoline? Our clothes will reek of gasoline before long."

"Yes, gasoline and diesel fuel," Eric said.

Gary piped up. "That's a good point. The clothes and stuff will air out, or can be washed. We have food coming and it won't air out. It'll be ruined. Do you think the hangar next door is for rent?"

"They offered it to me. I can get on that next week," Eric said wearily, "and I think it's okay for contamination. These hangars have been vacant for years. I didn't even consider it because we have so much space here."

"Maybe we should look at more tankers of gasoline then," Gary thought out loud.

"What are you guys so hepped up about gasoline for anyway?" Lynn demanded.

"It's pretty simple," said Eric. "Right now around the world as we saw in Zurich at the bank, nobody's taking the US dollar. The US imports two thirds of its fuel requirements. Somehow that has to be paid. If it can't be paid because no one will accept the dollar, where'll the US get its fuel? Our own oilfields are not nearly enough to supply us, so there'll be fuel

Operation Phoenix

shortages. Long line-ups at any station that can manage to get fuel itself. What little fuel that might be available is going to be priced through the roof. At a minimum fuel will be rationed. We expect fuel shortages so we grabbed some while supplies lasted. It helped that we had cash to buy with when every ones attention was focused on cash. But their attention will soon turn to fuel supplies as the pipeline of oil coming into the US empties and countries refuse to sell more to us unless the US pays in goods, or their local cash in advance. No more credit deals I'm afraid."

"Not only that," Gary added, "but there is something called 'peak oil'. The world pumped dry the fields that we know about, and we're having a devil of a time finding enough to keep up with the amount we are pumping now, never mind countries like China and India who are using more and more. The undeveloped oil areas such as deepwater take lots and lots of money, time and very advanced technology to develop. And the alternative energy sources are not developed enough. Imagine if every car in the US had to be scrapped and a new electric car bought? It doesn't stop at cars and trucks either. For instance, ten percent of California's electricity is consumed in moving water. With changing weather patterns bringing drought to some places they will not be alone in needing water to drink, especially since so much electrical generation relies on hydrocarbons. The more you think about it the uglier it gets."

"What about the strategic petroleum reserves? Can't they be used?" asked Lynn.

Gary shook his head. "Well even if they were full, which they aren't, they wouldn't supply the US imported fuel requirements for a month. They are strategic military reserves. You can bet your sweet bippy that the military is going to have first dibs on any fuel. The man on the street is not going to get any. Long before the average guy gets his hands on fuel, the

Operation Phoenix

farmers must have fuel to produce food. Of course various authorities will get their greedy little paws on any supplies because they're on 'official business'. How do you think the police or firemen in any city are going to respond to calls if they have no gas for their vehicles? Can you imagine fighting a fire on bicycles? The supply of oil will not go to zero because we do have our own oilfields, and unconventional gas supplies such as coal bed methane. It takes a long time and a lot of energy to get a new source up and running, decades under our current regulations. In the meantime, our problem is going to rear its ugly head in a month or less."

Eric said, "Let's get going. I'd hoped to do some shopping too. Why don't Lynn and I go shopping, and I'll deliver her home. Do you need anything?"

"That works for me. I have some other things I want to check on. If you run across any fresh vegetables, buy at least twice as much as you think I need. I'm taking some to Claude's tomorrow. Spanish onions too. If you find milk or bread, buy 10 times what you think I'll need. I'll freeze what I don't use immediately. I'll pick it up tomorrow. Is that okay with you, Lynn?" Gary asked.

"Sure."

They locked and alarmed the hangar. Back at the gate guardhouse, to show how important the $20 cash was to the guards, three off duty guards were present at the shack to pick up their cash. The Alden's were able to meet with them and become a face before leaving. They now knew personally, five of the ten guards at the site. All had been cautioned about secrecy and high levels of security.

Operation Phoenix

Chapter 15

Gary took the scenic route home since he wanted to get an idea about the level of crime, and an impression of how social disruption was proceeding. Shopping centres seemed nearly empty for a Saturday afternoon, except there were a lot of people hanging around the front doors. Obviously wanna be muggers. Those few drivers on the road seemed tense and drove accordingly. Road rage seemed to simmer just under the surface. *The atmosphere is sure electric,* thought Gary. *This could get ugly fast.* The power was out in a couple of areas that he passed leaving the traffic lights malfunctioning. At one such corner a fist fight was in progress next to a fender bender as Gary eased past.

About three blocks from the house Gary noticed a scuffle taking place on the sidewalk ahead. *My god, crime is getting blatant,* he thought. He saw the flash of a knife and slowed. A woman was under attack by three thugs.

"Shit, that's Jan Kerr," he swore and slammed to a stop. Reaching down he pulled out the .357 magnum he had rigged a hidden compartment for in the car. Jumping out of the car he yelled over the top of the car, "Hey. Knock it off."

One of the three, the one holding a knife and facing Jan, and obviously the informal leader, turned and took a couple of steps toward Gary. "Get the fuck out of here or I'll kick the shit out of you too. This is my chick."

Gary lifted the pistol from his side where it had been concealed by the car, flicked off the safety, and steadied it on the roof of the car. "Well, I don't like how you're treating 'your' chick so you get to fuck out of here. Now."

The thug took another step, partly aggressively toward Gary, and partly diagonally toward the safety of a lamppost, which was fine with Gary, because it tended to remove Jan from the line of fire. "You wouldn't dare fire that fucking thing around here," he yelled.

Gary took careful aim at the curb to the side of the thug's feet. Calling on his old billiard skills as to where the ricochet might go, he blew away about a yard of concrete. The sound of a bullet, particularly a heavy calibre round, ricocheting away, whining into the distance, tends to focus ones attention wonderfully. "Wanna bet?" yelled Gary. "Next one's for you. Move."

The leader turned and ran. Seeing their fearless leader in flight, the two lesser compatriots blinked stupidly, and then slowly seemed to get a telepathic message that their mother wanted them home safely and soon. They dropped Jan's arms, and began to keep time with their feet. Rapidly.

Gary hurried over to Jan. "Are you Okay?"

Jan looked at him wide-eyed. "It's a miracle you showed up. They were going to kill me."

"I doubt it, or not soon anyway, which might have been worse. Are you okay? You have a nasty cut on your upper arm."

Jan looked down at her blood soaked sleeve in shock. "I didn't notice. Yes, I think I'm okay."

"I have a first aid kit at my place, a couple of blocks away. We can look at that cut and decide if you need to go to the hospital, not that they are handling their load anyway. If it's not too bad, maybe we can bandage you up." Picking up her scattered groceries, and putting his arm around her back, he guided her to the car.

Operation Phoenix

Back in his living room they got her coat off, but the blood was beginning to congeal around her blouse and the wound. Gary grabbed his first aid kit, and wet a sterile bandage with alcohol. "This may sting a bit," and began to sponge the blouse loose from the wound. "We're going to have to get the blouse off that shoulder to get at the cut. So far it doesn't look too bad. It looks as if the coat took most of the force."

Sponging and lifting the blouse from the cut, they got it free, and then down from her shoulder. Gary finished cleaning the wound, and then sterilized it, making her gasp a bit. Taking a large adhesive bandage he carefully applied it a bit at a time, squeezing the cut together as he went.

Looking over his finished handiwork he glanced down and saw the gentle curve of her breast disappearing beneath her bra. Turning his head, he found himself about six inches away from her face, looking at her wide eyes and parted lips, and breathing her perfume. He leaned forward and kissed her tenderly and found her responding passionately. Soon clothes began to loosen. Gary picked her up.

"Don't, you will hurt yourself."

"Don't worry, I won't."

"Where are we going?"

"To the bedroom." As a response, she buried her head in his shoulder.

Later, during the afterglow, they were lying, loosely entwined, occasionally kissing softly and breathing each others air.

"I noticed you from the first," she said softly, "but you showing up the way you did today - well, it was fated to be."

"Well there's nothing quite so life confirming as the act which creates life, especially when you were facing death. And I noticed you too, although I must say you look even more beautiful this way than you do in your banker's suit," he grinned. "But a smart, beautiful lady with a great personality, what's not to like?" He sat up suddenly.

"Don't go."

"I wasn't. I was looking at your cut. Looks like the bandage hasn't moved, although it should have, as passionate as we were." He resumed his former position idly tracing a line up and down her ribs, her breast, and her back with is hand.

"I wondered about your hidden agenda when you bought gold in the way you did, and then silver, but as time has gone on, I've begun to think you are psychic, and can foresee the future. What do you see in store for us?"

Gary snorted. "I'm certainly not psychic. All I did was to look at what similar circumstances produced in history. I can't foresee the future so I don't know what will come of us. I'm divorced and I've always been pretty gun-shy. Every time before, when I got to that question, I've always run - fast. While I'm nervous I don't seem to be bolting from the corral, so maybe I'm ready."

"I'm divorced too. I know what you mean," she said softly

"No kids?"

"No. It never seemed the right time although I would like some."

"My two have been such a joy I've often said the only reason I would re-marry is to have more kids. It's insane but I love children. But as far as times go what's been happening around us will probably get worse, much worse. Sheer survival is going to be difficult, never mind babies. But maybe. Who knows? How many kids do you want?"

"I'd like three but I am not 18 anymore. I don't know how my body would react."

Operation Phoenix

Gary suddenly sat up in shock. "I don't think I've ever discussed the size of a potential family with a woman before. Certainly not this early in a relationship. And we're going to be busy trying to escape from this mess, so we'll have to run every minute. Something I should be doing right now."

Jan cupped the back of his head in her hands and said, "I don't want to leave you now." Drawing him down to kiss her, she silenced his concerns in women's age old way.

Later, he glanced at the clock on the nightstand and said, "I have to make a call before the stores close." He slipped on his robe and went to find Bill Cave, the butcher's number. He dialled and got Bill on the line.

"Did you get the chicken?" Gary demanded.

"Yes no problem, sixty cases. They're here now."

"Great, Bill. I just called to say that I'll definitely be able to take the frozen stuff early. I still don't have my schedule, but you need not worry about freezer space. I expect be able to take it off your hands by about Thursday. Okay?"

"Okay. I may work on cutting some of the meat tomorrow when I'm not distracted"

Back in the bedroom, Jan was sitting with her arms clasped around her knees. Gary slipped the robe off and crawled up the bed to kiss her. Jan leaned back and it soon turned into an intimate tender kiss. Gary looked down at her and said, "Before I was so rudely interrupted, you evil woman, I was about to ask if you would like a coffee or tea, and maybe something to eat."

"Definitely. But I think I'd like to shower first."

"Yeah me too. You shower, and I'll get the water boiling and pull out a few things for dinner. Then I'll shower. Coffee, tea, juice, milk or what?"

"It doesn't matter. I think I feel like a tea. I drink too much coffee at the office."

Operation Phoenix

"Tea it is." Gary slipped on his pants leaving the robe for her. He started the kettle boiling and cleared a bit of space in the fridge for Jan's few perishables. He pulled out some pre-made Thai spicy noodle sauce, and started defrosting it in the microwave. Just as the tea was about finished steeping Jan came out dressed in the robe. "Umm, smells good," she said, accepting a cup and sitting down at the breakfast nook table after a soft kiss. The doorbell rang.

"I wonder who that could be? I'm not expecting anybody," Gary said. "Who is it?" he yelled.

"Just me," Eric's voice came back. "I decided to drop off your stuff on the way home."

Gary let him in. Jan looked as if she thought being out of sight was the prudent thing to do, but before she got up Gary motioned her to stay, and let Eric in. Clutching the robe tight around her Jan was obviously uncomfortable.

"Jan, I'd like you to meet Eric, my son. Eric this is Jan Kerr. We met about a year ago at the bank, and she was the one who handled our overnight loans and bullion purchases." Gary conveyed the essential information casually. "Took you long enough. Did you have to go to many stores to get all this? I didn't get very much of what I had planned to do, done."

"It took forever. I think we hit every grocery store along the way."

"Hi, Eric." Jan rose and extended her hand.

"Hello Jan, nice to meet you," Eric mumbled, obviously uncomfortable at intruding. "I'll get the other load of groceries and be on my way." And he disappeared out the door. Soon he was back dropping a huge load of plastic shopping bags on the counter.

"Would you like to stay for dinner?" Gary asked. "I was thinking today about Thai spicy noodles, and my taste buds got all set for them. There's plenty."

Eric looked at Gary and said, "No, I don't think so right at the moment. I have too many things to do and the car is loaded and outside. I have to get my groceries in. I'll take a rain check. Okay?"

"Of course. Jan was attacked today, which I fortunately interrupted, and I think it was her bag of groceries that attracted them." Gary had received the message loud and clear. There was cash and groceries in the car. "See you later, and thanks."

Eric left.

Gary pulled out a pot and started to fill it with water for the noodles. Jan came up behind him and brushed his arm with her breast. "Eric seems like a nice guy. Can I help with dinner?"

Gary put the pot on the stove and turned the burner on. "Will you stop that, you insatiable woman? Have you ever had sex on a kitchen table?"

"No, but it sounds like fun," She grinned up at him.

Gary turned, slipping his hands under the robe, and pulled her bare pelvis to his, so she pressed against his beginning erection, before kissing her passionately. He turned her and moved her back against the breakfast nook table, forcing her to bend over backwards a bit. At her surprised and somewhat humorous look he laughed and said, "Hey you've got me pumped nearly dry now. I was hoping for a long slow, tender lovemaking session later." He swatted her bum lightly and said, "I have to get these perishables put away. Drink your tea. I'll get you to make salad if Eric brought the fixin's"

Gary swung the bags containing milk over by the cellar door. Then the bread. He took out a head of lettuce, and miraculously, a large bag of tomatoes, and put them on the table in front of Jan who ignored them. The rest of the bags he inspected, gathered up and then took the lot down to the pantry, where he put them away.

Gary prepared dinner and was able to find a candle, so the lights could be turned down. Along with a bottle of wine the meal was quite romantic. With Jan's nakedness under the robe, and the flashes of skin Jan seemed unconcerned about, Gary was very attentive.

Later they talked about her work. "Do you expect the bank to have to call many loans?" Gary asked.

"Oh yes. I've been working all week just reviewing accounts. I'd guess we might call, or demand more security on almost all of our loans." Jan held her tea cup up, obviously waiting for somebody to refill it. Gary did so.

Gary blinked as this factor that he had forecast and strategized about dropped into place. "Do you think that other banks will be doing the same?" he asked.

"I don't see why not. The banks all have the same problem. Risk has suddenly skyrocketed."

"Yes I guess so. Oh, by the way, I just thought, you know those forms for government that you fill out when you purchase bullion? How often do you send them in to government? Daily, monthly or what?"

"Monthly," she said.

"God, I wish there were some way mine could get lost for this month end, and only wind up going to government next month. With the government about to make gold ownership illegal, I could sure use the extra time." Jan might take the hint and solve a problem for him.

They finished the wine on the couch in the living room. Later the passion rose again.

Chapter 16
Sunday February 26ᵗʰ -- Day 13

Sunday morning after breakfast Gary explained that he had a meeting to go to and delivered Jan home. He mentioned that he'd like to arrange a get together with Lynn and Eric as soon as possible so they could get to know each other.

He bustled back to the house whistling all the way and loaded the trunk for the trip to Claude's. Then he drove to Lynn's and picked her up. At Eric's, one of the first things Eric said as they stood inside waiting for Eric to get his coat was, "This lady in your life is new?"

"Yes but I've been lusting after her for a while. One thing I really want to get done quickly is to have you both meet her. In matters sexual one tends to think only with your gonads. I don't mind doing that but not now. There is too much at stake, too little time, and no way out if I make a mistake. I'd like your opinion on whether you feel that you would be prepared to trust your life in her hands if it came down to that. If you have serious doubts after only knowing her for a short while I'll cut it short. I can't have her at the house for long without her noticing some things that are better not being noticed."

"Would you marry her today?" Lynn asked.

"Well it is early days, but that is about all we are going to get. Possibly yes. Very astute question, gets right to the crux of the matter. Probably." Gary blinked in shock. *Probably?! Are you falling in love my man?*

"What is she like?" Lynn asked.

Operation Phoenix

"I think she's good looking, intelligent, and fairly easy to get along with. I've dealt with her mostly on a professional basis. She was the one who handled our bullion purchases at the bank and I found her to be flexible then. She does know about how much money is involved but not about any of the steps we have taken since then. I had a bit of a job keeping her away from the vegetable crisper in the fridge." Gary grinned.

Eric interrupted. "I have a lot of things to do. Maybe I'd better take my car, leave Claude's early, and drop in at your house later."

"Okay but give me a go/no go on Claude before you leave. I have to set up most of the rest of the plan soon. If we're going to go ahead then the more time Claude has to think about what we have to say the more effective he can be."

They parked the two cars at Claude's. After Gary gathered up his packages out of the trunk they were admitted and introduced all around. Again they sat at the dining room table, chatting and drinking tea.

Eventually Claude said something about the security guy, and Gary said, "Do you ever run into Navy SEALs or British SAS people in your line of work?"

"A few SEALs in cases where ship was leased to the Navy on short-term basis. Maybe some were covert operations."

"Did you ever run across a Wayne Buckley?"

Claude jerked his head back a bit and then shook it. "More of your research, eh? You astound me. Yes I know Wayne. Fished him out of dodgy situation one time. They were in a rubber dinghy that had lost power with an armed speedboat coming on fast. He kept in touch ever since. Seems to think I saved his skin or something." Claude smiled. "He's top man and seems to have gone far."

"Would you trust your life with him? What sort of guy is

Operation Phoenix

he?" Gary squinted his eyes a bit and cocked his head slightly.

"If he were on my side no question. If he were against me I don't think my life would be worth two cents." Claude drew a deep breath. "He's a very proper trooper with rigid ideals. If he gives you loyalty his life is yours. His loyalty was toward the United States. He's very imaginative and improvises a lot. Makes him even more unpredictable than he has been trained for. Thinks really fast. Assesses situations accurately. A real catch if you can get loyalty. Otherwise I don't know."

"Any way to get his loyalty or assess whether his loyalty remains with the US?"

"Probably difficult," Claude frowned. "He's not stupid and very, very loyal. I might be able to get straight answer out of him."

Eric interrupted, "From what I see the big problem is that in any situation the security forces are the most dangerous to the leaders and the community. They're organized, trained, and equipped for mayhem. I think once people see that we're successful they're going to want what we have. We're bound to be attacked by individuals or groups, which may include countries. If the group or country is not the United States there seems little problem with his loyalty. Only if the country is the US do we have to watch where his loyalty lies. How likely do you think it is that in the initial stages of our approach that he might think it a good idea to adopt an undercover or sleeper role, still loyal to the US, but appearing to be loyal to us?"

Claude frowned. "That's possibility. I think in early stages it would be unlikely he would know enough details to try to be sleeper. He wouldn't listen further unless he suspected major chicanery. You plan for him to be part of discussion on our eventual destination, don't you?"

"We'd always planned that everyone would have a voice

Operation Phoenix

about where we would physically wind up. That's where they have to live possibly for the rest of their life. Particularly those people who were already in which boils down to the leaders," Gary said. "I'd expect, or hope, that before a definitive answer to that question were arrived at, that security would be in place as a leader. However since talking to you I now have a much better idea how to approach him. I think from the information you have given me I can largely bypass the sleeper issue and if he turns against us later then it's also possible for anyone else to do that as well. I feel safer with the issue now. May I also use your name as being associated with the effort should I think it wise?"

"Of course."

"Okay we have three possibles on our shortlist at the moment, but as of this conversation, Wayne is leading. Lynn you have been sitting there saying nothing. What are your views on this?"

Lynn shrugged, "You've been a head hunter for long enough that if you think you can bring him aboard without him being a sleeper, then I don't see any other issue to address on the subject."

"Claude anything new on the ship?"

"Not since I spoke to you. I want to get negotiations finished as soon as possible."

"You mentioned a half million price tag and I said I could have the money by today. Are you ready enough to need it?" Gary asked.

"Possibly. Laying hundred dollar bills on fender of a car makes their eyes pop and they spend it before they own it. I might be able to do the same thing with less than $500,000. Maybe you brought it in that bag. Did you?"

Gary nodded. "Yes and I agree with your auto analogy.

Operation Phoenix

Nothing like cash to make their eyes pop."

Claude frowned again. "I have run across rumour of another ship. It may have been pirated just from story. There's small 10,000 ton tanker in Singapore loaded with fuel distillates. They're asking two million US. From what I know cargo alone is worth more than that. You seemed very interested in fuels. Are you interested?"

"Wow," Eric grinned widely. "I think the answer is probably. We don't want any attention from the authorities now. Later it may be okay but not now. However the fuel could be critical to our success. Even if it were only for goods for trade it'd be worthwhile. Can you find out more?"

"I have a couple of questions," interrupted Lynn. "What exactly are the distillates, and do we have a free two million to spend?"

"We can swing the two million if the pick up of the cash is here in the US, but just barely," Gary said. "Distillates are usually gas, diesel fuel and heating oil. Do you have a closer idea of exactly what the cargo is, Claude?"

"Only second hand. Gas and diesel were mentioned. You know how rumours are. By the way did you know president was to address nation shortly? I thought we should watch," said Claude.

"No I didn't," conceded Gary, "and it's a must see. We need to know the official line. Back to our distillate tanker. Does anybody have an objection to Claude starting to sniff around?"

No one said anything and Claude turned on the TV. Small talk continued over the muted TV until the President came on.

"My fellow Americans. I speak to you today with a heavy heart. I speak of the economic terrorism in our financial markets. At this moment, America is under siege with the most diabolical scheme ever uncovered. Today we are a country

Operation Phoenix

awakened to danger.

"Yet, no scheme of an enemy, no crime of a consortium of enemies will divert us from our mission. We will not stop. We will never give up our freedoms.

"In the normal course of our generosity toward the rest of the world, and normal trade flows, we have availed the rest of the world with our largess. US dollars are sought and used worldwide. We have generously provided assistance, and lent countries around the world our dollar for their use.

"Our enemies have amassed a significant quantity of US obligations. Together they have sought to destabilize the United States by unexpectedly dumping these obligations in concert, in an attempt to drive the United States into oblivion. America has now entered a fierce struggle to protect ourselves and the world from a grave danger. The United States did nothing to deserve or invite this threat.

"These are sacrifices of high calling – the defence of our nation and the peace of the world. Overcoming evil is the noblest cause, and the hardest work. The objectives we have are worthy of America, worthy of all the acts of heroism and generosity that have gone before. Yes, there is work ahead, work that will demand the utmost of every American. By our actions, we serve a great and just cause.

"I have today ordered that every government department immediately cut spending by 50 percent. Where such actions result in default of our role of policeman to the world, and other world issues, we will withdraw our military bases, regardless of our previous generosity and the disruption that local reliance on that generosity will cause. We cannot be expected to continue to shoulder the costs of keeping peace in the world alone.

"At the same time, I have ordered immediate tax cuts across the board in an amount of 33 and one third percent for

Operation Phoenix

both individuals and corporations.

"The bank holidays ordered by the treasury have caused considerable hardship but we are Americans, and when the going gets tough the tough get going. That is a picture of America. People in these United States are proud of their honourable conduct and freedoms. We will sacrifice to maintain them.

"Immediately, effective at the opening of business tomorrow, I have ordered some of the restrictions of the bank holiday lifted. Individuals are permitted to withdraw up to $1,000 per week per institution of existing balances. Corporate current accounts will operate as they did previously in order to continue the normal flow of business, and to meet payroll needs.

"In order to keep jobs in America, all import duties are immediately doubled. Exceptions will be studied on a case-by-case basis, and rescinded where it is in the interests of America to do so.

"I have ordered that all debt obligations of the United States be converted into 30-year bonds at a rate of two percent per annum. All 401K and other pension plans are temporarily ordered to pay interest only on their holdings, which will result in a slight decrease in the immediate payout.

"Under the foreign exchange stabilization act, all foreign exchange and gold holdings are immediately converted into US 30 year two percent bonds at the price that prevailed at noon Eastern Standard Time on February 1st of this year.

"Once again we will apply the power of our country and its citizens to maintain our freedoms against evil.

"People of this country take pride in their freedoms. Our country has a tradition. No one who sacrifices will be forgotten by this grateful nation. We honour their sacrifices to America, and we pray they and their families will receive God's comfort

Operation Phoenix

and God's grace.

"Our financial system has performed superbly over the years. That is why so many people and nations want our dollars and our way of life. Americans must and will defend that way of life with all the resources we can muster. It is the American way.

"May God bless our country, and all those who sacrifice to defend our country and freedoms. Good day."

During the speech there had been silence with the only communication being exchanges of glances, particularly between Gary and Eric.

"Right. If we all hold our breath the Titanic will get lighter and won't sink. The capitulation is complete. If you can prove your rare gold coin is worth more than the price of gold then you get a worthless IOU that pays two percent in 30 years. Otherwise you get a worthless IOU which pays two percent in 30 years." Gary felt like he was sucking on a lemon. "If international trade wasn't dead before it sure is now. All those countries with US obligations up to their ying yang are not going to be happy with this haircut. But it's okay; he'll make a short prayer that everybody will receive God's comfort and grace. That is now the official American way."

Claude mused, "My pension goes down I guess. How much you think?"

"I'd think by at least two thirds. Mostly they were getting about six percent on the longer bonds and a fair return on whatever equities they had. What remains of the market, particularly the bond market, will definitely fall hard and fast tomorrow so the equity return will be negative. The interest rate will now be two percent, so knock off two thirds on that part, and then there is no payout of principal, so knock off a bit more. Two thirds is conservative. That's the slight decrease he referred

Operation Phoenix

to." As an afterthought Gary added. "I guess we don't have to worry about inflation though."

"Why?"

"Inflation is too many dollars chasing too few goods. What the government hasn't taken away, the banks will. There won't be any money to inflate with. I'll bet our local taxes won't go down. There'll be a lot of houses lost through non payment of taxes."

"You guys are a real bundle of joy, aren't you?" Claude said sourly.

"Sorry," Gary said contritely to Claude. "The thought just popped out. On the other hand this is just the beginning. There'll be worse, much worse to come. You're in the position that you can probably come out with a whole skin. This is only the 12th day after the crash. It'll take some time for this to sink in with the general populace. By that time hopefully you'll be on a ship, with armed guards and essential assets, safely off shore away from the maddened crowds."

Claude paused to draw a deep breath. "Okay it looks as if no other options now. We'd better get this thing rolling."

"Hey," Gary said. "Two weeks ago you were just listing your house because the crime rate was climbing. We've come a long way baby in a very short time. As long as we can stay ahead of events we'll come out on top."

"That's the only thing that keeps me from slitting throat. We have plan, some hope, and so far it seems to be working."

"That's all one can say," Eric said. "So far it seems to be working. New problems will arise but we have to keep struggling. I have to go now so I'll say goodbye."

Gary accompanied Eric to the door. Eric glanced significantly sideways at Claude and nodded once. Gary got the message. Claude had passed Eric's test. When he returned to the

Operation Phoenix

living room Lynn also discreetly signalled that she felt Claude was acceptable. The next hour was spent with Gary opening up on past events, future plans, forecasts and possibilities. The atmosphere was intense but filled with hope. Too soon for everybody Gary and Lynn had to leave. In parting Gary had opened up the possibility that there might be a female at his side.

    They picked Jan up and went back to Gary's. They chatted for an hour till Eric came, and soon the banter among the Alden's turned into a general laugh session between all four. It looked to Gary like Jan might fit well. Because everyone had to get up early Eric drove Lynn home. Gary and Jan retired to a tender session.

Chapter 17
Monday February 27th -- Day 14

Gary drove Jan and Lynn to work through extremely light traffic, dropping Jan off first so he could talk to Lynn. "I know you've just met her but do you have any impressions of Jan?"

"She seems like a nice lady."

"You say that in a way that is damning with faint praise," Gary said slowly. "The point is, knowing her a very short time did you see anything that would make you doubt that she was someone you would trust with your life?"

"Dad, I wasn't thinking in quite in those terms. I have a friend she reminds me of a lot. People would say my friend is moody, but really, it is more that if something is bothering her – look out. Right or wrong, she'll fight to the last drop of blood long after it becomes unreasonable to fight. She might be hard for you to live with."

"I'm really pleased you told me that," Gary said and paused to consider. "I hadn't noticed it but there is already some evidence that you might be at least partly right. She decided that we were fated to be and acted on that. Plus, she has climbed quite quickly in the corporate world and you don't get to where she is, and doing what she's doing, by being wishy-washy. If she's that way it's a personal decision if I can live with her. But it's a community decision if these traits are good or bad for the community."

Operation Phoenix

"She seems like a smart lady Dad. I don't think she would make many mistakes. On that basis I'd vote for her. For you I was just concerned that you might not have seen that side of her personality although I wouldn't have said so if you hadn't insisted."

"Personally I've never had a big problem with people who were willing to stand up for their opinions or values. Circumstances often modify the amount one can defend these positions, but if you know the consequences and ramifications of your actions and choose to go ahead anyway, then I think that is great even if your view opposes mine. In this case I see the big danger as being that a situation might arise where we come to loggerheads and she might be vindictive afterwards. That could badly damage the community."

"I don't see her as being vindictive, except if she's set a course that damages someone in some way, I wouldn't expect her to necessarily vary that course."

"Well should I decide to go ahead, we as a community will have to watch for that stubbornness. Personally I haven't seen too many warts but that is to be expected when you're thinking with your emotions. There will be some warts for sure." Gary changed the subject. "What did you think of Claude?"

"Claude's really wise in the way that grandpa was. I think you've found a wonderful person."

Gary decided that while he was downtown and since it was not yet 8AM it might be smart to check on 40 foot ocean going steel containers, so he called Chris to see if he knew a place to buy good used containers.

"Try Containerhaus over in Jersey. They do a lot of container trading."

"Do they do refrigerated containers too, Chris?"

Operation Phoenix

"Not too many reefers around on the used market so far as I know. I'd be afraid of used refrigeration systems anyway. They don't last that long. That box in front that contains the automatic refrigeration system, its gas motor and its gas tank gets bounced around a lot. They can tell you if they have any, or where to look."

"Great," said Gary. "If I buy several may I spot them in your yard? Normal rates."

"Sure but I only have a limited number of flatbed trailers capable of hauling containers, and no roll off trailers."

"Okay," said Gary. "Do you have the number for Containerhaus?"

Chris gave the phone number to him and Gary called to make an immediate appointment and get their address.

The Containerhaus yard was huge and it took Gary a while to find the main entrance. From the outside it looked like one continuous container half a mile long. The containers were stacked five high along the fence. Once inside the yard there was more open space because the containers had to be inspected and sorted according to their quality. Judging by the few trucks and trailers in the yard they weren't doing their usual volume. Just the area where tractors dropped containers was active. The clerk said that most of the incoming containers were on a consignment basis, and were not owned by them. A five high container forklift was busy moving containers to the edges the closely stacked storage areas.

Gary viewed and purchased, subject to inspection and acceptance by Roy Bryant, 14 dry cargo containers at $1500 each. In addition, they had a large number of refrigerated containers contrary to Chris Habels assertion. Gary thought that Chris might be right in terms of used refrigeration systems being suspect. He purchased six new reefer containers at a cost of

Operation Phoenix

$15,000 each. He also noticed five flatbed trailers and three roll off trailers that they were willing to part with and purchased them, again subject to inspection. He left a deposit of $90,000, more than covering what he wanted to take out on a rush basis. Four of the dry containers, four of the reefer containers, and three of the trailers were to be picked up immediately after inspection, and the balance picked up and paid within a week.

He called Roy to arrange an ASAP inspection. Roy was able to commit to first thing the following morning. Gary also asked Roy to find out where one could get a container lifter that could offload full containers from the flatbed trailers and back on later to free up trailers.

Back at home, Gary took time to familiarize himself with Wayne's file, and update it with the new information Claude had given him. He looked up Wayne's address, and located a nearby Raddison Hotel, which should be nice. He phoned to make sure the bar and restaurants were open. Then he called Wayne and got an answering machine. He did not leave a message. *Not my day,* thought Gary

Just then the house alarm went off. Gary grabbed a pistol from his desk drawer, and first peeked, and the slipped out the front door. Two male teens were attacking his armoured garage door with a metal pry bar.

He levelled the gun at them and said in a normal voice, "This gun shoots bullets at 2500 feet per second. Do you think you can run faster than that?"

They took off anyway. Gary fired one shot in the air and levelled the gun again. This only served to increase their speed. *Crazy kids,* thought Gary. *Immortal, indestructible, and infertile. Oh well, I hope getting 'shot at' at this address serves as a deterrent.* He went inside and turned on the perimeter alarm which he'd forgotten as he came back in. He checked that the

Operation Phoenix

garage door had not been damaged and went back to his phones.

He called Nils Jensen at Foremost bank as he had promised.

"Gary. Great to hear a voice that's not screaming and panicking."

"Is it that bad?"

"I share this with you confidentially. We're pretty much shut down," Nils said. "Everybody's pulling everybody else's line of credit and calling the loans. It's impossible to do an international transaction. Buying power only comes about as a result of producing something you can sell. If you can sell something, you can automatically buy something else. If you have nothing to sell, you can buy nothing. Wal-Mart, and everybody else who relies on importing stuff from China and all these low cost nations are out of business. They will have no products to stock their shelves as soon as whatever is now on a boat runs out. We can't even deal with our own branches in places like oil countries. We don't have the foreign exchange here to transfer to them, and nobody's taking US dollars for anything. So, they can't pay for cargoes of goods, and especially oil, which is going to hurt the US a lot. Better top up your gas tank now."

Gary smiled to himself and thought, *Despite his job of moving millions and billons around, he still thinks in terms of one, two, three, many. Reduce everything to the simplest terms to view the logic, and then just add zeros.* That was common among traders. They even called a one million trade 'a dollar'. "Yeah, and keep a few barrels full of fuel in your garage for later. I hear the banks may be pulling some corporate lines of credit?"

"Never mind corporate we're pulling lines of credit to about half the banks we are dealing with. Some are pulling

Operation Phoenix

ours."

"Half the banks!!" Gary was aghast. "If it's half the banks then it must be 90% of the corporate loan accounts being called."

"Don't forget, the banking system is the problem. In normal times the banks take deposits, or borrow from people who have the right to take out their money in a maximum of 30 days. Then the banks turn around and lend it out long term on say a 30-year mortgage. In times like these the banks are caught in a bind. People are demanding their money, today, but the banks have the money all loaned out for 30 years, or some other long term, so they can't get their hands on it, They call every loan they can. Uh, Huh."

"Right," said Gary. "The Fed does not print money. They can only lend it out to create credit due to the multiplier in the fractional reserve banking system. If the banks won't borrow then they can't lend it. As I recall the head of the central bank said in testimony before congress in 1934, 'We tried to increase money supply in 1929 and '30. The windows were wide open. We even tried lending 100 and they only had to pay back 98, a negative interest rate. But we were pushing on a string'. People think the government can simply print money. It can't. It can only create credit if the banking system is operating normally."

Nils was emphatic, "Because the dollar is not just American any more we can't simply seal off our borders. The dollar is worldwide. We've made things worse by outsourcing many of our jobs and production to third world, cheap labour countries, and now we don't even have the machines needed to produce what would be needed if we were to become isolationist. They're all in China or somewhere. If companies like Wal-Mart or manufacturers, can't get supplies that are coming in by boat they're out of business. The banks have to

Operation Phoenix

seize to stop losing money no matter what else happens."

"How long do you think we have before banks start failing?" Gary asked.

"The action that the government took in limiting withdrawals should hold it off a bit, but without that, I'd have said by next week the banks would start failing. Now I don't know. It'll depend on how fast the ordinary guy takes to panic,"

"That's not helped by our current outlook on life," Gary said. "The average little government welfare lackey who has untold rights, no responsibilities, and needs his government to solve all his problems, has this idea that if I want something, I need it. And if I need something and can't get it by myself, then somebody should give it to me, preferably the 'gummint'. As if the 'gummint' wasn't all us taxpayers who have to pay for it. Looking at how crime has skyrocketed in the last week while the banks were closed, it's a very short step to 'and if somebody doesn't give it to me, it is my right to take it'. Did you hear that the police were only going to respond to what they call serious crimes because they were swamped? Sounds like no blood, no response."

"I'm seriously thinking of packing up and moving to Canada," Nils said thoughtfully. "I worked there for a few years and I liked it."

"Better do it fast. By your own words you may have as little as a week to do it," Gary teased. "Anyway, I called to say good luck. I really enjoyed our relationship." After hanging up he thought, *Seriously thinking of packing up and moving to Canada? He's right in the thick of it, and knows what's going on. Why isn't he doing something? How can a person so brilliant about one thing be so blind to another? Bankers have their nose so buried in their ledger books they can't see the rest of the world.*

Operation Phoenix

Gary tried Wayne Buckley again, and this time his luck was in.

"Wayne Buckley?" asked Gary.

"Yes."

"My name is Gary Alden. Your name popped up as being an honourable and able handler of men, as well as being a strategic tactician. I was wondering if you might consider doing a job that I think is unique and very exciting. Are you now committed to a formal contract for your services?"

"No, I'm officially retired but I've been keeping my eyes open."

Gary said. "I'm surprised that someone didn't snap you up instantly. You must be selecting propositions that you look at very carefully. Can you tell me why you might have rejected what were obviously many traditional offers?"

"I suppose there are two reasons. One is I want to be more entrepreneurial, more in charge of my own destiny. The second is that the fu…ah frigging world is changing in ways that I don't like. The United States I served is not the US of today."

"What you have just said makes me very excited. I really believe that what we're trying to do, if anything, is over idealistic. It would certainly leave you in charge of your own destiny. I'd very much like to meet with you soon, today if possible, and then also have you meet with the other key people you will be working with quickly. Would you have some time later this afternoon for a coffee or a drink?"

"I suppose so. What the hell is your hurry?"

Gary responded. "Well first of all as I said I'm very excited. We also want to get our core people on board and working as a group as quickly as possible. In the past two weeks the world has changed dramatically and we expect that rapid change will continue. So there's a great deal of time pressure there. Where would you prefer to meet? Somewhere, maybe a restaurant or bar where private conversation is possible. Or a hotel. The Raddison is near you isn't it? I've never been in that particular hotel. Would the bar or the restaurant be preferable for a quiet conversation?"

Wayne paused. "The restaurant would be better. We can get an isolated table back in the corner if we do it before 17:00 hours when the restaurant starts to fill up. How about 15:00 hours? Will that give us enough time?"

"I know these sessions," Gary laughed. "If everybody gets excited, there's never enough time. Nevertheless I would hope to keep it to basics to see if you want to take the next step, meeting the rest of the gang. Just give you the concept so you have time to think, and hopefully come up with some new ideas, new ways of looking at things, and concepts to bring to the party. Sometimes people get fixated and don't see the forest for the trees. Okay Raddison restaurant at three it is."

Gary called Eric and gave him a quick rundown on what had happened this morning and asked him, "What did you think of Jan and Claude?"

"Jan's a good looking lady and seems to be smart. Claude is one of those wise old birds that should be smoking a pipe in his rocking chair to fill out the picture. I just don't know if he is long enough for his feet to reach the floor. They get my vote. I gotta run. I have to get that second hangar deal completed and I think I have found some more fuel tankers."

About 2PM he headed out to meet with Wayne. On the way he noticed two bundled up ladies standing in front of a garage with various articles placed on the driveway. Large signs proclaimed "Garage Sale." Since the weather was clear, and the temperature was just over freezing, that was okay. *But a garage sale on a business day? In February?* Gary shook his head.

Operation Phoenix

These people weren't just getting rid of junk. They needed money badly. Probably some combination of bank holiday, bank seizure, unemployment, and possibly rent coming due.

The Raddison was much like chain hotels everywhere. A bunch of strawberry boxes piled on each other around a sparkling entrance and driveway. Gary walked into the restaurant and looked around. The restaurant was empty. The only person watching newcomers attentively was seated back in the corner privately and appeared to be about five foot nine or ten and built as solidly as they come. No particularly bulging muscles, but solid everywhere. Reddish blonde hair in a crew-cut with a neat goatee. Gary ignored the waitress hurrying over to seat him and walked directly back to Wayne. Putting out his hand Gary said, "Wayne Buckley I presume?"

Wayne rose and they shook hands. It was only when he moved that the attentive could see the muscles ripple under the skin. However one would have to be pretty inattentive not to realize that messing with this man might not be in ones own best interests. He was a solid, densely packed bulldog. His handshake was incredibly gentle, as if he were afraid of crushing lesser mortals by accident. Gary's interest was piqued because the accepted norm was a firm handshake.

The waitress who had followed Gary asked, "Would you like a menu?"

Gary ordered a toasted bacon and tomato sandwich with a large glass of Clamato juice because he hadn't eaten yet. Wayne just had the juice.

"Been waiting long?" Gary said to get the conversation rolling. "I thought I was a couple of minutes early."

"You were, but I got here at 14:45."

"When we spoke on the phone you mentioned something to the effect that the US was changing in ways that you did not

Operation Phoenix

like. Were you referring to events over the past couple of weeks or over a longer time frame?"

Wayne leaned forward, putting his weight on his forearms on the table. "Appointing myself master of the obvious I think this country is moribund through and through, but fucking well particularly corrupt at the top." Wayne gulped a bit obviously trying to swallow the swear word. "The USA is rotten to the core like the Roman Empire before its descent into oblivion."

"I happen to think the same way. I think the events of the last couple of weeks are simply the results of the seeds we have been sowing over the past decades. We fear what these small beginnings will grow into."

"Yeah. It's a frigging slow motion train wreck ...... in progress," muttered Wayne.

Gary frowned mentally. *This is far too easy,* he thought suspiciously. *If it looks too good to be true it probably is. I think I will just stay on philosophy as much as possible and avoid details.* Smiling mildly he said, "What parts of the situation bother you most? Why do you say 'the US today is not the USA you served'?"

"Patriot Act II has brought us much closer to Stalinism than I ever believed possible in my worst nightmares. It was passed without anyone, especially those voting on it, being able to even read the document they were voting on. This is damned well no longer the land of the free. There are too frigging many people who think that freedom is free. Citizens must be vigilant. Then last night in the president's message every department gets cut by 50 percent. So far as I know my pensions come out of each year's appropriation and aren't funded in any way. So I'm likely to take a 50 percent cut in my pension. Fine way to treat someone who offered his life for his country. 'America always remembers those who sacrifice for her', indeed!"

Operation Phoenix

"Ah yes Patriot Act II. That's but one of the many reasons you and I are meeting." Gary paused as the waitress brought their juices..

"And you've connected up the dots in today's picture?"

Gary looked at Wayne and said intensely, "Yes this is a gigantic financial tsunami destroying the world financial system. What makes it worse is that it doesn't look as dangerous as a wall of water but then you can't see disease either. But mankind has learned to fear the symptoms of disease and react. This kind of event only comes along once in several hundred years so we have no learned reaction reflex."

Wayne nodded. "And today we are totally reliant on the gigantic machine. If one small part stops functioning the whole machine waits till it gets fixed. If the computer goes down we have to wait till it's up before we can do the simplest transaction. What is more Americans think they have a strong individualism and not a lot of mindset for collectivism, but they now rely on their leaders to give them a simple, sound-bite solution that makes all their problems, including the heartbreak of psoriasis, go away. There is neither a simple nor a one size fits all solution. "

Wayne's instant grasp of a new concept outside his field of expertise impressed Gary immensely. But it still sounded too good to be true. "Exactly. The good old USofA, and the whole world for that matter has mortgaged its soul more ways than I can tell. We have squandered our birthright. Sooner or later the day of reckoning had to come. After the events of the past couple of weeks we think that day is now. That means we're going to have to be very innovative."

The waitress brought Gary's sandwich and he took a bite.

"How many people are involved in your plan now?" Wayne asked.

Operation Phoenix

"Initially it was just my son, Eric and myself doing the research and forecasting. As events unfolded my daughter Lynn became a believer. Subsequently we recruited one Claude D'Antonio to handle the transport end of things. Otherwise at this point, there is no one who is aware of our intentions, although that will soon change."

"Captain Claude D'Antonio who lives in Jersey?"

"Why yes." Gary put on his best surprised face, eyebrows raised. Gary didn't think it would matter even if his fake surprise was discussed by Wayne and Claude.

"Well if he's aboard, I'm aboard," declared Wayne.

Gary was surprised again, but didn't quite know what emotion to show so he continued in an effort to keep control of the conversation.

"Basically we are thinking of entrusting a very critical function in the community to this position. No one, myself or anyone else, can decide alone that some one person is in or out. We have to reach a consensus. Later for instance, on people you might recruit, events may force us to rely solely on your opinion of whether someone meets the community requirements. In theory we'd prefer that each person in the existing community have a voice and opinion on the suitability of each new person that joins us. After all we'll each have to live in close proximity to each of the other people. It's not that we are looking for people who think like we do; in fact, diversity of opinion is essential. We need rebels. But we do have to be able to trust or predict how every other person in the group will react in a tight spot."

"That's a good concept. We emphasized it a lot in the SEALs. Everybody has to rely on everybody else, while being a whole person themselves. Where do I fit in all this?" Wayne asked.

Operation Phoenix

"In any society, large or small, government exists for only two purposes," Gary looked at his binder and lined it up with the edge of the table. "The first reason for a government is to provide a framework for the society to successfully operate on, a rule of law. The second is to protect the citizenry from enemies who might do them damage in some way. There are no other valid reasons for a government to exist. Government does not exist to take from Peter to give to Paul while skimming a percentage for themselves. Your field will be the second part. We think a community can be viable if it has mutual goals, support, and protection.

Wayne pondered for a moment. "You frigging well don't think small, do you?"

"There's a critical level, or a critical mass below which things will not work. I don't feel small has as much to do with it so much as practical. Either do the job or don't. Going only half way is a total waste. I could have taken my investment winnings and retreated to the wilderness, but sooner or later I was going to need something critical, salt, or a doctor, or something. It wouldn't work except in the short term."

"True." Wayne's brow furrowed slightly and he looked down at his hands. "But there's a critical mass in a technological world that might be very large."

"Agreed. But we think the world may have to go back to horse and buggy for many things," Gary leaned forward intensely. "We will only do so to the extent our enemies will also be forced to. That's why I wanted to give you only an outline of the problem at this meeting. You're a strategist, and I don't want to impose any boundaries on you that exist only in my mind. We made a forecast of what events might transpire due to forces we observed over the past years. We positioned ourselves accurately enough that we were able to amass some resources during the crash that just happened. Not a lot in terms of the numbers government and big business throw around, but for an individual or family, more than adequate. We felt we could use these assets in such a way that their effect would be greatly multiplied. First we'd like you to contemplate our assumption that violence and desperation will continue to escalate and form your own opinion. Having formed an opinion of where things are going, what measures would you take next? You have some, but limited resources in a financial sense, and none in a military sense. We're not a government buying $700 hammers."

"You're pretty vague as to how much frigging money I have at my command to do the job."

"To a large extent that's intentional because of how we see the world developing." Gary said slowly, "For the balance resources are allocated as events direct. Claude is just in the process of acquiring a multi-million dollar asset for a fraction of that amount. An asset that I think is essential for us to go forward. People still think in terms of dollars and to some extent we still must, but in a situation where you're starving because no food is available at any price how much value are dollars? Food's the valuable thing. Your forecast of coming events should give you an idea of whether food or dollars might be more valuable, and how to get stocked up on whatever is more valuable so you can trade for what you want and need."

"How much does this job pay?" demanded Wayne.

"I gave Claude a quantity of cash and a job to do, and told him to set his own salary. Until we get this thing organized I expect him, myself, and my family for that matter, to take what he needs to live comfortably and safely, and use the balance to increase assets for the community and incidentally for himself. In this financial tsunami we think paper money will become valueless. If the community is successful then the money is incidental. If it's not it's me personally who bites the bullet. You've invested some time that's it."

"That's an odd way to run a business." Wayne frowned and twisted his fingertips together as if he were tearing a small piece of paper to shreds..

"We go back to something you said on the phone. I commented that honour seemed to be lost and you agreed. This isn't a business venture although we do have to be profitable to stay alive. This is about building a tightly knit community for our mutual benefit and safety. A community based on humanistic values. This doesn't mean that everyone owns everything nor that individuals are not rewarded in relation to their contributions, or that we aren't responsible for our own actions."

"Sounds like true democracy in action," Wayne observed as he leaned back, still not taking the weight off his forearms on the table.

Gary paused for another bite of sandwich and a sip of juice. "The circumstances existing last month, or last year, are gone forever, and who can say what will be reasonable next year? I simply expect you to be honourable and reasonable in the circumstances bearing in mind all the contributions others make. Right now we're building an infrastructure. Personal profits will come later. If you want to be a nine to five working stiff with the so called 'security' that entails, and a regular pay check denominated in present day dollars, then we can discuss that. If you want to be a leader in charge of your own destiny it requires a different kind of thinking. If you want a big salary it's up to you as a leader to arrange the value to justify it."

Wayne drew a breath while pausing. "Ah. Frigging well put up or shut up. You're right. This is a changing world and

Operation Phoenix

changing my thinking at this stage in life isn't going to be the easiest thing, but it seems to be the only viable alternative. Okay, what's the next step?"

"We have to get you and everyone acquainted and firm up some immediate plans. Unfortunately I think time is exceedingly short so we'll have to move fast and make some snap decisions without sufficient data. I'll try to set up a meeting for somewhere for tomorrow night. Are you free tomorrow night?"

"Yes, anytime."

"Okay. I'll call you later tonight as soon as I get everyone onside," Gary said as he stood up and shook hands with Wayne, and left some money for the bill.

Chapter 18

As soon as Gary was in his car he phoned Lynn to coordinate her pickup from work and to arrange for the meeting tomorrow night. She told him, "I've found the financier for the hospital that is for sale. It's Medical Venture Capital, here in New York."

"They must be small. I don't recall ever seeing that name. Maybe they might be in trouble too, I hope. I'll do some financial investigating before we make the next move on the hospital. You carry on locating pharmaceuticals. I'll pick you up about five. Stay inside till you see me."

Gary picked Lynn and Jan up and the conversation turned to small talk as they escorted Lynn to her apartment.

In Stamford, the new Union Bank of Switzerland building caught his eye as it always did. They had built a trading centre as big as two football fields. Right across the street the Royal Bank of Scotland had built their new US headquarters. Numerous hedge funds and Fortune 500 companies had located their offices in Stamford and various parts of Fairfield county. In fact, the influx of financial entities had turned all of Fairfield county and Stamford from a sleepy, gritty manufacturing town, into a new and growing financial centre. Turning onto Broad Street, usually clogged with traffic at rush hour, the traffic was light.

"Where are the busses?" Jan suddenly exclaimed. Normally long lines of busses added to the rush hour traffic mayhem on Broad Street.

"Don't know. Probably the drivers are refusing to drive, either because of no pay or because of the increasing crime, or The Transit Authority can't protect them and pulled them off for safety reasons," Gary shrugged. "Are you going to stay at my place tonight?"

"I'd love to but I have to do some washing soon. I'm about out of clean clothes." She shook her head slightly.

"I have to be out tomorrow night till later. Why not pick up your laundry and do your washing tonight at my place?"

"That sounds like a good idea. I'm getting paranoid about the crime rate. I'd feel better being with you." She smiled at him.

"Yeah, I like your skin next to me too," he grinned back. "How's the shoulder?"

"You are a medical marvel Dr. Alden. I don't even notice it,"

"What's that big watch thing you have on your right arm? I try not to wear a watch at all and you have two. I find that people tend to run their lives against the watch. They see they have only five minutes to get there, and they do stupid things like switching into the moving lane just as it is coming to a grinding halt, or running over somebody in their rush. They will get there just as fast and with no ulcers if they just act normally."

"Oh, that's my pedometer." She said proudly. "Everyone who is anyone has one. It counts how many calories you have used during the day by counting the number of steps you take."

Gary didn't respond, partly because he was a safe driver, and driving safely requires a lot of attention, and partly because he disliked show toys. In the current circumstance with food in short supply how many calories one was able to take in were far more important than how many one had used. A small corner of

Operation Phoenix

his mind followed this train of thought. Mental note: *get started on the business of trading for goods instead of simply buying things, soonest.*

Back at Gary's refuge of peace and tranquility, Gary broiled steaks to perfection, or nearly so, and prepared his 'world famous rice pilaf' and a tin of asparagus tips. They sat down to dinner and Gary asked, "You look a little frazzled. How was your day?"

"If this calling of loans goes on, we won't have a bank left when we are finished. We sent out notices this morning on way over half our loans and I hear they've done the same on 90 percent of credit cards and personal lines of credit. Incidentally, I grabbed all the paperwork regarding your transactions and forgot they were in your file, which is a fairly normal place for them to be forgotten."

"Thank you. That is a tremendous relief." Gary said emotionally. "Are you calling interbank lines of credit?" Because he was her lover, was close to the banking community and spoke banker lingo, he had been accepted, in her mind, into the banking fold. Bankers are like that. Favours and information pass readily among the community in a manner that would horrify the non-banker. The same with lawyers, doctors and almost any other group. They are discussing cases, not personal information.

"I don't know about our foreign exchange and interbank loans but we're calling everything else on the slightest pretext. Where will it all end?" Jan asked rhetorically, frowning.

"I would expect a lot of banks to fail, far too many for the guarantee insurance to cover the accounts of depositors. How are other world banks doing?"

"I was talking with Swissbank in Zurich today. The guy sounds like he could lose his job, but I don't think there is a chance his bank would fail. They are part of the big three Swiss banks but they are covering their asses, although not to the extent we are."

"But if a lot of the loans you are calling don't pay 100 cents on the dollar, and if a lot of smaller banks go under owing you money, won't that force you into bankruptcy?" Gary asked, knowing full well it would.

"Oh no. We're big enough that the government would bail us out in a worst case scenario, but I wouldn't be affected. I have to work out the loans of my clients. What's your meeting tomorrow about?" she asked.

Ha, thought Gary. *Bankers can afford to take stupid risks because the 'gummint' will bail them out. Sorry babe, but the 'gummint' can't possibly take on the hundreds of trillions of dollars of debt that is now going down the tubes One bank, yes, but not the entire financial system..* Aloud he evaded. "Strategy session. An attempt to coordinate the information we have and guess possible futures."

"You seem to be leaving me out of some important parts of your life. What do you see in the future?" Jan sounded thoughtful but hurt.

"Well for the future I see Armageddon. Lots of blood on the streets. As to you I've been struggling. Before even thinking how you might feel on the subject I've been trying to figure out how I feel. As irrational as it seems I'd love to have more kids. We have only been seeing each other since last Saturday. Particularly as it regards how gun-shy I am, I've been struggling with the idea of asking you to marry me, and this is just too fast. Yet the situation demands fast action. I still believe that marriage is 'till death us do part' and I want this to work, especially if kids are involved. It's just too fast. Are we better off to simply walk away while it is simple? I don't know."

Operation Phoenix

"Oh you poor dear," and she reached across the table and placed her hand on his. "I know what you're going through. I've been struggling with the same thing. I don't have as much sense of urgency as you seem to. Why the urgency?"

"How much has the financial world changed since the crash? The average guy is going through the motions, waiting for normalcy to return. He has no idea how dramatic the changes are nor where the world might go from here. He thinks now that the bank holiday is over, that he sees light at the end of the tunnel. He doesn't know it's the headlight of an oncoming freight train and that the banks and the financial system are the problem. The rate of change, already blindingly fast, is going to accelerate. You think that crime is bad now just wait till people get more desperate."

"The banks won't disappear. The government couldn't allow it." She shook her head a bit belligerently. "Society would collapse."

"I'm afraid so. In every collapse of an empire I have been able to study there have been great numbers of deaths, even in the most recent example, the collapse of the USSR. In the three years between 1991 and 1993, the average life expectancy of a Russian fell by five years.

"Imagine it for a moment. Normally, even when there is a catastrophe and many die out of a population of millions the average lifespan will only change by a fraction of a day. How many people had to die prematurely to lower the average lifespan by five years? What percentage of the total population had to die to lower the average by eight percent? Not only old people died but young people too. Admittedly they had wars going on in Chechnya and Afghanistan at the time. The government was over a year behind in paying pensions, which by then because of inflation and currency debasement, would only buy a loaf of bread a month. Soldiers were selling their guns for food. All that despite the billions the rest of the world gave them. They died like flies. The currency was worthless. As memory serves the Ruble fell from something like four or five to the dollar to, I think it was about 8500 to the dollar."

"Is that where your gold and silver comes in?" she asked.

"Partly. The Russian government had been selling its gold reserves on the open market at the then regular world market price of US$12 per gram. Then they smartened up and started selling it on their own black market at US$20 per gram. That gram of gold which I think had previously sold for about 50 to 60 Rubles, was now fetching 160,000 Rubles, if anyone would take Rubles for gold. In the rest of the world the price had actually gone down. All this happened in the space of a few months. That was at a time when the US, the World Bank, the IMF, and the rest of the world was pumping billions into the USSR in an attempt to rescue some of the people, and prevent the collapse from spreading. Despite how horrible it was, less people died so the effort did do a great deal of good. Recently the US has been alienating more and more of the world. Who can, never mind who wants to, rescue the US? It's simply too big."

"That's unbelievable. Are you sure?" she had ceased eating but was still holding her fork straight up.

"Of course I'm not sure. 'History does not repeat, but it rhymes', to quote somebody. No matter how it goes the outcome does not look pretty."

"So what would you suggest?" Jan shifted forward in her chair.

"Well, in your case, or our case if we're together, I'd suggest the most valuable resource you have is your Rolodex, your various contacts and data bases. Trade is going to fall dramatically because the banks will either fail or no longer extend credit to each other. Because many of the names on your list will fall off and no longer be contactable, you need a huge list of people everywhere. In Russia, during its crash, no one had any money even if money had value in purchasing food. Those that were not just out to rip people off were trying desperately to trade whatever they had too much of, for whatever they needed." Gary sipped more wine.

"The problem in Russia was that there were so many people trying to steal, who didn't have what they said they had, that you couldn't trust any stranger, and even those you knew, just a very little bit. Not only will your contacts be valuable for information as to what's available and what's needed, you might be able to trust them just a bit, enough to get a deal going. One deal a year, on a shipload of goods will be enough to keep you in very fine style. I would be assembling a database of every name and contact information of anybody that ever did business with your bank. Who knows how valuable it'll be and information is very small and easy to carry whether you ever get to use it or not," Gary emphasized.

"That sounds reasonable. Anything else you would do?" Jan asked. She held up her glass and waited patiently for somebody to refill it. Since Gary was the only one there he obliged. "Well I'd put top priority on this over and above your work. You may have less than a week to assemble this data and get it out of the office. The other thing I'd do is to collect the name of every principal, and product information, on every loan the bank is calling. These people are likely to be desperate to save their businesses or themselves, and some deals may be available. At least you'll have one end of the deal who has product available at a discount. Then it will only require the other end who needs what."

Operation Phoenix

"Good lord you think of everything, don't you?" Jan's eyes widened.

"Far from it. I just play the odds, like a fisherman. Fish where the fish are, and you're more likely to get a bite. It pays to keep your eyes open for things other than what you are looking for." Gary was in full stride.

"What do you mean keep your eyes open?"

"One of my heroes is a guy named Mark Rich. I don't know how many of the stories are true, but I do know he's rich. Apparently he was born and raised in a poor area of New York. He got into the commodity trading pits in the market, and did quite well trading his own account. Then he realized he could do better with better information. So, he bought an oil tanker. The captain's real job was to report on who was loading what for where. From this information he had an edge, and did even better personally."

"Smart guy. Knowledge is power." Jan recited.

Gary continued, "One day, in September 1990 I think it was, when Russia was collapsing, Mark was apparently in St. Petersburg on other business. He happened to go down to the docks. At the time transport, particularly rail transport, was all screwed up in the USSR. They used to have central control, so somebody made sure that empty rail cars were sent to where they would be needed. When central control broke down, nobody paid much attention to the empty rail car. It just sat and rusted where it was. Thousands and thousands of rail cars were piled up in Eastern Siberia, whereas Moscow and St. Petersburg had none. Anyway, he was down by the docks and he noticed this huge pile of potatoes. He asked the port supervisor, what was going to happen to the potatoes?"

"Did they come in by boat?" Jan asked.

"Probably, likely from the Ukraine. Anyway the

Operation Phoenix

supervisor shrugged, and said, 'I guess they're going to rot. It will freeze soon, and we don't have rail cars to ship them to where people are starving'. Mark said, 'Okay if they're going to rot anyway, I can have some ships in here within two days.' Note the plural, ships. That's how big the piles were. Mark agreed to pay the supervisor some minuscule amount per ton to have the potatoes loaded aboard those ships. To the Russian it was a huge amount of hard cash in total, and crime was common as a measure of survival. So the supervisor did it. Disregarding the morality of what Mark did now comes the interesting part. What did he do with the potatoes?"

"I don't know." said Jan, "Sell them to supermarkets?"

"Nope for a couple of reasons. First they were probably bruised from being dumped as loose potatoes into the cargo hold of a ship so they were not very saleable. Secondly governments frown on transporting bits of dirt and the attendant foreign microbes into our food chain plus they had to be processed rather quickly because bruised potatoes spoil pretty fast."

"Animal foods," guessed Jan.

"Nope again. The foreign parasite problem keeps them out of the food chain, and there is not a large black market for bruised potatoes."

"I don't know. What?" Jan asked.

"He had them thoroughly washed, crushed, and made into alcohol, a process that does not mind bruises and kills microbes. Alcohol is saleable anywhere at good prices. Now I don't know if he actually did this, or even if anybody ever did this, but it sounds like his kind of deal, and it does demonstrate that keeping your eyes open and using a little imagination can be very profitable."

"That's amazing. What other kinds of deal did he do?" Jan was leaning forward avidly.

Operation Phoenix

"Well, another story that is attributed to him was that he found somewhere in Southern Asia, The Philippines I think, during the rioting when Marcos was being deposed or something, 38,000 tons of raw sugar sitting going to rot. Got it for pennies. Again he sent in a couple of ships and loaded it onto them. He sent it to a sugar refiner and had it refined on a tolling basis. The refiner took their payment in sugar. Now he has a product that won't spoil easily. He found out that some hood in Eastern Siberia had gained control of the sugar market for pretty well all of Siberia. I don't know if the hood was not a good mathematician, or he simply liked easy numbers, but he established a simple retail price for sugar. US$10 per pound. "

"Ten dollars a pound!!"

"Yep. Mark traipsed around to visit the hood and suggested that the hood buy or he would sell to the competition and break his corner on the Siberian sugar market. The hood bought at a high price, or rather he had available a quantity of an obscure brand of aviation fuel which he was willing to let go for pennies on the dollar. So our hero has taken thousands of tons of something he paid pennies a ton for, and sold it at dollars per pound. He traded that for aviation fuel at pennies on the dollar, which he transported to St. Petersburg, where there was a shortage of that particular type of fuel, so again he got top dollar. He took payment in alcohol, vodka as I recall, which is saleable anywhere. There are any number of smallish, imaginative trading firms around which do that sort of thing, putting up little or no money, and making huge profits."

"That's really exciting," Jan exclaimed. "I want to think about it."

"These deals are not easy to complete because they usually require a lot of time. But with patience, imagination, and knowledge, the profits can be staggering. Ideally you put up little or no money up front or at least until you have the other steps in place. Your contacts could also prove useful in the next steps disposing of the product at good prices." Gary shrugged. "So it behoves you to get whatever data bases you can, just in case they might prove useful." These were the countertrade or international barter type of deals he wanted to work on with Wolfgang.

"Umm." Jan was deep in thought.

"I have to make a couple of calls. I'll be a few minutes. Would you clean up here a bit?" Gary asked, rising.

Jan looked at him blankly for a moment and said, somewhat reluctantly Gary thought, "Okay, I can do that while I'm thinking."

"Don't get in a rush. I'll come and help as soon as I'm finished," and he went into his office study and closed the door.

He called Claude, and caught him just in, and about to sit down to dinner.

"How did it go today?"

Claude sounded pleased, perhaps with himself. "I hoped to have the paperwork finished today. If I get signed tomorrow we'll own 25,000-ton, self-loading general cargo ship with container fittings. The people financing the deal had their loans called this morning. The cash on the fender trick worked a charm. I let them hanging on the hook at $400,000. Then I put all back in bag, slowly. I thought maybe they were cry."

Gary laughed in delight. "Perfect execution."

"Famous last words, but if we get clear title, I don't care what they do with cash or their books. I could see wheels turning in their heads. I hope they won't wake up from whatever dream they have of that cash before sign."

"Which ever way it goes I am sure you will have done the best possible job," Gary said. "I thought $500,000 was a steal

Operation Phoenix

but $400.000? I don't know what is greater than a steal. Grand theft maybe."

"I have more news," Claude continued. "I was talking to someone who should know about Singapore tanker. He thinks probably is chicanery involved but ship hasn't been pirated. We might able to get clear title. I think worth following up on."

"Absolutely great. Do whatever is necessary. Charter a jet if necessary. But be very careful you have a way to get back. This financial system is going to blow up soon. Banks around the world are panicking. Don't trust any financial institution for more than 30 seconds, and even that's risky," said Gary.

"Is that bad?"

"Well it's not written in stone but all the signs are there. Every banker I've talked to, including my girlfriend, who I want to talk to you about in a minute, is quite disturbed. It looks real grim. Banks may start to fail as early as next week. Anyway my news is good news/bad news. I met with Wayne this afternoon."

"Were you impressed?" Claude asked.

"Yes very. He's damned smart. What puzzled me was how anti US he was. Almost as if he'd been briefed. The reasons he gave sounded legitimate and I certainly agreed with all of them. I think I was fairly careful when I was searching for him but in the end, both he and the people I was asking are often part of the espionage/counter espionage world and they pick up on clues pretty fast. As the interview went on I felt more comfortable but it was just a bit too easy. If things don't go the way I expect them to I am usually not considering some factor that I should be. Everything in his story hung together but I'd like to arrange a meeting with all of us to get more eyes looking, preferably tomorrow night. Are you okay with that?"

"Yes, I can make tomorrow," Claude answered.

"What I'd like to do is set a time, say 7 o'clock, at your

Operation Phoenix

place. We'll arrive half an hour later. That will give you a chance to talk with him. I'd like your opinion as to whether his switch in loyalties is real. Essentially he is saying the US of today is not the US he served. I agree but I expected more resistance from him. Either we have hit him at exactly the right time or he's being not truthful. I think you have a better chance of judging how real this change is."

"Yes," Claude agreed, "I be best one for that job. I'll try."

"If I didn't have access to your knowledge but all things considered, I'd probably vote for him anyway. I would feel a lot more comfortable with that vote if I think you're comfortable. Do you need us to bring anything?"

Claude said, "Do you have coffee? Wayne swills it by bucketful. I have none."

"Yes I have a pound of very nice coffee I can bring. I have told him that we are thinking of a self-sufficient community, that his job would be to protect us from enemies, that I had given you a sizable sum of money and sent you out to buy an asset for the community. I said I'd told you to set your own salary. Other than that I stayed on philosophy for the whole time and tried to not give him any more solid detail because I was suspicious. I left him with the problem of setting a strategy for the community protection. When I come in I would like you to give me a nod if you are comfortable about his loyalties or a shake if you are not. Okay?"

"Sounds workable to me," said Claude.

"The second thing I wanted to discuss with you is my girlfriend." Gary briefly described how he met Jan, and subsequent events, including possible marriage. "I hope it's a policy that new core members who might gain access to dangerous information, be vetted by the existing members. I'd be very interested in your opinions of her. People don't think straight when the issue becomes all entangled with the sexual thing."

Claude paused to consider. "I know why you want to check girlfriend. That's perfectly in character. Okay we find some way of casually meeting her, same as Wayne's girlfriend Mona, who I have met. Same thought has occurred to you?"

Gary nodded forgetting he was on the phone. "Yes it has. What do you think of her as a core member? I think we all might have to move to a common place for mutual self-protection. We can't chatter about common problems in front of a non-core member. I don't like us so spread apart and vulnerable individually where we would not be as a group."

"She's little bit different. A nurse, seems like smart lady, and close-mouthed. I think she has child, teen-age boy. He's a bit wild from what I hear."

"Damn solve one problem and two more pop up." Gary said. "One step at a time. First get Wayne onside and Jan next. If Wayne doesn't see the good in checking his girlfriend at first, then being part of a group effort to check my girl-friend should convince him the vetting process is serious. I have another question."

"Shoot."

"I checked with a vet who thought moving animals by sea would have a problem with diarrhoea. In turn salmonella is often part of diarrhoea. Salmonella can be fatal to humans. When you're fixing the ship can you bear in mind we have to flush that waste over the side, or at least keep it out of human contact?"

"Yes, should be able to do that," said Claude.

He called Wayne and set up the 7PM meeting at Claude's house.

Then he called Bill Cave the butcher, and arranged to back

Operation Phoenix

up a couple of reefer containers to slaughterhouses. He wanted an additional 60,000 pounds of frozen chicken loaded into the front of one reefer with Bill's shipment of butchered meats loaded into the back of the same container. The other reefer was to be loaded with red meat, 50 percent beef, 30 percent pork, and 20 percent lamb, mutton, and/or goat, as availability dictated. He wanted whole sides plastic freezer wrapped and frozen. He wasn't very worried about legal road transport weights, as he did not expect to be transferring them far by road, simply that the containers be filled to the maximum that could be safely stored.

Gary went back out to the kitchen where Jan was just putting away the dishes.

"I told you not to get in a rush and I would help you," Gary said walking up behind her, wrapping his arms around her waist and kissing her neck. She leaned back against him.

"I was thinking and didn't notice what I was doing," she said in a slightly peeved tone.

Gary cupped a breast with his left hand and began stroking her belly with his right, while continuing to nuzzle her neck.

"Stop that. I'll drop these dishes."

"Well put them down then. But you just said you could do these domestic things automatically while thinking about something else. Besides we have not tried sex on the kitchen table yet," he teased.

"You're incorrigible," she laughed, putting the dishes down, turning, wrapping her arms around his neck and giving him a big wet kiss.

"I'm incorrigible?" he asked as he pushed her bum back against the counter with his pelvis. "Look who's leading me on by flaunting her beautiful body within easy reach. I'm just a poor dumb farm boy having trouble keeping up with these smart

Operation Phoenix

city slicker bankers, who take every drop I have and then want more."

The phone rang. Gary reluctantly stepped away to answer it but not before giving her a quick kiss as if to say, 'later baby'.

It was Eric.

"Oh, hi. How's it going?" Gary said.

"I have six tanker trailers lined up for inspection tomorrow. I'll be using Roy Bryant as soon as you get finished with him. Those cash payments sure work magic everywhere. The second hangar is leased and I've ordered it alarmed tomorrow. I have a line on some 45-gallon steel fuel drums. I'm about out of cash. Where do you think is the best place to go first?"

"The clunker cars I would say." Just then the house alarm went off. "Ooops, gotta hop. I just got an alarm here. Probably some kids taking a shortcut." and Gary hung up.

He went onto his office study and switched on his infrared detectors. Five blobs coming across the lawn towards the house. Jan came into the study. He took a pistol out of the desk drawer, stuck it in his waistband, turned on the P.A. system, the floodlights, and a controllable searchlight, which he played across their eyes partly in an attempt to temporarily blind them. He keyed the P.A. system and said. "You guys are trespassing. Get to hell off the property or I start shooting."

One of the guys obviously shouted something.

Gary keyed the P.A. system again. "Sorry I can't make out what you're saying. These are your choices. Off the property in 30 seconds or I start shooting." He then flipped off the lights.

They milled about not moving much. Gary said to Jan, "When I say 'now' I want you to flick on this switch. Okay?"

She nodded, her body tense.

Gary went to the front door flipping off lights as he went

Operation Phoenix

so that he would not be back-lighted. Unlocking the front door he said "Now," and opened the door. The floodlights came back on. Gary again carefully aimed to consider where his ricochet might go and fired at the stone wall surrounding the house. The gunfire and the ricochet had all five were over the fence in a flash.

Gary came back in, reset the alarm and laughed. "I wonder if any of them peed their pants?" he said. He went in and shut off the floodlights. Jan still looked tense, so he said, "Don't worry. I was just trying to get a reputation locally for shooting first and asking questions later. Anything those five had with them was unlikely to get them in here. That decorative ironwork on the windows would take a large truck with a strong steel cable to pull off. The doors are steel with an oak veneer. You're pretty safe in here."

Jan still looked concerned. "This is the second time in less than a week I've heard you shooting and the bullet whining away."

"Ah, but the ricochet whine was intentional. I shot where the bullet was sure to ricochet and the sound makes it much more scary."

"Well it works. It scares the hell out of me." Jan shivered and Gary gathered her up in his arms.

"Don't worry. No one can be 100 percent accurate with a handgun but I'm far better than most. I spent much of my childhood shooting varmints. The game was to go out with 10 shells and come back with at least 11 tails. I did it every night when I went for the cows but didn't hit any farm animals. Always know where the bullet might go accidentally," Gary said. "Come on. Let's go to bed and cuddle. We have to get up early anyway. I have a heavy day tomorrow. But first I have to call Eric to tell him we're okay. He knows the alarm went off."

Chapter 19
Tuesday February 28ᵗʰ — Day 15

After dropping Jan and Lynn at work Gary spent much of the day buying things and directing Chris where to drop containers next. Roy was hard put to keep his inspections ahead of the purchases of the Alden family. Late morning after inspecting enough trailers and containers to get Gary in business, Roy left to inspect tankers for Eric, before returning to Containerhaus to finish his inspections there. Chris and his crew immediately began yanking those new tankers over to be filled with gas and diesel fuel.

Gary contacted a sugar refiner and made arrangements to fill a dry container with 44 pallets of five pound bags of sugar. The pallets were stacked two high in the container and weighed just under one ton each, so the container was over the legal road weight, but just within seagoing limits. He did the same thing with bags of rice. Chris' crew picked up and dropped containers thither and yon, including two reefers at slaughterhouses for the ordered meat.

Gary was so busy wheeling and dealing, dropping off cash and deposits to pay for all his dealings that he barely had time to contact a dairy. His request for a container full of fresh milk was met with a shrug. The transportation problems, the bank actions and the labour problems had them in total disarray. Even the offer of cash payment would not budge them although it obviously interested them. However with cash in advance, they agreed to a container of fresh milk in two days, chilled within a

Operation Phoenix

degree of freezing. They had no powdered milk. Gary tried other milk processing plants till he found one open with powdered milk on hand. He ordered two containers of dry powdered milk. Aside from personally detesting dried or evaporated milk, finding enough potable water to mix it with could be a problem later.

Last night he had asked Jan to find out what she could about Medical Venture Capital, the financier of the hospital Lynn was looking at. When he called to make arrangements to pick her up after work he reminded her about it.

"Oh I haven't had time to do any personal stuff today. In fact I have to work late tonight. Pick me up later. We have to follow up on a huge number of loans. There aren't many staff who can get in these days."

"I have a meeting and I don't know when it will finish." Gary said. "I'll tell you what. If you'll contact your venture capital people right away to get whatever they have, and print out a couple of current credit checks, I'll pick you up on the way home but it may be quite late. I really need that data and I need every detail I can get."

"That's okay. I could work here all night and still not be caught up."

He called Lynn and they arranged to have dinner at the company cafeteria which was still open and drive directly to Claude's. Gary took advantage of the suddenly free time to contact a flourmill he had researched previously. He wanted a container load of nitrogen pack flour. Flour has a 'B' vitamin that slowly oxidizes and turns rancid over time. Replacing the normal air which contains oxygen, with pure nitrogen stops the oxidation process. Rather than a one to two year shelf life nitrogen pack flour has a near indefinite shelf life, providing the pest eggs have been smashed by using an entoleter, a rapidly

Operation Phoenix

spinning drum with spikes.

The mill said that they didn't keep anywhere near a container load of nitrogen pack flour in stock and that delivery would take two days. Gary abruptly decided to purchase two rather than one overweight containers of flour providing they could have both containers ready by Friday noon, which they agreed to. Another two dry containers and more cash deposits on the agenda for tomorrow.

It was not quite five when he parked to wait for Lynn to come down. He tried and luckily reached, a mid-sized specialty bakery that was open. He ordered a container of heavy breads, because the community would have no facilities to bake. The bakery found a container of heavy bread unusual, especially with a new customer, but because Gary was offering cash agreed to order the ingredients tonight because they would always use them anyway. They wouldn't start baking until they had a deposit in hand but delivery was expected for Friday morning providing Gary got the deposit to them early tomorrow. A reefer container and more cash on the agenda for tomorrow. Despite how fast he was moving Gary was not at all happy with the limited amounts and variety of food he was obtaining, or likely to obtain with so many businesses closing. Not only that, but he was having to pay top dollar for the food he was purchasing.

Lynn came down and they went for dinner. "I think I can source a complete range of drugs and other medical supplies if we can find someone to sign for them. When will you let me know about the hospital?"

"We can sure use the hospital equipment if we can purchase it because we will be in isolation," Gary said. "Hopefully we'll have some financial data tonight if I can get Jan off the business of saving her bank. She has this stubborn bee in her bonnet and still hasn't realized in her heart just how

Operation Phoenix

serious things are. She has this vision that if she can just save her bank her world will remain unchanged. I think the bank is her security blanket. She says not too many staff are coming in these days but she's still trying."

They arrived at Claude's house almost simultaneously with Eric, who'd grabbed a burger at a fast food drive through that he had found open. The temperature had been falling steadily all day and a few flakes of snow drifted through the patches of fog.

"Got the tankers filled but the wholesale price of fuel has gone up by 75 cents a gallon," Eric said.

They entered Claude's house and Claude immediately gave Gary a vigorous nod of approval for Wayne. Gary had come in with his pre-assembled load of stuff, his leather binder, his briefcase of cash, and the coffee for Wayne. They got settled around the dining room table, and Claude started water boiling.

Gary smiled, "Well Wayne I hope you have a bit more information. Before we start answering questions I'd love to hear your assessment of the overall situation, albeit you have only had a few hours to think about it."

"There is an old adage that goes along the lines of 'If you will probably lose the fight that is looming, don't be there when it starts'," Wayne said. "From what I surmise about your plans I think you're headed in the right direction by trying to find an isolated spot and set up a self sufficient community. Recognizing what's happening, or can happen, allows us to prepare and gain advantage or at least avoid losses. I think the systemic problems in the US are now irreversible. There's frigging desperation in the air. You can smell it and feel it. Desperate men in high places are scrambling to save whatever they can for themselves as their kingdoms crumble around them."

Operation Phoenix

"So far, in theory at least, we're in complete agreement," Gary said slowly. "Where do you think would be a good spot to avoid conflict? What things do you think are most important to carry out these goals?"

"Morale would be the most important thing. Willing people are extremely inventive if they are allowed to be. Second you should have a variety of skill sets. Then you must have at least the bare minimum of tools to put that knowledge to work; so these people can be effective. Last but probably most important, conditions have to be conducive to success."

"What do you mean, 'conditions have to be conducive to success'?" Eric cocked his head slightly and frowned.

Wayne drew a breath. "Essentially I mean locations where man does not need supplemental things like technology to live. Generally, places where mankind has survived for millennia would be a good starting point. They were successful because conditions such as available food, water, and ability to take or make shelter, were enough to carry on."

"Do you know of any such places now?" persisted Eric.

Wayne leaned back in his chair, swivelled a bit, hooked one arm over the backrest while keeping his other forearm on the table. "I know of any number. Unfortunately for this discussion most are like the east coast of Japan. It has a good delta to survive on. It was so good that the population had reason to grow and now the population density makes such a location unsuitable for our purposes. Or you might think of Switzerland with high mountains throughout. For people dug into the mountainsides it's frigging uninvadeable because even today a ground force, including tanks, would be vulnerable to big rocks being rolled down onto them. Or Great Britain surrounded with a huge moat of water, making invasion difficult. Moving from the general to the specific what's needed

Operation Phoenix

is a smallish area that's suitable for survival but where communication is difficult. There should be some barrier such as high mountains surrounding the area, but the remoteness and the small developable food growing area make it uneconomic in today's world."

"Do you know of any such specific places now?" Eric persisted.

"I believe I know of several possible places, just look at a map. Any place that has no towns or roads is pretty isolated. Or look for areas where there is no cell phone coverage. Then ask why they have no towns or roads. The mountains on the west coast of the Americas could be good but earthquakes and changing weather patterns might be a problem. There are isolated spots on the east coast, particularly Canada and South America, but usually this means poor growing conditions. There is a great deal of lightly populated coastline between Guyana and the Para province in Brazil, all near the equator. The north coast of Australia or Queensland is a possible but Oz is only eight percent arable land, and is the second driest continent after Antarctica which would be safe but…" Wayne shrugged and grinned. "I'm sure there are others such as Pacific islands, but uninhabited islands seldom have good soil which is why they are uninhabited."

Lynn interjected. "Where would you see your skills best utilized if you were part of our group?"

Wayne took his arm off the back of the chair, swivelled a bit more, and smiled at Lynn. Gary had noticed him checking her out a couple of times. "I'd think the use of my knowledge would be the most effective thing to do. I'm a military strategist and a teacher. As a strategist my job is to figure out what the enemy is going to do and take countermeasures. Or perhaps it might be called doing the unexpected which throws all their

Operation Phoenix

plans out the window. I'm frigging good at that. As to teaching the learner must understand the larger objective first. Then they can more easily understand what's being done and why. Once they know this they can be inventive with the how. Some ideas will be more suitable than what I come up with. That doesn't mean that everyone has to know everything but they do have to understand in которой direction we are pulling as a group. I have to give my knowledge to others so we all act in unison even if the circumstances change."

"Can you teach me to strategize?" Lynn asked.

"Strategizing techniques can be taught," Wayne replied. "You strategize now just not militarily. Have you reached most of the goals you set for yourself many years ago? In the fullness of time how good were those goals? If the goals were good and you have made substantial progress toward, or met those goals, then you strategize well already."

Claude added, "If you changed your goals when you gained more experience then your analysis of what were good goals for you was faulty. Everyone changes mind at least a little as they get experience and more information."

Wayne had turned his head to listen to Claude but Gary kept his attention on Eric and Lynn sitting to his right. Lynn felt his eyes on her, looked at him, shrugged slightly and nodded yes. Eric became aware of this byplay and deliberately, but almost imperceptibly, nodded yes. Claude sitting somewhat directly across from Wayne, seemed aware of what had happened.

Gary said, "I think we've reached a consensus. We'd like to have you join our group as a core member Wayne. We have a number of urgent jobs to do right away so we can get the group working together effectively quickly. We, as a group, have to decide whether to invite a couple of people for the community.

Operation Phoenix

You have a lot of information to absorb as to exactly what our position is and where we think the world will go from here. Then you can formulate your own opinions and strategies. Would you like to join our community?"

Wayne looked surprised. "Once you get to marching you fu…ah frigging tramp right along don't you? A little over 24 hours ago I'd never heard of you."

Claude laughed. "You learn to respect his research. He continually astounds me."

"As I said before, 'If Claude is in, I'm in'." Wayne declared. "But I do need a lot better handle on what you are doing."

Gary grabbed the briefcase, "Well, first to induct you into the group. You need some tools with which to do the job," and he worked the combination locks. He turned the case to Wayne. With a questioning look at Claude, Wayne snapped the latches and opened the lid. "How much?" he said.

"Two hundred thousand dollars. You decide what it is to be spent on. All I want is a full and complete accounting. That's all. We do have more funds but at the rate Claude, Eric and I are spending we may run short soon." Gary grinned at Claude. "In fact one of our immediate goals is to spend it quickly while paper cash is valuable to people. They used to value things like bank accounts and checks but the recent bank holiday makes cash much more appealing and very effective. We don't expect to have much paper cash shortly. We're spending it quite quickly on things we deem vital."

"What the hell will take the place of what you call paper cash?" Wayne asked.

"Actually I call it fiat, something that has value because the government says it has value. I expect there will be efforts to prop up the idea of fiat, or paper money but I expect the real

Operation Phoenix

storehouse of value will be in commodities. Food for instance," Gary said. "Claude, any progress today?"

"Yes we're proud owner of 25,000 ton dry cargo ship. I haven't decided what to call her yet. Do you have any preferences? She cost us $450,000 in the end. As well I think I have to go to Singapore."

"That's fantastic. Recruit somebody and get started bringing her up to snuff especially if you are going to be gone. Buy fuel, every ounce she can carry. Fuel is going up by the minute. Eric just told me ordinary gasoline at the wholesale level here in the US is up 75 cents a gallon today. I don't think anyone really cares what she's named just so long as it's not attention getting." Gary said.

Gary interrupted that train of thought to deal with, what for him, was becoming a major problem; Jan, and her access to information. While the idea of having children was immensely appealing, that alone, along with the sex, was not enough basis for a marriage although he was beginning to think he was in love. This early in the relationship everything else was excitement. He proposed that they go to his house to pass on her. He would pick her up before proceeding home. Lynn would go with Eric who could later drive her home. Claude would ride with Wayne so he could fill him in.

"And the other person who needs to pass inspection being my girlfriend?" asked Wayne.

"Yes. Everyone with access to damaging information, male or female, has to be vetted, especially while we are still in New York. First you have to decide whether you want her by your side permanently. Or can she somehow remain a non-core member without access to details, for long enough that we can get underway to where ever it is we are going. I can't think how that might work without endangering her. Once underway the details need not be so much of a secret. I have that problem with Jan. I don't think you're living with her full time so you have some decisions to make, about yourself, her, and her son before this becomes a question that requires solving," Gary said.

"Her son!!" Wayne blinked and looked at Claude. "I see what you mean."

"Well it's short notice but the circumstances are rushed. Does anyone have any objections to that plan? I can call Jan and try to set it up," said Gary.

Wayne said. "Those plans are okay with me." Claude nodded. Lynn and Eric looked overjoyed. Gary asked to use the phone, and dialled Jan at the office.

"I have friends coming over to my house. I hoped you might come over and meet them and see what you think of them. Are you free tonight?"

She laughed, "For you, I'm never very expensive. Of course I'm available. When have I ever refused you?"

"You have a one track mind. Okay, I'll pick you up in about half an hour. Don't come outside till you see me."

"With a teacher like you it is easy to get bogged down in that one track. You even want to do it on the kitchen table." There was a smile in her voice. "Okay I'll be ready, and I'll bring the file on Medical Venture Capital with me. We're part of a syndicated loan to them so it's quite extensive."

"Okay, bye."

"Okay we're on." Gary announced. "Have we anything else to do here?"

With no response, Gary said that Wayne and Claude should follow Eric.

Wayne looked at Gary in a very speculative way with a half smile on his face, and snapped the briefcase shut. They paraded out to the cars, warmed them up, and set off.

Operation Phoenix

Gary picked Jan up and drove home. Once inside with their coats off, and introductions finished, Gary led them on a tour of the house, emphasizing the security features. When they got to the basement and the pantry, Wayne's eyes widened in surprise.

"Shit. You've got to have a ton of food in there."

Gary said. "It all started off with a fairly simple idea. If I used a tin of peas I bought two. If I used another tin of peas I used the oldest tin, and replaced it with two new ones. Because I was using peas at this rate I knew I would probably use them again in the future at this rate. At the end of the year I took inventory of what I'd used. Thereafter I looked for specials and mostly bought by the case. It works pretty well for everything except things like milk and fresh vegetables."

"Two large deep freezers," noted Wayne.

"Yes, I keep milk and bread frozen in the one. In the other I keep meats and so on. The shelf life is not as good as I would like. Long storage gives the meat freezer burn. The plastic covering bread is not right for freezing and it tends to dry out. Milk solids tend to separate so you have to shake or stir well." Gary said.

Back upstairs Gary pulled out coffee and tea ready for the water that he had plugged in on his way through the kitchen. Jan insisted on doing the honours and Lynn stayed with her. The men went into the living room and made small talk about everything but what was on their mind, the continuation of the meeting at Claude's. "What do you think of my security system?" asked Gary.

Wayne said, "One of the better home systems I've seen. Of course it could be a lot better, armed guards for instance, but in an unobtrusive way it's very good."

Gary mentally slapped his forehead and resolved that

tomorrow there would be armed guards, which had slipped his mind.

The women came over with the beverages and Gary steered the conversation towards Jan's job and the situation with the banks. Then he tried to stay out of it as much as he could.

While describing the difficult job of being a banker Jan mentioned that there had been several brawls and near riots at their branches, with people pissed off that they couldn't get their money. Added to the number of disgruntled clients they were foreclosing on, and bankers were constantly walking on the knife-edge. Both Claude and Wayne seemed interested asking a number of questions which spurred Jan into talking more. An hour later Claude insisted he was tired so everyone gathered up their things and left.

"So what did you think of them? I'm thinking of some pretty close relationships with them," Gary asked Jan.

"That Wayne is real sharp. It took me a while to notice how searching his questions were. You said he was a navy SEAL? Cream of the crop obviously, probably within the SEALs too."

"And Claude?" Gary continued.

"Claude's one of these quiet guys and very little gets by him. Smart too. I liked him."

"If I, or we, were to enter into some kind of arrangement with them how comfortable would you feel living and working in close proximity with them?"

"I would love to be with Claude. Wayne? He's a military man and doesn't think as people on the street do. In matters military I'd think he'd be superb. I don't think I'd want to be married to him. The military would always be a mistress I couldn't compete with."

"And what makes you think I would be different? I get all

Operation Phoenix

involved in whatever project I'm working on at the moment," Gary demanded.

"Yes, but in the end you'd be married to me and I'd know you were working for me and the family. With him he's married to the military and would be working for the military. I'd just be a mistress he visited occasionally." Jan shrugged.

They bantered about till the phone rang. Gary ran into the office and scooped it up.

Claude was on the phone. Gary asked, "How did Wayne react on the drive over here?"

"He thinks you're awesome. He's already bubbling over with plans. I see we're going to move to common area soon. He agrees that we're terribly exposed."

"Yeah I talked to Jan and she thought Wayne would be militarily brilliant but that she wouldn't want to be married to him because of the lifestyle he likely lived."

Claude paused, "That's quite insightful. I thought your lady was very smart but not necessarily street smart, and maybe bit stubborn. Perhaps I'm wrong. You're gathering some very intelligent people around you. She's smarter than average by a long way. If she were wife I'd vote for her as community member. She'll do the best she can at any job she undertakes, and you could not ask for more."

"Thanks Claude. I owe you one."

Gary, deep in thought, walked back to the loveseat that Jan was sitting on in the living room. He now had some slightly shaded opinions on Jan. Claude thought she might not be street smart. Maybe he meant shallow. And possibly stubborn? Probably what Lynn had referred to, a certain fixation on a bee that she got in her bonnet. None of these opinions were necessarily damning but neither were they wholehearted support. They'd all voiced the opinion that they would vote for her but as Claude had expressed it 'if she were your wife'. Gary decided to try to gain as much time as he could to get to know her better before a final decision. He definitely had feelings for her although he couldn't say how many of them were spawned by their mutual interest in having children or the usual lust that came with a new relationship. From his headhunting experience he had learned to listen closely to the opinions of others. Obviously his gonads had not learned this lesson.

"Well" he said, "Claude seems to like you and thinks you are a pretty smart lady By the way did I tell you I asked Eric and Lynn to move in here? It's far too dangerous getting into and out of those apartments. Can you live with that?"

"That sort of rules out sex on the kitchen table doesn't it?" She grinned at him.

"Yeah, it also rules out screaming, big moaning and playing tag naked," he grinned back. "Little moans are okay. Can't wake up the children you know. Seriously I don't see any other option."

"Where would you put them?"

"One in the rumpus room in the basement, one in the spare bedroom next to the office up here. I've been going to get round the clock armed guards for the houses. Maybe if we got guards for your place too not only would it protect the house when you are away but we could sleep over there often." Gary suggested.

"That would be good. At least I don't have to worry about yelling a lot," she grinned.

"Okay. I'll get guards tomorrow."

Operation Phoenix

Chapter 20
Wednesday March 1st — Day 16

Next morning Eric, who was playing chauffer and guard today, came by to pick Jan up. Gary went outside to talk to him while waiting for Jan, trudging through the three inches of fresh snow that had accumulated overnight. Patches of fog remained. "Did you see the retail price of fuel this morning?" Eric asked. "It's $7 per gallon."

Because Eric had to stop later at Roy Bryant's to pay him, Gary gave Eric a list of containers to be dropped today for Chris Habel, just down the street. "Make sure he's paid up to date and ask him if he needs anything. We don't want him immobile for lack of fuel but neither do we want to subsidize his other customers with cheap fuel. He may want to buy a tank himself. By the way, be sure to check with Roy about those container stackers to be used for offloading full containers from flatbed trailers. We are going to run out of trailers very quickly at this rate."

"Yeppers," Eric said as Jan came out. They left to pick up Lynn.

Gary went back inside and stripped his remaining cash out of the fridge. Now all the cash he had at home was his office safe. The cash was certainly disappearing quickly. Would they have enough to do the job?

Since it was still early and he was in the peace and tranquility of his home, able to relax and think, he sat down with the Medical Venture Capital file Jan had provided. It was easy to see that they were probably in trouble, just as the rumour had it. They were relying heavily on borrowed money to finance their purchases, money that was not available now that the banks were calling loans. He put the file aside, and called the security guard company he'd looked up previously. Fortunately, owners of companies tend to work much longer hours than their employees, and the owner was in. Gary ordered six armed guards on a 24/7 basis. One for the Trambull space, two for Gary's home since it would likely become a central rendezvous point, one for Claude's home because Claude might be away for a time, one for Jan's house and one for Wayne's house.

Another possible would be Wayne's girlfriend's place, but he had to check with Wayne as to what he thought was desirable. Having a guard for Wayne's house was desirable even if there was no immediate need. Personally, Gary felt that soon everyone with assets would be clamouring for guards. Being an established customer would give him an advantage should he want to move the guards around to other locations. All told, to provide 24/7 coverage, 36 or 37 guards would be required. It was a nice order for the security company, and they treated him accordingly, even if coming up with that number of armed guards on short notice would be difficult.

He rushed off on his round of paying for what he had ordered previously. The security company was particularly surprised and pleased to be paid in cash, and in advance. He called Ron Thompson, the lawyer. For trading purposes as he envisaged them, he had asked Ron to prepare a simple set of documents that would give him clear title to anything he traded for or bought. While he was in the general area, he picked them up and paid Ron as well.

One thing he did learn in all his travels. The banks had been so diligent at calling loans that many companies had

Operation Phoenix

simply thrown up their hands and closed their doors. Others, such as the ones he was dealing with, were trying to work something out with their employees. His cash payments were welcomed, because it gave the company some wiggle room in dealing with the employee payrolls. Cash was becoming very valuable for everything except the even more necessaries such as food. By noon the fog had disappeared and the temperature was about 35 degrees, so the slop on the roads was disappearing quickly.

Gary called Claude, and caught him in.

"I'm glad you called," Claude said. "I've been on long distance all morning arranging things so I can leave tonight for Singapore. I spoke to principals. I explained we were dealing with cash payments in the US. I said I would need clear title legally. They seemed to be able to live with that. I figure that everything up to date will be legal. If there is chicanery, it will be what the cash is used for. I can't say that for fact. I recruited Bob Baker, one of the captains on your list, to go with me to bring the ship back. I also recruited Bruce Nott, a junior on your list, to take charge of fuelling and supplying our ship here. Fuel prices are nearly double original estimates. That should be done today. You'll have to get some money to him."

"Claude, you are awesome. I will dump $1,000 in your phone account to keep it working. I'll get $200,000 to Bruce today somehow, probably delivered by Eric. Leave me with a 'to do' list with contact names and phone numbers. We will also need some code words that tell us that everything is going okay with a Singapore transfer. I will use 'Amigo', something foreign in the mix, danger, and 'my friend' for normal."

"Those are good words. We'll use them. No code word is 'Amigo'," Claude said.

"Good, and use of both says 'I'm not threatened yet, but

Operation Phoenix

I'm scared as hell'. I've ordered an armed guard for your place. I'll leave security arrangements with Wayne. The guard should be there this afternoon. By the way, we do have some foreign currencies in Switzerland, not in a bank, so it will take a day or two to get them should an emergency arise. Good luck then, my friend."

"You too, my friend."

Gary called Eric on his cell phone. "Hi, this is your venerable father. How are things going?"

"Hi vénérable pop. I'm just headed back. I purchased fifty 45-gallon steel fuel drums. Habel is picking them up."

"Great. That about finishes up your initial chores doesn't it?" Gary asked.

"Yes. And thank goodness. I am about out of cash," Eric said.

Gary brought him up to date on Claude's trip to Singapore, noting that if Claude did spend another couple of million dollars, they would be very low on cash. He asked Eric to Go to Trambull, pick up $200,000, go to Claude's, pick up his 'to do' list, and then deliver the money to Bruce Nott. Money was on Gary's mind consistently now. Would they have enough to do what was needed?

"Can you be available for a briefing meeting with Wayne tonight?" Gary asked. "We have to get him started."

"Yeppers."

Gary called Wayne. "Are you up to a meeting tonight with Eric and me to bring you up to speed?" Gary began abruptly.

"Sure, I have about a million questions and ideas."

"We have something to do first. Claude's is leaving for Singapore tonight. We have to arrange security for him. Can I leave that with you? I've ordered commercial armed guards on a 24/7 basis for Claude's house and yours," Gary said. "Claude

Operation Phoenix

will call you directly for updates and instructions."

"Armed guards should do till we get ourselves organized. I may want to recruit some people I know. What should I pay them?"

"Pay them well according to today's circumstances," Gary said. "They don't need specific details yet. You know our general goals. Handle it as you see fit. Any mistakes you make will be yours to deal with later."

"Okay, see you later."

Gary called Wolfgang Perl. "Wolfgang, It's Gary Alden. I'm sorry I have neglected you, but things have been a bit frantic."

"Yeah, me too mon. Unfortunately, a lot of it's been chasing ma tail, bloody spinning ma wheels. Customers screaming, 'Why are my plans not going forward? Our whole company is resting on that shipment', or having nervous breakdowns because of the financial system problems. What a mess," Wolfgang groused.

"Did you have a chance to look into what goods might be sitting along the coast?"

"Yeah, ah did get some information Mon, but the data that's normally available is all screwed up too. Mostly ah got was what was on the docks, not what ah expected, what was on the ships. It might be enough to give us a start," Wolfgang sounded personally affronted.

"Are you free for a meeting early tomorrow night, say 5:30?"

"Yeah. I could make a meeting after work," Wolfgang said.

"Another thing that has come to mind; I might want to buy some things we find. Think about what would be fair as a finder's fee. I may also want to bring a lady I have been seeing who is a banker and seems to be interested in matters trade. Okay?"

"I don't know why not. We can work something out. Whether the money comes from Peter or Paul isn't important," Wolfgang said.

Gary called Jan to arrange to pick her up after work. He mentioned his meeting tomorrow night with Wolfgang regarding trade matters. "Judging from your interest in the Mark Rich trade stories, I wondered if you would like to attend."

"I'd love to follow up on that sort of thing," Jan sounded pleased. "Incidentally, something that might interest you. The brawls and near riots we have been having have spread to nearly every branch. The social security payments normally due today from the government didn't come in. It was officially described as a technical glitch. Rumour has it that in defending the dollar, the treasury raided every budget going, including the social security budget. They now have no money. We've had guns waved around at several branches, and at least three shootings. I hear the other banks are having the same problems. We are thinking of closing many of our less protected community oriented branches."

"Jasus Marphy," Gary exclaimed. "Now the shit has really hit the fan. Thank god I ordered an armed guard for your house. I'll pick you up at five. Kisses, lover."

Operation Phoenix

Chapter 21

As soon as Lynn got in the car for the trip home, she said that she'd probably be ready for a container Friday night. Gary gave her Chris Habels number and told her to make arrangements directly with him. They picked up Jan, and Gary noticed he was low on fuel. They pulled into an open gas station. "Holy Toledo, will you look at that. Ten dollars a gallon for gas. It was seven dollars this morning"

"Fill'er up," he said cheerfully to the attendant. Gary was cheery because he had over 150,000 gallons of fuel stored at the hangar.

Gary's cheery attitude astonished the attendant and made him suspicious that they were drive away thieves. To Gary's amusement, the attendant demanded a $100 deposit before he would start pumping gas.

About noon the snow and fog had disappeared, so the temperature was now above freezing. In the corner of the gas station lot at the curb, an enterprising lady had miraculously found some cut flowers somewhere and was selling them despite the cold. On an impulse, Gary went over and purchased all of her few remaining flowers. He gave the larger bunch to Jan, who looked at them and frowned.

As he gave the smaller bunch to Lynn, she said, "Thank you Dad, these are lovely."

This prompted Jan to say "Thank you" while still frowning. Then she turned to Lynn in the back seat and said, "Would you like these? They don't fit the colour scheme in my house."

He dropped Lynn off. At Jan's house a guard was parked in her driveway. While instructing the guard, he learned that one guard was present at every location. He promised Jan he would stop by later, and drove home. He instructed his guard, and then drove the car into his garage and off loaded his remaining cash. Locking up and alarming the premises again, he drove to Eric's.

On the way to Wayne's Eric noticed a woman with two crying children, sitting on a pile of green garbage bags and boxes on the sidewalk, probably for not paying the rent. Gary slowed briefly, but they realized they couldn't help everybody although the decision weighed heavily on them.

"It's one thing to discuss in the abstract, and know there will be thousands of deaths as she likely faces, but it's quite another thing to see it up front and personal," Eric said morosely.

"Yes, I keep telling myself I'm concentrating on protecting those who are dear to me, that my resources will only go so far. I tell myself that I'm building a small island of light for humanity to rebuild from the ashes. I said previously that I'd have no time for the grasshoppers that fiddled the good times away, but a small voice keeps nagging me. Worse, all group animals have an inbred urge to protect the females and the young. I don't think anyone having an ounce of humanity could not have these feelings. It's a real gut-wrencher," Gary shook his head. "Unfortunately, the more times we battle these feelings and win, the more inhumane we become. There is no satisfactory answer. We just have to do the best we can."

They spent the balance of the trip in moody silence.

Wayne's house was pretty much a standard brown brick bungalow from the '50's. A gated path ran up the left side of the house. To the right a carport. Other than strong screens over the

Operation Phoenix

basement windows it didn't look as if any effort had been made to beef up security. The glass along the side of the door and the large window in the living room looked to be ordinary with no reinforcement. Gary thought of the shoemaker's shoes.

They shook off the mood and got down to work at Wayne's kitchen table which was located at the far end of the house. Wayne led off by suggesting they compile a list of assets so they'd know what tools they had to work with. They listed estimates of cash, food, fuel, the ship, containers and equipment, and skill sets from joined and potential community members. "We also have a substantial amount of precious metals, but it's far too early to throw that in the pot yet," Gary said. "The only selling I would do in precious metals is if there was a distinct, urgent need for cash for a good and necessary purpose. It's likely to take a year or more for it become valuable enough to consider."

"Nothing military?" Wayne asked.

"Other than a few shotguns and rifles, some good body armour, and 25 or so hand guns, plus 25 cell phones, no," Gary answered. "We do have some other things, like garden shovels, purchased in small quantities. We had planned on trading for military stuff later. Given that the government did not make its normal social security payments today, the military may not have been paid. So trading time may be upon us shortly."

"No fucking payroll?" Wayne abruptly reached for the phone and dialled. "Jim, I've been out of touch. Someone said some government payments had not been made today. What's the payroll situation?" Wayne listened for a while and said, "I'll get back to you."

"They lined the boys up and started handing them cash, $100 each. Brand new bills. They said there was some kind of technical glitch. When they got two-thirds of the way through paying them, they ran out of cash and said the expected shipment of more cash had not yet arrived. It's not showed up yet, but they're making everybody wait."

Eric laughed, "Something technical all right. Technically they are bankrupt."

Gary said, "One rumour that was going around is that they were busy defending the dollar and raided every government budget around. I certainly wouldn't put that past them, because it's a natural. But the budget is in dollars, and they needed foreign exchange. I'm not sure how they cooked the books to achieve that. Whatever the case, the government can still print paper dollars, but they don't have any money. Some wheels fell off somewhere,"

"The US can't even pay its fucking soldiers," Wayne raged. "Every two bit dictator finds a way to pay his frigging soldiers. This is sheer stupidity. You have to keep the soldiers on your side no matter what." Wayne paused. "Sorry, I got carried away. I cannot believe how far the country I was proud to serve has fallen. I didn't foresee this. Obviously you did."

Gary raised his eyebrows. "For us, it could be a real blessing. Anything that's not nailed down is going to get stolen. Morally, I have a big problem dealing in stolen goods. But practically, that will soon be the only game in town. The alternative is to die. As I said, we had planned on trading for whatever we needed,"

Wayne looked at Gary intently, "What do you see as the next events, and why?"

Eric spent nearly 30 minutes telling him, leading from one historic event to another, covering common factors in any collapse. Then he added the icing on the cake by suggesting some factors unique to this age; super diseases like, AIDS, mad cow, SARS and bird flu; the current heavy reliance on technology, the energy crunch, population growth and others. He also noted that states and municipalities, not being able to borrow, would also be unlikely to make payroll for basic services such as police, fire and water.

"I thought I was a frigging history buff," Wayne said, his forearms on the table. "I guess I was a military history buff. This will take some thinking. I think the basics of your plan are brilliant. So far it seems to be working. If it works, don't mess with it. We do have a few immediate problems. First is the valuables transfer for Claude. What are your plans?"

"Once you came aboard, we thought you would be better at organizing this sort of thing, because it is your area of expertise," Gary shrugged.

"I can cover this end personally. I'll get whatever we need here. I have a friend in Singapore and can call up some reserves there. I'll have to call some markers," Wayne said.

Gary smiled to himself and thought *We all have our contacts and I was absolutely counting on you being able to protect Claude.* and said, "Personally, I'm concerned for Claude. If something goes wrong, it's going to take Claude some time to make a getaway with the ship, a lot more time than it'll take for the bad guys to make a getaway here with bags of cash."

"That's what I meant by calling up reserves. We need a group of people ready to get aboard the moment the deal is done. I think I can fix that up, provided people are where I think they are."

"Okay, you make arrangements with Claude when he calls. What else do you need?" Gary asked.

"I have three local SEALS I want so bad I can taste it. They're all up to renew their enlistments. One, I'm almost positive I can get. I have already talked to him, and we are having lunch tomorrow. One is borderline. I'm afraid the best one of all has already re-upped... ah re-enlisted. She's on leave, and I can't find her. I do have some people in mind at other locations."

Eric said, "If they have been loyal to the US, how can we be sure that they will be loyal to us if the US attacked us?"

Wayne paused in thought for a moment. "There are two reasons I can see. If the US attacked us, they would already be branded traitors, facing a US firing squad. Secondly, I think it's a matter of timing and circumstance. A couple of months ago, I was pretty disillusioned, an attitude that is quite common throughout the forces. Yet I doubt that I would have given credence to your forecast of events. My thinking had not progressed that far. Circumstances taught me, and look at me now. I'm in up to my frigging eyebrows. I know they're disturbed by what they see. Maybe they are ready too. We won't know till we talk to them."

"Yes, a good deal of our planning has revolved around being prepared to take advantage of circumstances as they occur. As Wayne Gretzky said, 'It's not my job to be where the puck is. It's my job to be where the puck is going to be'." Gary said. "I don't think anyone can disagree with recruitment being a top priority. I'm in favour of you pushing ahead with recruitment as fast as possible. Since recruitment is my specialty, I'll take over the search for the girl. If she is findable, I'll likely get her. I will need the name of the girl, and any personal details you can dig up; her friends, relatives, or boyfriend, where she's stationed and bunks, what are her hobbies and interests. Anything else you need Wayne?"

"Yes, a general parameter to clarify my thinking. Claude said you were looking at a community of up to 300 people. In my mind that means a military of up to 20 people. To some

Operation Phoenix

extent, they'll also have to contribute to the community when they're not engaged in things strictly military, in order to pay their way, especially if the numbers run over 20. We can't compete head to head with the massive US military machine. We must have more of a guerrilla structure, where every member of the community may be called on to fight. Not only will our military have to be specialists in for instance, driving a tank, a helicopter and a submarine, all in one person, but they must also be good teachers in order to train others. The special forces have moved a long way in that direction. We'll have to take it even further."

"Great minds think alike," grinned Eric with his boyish grin.

"Exactly. I couldn't have said it better myself," exulted Gary. "It took us a very long time to come to that conclusion. You have done it in a couple of days. Okay, the community's security is in your hands. Singapore and our local protection problems."

Dropping Eric off, he drove to Jan's. Her house was a neat little bungalow, on its own properly-manicured, postage-stamp-sized lot. Entering the house, he had the impression that she was ready for *Better Homes and Living* to come and photograph. Every proper thing was in its very proper place, down to the largish cobalt blue glass vase near the archway to the dining room and kitchen. She had obviously picked her colour scheme from some "in" magazine somewhere, because it was coordinated but didn't feel like a home, just a house. Playing naked tag would definitely upset the décor. Gary had noticed that trait about her clothes too. She had several skirts, jackets and blouses that could be mixed and matched, but he had never seen her wear anything unique.

Jan beamed when he looked around and said, "Wow,

Operation Phoenix

Better Homes and Living, eat your heart out."

After a tour of the house, Gary went to shower before bed. Jan followed shortly, and while Gary was showering, reached in and turned the cold tap on full.

"Waahh," and the sounds of Gary jumping and slapping the showerhead aside made her double over with laughter. "Jesus Christ, I damn near broke my neck in here," he complained. "Just you wait Henry Higgins, I'll get you." He stepped out of the shower while wrapping the towel around him. "I have half a notion not to shave," he said. "All my whiskers have retreated back into their pores from the cold. If you get whisker burn, it's all your own fault."

"Oh, poor baby," she giggled and kissed him on the back of the neck.

"Waaahhh," and he shivered and scrunched up his shoulders. "Out of here woman or I might cut myself shaving and bleed to death," He wiped the foggy mirror with the facecloth. She lowered the toilet seat cover and sat watching him lather, shave, wash his face off, and towel himself dry. He leaned over and kissed her, and said, "Just you wait Henry Higgins you'll get yours," and went off and climbed into bed, nude. He grinned as he heard her lock the bathroom door behind him.

Jan walked into the bedroom in a silky, ankle-length black sleeping gown. Gary was instantly attentive. Long silky sleeping gowns with a naked nubile body moving underneath were a weakness with him. Jan lay down on her side in bed. Gary spooned up to her, smelling her perfume, and trying to get a hand on her bare breast, preparatory to falling asleep that way. Finally, in frustration, he reached down and slid his hand under her gown up her side till he reached her breast. She shivered as his hand slid over her ribs and all thoughts of sleep vanished. He began to stroke her breast and manipulate her nipple. Then the other breast, and finally her belly.

Jan turned over on her back. "Is this normal?" she enquired archly. "More than once a day since the beginning?"

"Are you complaining? Ask me a year from now. If I still can't keep my hands off you because you are endlessly exciting, you'll know. I love the silky feel of your skin, your muscles moving under your skin, and the way the small of your back bends toward me when I pull you close." He suited his actions to his words by pulling her close. He began to stroke her back and ribs under the gown, firmly and slowly. Then his touch lightened as he reached down and lightly scraped his nails from the back of her knees, up the back of her thigh to her buttocks. He flipped up the gown and leaned down to suckle and manipulate her nipple with his lips and tongue. She rolled part way on onto her back to allow him access.

His hand moved from her back to her ribs and belly, stroking so very lightly that he was really not so much touching the skin, but brushing the microscopic hairs on the skin. Then his hand moved back down to her knees, and lightly up and down her thighs, never touching that crucial spot on her body. With each stroke up and down her thighs and across her belly, the distance between her knees widened imperceptibly. He began kissing and tonguing her other breast, and then moved his lips down her belly, breathing on those body hairs, and lightly brushing them with his lips. His hands continued lightly stroking her inner thighs. Seemingly accidentally, on one pass they lightly brushed her nether lips, tantalizing her. She shuddered and gasped.

Having seemingly discovered this new spot, he ran his fingers up her lips from back to front, and brushed her hardened clitoris. Very lightly, in a counter-clockwise motion he began to make small circles with the end of her clitoris. He did not vary the rhythm or stop until he sensed her stomach muscles begin to tighten in pre climax.

He found her 'G' spot and began to rhythmically stroke it from front to back, and then back to front, until he again sensed that her stomach muscles were beginning to tense. He went from spot to spot, rhythm to rhythm, exciting her, and then moving on to a new spot.

Finally, noticing that her response was waning, thinking this had been going on to long, and it was too much; he went back to her 'G' spot. He began rhythmically stroking it in a circular motion using the slightest bit more firmness. Her stomach muscles tightened, and a grimace began before he quit and rolled her toward him on to her belly.

"You bastard, you are doing that on purpose," she wailed. "I'm stuck now. I can't get down. Help me, I'm stuck."

He found her 'G' spot again, and began slowly, then faster, to lash it from side to side. She came up partially on her hands and knees. He didn't stop, lashing even more rapidly. The involuntary spasms of her hips hitting the bed heightened and then decreased as she slowly collapsed toward the bed. He didn't stop. The spasms did not quit, but turned into quivering shudders. He finally quit and positioned himself between her legs. Raising her boneless hips, her impaled her on his penis. In three or four strokes, she was pushing back, until they both reached climax. She collapsed again, a lump of jelly.

He stroked her back softly and tenderly. She murmured, "God, I thought I was going to die," before falling asleep with her gown still bunched under her armpits.

Chapter 22
Thursday March 2nd -- Day 17

Gary awoke to the alarm, as did Jan. He kissed her tenderly and asked, "Sleep well, lover of mine?"

"Like a log," she answered.

"See why I fall asleep so easily? I'm totally wrecked when you get through with me," he grinned.

She grinned back, stretched, and throwing her arms around him, kissed him soundly. Then she abruptly padded off to the bathroom.

On the way home from dropping Jan and Lynn off at work, he called Wayne on the car phone and picked up more personal data on the lady SEAL. By the time he arrived home, and settled in its comfort and security, he had mentally mapped out a campaign to find her. He called the unit she was stationed at, and asked to speak with Petty Officer Patti Wagner.

"I believe she's out of the country, sir," the clipped military voice said.

"That's too bad. I wanted to relay some time-sensitive, confidential information that might be important to her in her job. Do you know if she has re-upped, or whether she might be able to take part in a conference first?" Gary casually used the military phrase 're-upped' because it made him sound like one of the 'in' crowd, and therefore more trustworthy.

"I don't believe she has formally re-upped, but we don't expect her to return for another couple of weeks."

"Sounds like she went quite a ways on her vacation. I hope

she went somewhere warm," Gary tried to elicit more information.

"I wouldn't know sir. Would you like to leave a message in case she calls in?"

"Not just yet, only as a last choice," Gary said slowly. ""Do you happen to have a contact number for her, maybe her mother or something? I'd rather leave a message there so if her mother feels it to be important, she can get hold of her."

"One moment sir." The line hummed as he was put on hold. "What is this about sir?"

"It's a confidential matter for her personally that I think will benefit her greatly. Since you say she'll be back in a couple of weeks and her time will be committed, it becomes much more urgent that I speak briefly with her on the phone. She may decide this information is worthwhile, and if she does, she can amend her plans accordingly. I'm so confident that she will be interested that I'm willing to go the extra mile to reach her now. Later, she may not be in a position to react as she would like. Do you have a contact number for her?" Gary repeated almost word for word.

"Well, we are not supposed to do this, but her parents are at 519-543-9876."

"Thank you very much," said Gary. "I do appreciate this. I'm sure Patti will too, so you can rest assured of my discretion as to the source of the number."

Hmmm, thought Gary. *Not yet formally re-enlisted, out of the country, and I believe that is a Canadian area code. Could she be at home in Canada? I think I'm not quite ready to talk to any member of the Wagner family yet, including you my lady. I need more information since our Wayne seems to really want you, and we can't afford to slip up. Let's see. We know she is young, likely in her early 20's. We know she excels, and probably did when she was younger too, so she'll be memorable.* He used the reverse search feature on the Internet to connect the number he had with a name and address. It was on the outskirts of a town southwest of Toronto.

He looked up the city hall, called them, and explained he was looking to locate a high school that a person from five to ten years ago might have attended.

"There are only two high schools. What's the address?" the clerk asked.

Gary told him, and he promptly said, "Oh, that would be St. Jude's Secondary School. That address is in a new subdivision, only a few blocks from St. Jude's."

"St. Jude's sounds like it might be a Catholic school. Do you have separate schools for Catholics?" Gary asked.

"We used to have, but that all changed about 30 years ago. St. Jude's would service that area."

"Do you have the number for the administrative offices at St. Jude's?" Gary asked.

"Yes," and he gave the number to Gary, who thanked him and dialled the school.

"St. Jude's Secondary School. How may I direct your call?" a matronly voice said. It sounded like one of those old biddies who has been around for years and knew everything.

Gary said, "My name is Gary Alden and I have your strange question of the day. A few years ago Patti Wagner introduced me to someone, apparently her best friend. I seem to recall Patti attended St. Jude's. First, do you know if Patti Wagner attended your school?"

"Oh yes. I know her well. Quite a tomboy then, but very smart."

"That's her," said Gary. "Did she have someone she chummed around with a lot?"

Operation Phoenix

"Oh, yes. She and Allison Swift were a pair, but Allison is married now, and lives in Toronto."

"That's okay," said Gary. "Do you have Allison's name and number in your file? She will have changed her name."

"Clive and Olive Swift live just down the street from me, and the Wagner's are just across the street, on their old tobacco farm, part of the new subdivision. Olive's number is 555-9676."

"Thank you very much, you've been very helpful," Gary said. He went into his Colombo routine, saving the most important question till the last, as an apparent after thought. "Oh by the way, I haven't run across Patti in forever. Do you know what she is doing now? I heard she was a SEAL."

"Why yes. Yes she's a SEAL now, and doing very well. She's home on leave now, before she goes back to her mysterious duties."

"Oh, good. I must look her up if I get up there. Any idea when she's going back?" Gary asked casually.

"I think she's going back late next week."

This had turned out to be much easier than he had expected. That was the information he had hoped to get from Allison Swift. *Tobacco farm? That's interesting. Now to contact Wayne,* and he dialled, forgetting that Wayne would likely be at lunch with his first recruit. He left a message.

While he waited for Wayne to call, he tied up some loose ends. Wayne called.

Gary told him he had located Patti. "How do you want to handle Patti's recruitment? I can head hunt her in much the same way I did you, providing I can catch her in, or you can contact her direct."

"You were so frigging smooth at not giving anything away while you drew me in that I'd prefer you do it. I got home and found the only new fact I had was that Claude was in. The rest was you changing my thinking about current events. However, she might shy away from you, and I would be better. You would make a better decision"

"Let me try one shot at it," Gary responded thoughtfully. "I have an idea that might help us if it works. If not, I may drop your name into the conversation if need be, and you can contact her direct. Okay? The object in these cases is not to give out information before she makes some commitment such as traveling to here. How did lunch go?"

Wayne had a shrug in his voice. "About as I expected. We had to offer a good deal more money, but he's pretty much on side ideologically. I'm sure he would be all the way there if he had enough information".

"How about Claude?"

"I got a crew together for Claude, and I'm feeling better about that situation. He thinks they might do the deal Monday." Wayne said. "I'll take one commercial guard for my girlfriend's place."

"Great, that takes care of everything except moving Eric and Lynn to my place, and a common place for us all to go so protection is easier."

Gary studied what he had on Patti Wagner, and dialled.
"Hello?"
"Is Patti Wagner in?"
"Speaking."

"Good morn.... Ahhh Good afternoon" Gary stuttered intentionally, and put an embarrassed grin in his voice to establish rapport. "My name is Gary Alden. I'm a head-hunter, and your name popped up. I guess the basic question is whether you would consider change if conditions were right?"

"I don't know Mr. Alden. My first reaction is that I'm

employed at work I love for the best force in the world. Recent events have confused me, and I'm not sure what to think."

"I'm glad to hear you say that, because the function I want to talk about is a direct result of those events and their impact on the future. It excites me very much, and confirms what I have learned about you, that you are actually thinking about these things, as opposed to 99 percent of the population who can't see that far ahead. Would you be able to fly down to New York on Tuesday to discuss this further?"

"I suppose I could drive down Monday afternoon. Where would we meet?" she asked.

"At the moment, given the speed with which events are unfolding, that is still uncertain, I was hoping to coordinate things Monday morning early, but my being in New York Monday is slightly uncertain. Here is my number and address," and Gary gave it to her. "In the unlikely event I cannot be here, I would like you to coordinate with one Wayne Buckley at this number."

"Is Wayne involved in this?"

"Why, yes he is. You sound like you know him?" Gary tried to sound surprised.

"Yes, I do, quite well"

"That's good," Gary said. "We can save a lot of time. We'll expect to meet early Tuesday then. By the way, if you're driving down, be sure to top up the gas tank in Canada. I don't know what has happened today, but yesterday morning, the price of a gallon of fuel here had jumped to seven dollars per gallon, and by nightfall, it was up to ten, with many gas stations closed completely."

"Gas was just over four dollars when I left on leave, and everyone was screaming," Patti said thoughtfully. "It isn't that bad here. No shortages, but the price has doubled. Canada has good oil supplies."

"Oh, and one other thing I just thought of," Gary said suddenly. "If you're driving, as soon as you get into the US, purchase a hand weapon, and a large supply of ammo. We'll reimburse you. Pick a good one that you would like for your own collection, but a somewhat standard calibre, like a 40 calibre Glock, or a Browning high power."

"Jesus, things can't be that bad!"

"Oh yes they can. It is just that the wildfire has not had time to spread to Canada yet, but it will. I rescued my girlfriend from what she felt was certain death, about a week ago, simply because I had a weapon. A single woman is viewed as a soft target. New York is insane. Get a gun, and be careful."

"I'll be there for Tuesday," she said grimly.

Operation Phoenix

Chapter 23

Chris called. "The driver of the truck that picked up the sealed fresh milk container says it's awfully light, probably empty."

"Aw, shit, I've probably been ripped off. Break the seal and see what's in it. Let me know, and thanks for the prompt tip." Gary immediately called the fresh milk company. The phone rang and rang. He looked up the number again, and dialled again. It rang and rang. *Damn, goodbye nearly $100,000. And it's my own damned fault. I should have seen it. That's why they only wanted cash upfront. I've got a receipt, but with two days head start, they're not likely to be found easily. Even if I find them, can I just walk up and take the money? Damn, I can't afford the time, never mind the money. Ah well, that's life I guess. Likely the bank was closing them anyway, and I just gave them a choice they couldn't refuse.*

Later as he drove down to pick up Jan for the meeting with Wolfgang Perl, the shipping broker, the traffic around her bank was at a near standstill. The reason was clear. A high-rise office building just down the street was on fire. Two floors, about ten stories up, were gushing smoke. As he inched closer he could not see any fire trucks. Just then Jan spotted him, ran over and climbed into the car. "The fire department hasn't even sent one truck the last I heard. Nobody is doing anything. I heard they called out the National Guard, but it had been decimated by conscription to fight overseas, so they aren't responding either. There are two floors on fire and I don't know how many dead."

Operation Phoenix

"Yeah, electricity is out in many areas too. Municipalities don't seem to be paying their people. There's not much garbage being collected either. It looks like only those things that run automatically such as phones and water are working, and then only till something breaks down. Even the internet and text messaging is starting to fail with phones and electricity failing. The information age is dying."

"I heard that there have been riots and shootouts between protesters, with martial law and reading of riot acts in over half the major centres in the US. Where will it end?" Jan said plaintively. "The whole credit card industry is shut down. Unemployment must be up over 25 percent."

"Probably over 50 percent. We sure do seem to be in a downward spiral."

In Wolfgang's somewhat small cluttered office, after introductions to Jan, and a general settling in, Gary said, "Wolfgang, something we didn't cover, and should have. I now have an interest in buying some things for my own account, either for consumption, or for an investment of my own for a later time. Before we get to the specifics of what you have, we should decide on a general method of handling my being a principal in a transaction. Jan may be doing some work in this area, so we have a possible conflict of interest."

Wolfgang's hair and dress was very armed forces. His dark hair was closely cropped and neat. His suit, shirt and tie were crisp and clean. "That's what I like about you Gary. If there is a potential problem, you get it out in the open right away." The conversation became quite confusing as Wolfgang put forth a complicated series of splits of profit and percentages depending on the circumstance. Any trade involving no cash made it difficult to establish a value anywhere along the chain of events.

Operation Phoenix

"May I suggest something?" Jan asked, smiling at Wolfgang.

"Of course luv." Wolfgang beamed at her. Wolfgang called every woman "luv".

Jan smiled back. "If you or Gary bought something for cash or some other product, at that moment the value would be established, either 'X' dollars or 'Y' tins of sardines. It seems to me that the payment should be a percentage of the purchase price, say one to two percent of the dollars paid, or one to two percent of the sardines paid. Whether you later agree on a cash value of the sardines or not, the sardines are yours." Jan was in her element, negotiating without seeming to. She was actually quite a hard worker.

"I like that luv," Wolfgang smiled approvingly at Jan. "Two percent of whatever is paid for the product purchased. That's fair because I don't spend all that much personal time in getting those lists. And if it is valuable enough to trade, I can always flog it."

"The lists will determine who owns what information only if I buy," Gary said. "In cases where we act as agents on countertrade or barter, the information goes into the pot and we split the profit 50/50 like we discussed. Jan, could you squirt our list of troubled companies and their products to Wolfgang this weekend or early next week?"

"Next week."

"So we can accept Wolfgang's list as it is?"

"I don't see why not," Jan said.

Wolfgang passed over his printed list.

"Do you have this list in computer format Wolfgang?" Jan asked.

"Yes, that's how I got it luv."

"Why don't we just email each other our lists so it will be

Operation Phoenix

easier to sort by product."

Meanwhile, Gary was studying the list. ""Hey, there's some good stuff on here. Much more of what we want for our own use than I was expecting. Ten containers of hard red winter wheat going to some restaurant in Peru. We'd be interested in buying that. I'm glad we brought this principal/agency thing up. Here is a distillery, a sawmill, and a canning factory from that company that builds a complete factory in a container, going to Africa and South America. I also see some stuff we can likely trade. Here are some containers of sugar, shipped by the refiner. I wonder if we can get them at a discount. There are so many sugar users that it should be easy to trade. Wolfgang, did you get the container weights on the lists you got?"

"Yes, but when I printed it off, it didn't seem necessary to include all that bloody junk for our discussion," Wolfgang said.

"Good, so long as we have it," Gary said. "By the way, the companies on our list are ones that we have dug up as being weak, and likely to have their loans called. It's just the tip of the iceberg. Our list is likely to grow rapidly."

"We'll have more product than we know what to do with."

"Yes, we are going to need to know what your offshore contacts want, and then go looking for it, plus a method of shipping. I do have occasional access to a ship, which will likely continue running even if US fuel supplies drop. Incidentally, our list is all Jan's fault. She's a senior banker, and has access to all sorts of credit files like Dun and Bradstreet, and she knows how to read them," Gary said.

Wolfgang blinked and beamed at Jan with newfound respect.

"Have you done much work with your offshore contacts?" asked Gary.

"I can see in retrospect, not so much as I should have,"

Operation Phoenix

Wolfgang confessed.

"Well, it looks as if we have a direction, and a two part agreement. Is there anything else you need?" Gary said as he rose.

Wolfgang shook his head, and grasped Gary's outstretched hand and then Jan's, again beaming at her smile as they left.

Once inside the car, Gary whooped a delighted laugh and pulled her over to kiss her soundly. "You are one dangerous lady, with an evil dangerous smile. I thought Wolfgang was going to drool. You got him to agree to two percent, and I was worried I might not get him below five percent without a fight. If they are not consciously negotiating, people always just pick the most advantageous deal offered. I noticed you offer one or two percent, not one or five. I keep wondering what our kids will be like. I'm reminded of, I think it was Winston Churchill when some voluptuous movie star sashayed over to him and cooed that they should consider having children. 'With my beauty and your brains, they would be awesome.' Winston shot back, 'Yes, but think what they might be if they got my beauty and your brains'."

"Well I must admit, you're very cute," she grinned wickedly.

"Ooof, that was a low blow you wicked lady," Gary grinned. "By the way, did you see what was on that list?"

"Why would wheat be of interest to you?"

"My bet is that there is something else in those containers, tanks, missiles or something else heavy being smuggled. Sure, we want the wheat, if that's all there is in the containers, but who ships ten containers of wheat to a restaurant in the outback of Peru, a known hot spot? That's why I wanted the container weights. Did you also see the five containers of tinned salmon? They make the best trade goods. When the USSR went down,

Operation Phoenix

some German guy traded a container of tinned salmon for a fully equipped MIG fighter jet. Everybody in Germany had a fit when they discovered the missiles on it were still live. All he wanted was a tourist attraction so kids could climb on it."

As they drove home, Gary exclaimed, "My god, there are a lot of carelessly parked cars along here. Here's some nut that who couldn't even be bothered parking. Just abandoned, with a parking space 2 cars up," said Gary as he manoeuvred around it. "Wait a minute, these cars look abandoned. They likely ran out of gas. There's a truck."

"How much gas have you got?" Jan asked.

"Full. I tanked up at $17.50 a gallon just before I picked you up. Took me a while to find an open station."

"$17.50," Jan said slowly and thoughtfully. "And there are almost no moving cars or trucks on the road." On the way home there were a fair number of stalled cars, but no road blockages in either direction.

As he drove, Gary thought about Jan. She was a hard worker, and very smart in a business sense. But her world revolved around her job and the bank, which represented an order and a world that she was in control of. Believing that the bank was a sacred institution made all the world her servants. She would not give up this world for change lightly. It was her security blanket.

Back at his house, he studied the list of containers, ticking off many as being of interest. He found a wide variety of canned goods, salt, soaps, spices, foods, insecticides, fertilizers, epoxy resins, fibre optic cable, coffee and tea, hand tools, nails and fastening devices, window glass, machines and electronics, a complete range of goods, all on the original list of desired products he had initially given to Claude. *This is becoming more interesting by the minute.* he thought, excitement rising.

Operation Phoenix

    Then he drove back to Jan's and turned his attention to her body, which he still couldn't keep his hands off.

Chapter 24
Sunday March 5th -- Day 20

The next morning Gary hung around Jan's somewhat longer than he should have. The sky was clear, the sun was shining, although it was still below freezing. He didn't want to get moving. He had been running at top speed, reacting to oncoming crises'. Maintaining a calm exterior while his stomach was knotted with tension about the cash situation was taking its toll. He had a ton of work to do, but he was loath to leave Jan. He justified to himself what he wanted to do, by inviting Jan over for the day on the grounds that it was Sunday, a day of rest. He did call home and alerted Lynn, who answered the phone, that he and Jan were on the way.

His cash position was beginning to worry him a lot. While it was necessary to spend cash as quickly as possible, while it retained value, the sheer unexpected size of his market windfall had caused him to unthinkingly misallocate funds. He had spent way too much on precious metals, and bought much larger quantities of some commodities such as food, and fuel, than he had money for. Since he didn't know where a black market for precious metals was, or even if one existed yet, the precious metals were essentially useless to him. With large expenditures, like Claude's fuel tanker, the hospital, and the armaments he still had to discuss with Wayne; surely his available cash would not cover. In fact he was not even sure exactly how much cash was available, with the community spending wildly. More cash would have to be obtained somehow. Lots more cash. And

Operation Phoenix

quickly.

He was no sooner home than he sequestered himself in his office with the door closed. He sat down with his face in his hands. He needed a plan, desperately. It was as he had told Wayne, getting the job only half done was worse than useless. Eventually, he called Chris Habel at home. "Hi Chris. Sorry to disturb you on your day off, but I've been neglecting you and I have a couple of things I'd like to discuss. Can you get fuel, and if so at what price?"

"Usually," said Chris. "We're talking $40 per gallon as of yesterday, and rising daily. Drive around enough to find it, and you've used enough fuel to double the cost."

"Do you think you and your guys would be interested in taking a tanker each of diesel and gas off me at a 10% discount from the retail price of fuel? I thought maybe fuel would be scarce enough that it might be worthwhile to load up four to six 45 gallon drums of fuel into the back of a pickup truck, head over to one of those roadside fruit stand kinds of spots, and sell it by the gallon. That would mean that a 45-gallon barrel at $40 a gallon would sell at $1,800 or $180 for you. If you got four barrels on a pickup truck, your part would be $720 per load," Gary said.

"I think we could get six barrels on a pickup."

"All the better," Gary enthused. "Your share would be $1,080 per load. You could say, split it three ways; one third to the driver; one third to you for administering, and one third for costs. With six trucks, we could be talking $40,000 to $80,000 a day in turnover. Eric bought 50 steel drums. I need you to deliver five here, full of gas, but you should be able to get six or seven pickups out on the road."

"If the drivers were making $350 per day, they'd be making at least as much money as they would driving long haul, and certainly more than they're making today, sitting at home. You're about our only regular customer. Most gas stations are closed. I think it could work."

"Okay we can try that for a few days," Gary said. "Yank a couple of trailers out of the hangar and sell them at the going rate for fuel. When the boys come in, either to reload or at the end of the day, check to be sure everything has been paid for in cash. Hold your ten percent and get the other 90 percent to me that day. I need cash, and I need to be paid daily. All costs belong to you. Does that sound workable to you?"

"That sounds very fair. Do you mind if I purchase some fuel from you?"

"Not at all. I don't care who buys as long as it is at the going price and I am paid in cash, No credit or credit cards to anybody."

"Anything else?" Chris asked.

"Was it you that said you had been a vet in a previous life?"

"Yes," Chris responded. "Why?"

"Do you maintain contact with the field, both as to your license and knowledge, and where and how animals might be marketed?"

"I've kept up my license to practice. I have some hobbies in that direction, and we do own a farm, but what do you mean, 'how animals might be marketed'?" Chris sounded puzzled.

"I'm interested in purchasing animals capable of throwing one or more offspring, in good shape and healthy. Pigs, cows, horses, goats, sheep, chickens, rabbits, anything that's a commercially farmed animal. I don't want specialty animals like racehorses, Clydesdales or ostriches although I'll take them if nothing else is available. I want a sturdy all round, good general-purpose animals. Also, do you know where to get things

Operation Phoenix

like harness and horse drawn equipment that you would use every day with those animals? The object is to set up completely self contained Amish type farms." Gary said.

"Yes, I could be of some help. Those kind of animals are my life, and I miss them. I do have some here on the farm."

"I'm anxious to get started on this. Let me know how you'd like to be paid for this search. I'd also like you and Roy Bryant to meet with my partners as quickly as possible. I want to get Roy's help to buy some machinery. Can you be available, probably Tuesday night, if I can get my gang together? It'd be an opportunity for everybody that is working together, to get know each other. Maybe ten or so people."

"Yes, of course," said Chris. "I've been curious about you and what you're doing, and this would be a wonderful way of scratching that itch."

Gary laughed. "Either that or raise even more questions. By the way, have you and your family been suffering any effects of the recent crime wave?"

"You mean other than having been put out of business by fuel shortages and high fuel prices? Other than the fact it is almost impossible to get any groceries? Or that people from the cities are invading, begging and stealing? Or that a neighbour was kidnapped yesterday in a home invasion and we're afraid to let the kids walk three blocks to school, or what?" Chris asked cynically. "I've been looking seriously at getting away. I have to do something and I'm not sure what."

"We'll discuss what we see as the current situation, and where we think events will likely go at the meeting. I may be able to find some personal time for you later in the week if you want to carry it further. Do you have Roy's home phone number? I think I'll call him too," Gary said.

"Same number as his office. He has an extension in the

Operation Phoenix

house. If he's there he'll pick up."

"Great. Call me as soon as you have anything set up on either of the fuel or the animals. I want to move forward quickly," said Gary.

Gary called Roy Bryant. They arranged consulting fees for Roy to find a complete metalworking machine shop, a sawmill to make lumber, stone cutting equipment, and a woodworking shop. Again, he invited Roy to meet the rest of the team. Both Roy and Chris were pretty reserved in the enthusiasm they showed the world, but Roy seemed as enthusiastic as Chris, and for the same reasons. Business was near zero, and crime was rocketing. Their personal situation was becoming untenable.

Gary left his office and went into the kitchen where Jan, Eric, and Lynn were laughing and talking amicably. He walked up behind Jan, slipped his arms around her waist and kissed her on the neck. "Have you trained them to call you 'Mommy' yet?" he grinned. Lynn looked like she might have swallowed a worm, so Gary got serious fast.

On Friday, as a wrap-up to the week, Wayne, Eric, Lynn and Gary had met. Gary had reported on his meeting with Wolfgang and Jan. He also told them of his lack of decision about whether to admit Jan to the group. He described the list Wolfgang had given them, and said that a huge percentage of what he saw the community needing was on that list. He wanted to make a trip down to the docks to snoop around.

Lynn said, "Dad now that you have found who I should be negotiating with I am about ready to begin bargaining for the Connecticut hospital. I have also found another hospital that is in receivership. But I have no experience negotiating. What if we're eyeball to eyeball and I gotta go potty?"

"Don't sweat it sweetie. You are famous at work for integrating people from mergers into your company, and making them like it. It's the same thing exactly. Circumstances for them have changed. These are the new rules they have to work under or walk away. They are nice people but they have to understand and accept that it is best for both of you that they do work under these new rules. Maybe we can get Jan to help negotiate. Bankers do these sort of negotiations daily. Since we are going after the equipment and pharmacy only, not the building, we can pass it off to Jan as trade goods. We don't need to lie to her, just let her assume it's trade goods. We can even pay her two to three percent of the total as a commission, whether she joins us or not."

They discussed Chris Habel, Roy Bryant, and a potential meeting to bring new members, such as new SEALs, Bruce Nott and the D'Antonio children into the community for Tuesday night. Wayne promised to bring Claude up to speed.

With Fridays meeting in mind he had to get Jan onside. "Jan, that data you got for me on the Medical Venture Capital Company, the ones that invested in that Connecticut hospital, have the principals got their personal assets locked up in the company?"

"Pretty much, as I recall. We try to make it as painful as possible for principals to walk away. It makes them work harder to avoid failure."

"I really want that equipment and those supplies. Not the building of course, but I think the rest will be extremely valuable. I was hoping to get the contents of that hospital for as little as a quarter of a million dollars, but we probably have to go somewhat higher. Do you think the principals might take a chance on nobody finding out where the equipment disappeared to, to snitch a quarter of a million for their own personal use?" Gary asked.

"Oh yes, that happens a lot. At the bank we know how to

look for it, although sometimes they effectively get away with it."

"Would you be willing to help me negotiate with them? I've never done this sort of price negotiation before," Lynn asked hopefully. "It would pay three percent of the total as fee."

"Sure. I've never done quite this sort thing, or from this side of the table, but all banking is arranging to get the best deal for your side. I have to be careful how much time I take off from work. There's a huge amount of work to do, and not many people to do it." Jan was coming around. Taking time off work ran counter to everything Gary thought he knew about her motivations. Or was she doing it because she felt she had to support him?

"We don't care how they do it, or what they do with the money, so long as we can get clear title and are able to strip the equipment out," Gary said. "We have to be able to complete the whole deal quickly, hopefully next week. Lynne says there's also another hospital in receivership. If we got the equipment and supplies from both of them, all the better. But if we're negotiating with two, we have a much better chance of getting one at least. What we don't know is how to deal with the receivers."

"Unfortunately, I have all too much experience dealing with bankruptcies," Jan laughed. "If they're motivated, receivers can move pretty quickly."

"Good," said Gary. "Here are some forms put together by my lawyer. Get them to photocopy them onto their letterhead, sign with their title and seal with the company seal. Did you send that list of companies off to Wolfgang?"

"No, but I'll do it right away."

"What about Wolfgang? Do you think he would be easy to work with closely?" Gary asked.

Operation Phoenix

"I don't know. Nice guy but he isn't very aggressive. Very understated, but that's not necessarily fatal. What other lights is he hiding under that bushel?"

Gary went back into his office and again closed the door. He called Wayne and found him preoccupied with the Singapore deal. "The representative is en route and scheduled to arrive here about midnight although flights are getting pretty erratic. He said that was the only inbound flight he could find. He'll be able to do an 8AM exchange, which would make it evening in Singapore. I've just started working on a place to do the exchange. What space do you have?"

Gary said, "The hangars, which you know about. There's a long narrow space, in a turn of the century building in Trambull. The space on one side is a retail store front, with papered over windows, and at the back is a loading dock and man door. We also have private garages rented. One is at the rear of a residential property, in a quiet area in Greenwood, all built up with older three story brick homes for large families. The garage itself is cinder block with two dirty, small high windows, a sheet metal roll-down door, a workbench, and it contains a vintage car for rebuild. A narrow driveway passes alongside the house to the garage from the street."

"That sounds good. Limited access otherwise?"

"Yes. There's a high solid board fence on three sides of the property."

"Could Eric act as street guard?" Wayne continued.

"Wait, I'll check." He went to the door and asked, "Eric, are you available tomorrow morning for an hour or two?"

"I could be," the answer came back.

"Okay, he's available. Would you like to see either or both spaces later today?"

"Definitely. There's frig-all to be gained by going into this

Operation Phoenix

cold," Wayne said.

"Have you talked to Claude recently?" asked Gary. "Given the state of the US dollar, I'm very uncomfortable not knowing why these guys want US dollars. This deal should have fallen through."

"I talked to Claude a couple of hours ago. He thinks this is going forward only because it is a cash deal. They seem to have something they want in the US costing two million. Claude suspects arms. He has checked the quality of the cargo, and seems happy with the condition of the ship." Wayne said.

"As long as his easy getaway is arranged. Is there some device that can check the ship is not transmitting its position for potential pirates or something?"

"I've already arranged for that. Among other things, I've got some GPS and radio scramblers. I've also arranged to move a Bofors gun and half a dozen heavy machine guns aboard with our guard crew when we take possession. The ship should sail shortly after," he said.

"Humph," Gary said. "One day I'm going to learn to keep my mouth shut around professionals. It's just that some parts of this deal don't smell right to me. I guess if all we get is the ship we won't have lost anything, but I wish I understood why they were baiting the mousetrap."

"You're not the only one but Claude seems to be happy with the arms theory. Maybe he knows this crowd. By the way I need some cash, and by next week I am going to need some foreign cash."

"Ouch. Almost all of our foreign exchange is in Switzerland. I do have some here, but I kept it merely for walking around purposes, so it is not significant amounts. I expect I could get more, but it would take a while. How much US do you need?" Gary asked.

"At least $150,000. Then I need foreign exchange to pay off the chopper to fly the guards off the ship, and to pay the guards."

"Okay, I'll give you the US dollars this afternoon. I guess I'll have to go back to Switzerland soonest. Will I have to travel on to Singapore or will they take a deposit in a Swiss bank?"

"A Swiss bank will be okay I think, but I'll have to check. I'm off to recruit three to five SEALs as soon as we finish interviewing Patti Wagner. By that time, the ship should be well underway."

"Yes, I guess that's the priority. What's happening between you and your girlfriend? Should she be at this meeting? I suppose she doesn't need to be done early, but with Claude's children there, two of which are doctors, it might be good if the medical people met."

"I can't give her full details, especially if those details are to convince her son. She seems to feel I'm forcing her to choose between her son and me. She worries he's headed for the wrong side of the street, which he frigging well is," Wayne said. "I don't think it would be useful for her to be at this meeting anyway. Later, when we are ready to move and the information can't hurt us, I'll be able to give her more information."

"Damn, sometimes life is such a pile of shit," Gary burst out. "Look Wayne, I am sure everyone is willing to bend a long way on this. Whatever you need. But, I guess you're right. It's not time yet. You decide when and how you will handle it."

"Thanks. I guess I never was a very conventional guy, which is probably why I am both a SEAL, and divorced. Women need stability, and in this situation, I can't promise that," Wayne moaned.

"I hear you. I'm going to have to become a lot more conventional if my potential marriage is to succeed. Having children will make it a lot easier, but it certainly isn't going to be easy. I don't envy you one bit. In fact, I don't even envy me," Gary commiserated.

"Well, let's get on with it. I'll be over about 14:00 hours to pick you up," Wayne said abruptly.

"Okay, see you then."

Finished with confidential matters, Gary opened the door to the office.

Chapter 25

Gary got on his computer to retrieve Wolfgang's list of goods sitting on the docks. He compared the hard copy that he had worked on and made up a new list containing all the data available for those products he had an interest in. His first attempt to cull the list left him with over 2700 containers out of the many thousands available. That was still too many so he began to prioritize the list by breaking it down into three groups; those items definitely needed for the new community; those goods that would be nice to have for the community; and those items that would make good trade goods. A number of things like sugar, appeared in each of the categories. The community would definitely need sugar. It would be nice if they had a safety cushion in case the original estimate was short. The balance would be invaluable as trade goods.

Finishing his container allocation so he could vary the numbers easily, he began to research independent fuel dealers from a file he had created earlier. The dealer that seemed to suit his needs best was headquartered in New Haven, with a single owner. He researched this man as much as possible through the Internet. As he was finishing, Jan came in through the now open door, and stood beside him, watching what he was doing. Gary reached around and began rubbing her back and buttocks.

"Whatcha doing?" she asked.

"Trying to dig up whatever dirt is available on this independent fuel dealer. Do you still have access to any of the credit files at the bank?"

Operation Phoenix

"Yes, some of the databases I can access from outside but some I have to be at a bank terminal," she answered.

"I'm very interested in this gas company. I have to leave soon to meet with Wayne. Can you dig up whatever you can on Peter Rosen of Friendly Gas Bars in New Haven? I'm looking at the idea of dealing with him in the bulk purchase of fuel. I want to know if he has the cash to swing a deal, say half a million dollars at a time. I need someone who still has the capacity to buy fuel in wholesale lots, but is having difficulty getting supplies. The majors, who don't have enough for themselves, will be squeezing most independents. If I can find someone who has the financial ability to pay, and who is located near the coast where we might be able to offload from a ship, they could make a great trade partner later."

"Okay, if you'll get off the computer, I'll find what I can."

"Here's the folder to save whatever you get on him," Gary pointed out as he moved away.

Jan fiddled with the computer for a few minutes, and said, "Got it. Essentially no debt, except a couple of small mortgages. A cash rich operation. In business for 15 years, and looks to be growing fast, twenty-one stations. Pays on time, all the time. Unusual. One would expect a few disputes, or errors that show up as late payments. Looks good."

Gary leaned over and kissed her tenderly. "You are one smart, beautiful and sexy lady."

She threw her arms around his neck and proceeded to kiss him soundly. "That's one of the things I like about you. You are spontaneous, and occasions are when you make them, not on some specific date like February 14th or whenever society says it should be." She kissed him lingeringly again.

"Hey, stop that, or you'll become a permanent feature around my office by getting screwed on the desk."

Operation Phoenix

"You're all talk, no action. First the kitchen table, now the desk." And she walked out, swivelling her hips.

Gary watched her departure with interest. *When I am around her I can't keep my hands off her. When I am away, I tend to focus on the current emergency. Mostly I think of her as a female, and occasionally of her business skills. Strange. Why do I hesitate about her as a community member when I want her as a wife? What is my subconscious telling me? It's like that gross fat cow model we had in art class. Everybody drew her as 'pleasingly plump', even the female artists where no sexual attraction entered the picture. We see only those things we want to see.*

The phone rang. It was Wayne. "Shit, I'm going to be late. The cops have got a roadblock set up, and they're threatening to hand out tickets left, right and centre. Have a speck of dirt on your windshield, or a wiper streak, and they claim it's obscuring your frigging view. Of course, you can avoid the ticket for a small contribution to the benevolent fund. No receipt, and no tax deduction."

"What's the going rate?"

"Twenty bucks." Wayne said in disgust. "Sounds like Colombia or some other frigging two bit third-world country. People who can afford gas automatically qualify as having money to extort. Very selective process."

"It was certainly predictable, but for them to be this organized this fast is unbelievable. Thanks for calling. I would have worried otherwise. You'll get here when you get here. I have some things I can do in the meantime. See you."

Gary studied the file on Peter Rosen and the Friendly Gas Bars, and then dialled the gas bar nearest head office. "Is Peter Rosen in?"

"No, he's at the office I think. This is the gas bar."

Operation Phoenix

"Oh, sorry. Being Sunday I suppose there is no switchboard. Do you have his direct number?" Gary asked.

"It's 987-1234."

"While I have you, do you have any gasoline?" Gary asked.

"Yes, we have some. I think that's what Pete is doing, looking for supplies. At least that was what he was bitching about when he left here."

"What's your current retail price?" Gary asked.

"$44.50 a gallon."

"My god, it's getting terrible isn't it?" Gary sympathized.

"Yeah, I can't understand why the government doesn't do something about it."

"Who knows why government does or does not do something," Gary declared. "Is it that hard to get supplies?"

"Oh, yes. Thank God Pete owns a big 500,000-gallon tank down by the docks, and this station has four 10,000-gallon tanks in the ground. We'd have been dead without it. The majors hate us. The army is requisitioning their supplies, but we are too small to notice. He's trying to get supplies from overseas, but the big docks are all tied up, and our port can't take the big super-tankers. Then we can't get the foreign money to pay for it. It is very tough."

"Do you sell diesel, or just gas?" Gary queried.

"All of our stations sell both."

"Pete seems to be growing fast," Gary said leadingly.

"Yes, but I've got to go. I have a customer."

"Okay. Goodbye, and thanks." Gary hung up, added the details to his file, and smiled. "Thank you very much young sir, whoever you are. It was very profitable talking to you. I can only say I hate that customer for cutting off your stream of information."

Operation Phoenix

Gary pondered for a while, planning, and then dialled Peter Rosen's number.

"Hello?"

"Pete Rosen, my name is Gary Alden."

"How did you get this number?"

"I guess someone gave it to me. I have it in my file," Gary evaded. "I'm calling you to see if you wanted to buy some distillate fuels."

"Oh. Well, I'm always interested in fuel deals."

"I have two 10,000 gallon road tankers, one each of diesel and regular gas. Would you have an interest in them?" Gary asked.

"Probably. What are your terms?"

"Cash on delivery, no cheques. The price is $36.00 per gallon."

"That's too much. I'll pay you $10 per gallon."

"Nice try, but these are not stolen goods," Gary laughed. "Besides, someone else will be happy to buy. I'm offering you 20% off retail. Are you interested or not?"

"Why don't you come over here and we can talk about it"

"That sounds like a good idea. I can't make it today, maybe tomorrow just before noon. Can you assure me that you can come up with the $360,000 per road tanker in cash?" Gary demanded.

"That's a lot of money."

"If that's a lot of money, I guess there's not much point in trying to figure out how to get a small ocean tanker into the New Haven docks and off loaded without having the fuel seized," Gary said.

"How big a tanker?"

"Two million gallons, I'd guess. I can't remember how many gallons per ton," Gary said in a disinterested way. "10,000

Operation Phoenix

tons of it anyway."

"I can't come up with ten's of millions of dollars cash."

"Of course not. Neither of us would even want to. The price would be in gold, or tradable commodities. But as a first test, I am interested in whether you can come up with $720,000 for two road tankers of fuel," Gary said. "Do you still want me to try to get over to see you tomorrow?"

"Oh yes, we may be able to work something out."

"Okay, I have something going on in the morning, and I have no idea how long it will take. I'll call you when I am finished, and we can set up a specific time then," said Gary.

"What's your name again?"

"Gary Alden. Hopefully, I'll be calling you around ten tomorrow."

"Look forward to it."

Gary looked up the number of Wayne's lady SEAL in Canada, and dialled. "Is Patti Wagner there?"

"Speaking."

"Oh hi. It's Gary Alden. You were going to call me tomorrow before you drove down, but both Wayne and I will be tied up with something tomorrow morning, so I decided to call you instead today. What time do you expect to get down here?"

"I expect to start mid morning tomorrow. It'll take six to seven hours," she said.

"Things have been changing rapidly here, and not for the better. Be sure to stop as soon as you cross the border and arm yourself. I said we would reimburse you. Do you have enough cash to handle everything?"

"Yes, no problem. But will my US credit and debit cards work in there? I'd rather use them, and I can't get them to work here," Patti said.

"You know, I can't even tell you that. I have cards, but

Operation Phoenix

I've been out of the country so much. You can't seem to use US cards anywhere in the world. I haven't even tried to use them in the last month. I'd think they would work in the US providing the banks haven't failed or pulled your credit line. In the rest of the world, no one wants to take US dollars for any reason, and the US has completely frozen all foreign exchange. I'd be careful coming across the border. Any Canadian dollars you have might get seized."

"I'll watch for that." Patti sounded puzzled.

"One other thing. Wayne is on his way over here, and just called to say he would be late." And he explained about the roadblock tolls. "I also had to pay a bribe at customs to get waved through. You might be smart to have a few 5's, 10's and 20's stashed away about your person in case you need them."

"Jesus. What the hell's happening down there?" Patti exclaimed.

"Nothing that won't happen in the rest of the world. It will just happen a little later as this tsunami wave rolls around the world. Canada is just a short way away from New York. The effects will be felt soon enough."

"I'm beginning to wonder if I should come back," Patti said reflectively.

"Have people you know up there been being laid off?"

"My best friend's husband was laid off Friday. They export a lot of stuff to the US," Patti had a frown in her voice. "My folks have been talking a lot about the sudden unemployment."

"Sudden unemployment is one of the early signs that the shit is hitting the fan. A trip down would at least give you a look at what is happening, so you have enough information to make an intelligent decision. I think you'd better come directly to my house," Gary gave her the address again and directions. "I don't

Operation Phoenix

know how many people will be here, but someone will be. I have moved several people in for safety's sake. Park your car on the lawn, or at least inside the gates. There may be a couple of cars there already. I have a perimeter security alarm and guards, so it should be safe enough. If you leave at ten, you should be here latest by six. If you're going to be later than six, or if you have any troubles, please call. Where will you be crossing the border?"

"At Niagara Falls."

"Okay, we at least have some idea of your route down, in case of problems. Once we have connected up, we can put you somewhere reasonably safe, so you can have your meeting in peace. See you tomorrow"

"Right."

Gary ran Jan home, returned and fiddled for a while putting his files in order until Wayne arrived. They left immediately for the Greenwich garage. Wayne reconnoitred the site and the area and pronounced it suitable. He outlined the procedure he intended to use. They then left for the Trambull rental space.

Suddenly they ran into a traffic jam. "Shit, not another toll," said Wayne. "There aren't enough cars on the road for it to be anything else."

Gary took out two 20s and slipped one into each of his shoes. They worked their way towards the front of the line. "No blue uniforms," said Gary. "This must be some kind of gang. I wonder which came first: did the hoods learn from the cops, or did the cops learn from the hoods?"

A burly gorilla in body armour and holding a sub machine gun approached them. "There's a $20 toll to pass through our territory."

"Hey, jeez man. I just spent my last bucks on gas. Can't

Operation Phoenix

you just let us through?" Gary whined.

"Nope. Twenty bucks. Now fucking hand it over," and he gestured meaningfully with the business end of the gun.

"Okay, okay," Gary said as he raised his hands. "It's in my shoe. I'll have to get it," and he lowered one hand and slipped off a shoe. Placing the shoe on the seat beside him, he fished out the twenty, and passed it to Wayne, who passed it on to the gorilla. The gorilla waved them forward, and they were out. "I can see it might get exciting bringing that two million back to Greenwich on our return trip," Gary said. "Unfortunately, they are probably roving roadblocks, in place only for an hour or so before they move on, so they are not very predictable."

Wayne grunted.

As they drove through Trambull, suddenly Wayne's lips tightened. Just ahead to the right, a man lay on the sidewalk among the uncollected garbage, his blood pooling under him in the gutter. A woman was screaming and wailing over him. Back a few feet, a small crowd of onlookers milled around. Gary rolled down the window. A self-important but gaunt, and dirty young man came over to spread the gossip. "Does she need help?" asked Wayne.

"Nah, we called the cops and ambulance over an hour ago. Some guys came up to him and wanted money. He didn't have any, so they shot him. Just crazy man. Some guys from New York I think. I never seen them before. It doesn't matter much though, he was just a spic anyway"

"I guess the cops had other things to do," Gary said cynically, referring to roadblocks.

The skinny young man took him literally. "Yah, I know. They took nearly two days to get here when my aunt died last week. Man, she was starting to stink. There's a guy in the stairwell of our flop. I guess he's been there for a long time. The

Operation Phoenix

maggots are crawling all over him. It's too funny man. Sometimes it looks like he's moving. Really weird."

"How did your aunt die?" Wayne asked.

The thin young man looked at him as if he were some sort of mental retard. "She starved I think," he said blankly. "I guess she was too old. She was over 40."

"Yeah, over 40 is pretty old," Gary said wryly being 46 himself. "You say you live in a flop? Don't you live with your parents?"

"Nah, they put me on rations, and all kinds of rules. They won't give me any money, and they were going to move out to the country. I wanted to be with my friends, so we found a building where the landlord doesn't hassle us. We broke into the variety store, and we eat pretty good. There are big bottles of Pepsi, and lots of chips and there's ice cream in the freezer."

"When did you go to the flop?" Gary asked.

"Day before yesterday, but some of my friends have been there nearly a week."

"Looks like he's dead alright," Wayne said, nodding at the corpse. "That blood's turning brown from drying. You're right, that was a totally senseless killing. Oh well, nothing we can do here. See you," and he pressed the accelerator to move off.

At the rental space, they stopped at the front to alert the guard to their presence. He was asleep in the car. Because they were reluctant to have anyone knowing they had entered, they let him continue sleeping and went around to the rear, disarmed the alarm, and entered. Gary flipped back the tarp, moved a desk, and opened the safe. Gary felt Wayne's eyes take in the spectacle of 40,000 ounces of silver, as he yanked out the bags of money and closed the safe. They arranged and split the money into the two million for the transfer, Wayne's $150,000, and the balance. After recovering the safe with the tarp, they checked for onlookers, and stuffed the bags of money into the trunk of the car. After rearming the alarm, they drove back around to the front and contemplated the guard, who was still asleep.

"Well, he certainly doesn't have any sense that he is guarding something valuable, and that is good and bad," Gary said. "What do you think we should do?"

"Is there a loud alarm bell on the system?"

"The bell's right over there," Gary pointed. "I think it should wake him. On the other hand, it would be much better if he were alert in the first place. At least no one now knows we've been in to do a pick up."

"I vote for calling the company, and getting a supervisor over here right away."

"Good idea," Gary said, and he picked up the car phone, dug through his wallet for the phone number, dialled the company, and demanded to speak to the owner. After a brief wait, despite it being Sunday, the owner came on. Gary identified himself and where he was calling from, "I just stopped by to check things out, and your guard is sound asleep."

"One moment, I have to check who's there." He came back on. "I'm sorry. Things have been so hectic lately that some of the guards have been doing double shift. Jake is a really good long time guard, but I guess we've pushed him too far."

"How does that help me? I have several guards on a 24/7 basis. I pay top dollar promptly or in advance. I pay in cash, even during the bank holiday. Is this the reward I get for being an unusually desirable customer?"

"Oh, I know who you are. Can you go and wake Jake up and let me talk to him, please?"

"No, I want someone from your company to take the time, inconvenience and expense to come down here and wake him

Operation Phoenix

up. And I want him replaced immediately. Let him sleep at someone else's site," Gary stormed.

"I don't deny we're at fault here, but I don't think you understand the situation. In the current atmosphere the demand for armed guards is overwhelming. Almost anyone who has the ability to pay wants armed guards. We're turning away business by the truckload. We can't get experienced guards at any price."

"Oh, I see. Your former reputation for quality service is disposable in these circumstances. Okay, I'll go wake Jake up, but this isn't the service I contracted for. I am not happy with the implied threat, true or not, that you can easily replace my business. I like to think that I conduct my business in an honourable way. I expect my business associates to handle their own problems, and not try to shuffle them off onto me in the form of crappy service," Gary said as he got out of the car.

"My problem is, I need alert guards. I hired you to solve my problems, not compound them. One moment, I'm at Jakes car. I'll try to wake him," and he banged the phone on the window and yelled, "Wake up. Wake up."

Jake came to foggily, pulled his pistol, and then rolled the window down a bit. "Your boss wants to talk to you," said Gary, thrusting the phone at him.

"Herro." Jake was still pretty foggy.

"Yeah, I guess I was."

"Well, you knew what I was doing."

"Yeah, he looks pretty mad," Jake said, glancing at Gary.

A long pause, Jake handed the phone back to Gary. "He wants to talk to you."

"Yes," Gary said crisply into the phone.

"I recognize that we are at fault. These things happen. While I could swear it wouldn't happen again, I know it will somewhere. It will happen with any firm. It's the nature of the beast. However you are right, our reputation is very important to me. I will take a personal hand in this, providing of course you want to continue using our services."

"At this moment, I'm pretty angry," Gary said. "I will likely cool down somewhat. I usually do. The implication that this is happening on a fairly consistent basis at my sites gets to me. In the meantime, I'll be making some changes tomorrow or Tuesday. Not in the number of hours, but in locations guarded. However I can't give you details yet. In the meantime, I'll take you at your word that you will take a personal hand in this. My son or I will be in touch by tomorrow night regarding the changes."

"Yes, but please give me as much notice as possible. With fuel supplies the way they are, shifting people around is very difficult."

"I may be able to help you there," Gary said. "I have some fuel available at $40.00 per gallon, cash, providing you have a place to store it."

"I think I could take 1,000 gallons tomorrow. When you call, I'll let you know. My problem is that I don't know where I'll store it."

"Well, it's strictly a cash transaction," Gary continued. "I just saw an open station advertising gas at $44.50 a gallon but the price will be up tomorrow. I'll give you a discount off retail, so the price is $40 per gallon, firm for two days."

"Do you have heating oil?"

"No, just regular gas and diesel fuel," Gary said shortly.

"If I can find the cash, and storage, would you be willing to part with more?"

"Yes, 10,000 gallons on short notice."

"Would there be a discount?"

"Well," Gary paused, "I suppose I could. I'll tell you what

Operation Phoenix

I'll do. You come up with $390,000 in cash, and I'll drop the trailer wherever you want. The tanker is yours. That would alleviate your storage problems. I'll get another."

"You know that with these higher fuel costs we are going to have to raise our prices to everybody?"

"I've no problem with that, so long as it is in proportion. I will be willing to discuss it with you. In the meantime I'll call you tomorrow, probably in the afternoon," Gary finished up. Nodding to Jake he said, "Stay awake. What good is a guard who's asleep? Sleep at some other site."

As he got back in the car, Wayne threw back his head and laughed heartily. "You were the perfect picture of righteous indignation and rage, banging on that window with you phone while that poor bastard was glued to the phone on his end."

"What route do you plan to use to get back to Greenwich with this cash?"

"First of all, I thought it would be safer at your house overnight. You have only a short distance to go to Greenwich, and there will be both you and Eric. They're not likely to set up a roadblock at that hour. I'll lead my group around by the nose for a while, and show up at the garage at 08:00.

Sounds like a plan to me," Gary said. "I presume you want me at the airport to meet them tonight?"

"It'd be better if we had someone to watch the cars while I identify them."

The drive back was without incident, and they got Wayne's car into Gary's garage, fuelled the car, and Gary gave Wayne the $150,000 he needed. The two million was removed from the car and stacked in the garage. The balance went into Gary's home safe.

Later, at the airport, the short-term parking was virtually deserted. Wayne emerged with three well-dressed people, two

Operation Phoenix

heavies, and an impeccably dressed businessman. He introduced John Disney, the representative, and Norm and Henry, the heavies. They got into the cars. Gary followed them out of the garage as part of a group of the last few cars parked, something Gary had never seen before. They then went their separate ways.

Operation Phoenix

Chapter 26
Monday March 6th — Day 21

Gary and Eric loaded the cars and left for the Greenwich garage early. As yet the temperature was below freezing, with about three inches of snow on the ground, but with the cloud breaking up, much higher temperatures looked probable. Even at this early hour, there were quite a number of people walking on the roads out of the cities, dragging buggies, pushing shopping carts, or carrying packs because food shortages were becoming extreme. Gary unloaded the moneybags onto the workbench on the left of the garage. Wayne had directed Gary's street sweeper shotgun to be placed out of sight behind the overhead door track on the right of the garage. Eric's car was to be parked down and across the street from the driveway entrance with no footprints in the snow, so he might not be noticed, and therefore a surprise, and could come up behind any trouble.

Promptly at eight, Wayne pulled in followed by a rental car containing their guests. Wayne climbed out of his car and immediately dialled the security counterpart he had hired in Singapore. John Disney, and the first heavy, Norm, also got on the phone, presumably to their counterparts in Singapore. Gary dialled Claude. "Claude, great to talk to you again my friend. The representative, John Disney, and two heavies just pulled in." Gary gave the agreed on codeword.

"Gary, good to talk to you too, my friend. Everyone is here and ready to go." Claude returned the codeword.

Gary glanced at Wayne, who nodded. Gary said to John Disney, "If you're ready to go ahead, back the car up to the

Operation Phoenix

garage so you can load the bags into the trunk."

John Disney looked in enquiry at Norm, who thought about it for a moment, nodded, and said to the guy in the back of the car, "Henry, I want you to wait here at the sidewalk." Henry obligingly took his place at the corner of the sidewalk and the driveway. When he got out of the car, it became very apparent he was wearing a shoulder holster. Not bad for a guy who had landed only a few short hours ago, on a Sunday night when all the stores were closed. The theory that they might be engaged in something like gun running gained credence.

Gary opened the garage door, and walked with John to the workbench on which the moneybags were placed. Wayne drifted to his right and leaned against the overhead door track hiding the shotgun, one step away from the safety of the corner of the garage cement wall. Norm placed himself on the far side of the rental car from Wayne. "We'll be some time here counting and checking the cash. Would it be acceptable to you for two or three of our seamen to go aboard the ship and prepare her for departure?" Gary asked.

After checking with Singapore, John Disney agreed. Gary said into his phone, "Claude, my friend, are you there?" and then conveyed the information to Claude. Money counting took nearly half an hour despite the fact that they were only counting packets. When Gary enquired if John Disney was satisfied, John replied, "Eminently."

Gary asked Claude whether he was ready to go, and Claude thought they would need another eight to ten minutes. Gary conferred with John. "I can understand why you might want another ten minutes," John said. "May I suggest we do the formal exchange now, put the money in the trunk, and we will wait here the ten minutes."

Norm did not look happy and said; "We will move the car

Operation Phoenix

to the end of the laneway, near the street."

Gary shot an inquiring glance at Wayne, who didn't look too happy either, but shrugged and nodded. Wayne, John, and Norm were all talking on their phones. Gary got Claude's opinion and approval. "Okay, they are ready to hand over the papers my friend," Claude said.

"Is everyone ready to go ahead? Last chance to object," Gary said loudly. Nods all around. "Okay, go."

John Disney picked up the bags and struggled over to the car. Claude said into his ear, "My friend, we have the papers."

"Okay everyone, the formal exchange is complete," Gary said, primarily for Wayne and Claude's benefit. Wayne continued on his phone for a moment, and then got on his radio. Gary knew he was talking to Eric.

Claude's voice came over the phone. "Here comes the cavalry, my friend. The trucks are alongside. My crew is headed for the bridge and the boiler room."

About a minute and a half went by, when suddenly Norm looked with surprise at Wayne, and said to John Disney, "These guys are SEALs, and they're moving fast to secure the ship. A crane truck is lifting a Bofors gun onto the stern to secure it, and they have heavy machine guns. Tense, but nothing negative yet."

John Disney drove the car to the end of the driveway, got out, and beckoned Gary over. Glancing at Wayne, and watching for any developments, Gary went over. "What is your line of business?" John asked.

"Up to a month ago, I was a poor consultant, but now, I guess you could call me a commodities trader, although we might consider other things. Are you expecting to do any similar deals in the future?" Gary asked to regain control of the conversation.

Operation Phoenix

"No, we don't expect to do any more deals in US dollars," John laughed. "This was a special circumstance, and we were glad you were prepared to move quickly and in cash. I liked what I saw today. Would you have an interest in further deals? We deal in anything that will turn a profit."

"Well, I never say never because circumstances change things, but there are some deals we would tend to shy away from. Still, talk is cheap, and I think we might have some mutual interests in the future. Let's keep in touch."

"Capital idea sir," John enthused.

They exchanged business cards and private phone numbers, and chatted for a few minutes. "I suppose it is about time," John said. "Let's check on our people at the other end."

As he walked back to Wayne, Gary mused on Wayne's strategic abilities. Wayne had taken the elements of the situation and arranged them so that little communication was necessary, and no orders would be needed. Any actions required would be apparent to all if some wheels came off somewhere. In fact, Wayne had probed much deeper into what could go wrong than Gary was likely to have done. *It is sure good to have Wayne's experience and knowledge with a couple of million and Claude at risk. Me too for that matter.* "How is your end holding up, Wayne?" Gary asked.

"They'd probably have to blow up the ship to dislodge us now."

Gary checked with Claude, and when he confirmed they were casting off, turned and waved to John. Norm and Henry climbed into the car, and they were gone. Wayne radioed Eric to come in.

They cleaned up, locked up, and Eric left. Gary asked Wayne if he had time to come with him to meet Peter Rosen of Friendly Gas Bars, and explained the situation.

Operation Phoenix

"Sounds like I should be there, and I will be," Wayne declared. "I'm going to have to assign you a personal bodyguard the way you zap around thither and yon. You're too exposed to people who have the potential to be bad cases, and you are quite cavalier with valuables. You're good for someone untrained, and very aware of your surroundings, but you are not god. I think Patti would be best. She's smart and innovative"

"Just what I was thinking a minute ago," Gary laughed. We had millions, Claude and me at risk and I was treating it as if we were buying some bread. As far as your SEAL guards go, I don't know Jim at all, but I am impressed with the little I know of Patti. For instance, I'll have to get some money to your crew in Singapore fast. That means travel. I'm not sure Patti, as a female would be suitable for that, no matter how professional we both were. Jan might have some very large objections. I'll have to run it by her, ASAP. But lets get on with life. We have a very full plate."

Pete Rosen turned out to be a big burly guy, maybe six foot three and near 250 pounds, very little of it fat. The office had maybe ten people, and generally mirrored Pete's office. The walls and floors were clean and bright, but the desks were littered with papers. Everyone moved purposefully. In Gary's mind, this was a sign of busy people actually multitasking. It appeared to be an ordered disorder with few deadlines missed.

Pete's negotiating style proved to be very much like what Gary had already experienced. 'Come down to my turf where I have a huge psychological advantage, and maybe we can work something out.' He seemed to realize that in the present circumstances that Gary was invaluable to him, but he wasn't going to let Gary screw him without getting some kisses back.

He was extremely interested in Gary's ability to provide a continued supply of fuel. He seemed to feel his long-term needs

Operation Phoenix

were a major trump card. Gary was all too aware of the risks, especially where there was a grave danger that the authorities would seize what they wanted on the flimsiest pretext.

Gary said, "Getting you a continuous supply of fuel very much depends on three things. First, we have to be able to get in and out of here without the cargo or the ship being seized. Second, is your ability to take delivery of, and pay for, sufficient quantities to make the operation worthwhile. I note that you have one 500,000-gallon tank down by the docks. How easily could you get a second? Our ship contains both diesel fuel and regular gas."

Pete interrupted. "First you contact me on a Sunday at my private unlisted number. Then you tell me about a tank that I have been trying to keep a very low profile on, lest it be seized. Where are you getting this information?"

"Most people down on the docks know it is your tank. If the authorities get off their fat butts and take a walk down there, they'll know too. To continue, the third factor in getting a continued supply rests on our ability to find continuing profitable supplies, which we have not attempted to do yet. You're concerned with our ability to continue supplying. Our concern is that somebody who always seems to have some fuel will come to some authority's attention. In a best-case scenario, we just lose a valued customer. In a worst case, we also land on the radar of the authorities. It's a chance we all take, but there's no point in begging for trouble. We have to get our ducks in a row first. Are you interested in doing a deal for two road tankers of fuel or not?"

"Put that way, you are giving me the option of closing up shop today, or waiting till the authorities arrive and close me up," Pete grumbled.

"You have been in business 15 years. In that time you

Operation Phoenix

have grown to 21 or 22 stations. You've done that with only a couple of small mortgages, and a prompt payment record that is so prompt it's almost suspicious. To have grown that fast you must have made some very good decisions, decisions that have gotten you over whatever your immediate problem was and back to the business of making a profit. Now the world has changed dramatically. If you choose to get out of business because the world has changed, or choose not deal with us because you don't like the colour of our eyes, that's fine. I have a couple of road tankers of fuel that are surplus to my needs, and not enough cash to cover my needs. I want to sell those road tankers. The US is crying for fuel. There are risks, but there are big rewards. If we're to do business, the first step is to complete the first deal, and then look at whether we can to do a second deal. We've gotten side tracked onto all sorts of theory. The question is; do you want to buy two road tankers of fuel?" Gary said impatiently.

"No. You scare the hell out of me," Pete said abruptly.

"Sorry about that. I guess we have nothing more to do here then," and Gary stood up.

"Wait," said Pete. "It's just that you have so much information on me, and what do I know about you? You could easily be the Mafia for all I know. In fact, there's still the possibility the fuel is stolen. Do you have a business card, and maybe I could get back to you?"

"I certainly have no objection to giving you my business card," Gary said as he dug one out. "However, I'm not sure what good it will do. I expect to sell those tankers of fuel today." He handed over the business card, still standing.

"One moment," Wayne interrupted. "I know how disconcerting his information can be. I just joined him as a partner, and it scared me how much he knew about me before I even knew his name. I don't know yet how he finds time to do all the things he does, never mind research. He forecast the market crash, and since then has been doing an excellent job of staying ahead of events; and guessing what crisis will appear next. One of the early things he did was to purchase fuel before the shortage became apparent, so the fuel is legit. Of course that is profitable for him. Why shouldn't it be?"

"Oh," mumbled Pete, "I just feel he knows every secret I own."

Gary sat back down. "I guess I've been in too much of a hurry on this. Before the crash, I anticipated a fuel shortage as a result of the crash. I gathered the names of independent dealers across the country. Your location, and present circumstances narrowed it down to your being of interest to me. You were accessible to ocean supply. The credit bureau gave me 90 plus percent of the rest. I doubt over the years that I've talked to more than two or three people about you. You have grown fast, are aggressive, and didn't make mistakes. You adapt well to changed circumstances. In fact, you've done so well that you could easily be a front for Mafia money yourself. If you look at events over the last month, the change has been massive and at blinding speed. Yet you are still pumping gas. That says a lot about you."

"It says all that in my credit report?"

"Of course not," Gary said. "The credit report said you were in a position to weather this kind of storm. All it took was one phone call to ask 'do you still have gas?' to fill in the remaining blanks."

"Oh." Pete was silent for a time and then heaved a sigh. "You're one sweet talker, you are. I guess I need fuel, and I don't see much on the horizon. When can you deliver?"

"When can you get cash? I don't know for sure when I can

Operation Phoenix

deliver till I ask my trucker, but I could probably deliver some, if not all tonight."

"On short notice I don't know how much cash my bank can come up with. Probably not $750,000 anyway. Half maybe," Pete fiddled with some papers on his desk.

They arranged a later call to settle the details. Outside, Gary thanked Wayne for intervening. "I'm worn out and I'm getting heavy handed. Deadly kinds of mistakes, I'm afraid. By the way, what's Claude's itinerary?"

"A chopper picks him and the SEALs up four to eight hours from now. He catches the first available flight back. Singapore Air Lines used to have a direct flight to Vancouver, and there were other direct flights to Toronto. Once we get him into Canada, we think we can get him across to Toronto or Montreal if necessary. John Disney told me that the flight he took seemed to be the only overseas flight to New York. Once Claude's in the east, we'll find a way to get him down here."

Gary wondered aloud if he would have to travel to Zurich or Singapore to pay the Singapore crew. Wayne surprised him by saying, "I've already paid it. Wire transfer from a Swiss bank. A quarter of a million Euros, of which over 100,000 was for the guns and ammo. Those Bofors guns are not cheap. Then there was the chopper, the trucks, and some other stuff. The rest is for the guys."

Privately, Gary didn't know much about Bofors guns, but he doubted they could be purchased for as little as a quarter of a million, never mind the heavy machine guns and ammo. Wayne was obviously spending goodwill, and Gary was concerned he was overspending. "I'm just a poor country boy, and I have a psychological thing about the word million, but Claude's safety was certainly worth it. How do you want me to pay you? Certainly not in US dollars," Gary said.

Operation Phoenix

"I think your silver idea is a good one. How about in silver?"

"At what rate per ounce?" Gary wanted to know. They decided to get a quote in Euros from a major bank in Switzerland to determine the number of ounces owed. "Oh yes," Gary said, "and we will add a percentage for your risk."

"What risk?"

"That I might have had a heart attack at the mention of the word million," Gary grinned. "Your paying was very trusting, and flattering to me."

."Well, there is that," Wayne grinned back. "I'll call it 250 thousand if I ever have to do it again."

At the apartment hotel that Wayne had found for better security in Hamden, the perimeter fencing was going in today. Eric and the SEALs would begin to move tenants today, and would headquarter in a couple of vacant suites starting Wednesday morning.

Wayne dropped Gary off at his house, refuelled his car, and Gary started for the docks. He phoned Chris to find the retail gas business was going gangbusters. In three hours, Chris, and a couple of other drivers had sold most of their load, and would have to go back to reload. Gary alerted him to a possible need to haul tankers tonight to Pete, and the security guard company. He called Lynn on her cell phone.

"I have made contact with Medical Venture Capital Company. We have an appointment for this afternoon. I dropped the word 'cash' into the conversation and they are so eager, I suspect the lack of money spawns all sorts of evil." she said excitedly.

"Great. I'm on my way to the docks. Those containers are becoming more important by the second."

Operation Phoenix

Chapter 27

Gary arrived at the dockyard gates where the security guard stopped him. "Who do you want to see?"

"I am trying to arrange a way to redirect some containers out of here, and I need to know exactly what documentation and stuff I need, as well as someone to authorize it, preferably the harbour master."

"Not many staff are in these days except the harbour master. I'll check if he's available." The guard phoned. "He can see you now. Park your car in the lot to the right of the administration building, go through the main doors, and take the elevator to the top floor." Beyond Gary could see the container moving cranes, now idle, and giant stacks of containers.

I presume there is a parking fee?" Gary said pulling out a $20 bill. "Would you keep an eye on my car while I'm gone?"

"Why yes there is. Park your car by the handicapped spot. I can see it from here."

Gary said, "I was wondering whether your workers came in much these days?"

"The guys come in anyway, despite not getting paid, particularly the night shift. I'm not sure why, there isn't much for them to do," the guard grinned a knowing grin.

"I imagine there is quite a lot of theft around here. Is there more theft lately?"

"Yes, I suppose so," the guard said slowly. "I hear there was a couple of trucks went out last night, so I guess there's more stealing going on. But I guess it is all over. Did you hear that they announced the army was bringing in a convoy of trucks of food? It turned out that it was 37 trucks for all of New York. They were stopped and looted before they got anywhere near the distribution point."

"No, I hadn't. Have the armed forces been in to pick up containers?" Gary asked, thinking about the army being called out to deliver food to the masses.

"No, they have some stuff here, but they haven't picked it up yet."

Obviously they hadn't been in for food either. It appeared nobody in authority had thought that food might be sitting on the docks, not just at the food packers.

"Thanks, you have been a big help," and Gary peeled off another 20 before he left for the harbourmaster's office. Following the signs, he poked his head into what appeared to be a deserted reception and secretarial office. He looked again at the door. The sign was 'harbourmaster' all right. "Hello, Hello," he sang out

At the far end, a portly man of about five foot nine appeared. Gary said, "Hi there, my name is Gary Alden. Are you the harbourmaster?" Suddenly a quote from a gunrunner Gary had once met ran through his mind. *I've never met a fat official yet who was not bribable. Now why did I think of that right now? Probably because he is so greasy."*

"Good afternoon." The smiling harbourmaster bustled over, took Gary's hand, and pumped it like he was going for oil. "Come in, come in. Jack Sopper at your service sir," he said effusively, with a definite Brooklyn accent.

Gary said, "I've been looking at redirecting some goods you are currently storing. I wondered what hassles I would find in the process."

Jack got a calculating look. "Lately it is very difficult.

Operation Phoenix

Nobody knows when title has passed, and the banks are effectively no longer guaranteeing anything. To add to our woes, very little is going out of the yard, so we are full to the gunwales. If you had a specific container, it might take some time to dig it out."

"I was thinking more of exactly what documentation it would take to be able to remove containers from this location," Gary repeated.

Jack frowned elaborately. "Normally, all it would take is a phone call from the broker to redirect a shipment. But our lawyers have cautioned us that given the current circumstances ownership is so unclear that we would have to be absolutely sure there was no impediment to title. Either the shipment goes to whomever it was directed, or we have to check that the person making the redirection has the authority to do so. How many containers were you thinking of moving?"

Since this could be nothing but a bureaucratic stall, Gary said, "I was hoping for around a thousand. However, I expect that theft and vandalism has gone way up, so even if we were to secure any given container, I can't say whether I would want to take it. Has theft gone up recently?"

"Yes, unfortunately it has. I can't really say I blame the boys. We learned Friday that our pensions are gone. We haven't been paid since the first of February, and it looks as if we will not be paid soon, if at all. If somebody gave me a million dollars cash, I would be out of here so fast it would make your head spin," Jack said with finality.

Gary knew what that meant. One million dollars was the bribe price. "Well, I don't exactly keep millions of dollars cash in my hip pocket, but I suppose anything can be done if one is really interested."

Gary had just boxed himself in. He had only wanted to

Operation Phoenix

keep that option open in case of emergencies, not move further down that road. He tried to retreat a bit without blowing it entirely, "But I have never considered anything illegal. Back to my original question: 'What kind of documentation would you require to redirect certain shipments now in storage?' Surely a transfer of ownership letter from the shipper or receiver would be adequate?"

"We would pass the documentation over to our lawyers for their opinion. I'd expect that opinion would take some time and expense, since they have already voiced their concerns about the legal limbo that exists," Jack said in perfect bureaucratic stall mode.

There is no way of Gary going to do this legally before the goods were stolen. This guy really wanted his bribe. With things deteriorating as fast as they were, it was also unlikely he could get supplies fast enough elsewhere. Gary realized he was in the process of inventing what would become an organized black market.

"I see. I have to decide whether I want to do this. I was looking at about 1,000 acceptable 40-foot containers. You are looking for a million in cash. That is about $1,000 per container. You probably have many tens of thousands of containers stored here. I know there are listings of those containers stored here showing; shipper, content and weight among other things. Where can I get a current list?"

"I have a file available which was highly accurate up to about a week ago when our girls decided it was too dangerous to come into work. On the other hand, not much has moved in that time. Would you like me to e-mail it to you, or would you prefer a hard copy?" Jack asked.

"Hard copy," Gary replied. He didn't want his address on Jack's computer. "I thought this might be available on the

Operation Phoenix

Internet?"

"The Internet version isn't all that accurate, but here's the address and a password." Jack wrote both on a scrap of paper as the printer spat out sheets of paper. Jack gathered up the sheets, slipped them into an envelope and handed it to Gary.

"Is that the site that lists ships anchored and waiting to dock?" Gary asked.

"Yes, you just click on shipping."

Gary pursed his lips and pondered. "I'll call you tomorrow afternoon or before for sure. What is your direct number?"

Jack fished out a business card and handed it over, while waiting expectantly for Gary to reciprocate. Gary ignored the implied invitation. "How would you handle the paperwork if the indicated containers were re-directed to some other mode of transport?"

"What paperwork?" Jack grinned. "They just vanished. Who can tell what those naughty union boys did with them?"

"I see. Okay, I'll call you tomorrow afternoon or earlier," and Gary left.

Back in the car, Gary called the guard company, and got the owner. "It's Gary Alden. I'm calling to get your decision on how much fuel you need."

"I don't know Gary. I think I'm in a real mess here. I just got back from the bank and the doors were locked, with a handwritten sign, 'closed'. I don't know whether that means another bank holiday, or if my bank is closed temporarily, or what."

"Have you phoned them?" Gary asked.

"No answer on the phone, although there were people inside when I was there. The handwritten sign just said 'Closed'. Thank god I still have my deposit."

"I think you're right to worry," Gary said, "but I don't see

Operation Phoenix

much more I can do for you."

Gary hung up and swore to himself, "Damn, I needed that $400,000." *It looks like today's the day the banks begin to topple.*

In turn he called Eric, Wayne, Lynn and Jan, relaying the banking situation. Claude was next on his list. Surprisingly Gary caught him at the Singapore airport awaiting a flight to Toronto. "Claude, I'm sorry to be calling you at such an ungodly hour. Actually I thought I might be waking you. What time is it there?"

"Nearly 4AM. What's wrong?" Claude sounded alarmed.

Gary explained the banking situation so Claude might take pre-emptive measures, and then brought up a question that to him was even more important. "Claude, I have a moral 'limbo bar' problem. On one hand, I had always expected that we'd conduct ourselves in an honourable way, regardless of how the people around us reacted. I had hoped that I'd be able to buy or trade for the supplies that we needed, and if the someone chose to evade taxes for example, that was on his conscience. The way the social situation is deteriorating, even if we found the supplies we needed, it's improbable that we will find the owners to buy from."

Gary paused before continuing. "We've been offered about 1000 containers, sitting on the docks, containing probably 90 percent of what we need, for a bribe of one million dollars. I had expected to get into some pretty gray areas, but I'm having a problem reconciling trying to live a relatively honourable and trustworthy life with knowingly receiving stolen goods, or helping in the stealing of them. At the moment, I don't see any other way. This is a community decision. What are your thoughts?"

Claude's silence was shorter than Gary had expected.

Operation Phoenix

"When in Rome, do as the Romans do. We can't successfully fight for our lives while obeying Marquees of Queensbury rules. I don't see another choice either. Admittedly, it's very slippery slope we're on."

"God grant us the serenity to accept the things we cannot change, the courage to change the things we can, and the wisdom to know the difference. Considering that at least among ourselves we want to be honourable, that would mean that we must at least inform Bruce Nott how deep the water is before he jumps in. I expected him to be inducted at the Tuesday night meeting. But since the union boys at the dock are starting to steal goods by the container-load, we'll have to start loading the containers on a ship ASAP, and that means his ship. Can we induct him only on our say so? Is he likely to want to go ahead under the circumstances? How do you think the others would vote?" Gary asked.

"Unless someone can suggest an alternative, I don't think they'll have a choice if we're to save any of what we have worked for. I'll give Bruce a little prep call. You induct him. I have direct flight to Toronto. There are no flights to New York. They're calling the advanced passengers now. I'll be in Toronto in 15 hours."

"I suppose crime is like experience. Do two or three every day and you will soon have experienced every one. You will be vaccinated against every one and be morally perfect. I'll send someone to pick you up, probably a SEAL. I'll hold the bribe decision till tomorrow so I can check with the others for an alternative and induct Bruce. See you soon Claude."

Peter Rosen of Friendly Gas Bars was the next to receive Gary's attention. "Mr. Rosen, it is Gary Alden. I was to call about your schedule of deliveries."

"Yes, I will take the tanker of gas tonight and the diesel

tomorrow. All at the prices we agreed on, right?"

Gary laughed. "Has the price of fuel jumped so much today? Yes, a deal is a deal. But dame fortune is smiling on you. I had committed a tanker of gas to someone else, at $40 per gallon, and his bank has closed its doors." Gary explained that would begin a domino effect of other banks closing, or at a minimum, another bank holiday. "My other customer can't pay for the fuel, so there is another tanker of gas available if you are interested. But if I were you, I sure wouldn't have any cash in a bank. I suspect you have a lot because all that inventory of fuel you had has been converted into cash, and I'll bet most of it is in the bank. If the banks close for a holiday or otherwise, cash will be blocked to you."

There was a longish silence before Pete said, "You still scare the hell out of me, but you're right, I have a lot of banking to do in the next hour or two. Call me on my private number when you are on the way tonight."

He called Chris who answered cheerfully. "Hi Gary. What's up? We are going gangbusters here. I'm on my second load."

"That's fantastic, and I need the cash. I called because I need you to do a couple of things. First I need a tanker of gas delivered tonight to the Friendly Gas bar offices. What do you think is the best time to do it?"

"We should be there at 9:30 or 10," Chris opined.

"Great, I'll tell him," Gary said. "Do you normally go about armed these days?"

"Of course. Carrying this much cash, and having a valuable cargo, it would be insane to do otherwise."

"Good." Gary said. "The other thing is; you recall that wooden box you are storing for us? I need you to put it in an empty container, along with a lift truck, and deliver it to the

Operation Phoenix

Trambull space tomorrow morning. I'll also have another job for the driver. I'll be there at seven AM or shortly after."

"It'll cut into our gas sales you know?"

"I know, but this and the meeting tomorrow night are even more important than the money. It bugs me, but a guy has to do what a guy has to do," Gary said. "Besides, I gather the price of gas has gone up again, so more profit all around."

"Yeah, okay."

"There may be loads tomorrow night after the meeting, to the Friendly Gas bar, at a time of your choosing too."

He then turned his attention to Bruce Nott. "Bruce, my name is Gary Alden. Did Claude call you to say I would be calling?"

"Yes he did, and I am looking forward to meeting you." Bruce said.

"I was hoping, since I'm fairly close by at the docks, you might have a few minutes to go into our situation a little more fully now." Gary asked for, and received directions.

Half an hour later he was walking up the gangplank of a ship he had paid for and never seen. She looked smart and elegant, black with deep red bands and trim. She was clean, somewhat bigger than Gary had imagined, and looked well maintained. Claude had outdone himself in her purchase Gary thought. The paint of the old name had been chipped off, ready for the new name. Bruce, tall, fit and blond, met him and escorted him to the captain's stateroom, which was also immaculate.

"To a layman at least, she looks pretty smart, doesn't she?" Gary commented.

"Yes, and I love her already. Claude has been hinting that she might be mine to captain someday." Bruce was bursting with pride, but was obviously trying to remain modest.

Operation Phoenix

"The captaincy is strictly Claude's call, but there are other aspects that the rest of us might have an input on. So far we have been impressed. But that's why I am here, to discuss your future, not necessarily limited to the role of ship's captain," Gary said. "We all wish that we could have gone through regular procedures, and that Claude could have been the one to have this discussion with you. However, events are moving so quickly that we don't have even the 24 hours to get Claude back here."

"Sounds serious."

"It is. I guess I lied to you when I said I needed a few minutes with you. We really need several hours on a matter this significant, but I don't have that sort of time available, so don't let any question pass unasked," Gary instructed.

"I have nothing that cannot wait."

They got seated in the captain's cabin and Gary said, "I think the best way to begin is to review conditions as they are today, then see where this might logically lead. Finally, a bit about what we are planning so you can decide where you might fit in all of this. That doesn't mean that you, or we, will necessarily get to these goals, or that it will not be hard work, or with no risk. It is just an opportunity to get us reading from the same page, and to compare possible futures. This matter is strictly confidential between you and your wife. Okay?"

"That seems to be a reasonable way of going about it."

They agreed on the state of society in New York and the US; murder, starvation, desperation, mass exodus from the cities, and near anarchy. Bruce agreed that the forecast of worse to come was probable. Without referring directly to certain actions they had taken, such as purchasing gold, Gary gave Bruce a précis of what they had done to date. Finally, he came to the crux of the matter, and began to touch on the plan for the

Operation Phoenix

community and survival.

Bruce interrupted. "Everything you have said is logical, and on the surface is a great opportunity. In fact, it is overwhelming. I do have a couple of questions. Is Claude part of this?"

"Yes, aside from my own family, Claude was my very first recruit. The meeting we're planning for tomorrow night was for most of the ten people now in to get to know some new people, such as yourself, and to decide whether to invite them to join."

"I see." Bruce pondered. "You said I was unusual, and circumstances were forcing your hand. Why are you asking me specifically now, especially when you were planning your meeting with me as a regular attendee in 24 hours?"

"That is a very insightful, intelligent and reasonable question. It's also one I do not want to answer with a lot of specifics right now. Circumstances are forcing us to consider doing something that in normal times, if we were to get caught, would be considered illegal." Gary tried to choose his words carefully. "It is not so horrific as murder, however, we could all face jail in normal times. The final straw on the camels back was that there was no visible way the community could survive if we did not do something along these lines. Unfortunately, you are never just a little bit pregnant. When you are fighting for your life, you don't necessarily restrict yourself to Marquees of Queensbury rules, so we will fight for our community."

"So, something is happening now, like stealing or aiding and abetting stealing," Bruce surmised. "You need whatever you expect to be stolen, so you have decided to join that daisy chain. I take it I am needed in this daisy chain?"

"Not necessarily needed. I could have probably involved you without your specifically knowing, or dropped you

Operation Phoenix

completely. However, at its core, the community is about intelligent individuals having as many facts as are available, making a decision and dealing with the results, good or bad. We couldn't let you go into this blindfolded. We'll never have all the facts about any given situation, but members of the community deserve as many facts as possible. Yes, if you were to join us, you would be directly involved."

"And why can't you tell me now?"

Gary laughed. "The first law of secrets is to never tell. If you were a member of the community, you would have a need to know, and a voice. If you're not committed, it would be rather foolish of us to advertise our activities. Since you're a potential member, you need to have a good idea of how deep the water is that you are stepping into. We cannot risk the community and its goals totally, but consistent with our view that you deserve information that's pertinent to a very important decision in your life, you must know that something exists. The less honourable way would be to let you proceed blindly, and then feel that you had been sandbagged. I'm giving some, but not all, potentially damaging information to you, so that I at least, feel comfortable that you realize the magnitude of the actions you might undertake. It's an attempt to balance all the factors, and that never happens perfectly, but we're trying to do the right thing by you."

"Yes, I can see that, and it says a lot about you." Bruce paused to think. "With the caveats that I have limited information, and that I want to consult my wife, I'm ready to join. I believe my wife is ready for change. In fact she's scared stiff. I would prefer she and the children were on board ship with me, especially if we were out to sea. I think I can say with ninety percent certainty that I'm committed."

"I think some more information is in order, but first a

couple of questions. Where do you live, and what does your wife work at?"

"I live quite near Claude. There are quite a number of marine officer 'widows' in that area. My wife's a teacher," Bruce responded.

"We should have had an armed guard at your house with all the crime around. That was a bad mistake. If your decision is to join us, I think you having your family move in here is great. We can provide a container, and your wife can hire someone she knows to help her pack and load the container. Same with the rest of the crew. The streets are becoming a jungle, so we may be shipping out rather earlier than we had expected. By the way, are you and the crew armed?"

"No, but I do have something that could be used as a gun safe," Bruce decided.

"Well, for the moment, I want you personally, and at least one security person armed at all times. I gather you have no arms on board? I'll bring some tomorrow. Before you leave tonight, I want you to give orders to prepare the ship to be moved to the container loading area some time after ten tomorrow morning, upon my order. If you decide not to join us, or can't make up your mind, don't bother to come in. Claude will land in Toronto tomorrow morning. I'm sending someone to drive him down," Gary said. "Who's in charge in your absence?"

"Jim Blanc will be duty officer tomorrow till 1500 hours."

"Who recruited him, you or Claude?"

"Claude. He recruited all but two, and he told me who he wanted. You're being rather blunt aren't you? If I am not going to join, stay home." Bruce sounded rather hurt.

"Well, if you don't join, you're rejecting the whole idea. However, if you have not decided, don't come in. I don't want

Operation Phoenix

you involved should you then decide 'no'. I'm sorry if I was blunt, I'm just in a hurry. I haven't closed the door to further discussions. When I asked who chose the guys, I assumed Claude knew he was recruiting potential community members. You couldn't have known. Your wife being a teacher enhances you as a family. We're going to need education, particularly for the children. She'll need whatever teaching supplies she can find, particularly textbooks."

"You said something about 'not necessarily related to my role as a ships captain'. What did you mean?" Bruce asked.

"Looking back in history, every time an empire or society has fallen, and that's definitely what is happening here, the people who did best during and after the collapse were the traders, particularly those with available transport. In sailing ship days, aside from warships, how were ships used? Almost exclusively for hauling goods that someone had picked up cheap at point 'A', because they were plentiful, and hauling them to point 'B' where they were in short supply and therefore expensive. If a common currency was not available, they traded their expensive goods at 'B' for something that was in large supply at 'B' and hauled it to 'A' where it was in short supply. In those days, usually the captain owned a percentage of the cargo, and each seaman was allowed space for a barrel to transport goods for him to trade."

"So how does that fit here? Why would a captain be important?" Bruce frowned.

"Since no one knew for sure exactly what conditions they'd find at a new port, the only judgment as to what might be profitable was the guy on the spot, reacting to those conditions. That was often the ship's captain, although it could be a professional trader or the owner. That's why the captain often owned a percentage of the cargo. It was a great incentive to select profitable goods to trade. He had to be smart, imaginative, and effective at getting to his goals regardless of the circumstances."

"Why do you think that I have those skills? I've never done any trading." Bruce asked.

"Any leader has to make many decisions in the absence of hard data. He will make mistakes, but they had better not be big ones, because the first rule is to survive. I think you are a long way from being 'there', but I think you have the potential. There's no crystal ball to tell us what the future will bring, but these same qualities, smart, imaginative, and adaptable will serve well to cope with whatever does come up."

"When would I start this?" Bruce looked concerned.

"We're not offering you anything yet but a seat on this ship, not even a captaincy. You have to be smart and aggressive enough to earn more. Right now you're one of very damned few being offered such a seat. The rest is up to you," Gary replied.

"I want to be on this ship," Bruce said grimly. "The question is whether giving up extended family is too big a price to pay."

"That's surely one of the most difficult questions possible. I'm sure that being away from a heavily populated area such as New York is best for your wife and children, again because of crime. As to your extended family, a rough rule of thumb might be; any skills necessary to survival in the 18th century, or the 4th century AD are likely to be essential basics today. The only exception to that is application of modern technology. Claude's children are doctors and dentists. We're going to need medical facilities, and we must keep and use that knowledge, or we'll regress towards the 4th century."

"Both my parents and my wife's parents are farmers, as are some of our siblings," Bruce exclaimed.

Operation Phoenix

"We certainly need those skills to be self sufficient. Put forward their qualifications for a skills assessment. What we cannot afford is to support idle, non-productive hands while we're building. Starting from scratch will take more energy and resources than we have. We do put more weight on people of childbearing age, although some with suitable experience, like Claude, are beyond that. In addition we'll need genetic diversity. Hopefully, we are going to be pretty isolated. Farmers are definitely a possibility. Do you have any other questions? I am running late."

"The minute you get out the door, I will have about a million, but right now I am just dealing with an information overload," Bruce confessed.

"Okay, call me on my cell anytime, but let me know before eight AM tomorrow whether you are in or not. I'll be on the road, and then I have to come down here after that. Give orders about the ship tonight in case you're not in. I expect Claude to be here very late tomorrow, but he'll be rather jet lagged. I, or Claude, can talk with you later."

They stood up, and shook hands before Gary left.

Chapter 28

Gary drove directly home. The clear warm weather made the roads nearly dry, and pedestrians, transporting goods in every imaginable way out of the city, was a slowly moving mass of locusts looking for food. At first Gary had made the mistake of slowing down to avoid people on the highway, but when he had to pull his gun to move someone blocking his path, he increased his speed to make it clear he would not be able to stop in time, and they scattered when he leaned on his horn. Thank god, it was a paved highway, with few sizable rocks, because a car with fuel obviously contained a hated bureaucrat with fuel, and a few threw whatever they could get their hands on. Most just lethargically shuffled along in dirty fatigue and hunger.

As Gary arrived, so did Wayne to pick up Patti. The yard was full of cars. Gary entered and said, "Hi everybody. Come on in Wayne." Wayne introduced Gary to Patti. Patti was slim, about five foot seven with her brown hair styled quite short.

"Patti," Gary smiled, "I'm so glad you made it safely. And to have you see us at our worst cannot be impressive. Believe me, it is not always this bad. Sometimes it's worse," he grinned. "You'll have to wait a few minutes while we try to get headed in a common direction." Turning to Jim, he said, "You must be Jim. Have you met Patti?"

"Yes I know Petty Officer Wagner quite well."

"Patti, have you met my daughter Lynn? - Lynn, if you haven't already started something, could you get a bite to eat for Patti? She's had a long drive," Gary said. "Patti, could you give Lynn a hand while Wayne, Eric and I have a quick meeting to bring each other up to date? Jim, if I can persuade both you and Wayne, I have a rush job for Toronto tonight." He led the way

Operation Phoenix

into the office.

Behind the closed door, he described his moral limbo bar question, and asked for reactions and suggestions.

Wayne said, "Is there any other way we could do this?"

Eric answered, "Have you looked at the streets lately? Power is out in many places. Fires rage unattended. The whole city would be aflame if the winter was not stopping the fire from jumping block to block. Telephone landlines are out in a majority of areas and cell phones are starting to fail. Houses and factories are abandoned and looting is endemic. People are walking out of the city to try to get to a rural area where there is food. I don't even see that we will have time to do what we need to."

"One way or another, what is at the docks is going to be stolen?" Wayne asked.

"This guy was so blatant with his demand for a bribe, it's sure to go to anyone who meets his price," Gary said. "Do you see any alternative?"

"No, I don't, which is why I asked the question," Wayne said. "There is an old adage, 'If you are going to lose a battle, don't be there when it starts, but check what you have to lose first'. It appears that we might lose it all if we don't do this thing."

"Okay, I will have to run this by Lynn," Gary said. "Claude and I thought you might vote this way, so we decided to start the induction process with Bruce Nott, the guy he left in charge of the ship. We have to start loading that ship, and we couldn't let him walk into this blindfolded. If his wife is onside, he is aboard. Wayne, we will discuss Patti after you leave, and I'll call you later. We might be able to induct her and Jim."

"I have worked with Jim and I vote for him," Eric said.

Wayne said, "I may have to drive down as far as Langley

Operation Phoenix

in my recruiting drive. I could be gone as long as Saturday."

"If Patti comes aboard, maybe you should consider taking her along. She may have some stuff to pick up. By the way, I found out that her parents are tobacco farmers. They might be useful if they are active and have seeds and equipment. Play it by ear. This is your field, but we do need farmers, just younger ones. - Any other comments? Okay, let's get back to our guests." As they exited the office, Gary noticed that Lynn and Patti were sharing a laugh.

Gary approached Jim, "As I said Jim, I have a rush job for Toronto. I know it makes for a long day but I have Claude coming in from Singapore. He lands in about 12 or 13 hours from now. It appears there are no planes flying into New York not even from Canada. He has to get back here urgently. Could I could get you to go and pick him up?"

"Sure."

"Great," Gary said. "I have to get you some money and I also owe Patti some expenses. Let's go talk to her." They went over to Patti who was chatting with Lynn.

"Patti, Jim here has to make a make a quick run up to Toronto to pick someone up. I have to get him some money. How much do I owe you?" Gary asked.

"Nothing, really."

"Come on. Did you get stopped by any roadblocks?" Gary asked.

"Two."

"So really, how much did you spend total?" Gary asked again.

"Maybe a hundred bucks."

"How much is fuel in Canada?" Gary continued.

"$2.79 a litre. I was paying $1.34 when I arrived."

"There's about four litres per gallon isn't there?" Gary

mused. "So three bucks times four is eleven or twelve dollars per gallon. It is pushing $50 a gallon here."

"I put 35 litres in to fill up."

"Did you pay a bribe to get through customs?" Gary asked.

"No but I was really stupid there. They asked me if I was carrying any Canadian dollars and I told them the truth, despite you having warned me," Patti grimaced. "I thought small amounts wouldn't be seized. They confiscated over $200 that I had."

"Okay, I want you to brief Jim on any problems he might encounter on his trip, and I'll get some cash," Gary said. He turned to Lynn and said, "Would you come into the office for a moment please?"

Once behind closed doors, he again explained his moral limbo bar question, and was again met with the question 'Is there any other way it can be done?'

"When you are standing looking at a judge, it's always obvious that there was another way. But, no, given the speed with which things are going to hell, I don't see any other way, and I don't think the community will succeed unless we have most of this equipment and supplies. We could probably get only a small percentage through the normal channels now, but I don't see us having the time available to stay in New York, even if the dock workers were not organizing to steal wholesale."

"A judge. That could be a serious distraction." Lynn said.

"You can always go to jail for stealing, or receiving stolen goods."

"You always taught us to be honest and do the honourable thing." Lynn frowned.

"That's why I raised the question. This is a moral issue. The question is whether survival is a higher moral issue. It's

Operation Phoenix

also true that some things are worth dying for. The question is; 'Is this one of them'?"

"Honour: the best of all the lost values. If only there was money in it. I suppose you can't be very moral if you are dead." Lynn changed the subject. "We are expecting to close the hospital deal on Thursday. Final price, $600,000 for well over $20 million in equipment."

"Fantastic. I'll have to scrape up some money."

Lynn left.

Thinking about Canadian dollars for Patti and Jim, Gary suddenly wondered what the exchange rate was. He got on the Internet to find quotes for gold, silver, and foreign exchange. His favourite US sites seemed to be down, showing 00 00 across the board. To get a quote for the silver he owed Wayne, he went to a German site that would likely have a quote in Euros. The quote would probably not be very accurate, because they would be giving out the official line, not the probably rapidly developing black market. Sure enough, silver was quoted at 157 Euros per ounce. Gold was shown at 3,723 Euros per ounce. He frowned. *"Gold and silver have both run up nicely, but I expected more percentage-wise from silver."*

He switched to the foreign exchange screen, and finally had his epiphany, although it took him a while to realize it. On the US to Euro quotation, there was no bid for US dollars, anywhere. US dollars were being offered at 4,380 dollars for one Euro. Last trade was 4,380, but there was no way of telling when that trade had occurred.

Let's see. Gold at 3,723 Euros, times 4,380 dollars per Euro makes $16,306,740 US per ounce. Good lord, 16 million dollars an ounce. He chewed on his tongue for a minute thinking about this.

Okay, lets look at crude oil. The price of a barrel of oil

Operation Phoenix

was around $150 a barrel, or about 110 Euros a couple of weeks ago. Start with crude oil; if oil was $150 per barrel, then the equivalent price due to dollar devaluation today would be 4380 times $150 equals $657,000 per barrel. And that's only if the Saudi's are willing to take even more useless dollars at the current rate.

We were paying about $4 per gallon for gas at the pump. Using these same mathematics, we should now be paying $4 times 4380 equals $8,760 per gallon. Pete at the Friendly gas bar doesn't know how good a deal he is getting tonight. I guess you won't be getting a ship full of fuel, Pete. The population can thank their lucky stars we still have a fair amount of domestic oil production to maintain this fantasy, and Pete can thank his lucky stars I need US dollars for something even more important.

He pulled up the commodities screen, to see what crude was selling for, and blinked. Crude was quoted at 41.75 Euros per barrel, not near 110 Euros where it had been prior to the crash. He suddenly knew why. Before the crash the US was a big user of oil, and oil was in short supply around the world, so the price was rising over 110 Euros per barrel. Now the US still wanted to buy crude, but couldn't buy fuel because of the dollar crash, whether it would like to or not. So now there is a glut of oil in markets all around the world, except in the US. The price for the rest of the world had actually gone down.

It's strange no one has mentioned with this. Maybe they did, but I haven't been paying any attention to the news, if indeed any news outlets in the US are still functioning. I don't recall receiving a newspaper recently, come to think of it. With people abandoning the cities en masse, I doubt many people in the US are diverting their attention away from survival to read the news anyway, so few will know. Outside the US, few would

Operation Phoenix

know that the dollar was still quite valuable in New York. Of those few, who might have the right resources, or the inclination to travel to New York to take advantage of it?

So, how could use this information to his advantage? A trader finds something that is relatively cheap, at point "A", transports to point "B" where it is relatively valuable, and trades it for something that is relatively cheap there to bring back to point "A", where the new product is relatively valuable

If I could get 10 ounces of silver over to Switzerland and sell it for 1570 Euros, and then exchange it for US dollars at around 5,000 dollars per Euro, I'd have about seven million dollars. With all the bills coming up in the next few days, a million plus for bribes, and over half a million for the hospital, that sure would be helpful.

The big problem was getting the money back to the US. There was no way he was going to get cash back into the US without it being seized as potential drug money. Getting the silver to Switzerland should be no big problem. He didn't think it was illegal to own silver yet, and ten ounces was small, even if he had to smuggle it. Or he could use an ounce of gold he already had over there. Never mind silver or gold, he already had Euros cash over there. He didn't even need to get the silver over there. He couldn't use the banks here; they would probably be on holiday by tomorrow. And anyway he didn't think you could trust wire transfers, even if they theoretically would be done in an hour. He was boxed in because he couldn't get legal money into the country.

Gary pondered for a time. *How did drug people move large quantities of cash around?* He really didn't know, but the stories he had heard always involved either crooked bank employees, or shipping it in among some other legitimate goods. With little or no air or ocean transport coming into New York,

Operation Phoenix

smuggling among other goods was pretty well out. Not only that but the events Gary anticipated made him leery of holding US cash for more than hours at a time. Shipping by boat would take days or weeks. The banks were pretty non-functional so they were out. You can't drive to Switzerland so you can't smuggle it out that way. You can't charter a jet because few, if any, private jets had the range for a round trip, although one might be able to refuel in Canada.

His thoughts ran around in circles, but something was nagging at him. Finally, he decided to give it a rest and let his subconscious work on it for a while. Besides, he had guests to take care of, so he dug some cash out of his safe.

He went out and gave Patti $300 Canadian and $2000 US, to include the pistol she had purchased. She thanked him.

He gave Jim $700 Canadian, and $5,000 US. "You might have some problems at the border with cash. I would stash about $500 Canadian and $4,000 US in various spots in the upholstery or something, so if you lose some of it, you lose it, and you can do your job anyway. Don't try to spend the US dollars in Canada, it won't work, and might draw attention to you. You shouldn't have all that much problem at the border. Come on and give me a hand. I have a barrel of fuel in the garage. We will wrestle it toward the front so we can tank everybody up."

Patti decided to come too. She backed her car up first, and they fuelled it, followed by Lynn's car, Wayne's, Jim's Gary's, Eric's, Claude's, and the two armed guards outside.

While they were fuelling the guard's cars, Gary asked, "You guys live in Jersey?" One said yes, the other, no. To the one who said yes, Gary said, "I am going to split you up. I don't want a second guard here tomorrow. I want you to guard a house that I do not have the address for yet, but it is near the one you were guarding up till today. I want 24/7 coverage on that

Operation Phoenix

family. Okay?"

"Okay."

Gary turned back to the barrel, and Patti was busy pumping gas with the hand pump. *Not afraid to get your hands dirty, are you lady? I'll bet there are few things you are afraid to tackle,* he thought. Aloud, he thanked her. They got the barrel back in the garage easily, since it was nearly empty. Gary offered up a small, silent but heartfelt prayer of thanks to Eric who had been busy labouring in the background, picking up details such as gas hand pumps and other supplies, and then to Lynn who had been working as hard as either Eric or Gary on her hospital and pharmaceuticals assignment.

Back in the house, Gary got two cell phones, two pistols, shoulder holsters, body armour, ammo, and some sealable plastic bags. He presented them to Jim. "I want you armed whenever it is possible to be. You will not be able to get the arms into Canada so don't try. They'll just be confiscated. You'll have to hide them in a culvert or something this side of the border, and pick them up on the way back. One is for you and one is for Claude. Do you drink coffee?"

"Show me a SEAL who doesn't."

Gary began to make a huge pot of coffee and found a large thermos on the shelves under the counter. He started making up some sandwiches. "Patti, are the restaurants open in Canada?"

"Pretty much."

"Okay Jim don't forget to stock up with food for the return trip. Do you need anything else?" Gary asked.

"I'd rather take my own pistol if you don't mind."

"By all means. Whatever you feel comfortable with. Handle this as you see fit. I just noticed I am getting all uptight about one thing, and blindly trampling on everybody and everything else. I say you are on your own but nit-pick on

Operation Phoenix

details. Sorry. The object is to pick up Claude and get both of you back here safely, as quick as humanly possible. What do you need to do that job?" Gary asked contritely.

"A road map?"

"I have one," said Patti. "I'll get it."

"Anything else you need?" asked Gary.

"No I'll change clothes and get started. That seems like a lot of cash for a simple trip to Toronto."

"I'd rather you had too much rather than not enough to do the job. Here is my card with phone numbers on it. Don't hesitate to call at any time. You should probably use the cell numbers, land lines are failing a lot. I'd feel more comfortable if you have a chance to call me after you have connected with Claude and have an idea what your itinerary back is going to be."

"Okay will do," and Jim went to his kitbag to prepare.

"Anybody else for coffee? Wayne? Patti?" Gary asked. "I'll make another pot."

Patti looked at Wayne in enquiry. Wayne said, "I'll take a pound or two of that coffee if you don't mind. I'm out."

"No problem, but we will have to conserve because I only stored supplies for one person for a year and now we have about ten coffee hounds slurping it. I hope to get more this week but it's far from sure at this minute," Gary said. "You're leaving too?"

"Yes, I have a lot of things to do before I can sleep," Wayne said. Gary went to get the coffee. Good byes and good lucks were exchanged before the SEALs left.

The family gathered in the living room. Gary said to them, "I just had an epiphany," and he described the silver price and US dollar price in Euros situation. "The problem is, I can't figure a way to get the US cash back here from Switzerland to

Operation Phoenix

spend it here where its value is greater."

Lynn cocked her head and said, "How about Canada?"

Gary went blank for about half a second and then exploded. "Oh, for Christ's sake. It's so simple and so perfect. Lynn it's brilliant. Canadians will probably have a lot more US cash on hand than even Switzerland. I was beginning to worry how much gas we would have to sell to meet our commitments. Perfect. By the way, what do you think of Patti?"

"I like her. She is smart and fun. I think she would make an excellent addition to the community."

Gary then raced for Jan's house. After kissing her perfunctorily, he immediately asked her, "I'm only here for a few minutes. I need to talk to you about two things. First, Wayne thinks I need a bodyguard because I am zapping about with valuables, and among some pretty dangerous people. He has proposed a very smart lady SEAL. Before accepting, I wanted to check with you. How do you feel about me working in close proximity with another female?"

"How long would it be for?" Jan asked.

"Good question," Gary said, realizing that the most intense period would be while they were still in New York. Later, at the community, Patti would not be needed as a guard and would also have other things to occupy her. "I would guess from one to four weeks, likely about two. I am starting to feel better about this already."

"I trust you, and I don't see any harm in a short-term arrangement. Why does Wayne think she would be best?" Jan asked.

"Wayne said she had the best chance of keeping up with my mind in the variety of situations I get into. Personally, I think he also feels she would be a modifying influence when I get tired and hungry and bitchy."

Operation Phoenix

"I think he's probably right about that. Go ahead."

"The other thing I need is some help with foreign exchange. I'm interested in Canadian dollar versus the Euro. Can we get on the net for a moment?" Gary asked. Jan tapped into her bank's foreign exchange network and found a quote; 3.25 Canadian dollars per Euro. The quote for the US dollar against the Euro remained the same; 4380 US dollars per Euro, still no bid for dollars. The former trillion US dollar per day market was trading zilch. "The Euro's strong against the Canadian dollar too!" he exclaimed.

"Yes," said Jan. "But that's reasonable. The Canadian dollar was always viewed as having features that were something of a proxy to the US dollar. Some of our mud has rubbed off on them too."

If the US dollar is 4380 per Euro, and the Canadian dollar is 3.25 per Euro, then the Canadian dollar against the US dollar would be 4380 divided by 3.25, or about 1350 US dollars for 1 Canadian dollar. Theoretically, one could get 1.3 million US dollars for 1,000 Canadian dollars. "Do you know anyone in Toronto or Montreal that is big in the cash foreign exchange market?" Gary asked.

"No, but Heidi in our foreign exchange department is forever going up there on correspondent banking business. She's even a member of the Canadian Foreign Exchange Traders club."

"You sound like you know her well."

"Yeah, we chum around a lot together," Jan shrugged. "She was the trader who I was on the phone with when you purchased gold."

"Can you call her up to see what's happening at the old homestead, and at the same time pick her brains for a couple of people each in Toronto and Montreal who might be able to put a

Operation Phoenix

sizable stash of US cash together on short notice?" Gary asked.

"How big a stash, and how short a notice?"

Gary considered. "Globally, I want to get as close to ten million as possible. I'll settle for as little as one million. I'll pay as much as $2,000 Canadian per million US, but she doesn't need to know that. $2,000 is twice the number we are seeing on the screen, and even that screen number is inflated. I want to be back here Friday morning latest."

"I know she doesn't need to know, but I'll have to have a believable story to cover what I need, otherwise she'll twig to it. She might anyway, she's a smart woman."

Gary considered. "I was going to say that I thought it wouldn't hurt if she twigged, but didn't act for a couple of days, but forex traders react in split seconds as a way of life. We have to find out who acts as a warehouse for the mom and pop foreign exchange dealers to buy from, at a minimum."

"I suppose I could develop a Canadian cousin who wants to buy because he thinks dollars will go up," Jan mused.

"Sounds like a plan to me. I'll be back late, probably around midnight. Is there anything you want, food or anything?"

"Yes, some chicken if you have it," Jan said.

"No problem," Gary said as he kissed her and rushed out. "See you later."

On the short run home, Gary called Wayne. "We voted on Patti and Jim, and both are 'in' if they want to be. I talked to Jan, and Patti is acceptable as a bodyguard until we get offshore at least. I think I've found a way to come up with some more US dollars, a few million. If you see something you want that is for sale, a stealth bomber for a million or something, check with me. We might be able to swing it, or perhaps trade for it. We probably have to buy another cargo ship. I'll know by Thursday night for sure. I may have to leave for Canada tomorrow night."

Operation Phoenix

He had no sooner gotten home than Jan called with the information about the movers and shakers in the cash foreign exchange markets at Toronto and Montreal, along with an introduction by Heidi, who thought that four to five million might be available in Toronto. Jan also imparted the information that almost all of her banks foreign exchange department had been laid off because foreign banks would neither deal with US banks nor would they consider any deal involving the purchase US dollars. The rumour was very strong that a bank holiday would be declared. Most US banks were insolvent and likely to close their doors. "Heidi is getting pretty desperate. I am going to give her some food."

"Okay, I'll get some rice, chicken, bread, powdered milk and beef for her. Maybe Lynn and Eric can deliver it over to you or her later," Gary said.

Gary dialled Chris's cell phone. "We didn't make plans on how we were going to hook up tonight. Something has come up. Could we do it at my place?"

"I don't like to stop the truck for any length of time, but I have wads of cash I'd like to get rid of. I'll stop by your house about nine?" Chris answered.

"Perfect, here at nine. I have to run up to the hangar and get some stuff. Anything you need? Bread? Rice? Meat?"

"All three. We are getting pretty desperate," Chris said. "It's dangerous to go shopping, and you can't find much, particularly protein foods. Thank god we live on what might be called a farm. We do have some things, so we're less desperate than city folk."

"How about Roy Bryant? Is his family in the same shape?"

Chris drew a deep breath. "Yes, I'm afraid he is. He's really badly off."

Operation Phoenix

"Okay, I'll think of him too. See you around nine," and Gary hung up.

Gary went back out to join the others. "I'm really tight for time. Eric, if I drop some food off at nine, would you take Jan and maybe Lynn to go over to Heidi's to drop it off?"

Eric nodded.

"Okay I gotta hop," and Gary left for the hangar, where he stuffed the car with four cases of chicken, eight large pot roasts, bags of rice, and as many bags of powdered milk and bread as he could get into the car. He called Roy Bryant.

"It's Gary. I wanted to know if you were home. I have a couple of things to drop off."

Roy sounded puzzled but said "Sure". Gary did not enlighten him but said he would be over in a few minutes. Gary hadn't thought about how cold driving a car full of frozen goods might be. The pile of stuff sitting on the passenger seat beside him seemed especially cold. Every time he turned the steering wheel, he somehow managed to bang some bare skin on something frozen.

At Roy's house which was set back from his Quonset hut garage, he grabbed a case of chicken and went to the door. Roy answered. Gary walked in, and Roy eyed the case. "Whatcha got there?" he asked.

"Where's the kitchen?" demanded Gary. "This stuff is frozen, and it's cold. I thought you could use it."

Roy pointed as both he and his wife watched in puzzlement. Roy's wife was a light brown as Gary thought a Peruvian should be.

"Back in a sec," said Gary as he hurried back outside. This time he came back in with a tray of bread with two pot roasts on top. As he entered the kitchen and started unloading the trays, Roy said, "Is that frozen chicken like the box says?"

Operation Phoenix

"Yep," Gary said. "Back in a sec," as he hurried outside with the tray. The children stared curiously as he returned with a bag of powdered milk. On the next trip he brought a bag of rice.

"It's like god answered our prayers," Roy's wife said. "We're at our lowest point ever." She was nearly in tears.

"Are you sure you can spare this?" Roy said.

"Oh yeah, I bought it with this kind of situation in mind. I'm sorry I didn't get a larger range of stuff, but time was very short then. Dried potatoes and freeze-dried food would have been good. Are you guys coming to the meeting tomorrow night?"

"I'm coming with Chris Habel, who seems to have some fuel left." Roy answered. "I didn't know our wives were invited too." Roy's wife began opening the case of chicken to peer inside.

"Oh yes, we much prefer the wives be along, but we also understand that leaving the kids alone and unprotected in today's world is foolish. Well, I gotta hop."

"Wait, wait," Roy's wife said. "How can we ever thank you? Won't you sit down for a while?"

"Roy has been thanking me, well, ever since I met him by doing a superlative job of looking out for my interests. It's my turn to look out after his interests. I really have to go. I have a lot to do before bedtime. See you tomorrow night."

Gary dropped a similar load at Chris' house before racing home to find Chris waiting for him. Chris thankfully handed over $58,800, and allowed as to how it would likely be more tomorrow since the price of fuel had already gone up to over $50 per gallon. Gary then followed Chris down to the Friendly Gas Bar offices.

Pete dipped the tanks, sniffed the dipstick, did a couple of simplistic tests, such as pouring a bit into a jam bottle lid and

Operation Phoenix

igniting it. He got a satisfying whoosh. He also did a couple of other tests that Gary didn't understand, but in the end he seemed satisfied.

Pete showed why he was so successful in business. With only a few hours to bank closing, he had somehow managed to pick up a substantial portion of his bank balance in cash and wanted the three trailers of fuel delivered tonight. Gary and Chris huddled and compromised by delivering two tonight and one tomorrow. Chris dropped the first load and immediately hustled off for the second. Just over an hour later he was back and Pete handed over another $360,000 in cash.

In the midst of all this, Bruce called to say that they were on board.

After Gary returned home, laden with cash, he found Eric and Lynn still up waiting for him. Gary dumped his cash in the office and came back out, wondering at the nervous body language of both Eric and Lynn.

"Dad," Eric began, and Gary's antennae shot straight up, because he and Eric tended to treat each other as equals, and Eric almost never addressed him as 'Dad'. "I think we've found someone we should think of for the community. We took some food over to Heidi, and that is one smart lady. She's an electrical engineer and a computer programmer."

Lynn interrupted, "You should see her light art. She uses computer-controlled lasers to paint with light. It's amazing. I've never seen anything like it."

"An imaginative artist, electrical engineer, and computer hotshot combined sounds good to me." Gary knew that many banks automatically short-listed anyone with an artistic 'inventive' ability, so this combination did not surprise him. He frowned. "I do see one problem. She and Jan are friends. We can't bring her in to the community without my settling Jan one way or another. It sounds strange, but I really do want more children. Jan and I seem to get along well. It's early days, but I think I love her. We haven't got much more time, so it is decision time, I guess. I'll let you know tomorrow."

Gary left for Jan's, deep in thought. In the end, like most of humanity, he convinced himself of the rightness of doing what he wanted to do anyway. He sensed that Jan had her warts which he now found endearing but probably wouldn't later. He knew that if he didn't do this mad, impetuous thing, right or wrong, he would wonder and regret it all his life. He wondered if Eric were doing the same thing with Heidi. He seemed to be very anxious to bring her aboard. If so, Heidi must be an exceptional lady. Eric tended to be conservative and very selective around the opposite sex.

Arriving at Jan's, he found her curled up in her negligee, working on some bank papers while waiting for him. She put that aside as they prepared for bed. In bed, assuming their usual spoon positions, Gary began rather abruptly. "Could you take living with my kids? You'd become an instant mother without all that trouble. But then you wouldn't have all the fun that goes with it either," he grinned.

"Yes, I like Eric and Lynn. They are fun people. Having them around will be fun, and the situation is dangerous and demands it," she said.

"And how do you think about making your own kids?" he asked.

"I already told you that I would like to have three. Oh, are you proposing to me?"

"Well, I do think that young children need a stable family atmosphere with a mother and a father. Usually that's best accomplished by getting it right legally," he grinned.

"I suppose we could always get one of your other kids to

baby-sit."

"I doubt that. Lynn would likely tell us very early on that she doesn't do babysitting," he grinned. "But you're doing this all wrong. You are supposed to say, 'Oh, yes, yes, yes'."

"Oh, yes, yes, yes," she laughed, turning over, putting her arms around his neck and giving him a chaste kiss.

Gary felt overwhelmed, and began rubbing her ribs. They consummated the deal, but for some strange reason she was not as passionate as usual. Gary put it down to the lateness of the hour and the tension in the atmosphere. Later, he invited her to the induction meeting before falling asleep.

Operation Phoenix

Chapter 29
Tuesday March 7th ¾ Day 22

Gary was up by six, leaving Jan to sleep. The first thing he did on arriving home was to check for a fax from the bank in Switzerland that he had phoned. His immediate interest was the bank report on the price of precious metals. Silver was quoted at 171 Euros, rather than the 157 shown on the website. Dividing Wayne's 250,000 euros by 171 came out to approximately 1462 ounces.

After a quick shower, shave, and breakfast he and Eric left for the Trambull space. They opened the office safe and moved aside the gold that Eric had been delivering from the clunker cars, and pulled out 4000 ounces of silver, of which 1750 was for Wayne. They put the 4,000 ounces of silver in bags, replaced the gold, relocked the safe and re-disguised it with the tarp. The Habel driver arrived and backed a container containing the boxed safe that had been stored, and a forklift truck, up to the dock. The driver used the forklift to bring the box out. Gary sent him for another container, just to get him out of the way.

They opened the boxed safe and removed the last of the money from their stock market days. Gary managed to stuff an additional 900 ounces of silver into the boxed safe, and they relocked, and re-boxed it. Using the forklift, they moved the office safe and the box into the container, followed by the office furniture, tied it all down and covered it with the tarp. Except for the forklift truck, the space was now empty.

The Habel driver returned and backed the second empty

Operation Phoenix

container up to the dock, and then hooked up to the first container containing the office safe. Gary locked and sealed the doors of the first container, and the driver left to drop the container at Habels storage. Chris would yank it over to the hangars later. Gary immediately left for home with the money and 3100 ounces of silver. Eric stayed to move the forklift truck into the second container. When the driver returned, Eric and the driver would pick up the two other publicly-stored, boxed safes, drop the forklift back at Habels, and finally drop the container in Gary's yard at home. Gary would immediately begin loading the container with whatever boxes had been packed in his house, covering the boxed safes.

All this time the guard, who was hopefully guarding the front window side of the space at least, had not challenged them. Gary wondered if he was sleeping, but was not going to disturb him in any way. There was no point in having anyone unnecessary know that he had visited and possibly removed something. That lack of knowledge might muddy the trail a bit if someone came snooping around later.

Once Gary was home, he counted his cash. The total now was $1,070,000 US. He took the one million, arranged it in gym bags, and loaded it in the trunk of the car, leaving him with about $70,000 US for other needs. He also had about 70,000 in foreign cash, primarily Canadian dollars. He pulled out some pistols, ammo, shoulder holsters, soft body armour, and satellite and cell phones to put in the car. As he was doing this, Patti arrived, looking very business-like in a jacket and slacks. Her shoulder holster was not very noticeable, but on closer inspection, it seemed somewhat larger than usual. Probably a machine pistol whose cartridge case would make it quite bulky. "Are you wearing body armour too?" Gary asked.

"Of course."

Operation Phoenix

"Great. Anything else you need?"

"Just the plan."

"Well, first we're going down to the docks with a million dollars in the trunk to try and bribe someone to steal about 1000 containers of goods for us. We, the whole community, had a very big moral problem with actually doing this after it was offered. In the end, we decided that since the theft was already underway, and our whole project would fall apart without those supplies, it was critical. But I still feel uncomfortable with that," Gary said.

Just then the phone rang. "Gary, it is Claude. We've had a couple of hours sleep and are across the border. We've picked up our arms and are on the way."

"Fantastic. We've been missing you. You did a superlative job in Singapore. I'm afraid I may have another assignment for you. If everything works out, we may need another one or two ships. Something for you to think about on the way down," Gary teased. "By the way, the present community voted on Jim, your driver, and he's in if he wants to be. If you get a chance to induct him, do it. Anything you need?"

"Nothing extra 24 or 48 hours a day wouldn't cure. You're hard task master. More suitable ships are going to be hard to find. Not many good ships are sitting around empty."

"Not me bro, not me. I'm not the hard taskmaster, you are. You came up with this Singapore thing. It's all your fault. If you weren't so damned good, we would not be where we are. You are awesome," Gary enthused and hung up.

Gary turned to Patti. "Let's get those cars exchanged in the garage." They left for the docks, with Patti driving. Gary dialled Jack Sopper, the harbourmaster. "Good morning. It's Gary Alden. I spoke with you yesterday. Do you recall?"

"Indeed I do," Jack was all syrupy.

Operation Phoenix

Jesus, he's greasy even on the phone, Gary thought. Aloud he said, "I promised to call you today. I can be in your area in about an hour to discuss this matter more fully with you. Will you be able to see me?"

"Certainly, certainly. It would be my pleasure," Jack gushed.

"I'll have the guard at the gate call you when I get in."

"Good, good. I look forward to it. See you then," Jack said effusively.

A problem that had crossed Gary's mind a number of times resurfaced. Turning to Patti he said, "Tell me, how conversant are you with hostage situations?"

"I've been involved in a couple. I've had extensive training. Why?"

Gary frowned. "In the present circumstances, it's only a matter of time until someone gets kidnapped. It'll be our growth industry. We all need some training in what to do in a hostage situation. Can you set up a course to cover what to expect, how to act, and how to avoid becoming a hostage, both as a hostage and as a negotiator?"

"Sure. Wayne's picking up the rest of my stuff. I have several texts. I think it's a good idea. I'd love to," Patti said. "I think we should also consider SERE courses, Survival, Evasion, Resistance, and Escape, which are really part of that problem."

"Good, we'll do that as quickly as possible," Gary said, and devoted the rest of the trip to comparing his list of containers on the dock to the list Jack Sopper had given him, as well as selecting additional containers of interest. Of course some would now be empty with all the theft going on. On the other hand, almost any full container had value, and Gary had eliminated many as simply being 'too much'.

The day was sunny, bright and warm, they were mostly

Operation Phoenix

traveling the back roads to avoid the mass of humanity making its way out of the city on the highways. By and large this worked. The few pedestrians on the streets tended to stay on the sidewalk. They were making relatively good time till they came upon a man kneeling in front of a kind of shrine he had erected in the middle of the street. He had pasted pictures of food and various creature comforts such as plasma TVs over the shrine, and was kneeling in front of it, arms raised, praying incoherently but loudly to some god or another. They edged past, driving on the sidewalk to do so.

"If he keeps screaming at that volume, he won't have a voice-box left in an hour." Gary and Patti looked at each other, shook their heads and got on with it. The world was becoming weirder by the minute.

At the dock guardhouse Gary went in to see his 'consultant' guard, who reported that about 40 trucks carrying containers had gone out the previous evening. Gary pulled out $40, which disappeared quickly. He and Patti drove on to the parking lot. Gary decided that Patti should stay with the car, first because Jack would likely object to witnesses, and secondly because of their cash cargo.

Patti shook her head. "A million dollar cash cargo. No wonder Wayne wanted me guarding you."

"Hopefully by tomorrow, we will be carrying much more than that," Gary observed laconically.

Surprisingly, the negotiations with Jack were very simple. Strangely amateurish Gary thought. They settled on a cost per container loaded. Jack demanded $1,300 per container because he would have to pay off the dock foreman. Gary opined that the union boss was Jack's problem, but he settled at $1,200 per container. Jack wanted an upfront payment, which Gary refused because he neither understand, nor trusted the process Jack was proposing. Jack wondered how he could be sure Gary was sincere and suggested that a quarter of a million would be an expression of good faith. Again Gary refused, but offered to show Jack that he had the cash.

They walked outside to the car. "Would you pop the trunk, please?" he asked Patti. He unzipped the three mid-sized gym bags, laying bare their contents. Jack actually drooled briefly. "One million dollars," he breathed.

"Exactly one million," Gary said, picking up a pack of $50 bills and handed it to Jack. "The rest will be delivered later. I don't think we can get a thousand containers on the first ship anyway, so we'll have to send another, as soon as the first is clear of US waters."

"Okay, you've got a deal," Jack confirmed breathlessly. He ran his fingers over the other packs lovingly. In fact, he was so reluctant to part with the pack of bills in his hand that Gary insisted he count it, as part of the amount for the first containers.

"If you can clear a berth for my 25,000 ton ship, most or all of this can be in your possession as soon as you get it loaded, with more to come. Hopefully this ship will be loaded within 24 hours," Gary said, "and then we can get the next one in. That will take some time. I'll have to check."

"I'll have space cleared right away. How long will you be?" Jack asked.

"I would hope not as much as three hours. The ship is in the supply and repair facility. I need to get two copies of my list, which shows the containers I have as highest priority. The person in charge will give you a priority list in the order he wants to load it. He'll pay you per container loaded. We will not pay for empty containers, except possibly for reefers. We'll accept any still sealed container on the list. Unsealed containers are subject to inspection, and may be refused at our option.

Operation Phoenix

Okay?"

"Yes, let's get started," Jack said eagerly.

"Okay, we'll be in touch by ship's radio." They went back into the office. Gary got his photocopies and left. At the ship, Gary was happy to see an alert security guard posted. Gary and Patti loaded themselves with bags of money, pistols, ammo, and body armour, and staggered up the gangway. At the challenge Gary asked for Bruce, who hurried out. He was beaming. The first thing he said was, "The wife called. The armed guard has been in place since this morning. She's recruited a couple of neighbours and all three of them are packing."

"Okay, I'll get a container dropped this afternoon."

He dialled Chris. Chris said he could arrange it, but this was his last trailer. Gary asked that Chris buy half a dozen used trailers and any seaworthy containers he needed from the cash he was holding for Gary. Chris said they were getting $60 per gallon for gas. Business was even brisker than before as word was getting around. Gary asked if Chris could locate a quantity of standard two cubic foot empty cardboard packing boxes, and include them in the container going to Bruce's house. Gary would need more later, because there would be several more containers to be filled. Chris allowed that he had a few packs of flat boxes kicking around, and would have them thrown into the container.

Gary and Patti followed Bruce into the captain's cabin, where the money was put away, except for $1,100, Jack already having $2,500. Patti went back to the car to drive back to the container loading facility. Bruce gave orders to get the ship underway as Gary filled him in on the details, and gave him the photocopied lists.

Bruce issued firearms to the crew, along with strict orders about their use, while Gary went to the rail to get out of Bruce's

Operation Phoenix

way. They docked, and Jack Sopper soon bustled up. Bruce indicated the first containers wanted, and Jack passed the orders on.

The first container came across. Gary watched as it was approved, and immediately handed an additional $1,100 over to Jack, even before the container hit its fittings. At the third container, he handed the entire operation over to Bruce. Gary and Patti left for home. Along the way, he described to Patti the 'smuggling' operation he was contemplating out of Canada, and they began planning the operation.

Gary's wife had been Canadian, and he had lived in Canada for a time. Patti was Canadian, so they compared porous points in the Canada-US border, and made specific some of Gary's general plans. They debated using one or two cars versus a boat across Lake Ontario. In the end, they decided that two cars were better. While there was increased risk, the time at risk was substantially less. Another major factor was the physical size of this amount of cash. Gary was hoping to obtain as much as $10 million US. They couldn't put as much as $5 million into the trunk of either car. Some would have to visibly sit in the back seat.

Operation Phoenix

Chapter 30

They arrived back at the house to find that Lynn and Jan were out, presumably finalizing their deal for the hospital. Gary called Jan, and they were indeed in a meeting. "You will have to delay your closing until Friday. We can't get back here with money before three or four AM Friday morning earliest," Gary imparted the news as succinctly as possible.

"I'll make note of that," Jan said, skilled at not imparting information to others in earshot.

Turning to Patti, he said, "Patti, you might as well try to get some sleep. We'll have to use Lynn's bed because we weren't expecting you. If the descending hordes don't wake us, we'll get up about 5:30 to make some dinner."

Gary went to his bedroom, stripped off most of his clothes, pulled the coverlet over himself, and was asleep quickly, as usual. When he awoke he had a quick shower and went to the kitchen. Patti was up.

"Patti, would you like to have a quick shower? The bathroom is right at the end of the hall, and there are fresh towels in the closet to the right of the bathroom door. You will be feeling pretty grungy before we get there."

"Sure," said Patti. "I'll get my kit from the car."

Lynn came in, having dropped Jan and her guard off at Jan's house.

"Lynn, I had Patti catching 40 winks on your bed. I hope you don't mind? I couldn't find anywhere else to put her since I thought Jan would object to her sleeping with me," Gary

Operation Phoenix

grinned.

"Do you think I will get SEAL germs or something if she sleeps in my bed?"

Claude phoned from his house to say he had arrived back safely. "Do you know FEMA has set up a ring of National Guards with orders to shoot to kill those starving people trying to escaping to rural areas until looting is controlled?"

"That sounds like government. They did the same thing in Hurricane Katrina. Escape to safety and they drove you back into the flood until the looting stopped."

"How can people live? This is insane," Claude growled.

"The whole society is. They have lost their familiar way of life, and the shock is producing unsane reactions. Jack Sopper, the harbourmaster was so amateurish the way he went about his bribe of one million dollars, I'll bet it's his first time around at that."

"Yes, I wondered when you first brought Jack up as being bribable. I've known him for years. I couldn't imagine it," Claude said.

"He lost his pension, is getting no pay-check, and the dock workers are going home rich so I guess something snapped. People count their value in dollars and if it had been one container or 10,000, my guess is that his price would have been a million dollars. By the way I had Chris drop a container at your place for packing your house."

"I'll get my children to help me. Now I sleep."

The induction meeting at Gary's house went relatively well that evening, despite neither Claude nor Wayne being in attendance. As is usual with groups of people, they tended to group with someone they knew. In the next hour of mixing and chatting, Gary worked hard at getting them to mix so they would know more people that they would be living in close proximity

Operation Phoenix

with. As yet he could not directly say why in detail to them. He phrased it as that he wanted them to get to know people that they might be working closely with. The medical people were particularly hard to break up. One, the surgeon married to Claude's daughter, opined that while he might be operating on them, he didn't expect to be socializing much with truckers or repairmen, so he saw no necessity to meet them.

Gary quietly pulled Eric and Lynn aside to discuss this possible fault-line in the community.

"Lynn, you're the expert at melding groups of people together at work, so I thought we should leave you in charge of melding this one together. Because it's Claude's family, and he is a surgeon, it is going to be hard to dump him even now. Is he going to be a problem?"

"Oh, I think he'll come around. First, if he maintains that attitude, he will have very few people to talk to, and second, as time goes by he will rub against these people and they will become real people to him, not just repairmen. And if he doesn't change, he is not going to get many repairs done. I think it will work itself out."

Gary and the other community members present led the neophytes up the mountain and gave them a view from there by giving a few more details. Nods all around when Gary polled the existing community members with his eyebrows and questioning looks. More details and the induction of the new members was successful. Everyone agreed to begin packing for the move into the apartment hotel as quickly as possible.

Later Chris Habel confessed that with the time pressure no horses or sheep had been procured, but he had obtained pigs, cows, goats, rabbits, and chickens. Roy Bryant described a fully operative, working machine shop that he'd discovered. He also dropped the bombshell that he had located a container lifter that could stack full containers three high. Gary was beside himself with appreciation. "Go for it," he said.

Gary introduced himself to a cute, short, and very blonde woman of about 30 that had to be Heidi. "You must be Heidi. I'm Gary, Jan's new toy," he grinned at her.

"Hi Gary," Heidi extended her hand. "Jan has been hinting marriage. Congratulations."

"Well, she didn't exactly scream 'Oh, yes, yes, yes' when I broached the subject, but I'll wear her down. I'm hoping our kids will have her brains and my beauty. My first bunch got it the wrong way around," Gary grinned, indicating Eric and Lynn.

"Oh, is Eric your son? I think he's very cute, and very, very smart. I had a chance to talk to him last night, and again briefly tonight."

"What do you think of our general idea and plan?" Gary asked.

"I'm blown away," Heidi said. "I've been cowering at home, totally in shock, unable to think, or move. You hear such stories."

"What kind of stories?"

"Oh some neighbours were home invaded last week. The invaders beat up the husband with some kind of clubs or baseball bats, tied him up to a chair, taped his mouth shut, and forced him to watch as they defiled his wife. She was wearing a body stocking and they cut holes for her breasts to show, then they cut a big hole for her pubic area to show. Then they gang raped and sodomized her. Then they began torturing both of them. Apparently it was pretty vicious because they left them both for dead but the husband didn't bleed to death. But he is not a man any more. They neutered him, all for fun. They didn't take much just trashed what they had. She died. Apparently they cut part of her thigh off and ate it, because there was a big chunk

Operation Phoenix

of thigh missing and some cooked meat left. The husband didn't see that because he was unconscious and may still die."

"Then you hear stories about kidnapped women wearing a collar around their neck, and a chain, with burn marks all over their body, walking around nude as a sex and torture slave. One of the girls at the bank was rescued from those conditions. She said they rounded up a bunch of Latinos, raped, tortured, and killed one in front of the others as an object lesson, and then sold them off as slaves or prostitutes. I didn't know what to do. You sit there in shock, afraid to do something, and afraid not to. You are paralysed. This community offers hope. I don't want to ever go home."

"Whew,' Gary exhaled. "I can see why."

"Is there something I can do, some kind of work I can do, so I won't have to go home?" Heidi begged.

"You'll regret ever asking me if there is work to be done," Gary grinned. "The top priority right now is forex related. I am on my way up to Canada tonight to pick up US cash. You recall Jan asking you about that?"

"Yes and I gave her some names."

"Is there anything else you could do to smooth our path and make the whole thing go faster and more easily?" Gary asked.

"I could phone the guys tomorrow morning and get them started. I could also ask them special favours if necessary."

"Anything you can think of that will get us in and out of Canada with eight to ten million US dollars cash by Thursday evening would be wonderful. We expect to pick up about half in Toronto, and the other half in Montreal. But if it were available in one place that would be even better. We're expecting to pay between $1,200 and $2,000 Canadian per million US. Do you think that is reasonable?" Gary asked.

Operation Phoenix

"Yes the US paper is worthless but that'll give them a handling fee. Yes I think I could help there."

"Great, anything at all would be appreciated," Gary said. "We desperately need to buy many things for the community to survive. The second priority is to save as much of what you have as possible. I'll assign a guard for you so you can go home and pack. Because resources are so short, the community will need simple things like beds, and pots and pans. We will also need information that you as an engineer might have. Any text on any subject, your computer and mathematical skills and equipment, your laser and light knowledge, anything at all. We are going into unknown territory and can't possibly guess what might be useful or necessary. I'll get Chris over there to back up a container for you to pack your stuff in. You can hire someone you trust to help you to pack. Get Eric to give you a gun. Okay?"

"Yes," she answered.

"Something else to think about," Gary continued. "We need skills and the equipment to use those skills. If you know of any people you would trust your life with in a tight situation, who has, for example great computer skills, all the programming in every major field, let me know and we will investigate them with the idea of offering a position. We also need to know where to put our hands on a good computer server, storage units or any other basic equipment needed to use those skill sets."

"Sounds like you need to pack up a university and bring it along."

"Sort of, but we need more practical than theoretical, and all in one person." Gary replied. "Eric will also give you a cell phone and body armour. See Lynn regarding gun training. I'll call you tomorrow morning from Toronto regarding things you have done to expedite the forex deal. Thank you for coming

Operation Phoenix

with us. I think it was a good decision for both of us.

"I think a comment by the journalist Matt Savinar, sums up our current situation well. He said he wouldn't count on technology, the market, brilliant scientists, or government programs, to hold things together and to continue life as we now know it. But he did think we could lead happy, fulfilling lives, even facing the grim situation we are in now, with a lot of hard work, adjusted expectations, and a bit of good luck. See you closer to the weekend."

Gary hurried off to find Patti stopping only to give Jan a quick kiss and tell her that now she was a member she had better talk to Eric and Lynn and start packing. Lastly he stopped to give information to Eric for action.

Patti and Gary gathered gear for the operation, night and day vision monocular scopes, firearms, and large sports equipment gym bags, of which he stuffed two with crumpled newspapers. Because he didn't know how much the US cash would cost, and he wanted to get as much US cash as possible he took $39,200 Canadian dollars which he split into 4 packets of $9,800 each. Anyone carrying over $10,000 was automatically suspected of money laundering. He and Patty would openly carry one packet each. They hid the other packets in their cars. They left for Montreal at ten PM, an hour later than they had planned to start.

As they were driving up to the FEMA National Guard roadblock, there was a large crowd of urban refugees with their bundles and buggies milling about. Patty was ahead. She spoke briefly to the officer, waved something and passed the checkpoint. Gary drove slowly through the crowd, and noticed a bundle buggy of goods spilled at the side of the road, and then saw the bleeding body lying next to it. Off in the distance, there appeared to be several bundles of rags in the field. Obviously a

Operation Phoenix

group had decided to walk around the checkpoint, had been shot and were left to die and rot. He pulled up with extreme caution but the guard waved him through. The troops did not notice or seem interested in, the large gym bags stuffed with newspapers in the back seat as a test to see what might happen if they were stopped with a bag of cash later. Anyone with the fuel to drive a car was obviously important and not a looter.

As soon as he was out of sight of the roadblock, he phoned Patti. "What was that all about? How did we get through so easily?"

"I just waved my SEAL identification and said you were with me."

Operation Phoenix

Chapter 31
Wednesday March 8th —Day 23

While it may be legal to carry large amounts of cash, in today's world it is at least highly suspicious. Despite Gary and Patti's careful planning, if they were discovered, at a minimum they could expect to lose the cash. If they lost their own freedom, the whole escape might be in danger. They needed information but they had to be extremely careful as they scouted for it.

They drove along with Patti leading, keeping in touch by their cell phones where service existed, and practicing keeping a five to ten mile gap between cars. If they were successful in reaching their monetary goals they wouldn't be able get all the money in the trunks. The plan was to put those visible bags of cash into Gary's back seat. Patti would front run the roadblocks, with nothing extraordinary being visible. Patti, being young, female, and pretty, would be more likely to be able to sweet talk her way through. Gary, being behind, but with visible bags on the seat, would immediately try to exit the highway, or, at a minimum, pull over. If they lost Patti's load, at least it would be the lesser load.

About five miles short of the border and customs, they turned off the highway and drove west on a small road and then turned toward the border. Two miles short of the border they stopped and parked the cars. Patti took her pistol, went into the trees and buried it. Gary didn't trust his memory in the dark, so he found a culvert and tossed his plastic wrapped package into

Operation Phoenix

the end of the culvert. They sneaked to the border on foot.

The trees had been cut back by about 150 feet on either side of the border. Gary had once been through this particular crossing many years before. Local farmers and partygoers were its primary users. On the Canadian side, a farmhouse set back from the road by about a quarter of a mile, doubled as a customs office until nine PM. Other than that, only stern signs on both sides of the border, directing people to the nearest open customs offices were the only hindrance to crossing.

About 75 feet before they would come out into the clearing they stopped and Patti climbed a tree with her night vision scope. About fifteen minutes later, she was back down. "I think I see a passive camera but other than that it looks like they're relying on the electronic alarms I told you about."

"That's about the way it was when I went through it before. I think our plan of playing a dumb, lost tourist is still good. Lets get back to the cars. I don't want to inadvertently set off some alarms and alert them." Gary shook his head. *The 9/11 scare has not tightened up security anywhere except at the official border crossings. Right, the bad guys will pay attention to the stern signs telling them to cross at the official crossing. Standard bureaucratic thinking. As long as the voting public is inconvenienced, the illegal's don't matter. Government is perceived as doing its job.*

At the Canadian customs office Gary waited for Patti to clear before he drove up. It took a rather long time. Gary was beginning to worry that they might have triggered something on their little visit to the other crossing point. Although there were not many cars in the line, they all seemed to be moving very slowly. Patti finally cleared, and Gary waited till she was out of sight before driving up.

The guard asked him the purpose of his visit to Canada.

"I have a bit of business to do." Gary answered

"What kind of business?"

Gary was dumbfounded. That answer had always worked before. "I want to arrange some foreign exchange transactions which I can't now do in the US, and see if I can get a flight to Europe."

"Would you get out of the car please and pop open your trunk."

Oh, oh a car search. And I'm carrying nearly $20,000. For the first time, Gary was going to have his car searched crossing the border. The grilling continued at length although the search was very superficial. The questions seemed directed in a strange way, his background, where he was going, and what he was going to do there. Gradually, Gary realized that this was not related to the visit at the other border crossing point. Besides, they had let Patti go and she would have phoned to tip him off if her cash had been confiscated.

They didn't seem to be searching for contraband, but he was mystified as to the reason for the extra attention. Usually the delay was on the return trip at the US customs since the terror attacks of 9/11. Best to just go with the flow and not get too curious. Finally, after nearly 30 minutes of grilling they let him go. He and Patti stopped to refuel and have a coffee at a nearby truck stop where she had waited for him. Patti said the Canadian customs officer had said they were on a heightened alert because so many US economic refugees were trying to sneak into Canada.

They got into Toronto just before 10:30 AM. At the outskirts of Toronto, Gary dialled Heidi, "Hi, it's Gary."

"Hi. I contacted Alex Peterson at Brunswick Bank. He will have about six million ready for you by noon. He will also arrange to have his Montreal counterpart pull together whatever he can. The price is $1,400 Canadian per million. He also told me that he thinks there will be another indefinite bank holiday declared in Canada today after the bank closing."

"Ah, the tsunami now rolls into Canada," Gary exclaimed. "The Canadian banks have to be in trouble, even if it is because they not only lost a lot on their US dollar positions, but they won't be collecting on their US interbank loans, so they are underwater. The rest of the world is now following the US into the crapper. The world financial system is kaput."

"Yeah, but Brunswick is in better shape than most because they own Brunswick McCoy, the precious metals dealer, and they have done well there."

"Heidi, thank you so very much. The community owes you big time for this. I just hope we can repay you somehow. See you later." Gary knew that once he had the bankers onside, virtually anything monetary was possible. Never-the-less, it would be a relief to actually get the cash in his hands, despite the fact that he still had to get it home.

The Brunswick building was glass instead of glass and stone like Premet, but the rotunda was laid out nearly the same with a round counter for normal banking and a precious metals and foreign exchange counter and offices section taking up a large corner of the main floor. Over an hour early they located Alex and Gary introduced himself.

"You're early. We are still counting the cash," Alex said.

"I know, but in view of the possible bank holiday, I was worried about getting the Montreal part of the purchase outside the banking system today. I need to know whether I can send an armoured car service for pickup or whether I need to fly down before bank closing," Gary said. "Who do you use as your armoured car service?"

"We use Yenom Transfer primarily. I will find out from

Operation Phoenix

my guy in Montreal how he is doing with the order, and ask him about using Yenom." Alex walked over to a woman seated at a desk and spoke to her at length. She immediately picked up her phone.

Gary and Patti had discussed what might happen to her Canadian savings. After agonizing, she decided to buy silver. As Patti turned over the $19,600 Canadian she had smuggled over the border, she also turned over $5,000 Canadian of her own. Gary said, "Alex thinks there will be an indefinite bank holiday declared in Canada tonight, so whatever you do, get on the phone now and tell your family to pull as much cash as possible from the banks today. Empty any accounts you personally may have. It can't cost them very much. If they don't, they'll be like everyone else was in the US. They'll lose it all. They won't even be able to buy any food that is available," Gary said.

Gary purchased nine ounces of silver for Patti, while she called her parents

Alex came out and said the cash was ready. Gary took one look at the pile of cash and asked Patti to go to the cars and get seven gym bags.

Gary did a rough estimate of the amount of cash that was there and asked, "How much is here?"

"Six million even."

That was in the ballpark that Gary had estimated. He doubted Alex would try to cheat him out of a few dollars Canadian. The lady who Alex had talked to earlier walked in. "Jacques in Montreal has four and a half million he can scrape up on short notice. I talked to both him and Yenom, and you can pick up anytime after 6PM. Here is the address, contact name, and an identification code to clear the shipment. Yenoms charges will be $300."

Gary tucked the paper away in his wallet. "I was planning

Operation Phoenix

on stopping at $10 million, but what the hell, I need something to light my cigars with. I'll take the whole ten and a half million," he grinned. "Actually, I'm very grateful that you took the time and trouble to help me. I owe you a big one. Here's my card. I guess I owe you $14,700 plus $300 for Yenom." He pulled $4,600 out of one of Patti's envelopes and handed the two envelopes over.

"There should be $15,000 left in there. Check it please." She walked over to a bill machine, which soon began to rattle. She nodded to Alex and went out, but was back shortly, escorting Patti with her empty gym bags.

Sixteen thousand uncirculated notes take up almost exactly one cubic foot of space You can get about $1,140,000 of uncirculated $20's into a standard 3 ½ cubic foot, old bank bag, and about 1/3 less of circulated bills. Large hockey-style gym bags vary only slightly in volume and dimensions from old bank bags. They got the six million into five bags because of the variety of denominations.

Gary zipped up his bag with difficulty and heaved it off the table. "Ooof, this thing is heavy. May we borrow your trolley for a few minutes?"

"Sure."

He was relieved to have the cash finally in hand, but was beginning to worry about transporting it, because they were now alone against the world. He and Patti got the bags down into the trunks of the cars. While Patti guarded the cars he returned the trolley and phoned two of the most prominent US banks that had branches in Canada for rates on a US bank draft of over $20 million. He wanted a US based bank to disguise, for a while at least, that he had purchased the US dollars outside the country. After arguments about exchange rates, which Gary won because he knew he was on firm ground, he nipped over to one bank, about three blocks away, and purchased two bank drafts, one for $20 million, 357 dollars and 23 cents, and another for $5 million even. Both were to be made out to the Internal Revenue Service.

He returned to the cars with the drafts safely in pocket. They left to refuel. After swinging by a drive-through burger joint for a quick bite, they were soon on the road back to Montreal. Nearing the half way point of Kingston, Gary decided, *Enough. We have been going at high speed for the last 20 hours straight.* He called Patti.

"Patti, we're not going to get to Montreal by five in any case, and I'm falling asleep. The way we have it arranged, we are running almost 24 hours ahead of our expected schedule. Let's pull off in Kingston and get a couple of hours' sleep. We can take the bags into the motel with us. We have a long run afterward."

They piled the gym bags of money between the beds. While Patti was showering, Gary called Lynn to advise her of the accelerated itinerary. She told him that they were getting nibbles from the trustees of the second bankruptcy hospital.

"We can't have too much medical equipment. I just wish we had more medical people," Gary lamented.

"Claude's doctor children are inspecting the Medical Venture Capital hospital now. According to Eric they have some medical people they want to recommend. Claude has been on the phone all morning and seems to have something cooking. I'm ready to take delivery of the pharmaceuticals now that we have a doctor to sign." Lynn said.

"Okay, we have six million in our possession now, and expect to pick up another four later this evening. If we can get back to Stamford safely, we have lots of funds. After seeing how far things have deteriorated in Canada, I think we can expect more dramatic and disturbing change to occur shortly.

Operation Phoenix

Tell Eric I want everyone who needs money to be gathered at the house to pick it up tomorrow morning. I want whatever purchases are possible to be completed and paid for by this weekend. I want as much of this $10 million spent as possible. We are likely very short on time. Is Claude there?" Gary asked.

"No, he's gone off to meet with Bruce Nott, and to look at ships. Heidi is working on her lists, and packing. Jan is packing."

"Tell Heidi to try and locate as much computer equipment as possible, particularly the heavy duty servers, storage and software. I want to take delivery by the weekend if possible," Gary said. "I gotta hop."

He awoke to the phone, which he reached for groggily. As he picked up the phone, he became awake instantly at the sight of Patti sitting up in bed, holding one of the strangest and wickedest knives he had ever seen. "Yes?" he said into the phone.

"Your wake up call sir."

"Thank you," he said and hung up, still staring at the knife. "Where the hell did you get that?"

"I have worn it on my arm constantly since I came on duty with you."

"May I see it? I've never seen one like that." She handed it over, butt first. The blade, if it could be called that, was a triangular needle of about eight inches in length. It tapered from half-inch at the base, to a needlepoint. Each face of the triangle had been hollow ground to along its length produce three extremely sharp edges.

"It's made of the same steel as the armour plating on an Abrams tank so it's very strong, even where it's thin at the point. It's a specialty, close fighting weapon, designed to slip between ribs and then be wiggled around, cutting internal organs."

"My god, I never even guessed that you had it," he said, carefully handing the knife back to her. "Well, now that I'm thoroughly awake, I guess it is time to get moving."

They spent half an hour loading the cars, checking out, grabbing a bite to eat, and topping up their fuel tanks.

Chapter 32

They picked up the money in Montreal, and started for the border. At the truck-stop they had stopped at on the way up they fuelled again and turned west on a small road for a time. They stopped to empty Patti's car of cash. Using some mud they obscured the state name on Gary's license plate, turned a 3 into an 8, and a 7 into a Z.

"I'll call you when I clear the border," Patti said and left. Gary settled in to wait.

Gary was beginning to fret when the phone rang. "Clear," she said. They both hung up.

Gary started his car and maintained a steady speed, just below the limit. He drove a bit further west and then turned south toward the border. A couple of miles from the border the phone rang again. "In position," she said.

"In position, 2 miles," he replied, and hung up.

He continued to drive at the same sedate speed, ignoring the farmhouse cum customs office, ignoring the stern signs, until he located Patti parked near where they had parked the previous night. They hurriedly moved the cash from Gary's car into Patti's car and retrieved their weapons. They both turned around and drove off. Gary retraced his route, now a tourist who had unknowingly crossed into the US while lost. Once he came to the point where he turned east toward the highway, he stopped and scrubbed at his license plate. That trick was lame at best but it might confuse the issue if the camera was unable to discriminate between the real and the fake.

When the customs offices came in sight he dialled Patti

and said, "Entering," and hung up.

Re-entering the US posed no unexpected problems. Exiting the customs he dialled Patti and said, "Clear" and hung up. At the exit to the west he instead turned east, drove nearly a mile, turned and parked. He watched for tails and listened for aircraft for a few minutes and then started driving west. He drove until he found Patti and they carefully packed the cars with the moneybags. Patti left and after a few minutes, Gary followed.

They were barely on the road an hour when Gary received a call from Lynn. She sounded frantic. "Heidi has been kidnapped."

"Hold on. Slow down. How do you know that?"

"We heard that potatoes and canned vegetables were in at the shopping centre, so Heidi and I went to get some. On our way out we got separated and I saw Heidi being pushed into a car. I tried to catch them, but couldn't find them, and came home,"

"Oh my god, Heidi's worst nightmare come true," Gary burst out. "Listen, call Patti. She's a hostage expert. I already asked her to give a course in kidnappings and hostages. I'll call Patti for about ten seconds to alert her and then you call her for instructions. I'll call Wayne, and those two will take over. You call Eric to alert him and he can alert the SEALs. Okay?"

"Yes."

Gary immediately dialled Patti. "Heidi was taken hostage a while ago. Lynn will call you for instructions. I'll call Wayne. You two take over."

"Okay."

Gary called Wayne and quickly briefed him on all that he knew. "You two are in charge. Anybody that messes with the community will regret it."

Operation Phoenix

"Give me Patti and Eric's numbers," Wayne demanded. Gary did.

"I'll keep you informed," Wayne said and hung up.

Gary gave his attention to the job at hand, returning to Stamford with his cargo. That did not stop him from thinking about Heidi and the situation. Poor Heidi, in the wrong place at the wrong time. She had only been with the community a matter of hours and then this. There was little that could be done to trace her immediately, unless they had been extremely lucky with the mall security cameras, an unlikely prospect. The cameras would have had to catch the car and also its plate number to have a chance of a fast solution. Anything else would require slow digging. Even if they threw their entire resources at the problem, something Gary was willing to do, would it be fast enough for Heidi? If she wasn't already dead she was in the process of being sold into slavery, or it was a straight hostage for ransom. In that case she could be completely unharmed. If it were for ransom, the problem would likely tend to resolve itself during ransom negotiations. He followed the beams of his headlights boring a hole in the night.

Patti phoned about an hour later. "Cop cars in the centre median, sitting talking to each other. They are not moving out after me so far as I can tell. There hasn't been an exit from the highway in miles."

"Looks like I have two choices: pull over, or keep driving. I think an occupied car pulled over is more likely to attract a cop than one proceeding normally."

"You're probably right," said Patti. "Keep coming."

"Any news?" Gary asked.

"Not much. Some of the security cameras were pointed at the doors. Not much coverage on the lot. We probably have a good chance of seeing the snatch but not much else. Wayne is concentrating on pulling in more detective expertise, so you and I are going to be on the spot in Stamford. Once we see who pulled the snatch, and have faces we can back up and see if they have frequented the mall in the last month. If they have, and we are lucky, we might catch them talking to someone who knows who they are. Finding that someone will be largely a matter of waiting till they show up again. Otherwise it's a matter of pure detective slogging at this point. There are some clues, such as they have a car with fuel, but I don't know where those clues point yet."

"Okay you have enough to do without holding my hand. I'll get off here." Gary hung up.

Just outside Stamford, with Patti having already exited, a cop car appeared from nowhere, pulled up alongside Gary, and motioned him over. Gary complied. As the cop got out of the car, standing behind his door with drawn gun, Gary got out of his car because he didn't want the cop looking into the car with cash in the back. This seemed to make the cop nervous, because he barked, "Hands on the roof of the car." Gary did as he was told.

"Are you carrying weapons?"

"Yes," said Gary exasperatedly. "If you will calm down, I'll get it out."

"Slowly," said the cop.

Gary reached in and pulled out his pistol and put it on the roof of the car. It was legal for him to carry, but in the circumstances he wasn't going to create a row unless he had to. Give him his bribe and get on with it.

"On the ground."

"Okay, but I'm not going to drop it. It might go off accidentally, and I don't want to get shot." Gary picked up the pistol, exaggeratedly using two fingers, and laid it on the

Operation Phoenix

ground.

"Now back away."

Gary moved to the front of the car. The cop approached with his gun drawn, scooped up Gary's gun and ordered Gary back to having his hands on the roof of the car. He then patted Gary down.

"Pretty serious stuff you've got there. Body armour, shoulder holster, and a 40 cal Glock. You got a carry permit?" the cop asked.

Gary dug it out.

"What're you doing out this late?"

"A group of us have set up a mutual community protection plan. One of the girls was kidnapped last night. We've been running around searching for her all night."

"And you guys decided to arm yourselves and 'git them guys'. Maybe do a little vigilante shooting? This is a job for the police. You stay out of it."

"No," Gary said wearily. "I've been wearing this thing for nearly three weeks, and I have yet to pull it. Pulling a gun unless you intend to use it is stupid."

"Anyway, you changed lanes back there without signalling."

"I didn't... Oh, I see. And is it possible to prepay the fine?" he said resignedly.

"Yes. A small donation to the benevolent fund would cover it."

"Twenty bucks I presume. Wait, I'll get it," and Gary knelt down and took off a shoe. Extracting the $20, he handed it over. The cop stood there.

"May I have my pistol back, please?" Gary asked politely.

"I think I should confiscate it. You look like you plan on taking vigilante action."

"Oh I see. And is there a fine for that too?" Gary asked in exasperation.

"I can probably think of something."

Gary shook his head, knelt down, took the other shoe off, extracted its $20, and handed it over. He stood up. The cop stood there expectantly.

"What the hell do you want?" Gary exploded. "Do I look like a guy who has millions in my pocket? There's a bank holiday on you know. You're taking food from my family. In the meantime you're doing squat about a girl whose life, and worse, is in danger. Give me my gun so I can go home and sleep."

The cop's eyes narrowed, and then he seemed to reconsider. He took Gary's pistol, jacked its clip empty, handed the weapon back, stalked back to his cruiser and pulled away. Gary found three of the shells, reloaded his pistol with them, and drove on to exit at Stamford. The phone rang. "Where the hell are you?" Patti demanded

"I got stopped by a cop."

"And?"

"I managed to divert his attention with a little guilt trip about Heidi, and his bribe. Anyway, I'm off the highway, and on my way."

When Gary arrived at the house, they backed Patti's car into the garage and unloaded it. Then Gary drove his car in, locked the garage, and armed the alarms. He entered the house to find a red-eyed Jan and Lynn awaiting him. He gathered them into his arms. Jan said, "Poor Heidi," and began to cry on his shoulder.

Lynn said guiltily, "Dad, it's all my fault. We got separated."

Gary said, "If it's anybody's fault, it's mine for not giving

Operation Phoenix

everyone enough training. What is done is done and it wasn't done intentionally. She's been kidnapped. Now we have to get her back. I want you two to shower and get some sleep so we don't make mistakes. Is Eric at the apartment hotel?"

Both Jan and Lynn protested that they couldn't possibly sleep.

"You have to sleep for Heidi's sake. There's only one way to win this and that's to think faster than the kidnappers. You can't do that if you are falling asleep or numb. You too, Patti. The kidnappers are not likely to call in the next four to five hours, so I'll stand guard over the phones in the unlikely event they do call. You can relieve me in four hours Patti, and I'll go down for eight. Lynn, will you show her where Eric's room was? You can sleep there, Patti. I want you absolutely alert."

"Eric took his bed with him," Lynn said.

"Damn," Gary growled. "Patti, you go get showered if you want to. You have been going for about forty hours, with only four hours sleep. Sleep in my bed. I want you to wake Jan and Lynn in six hours. I want you two to take the money and go close that hospital deal. We absolutely need that hospital. Then you can start taking delivery of pharmaceuticals Lynn."

"But what about Heidi?" Lynn was aghast.

"That is unbelievably callous," Jan said firmly.

"While you have been standing around weeping, Patti, Wayne and the SEALs have been working on this full time. They have done an incredible amount of work. Either Heidi is dead by now, in which case we have some other urgent matters and standing around weeping is not going to help. Or if there are hostage negotiations, they will likely take two or three days. Is that not right Patti?" Gary asked.

"Yes, usually."

"So, either way, you won't help anything by standing

Operation Phoenix

around getting in the way. We have some of the finest minds available, with lots of experience, working on this. You need something to divert your mind, and the hospital deal needs to be done. I want you in bed," Gary roared.

"Patti," Gary ordered, "Shower or bed. I want your cell phone."

"Yes Sir." She handed it over and scooted for the shower.

Gary went into the office to set up a recording device. As tired as he was, it'd be easy to miss some obvious clues. The tape recorder was old and large, but it was a sophisticated model that had been the top of its line in its day. He had occasionally used it while head hunting if he thought he might want to review a conversation for clues.

He was just holding the fort while others slept. Moreover they couldn't lose sight of the main goals. Every individual in the community, including him, was dispensable. However he did think that Heidi was smart enough to give them reason to believe that she was a valuable piece of merchandise, better alive and well than dead or as a slave. A ransom situation was highly probable.

Chapter 33

In order to keep active and awake, Gary went out to the garage and brought in the bags of cash. Because he expected Heidi would advise her captors that Gary had cash, so they would feel disposed to keep her alive, the major problem was one of how frightened Heidi would be, and how much she would blurt out in fright. Would she mention the $10 million, or would she just say lots of money?

Gary knew that once an exchange was proposed, and assuming at least one side was willing to give a little, cash would be delivered. That did not necessarily mean that the hostage would live, or even be delivered, but the game was to keep the kidnappers tense and tired so they would make mistakes.

As a tentative plan, and for part of the negotiations, he decided that the story would be that most of the money had been seized at the border, and that they only had $2½ million left. Then he intended to make up as much as possible of that $2½ million with small bills, making it bulky, heavy, and difficult for the kidnappers to transport. If ten million became a sticking point then believably they would require at least a couple of extra days to get the extra seven and a half million, a further delay.

Happily, at the bank pick-up points, the bills had been stacked according to denomination. Little mixing of denominations had occurred while packing it in the bags. The job went quickly. A simple calculation showed him that all the

Operation Phoenix

fives, tens and twenties totalled $1,980,000. The remainder would come from 208 packs of fifties. He took five bags and placed equal numbers of packets of fives in the bottom of each, tens on top, followed by twenties. Lastly, he scattered the packets of fifties across the top of each bag. In total the bags weighed about 400 pounds.

Patti's phone rang. 'Patti's line," Gary answered.

"Who's this?" the caller asked suspiciously. Gary recognized Wayne's voice.

"It's Gary. I ordered everybody to bed to get some sleep, including Patti."

"Well get her. I need her. We're pretty sure we have found Heidi. Either she or one of the kidnappers appears to be moving around a house. Our resolution is only to ten yards, so we can't be sure. I need Patti to plant some listening devices," Wayne said.

Gary walked into the bedroom and, recalling seeing Patti wake up unexpectedly before, carefully approached her feet. Leaning over he gave one a nudge. Patti shot up fumbling for the dagger that she had obviously taken off in more secure surroundings.

"It's Wayne," He whispered as Jan stirred slightly. "Give me your keys, I'll fuel your car."

Patti tried to reach for her keys, cover herself, and answer the phone all at once. It didn't work. Gary noticed she was very slim, not as chunky as she appeared when she was dressed. Obviously her gear and body armour added girth. She said into the phone, "One moment," and casting modesty aside got out of bed to retrieve the keys. She grabbed a handful of clothes and went into the bathroom. Gary headed for the garage. Moving his car out he drove Patti's in and started to pump gas.

Patti came out carrying some things from her kit looking

Operation Phoenix

very fresh and able in her combat gear.

"Is there anything I can provide?" Gary asked.

"I don't think so. I have only till dawn to act."

"Where do they think she is?" Gary enquired.

"Here in Stamford. I have to go to Wayne's house to pick up some things first," Patti responded while getting into the car.

"Okay you should have enough fuel then." Gary gave it two more big pumps, removed the nozzle and replaced the gas cap. Patti roared off. Gary returned his car to the garage and fuelled it. After arming the garage alarm again he returned to survey his piles of cash and review his plan.

As he finished moving the packed bags into his car trunk, Jan padded out. "I can't sleep,"

Gary gathered her up in his arms, and kissed her tenderly. "Hi, sweetie. I missed you. You were asleep about an hour and a half. We think they may have found Patti, or at least one of the kidnappers," Gary said in a low voice.

"Where? Is she okay?" Jan exclaimed, fully awake now.

"Shhhh. Here in Stamford. My best guess is that they somehow used her cell phone to trace her. Beyond that, I can't say," Gary said, still in a low voice.

"Why didn't you ask?" Jan blazed. "It's the least you could do."

"Listen Jan," Gary said testily but still quietly, "these people are experts. They are busy, busy trying to save Heidi. Being my, or your source of news is way down on the priority list. You know all that I know. If and when they need us, or have time, you will get more information. In the meantime you can wait, just like everybody else."

"But, I'm worried," Jan said, pouting.

"So am I, and so is everybody else. Heidi will be more than worried if they don't get to her in time. She will be dead.

Operation Phoenix

Now go back to bed, and stop waking up the whole house," Gary hissed. "There won't likely be anything significant happening for a few hours at least."

"I'm going to get a cup of tea," Jan said firmly.

"Will you please keep your voice down," Gary hissed. "Everyone here's exhausted. You're exhausted. I'm exhausted. Lynn is exhausted. If we are exhausted, we will make mistakes and Heidi may die. I can't stay awake much longer and there has to be somebody awake and alert. The longer you stay up, the longer till I can get some sleep. Please go back to bed."

"No. I'm going to have some tea," Jan repeated. "I'll stay up. I can't sleep anyway. You go to bed."

"Please keep your voice down. Please." Gary then considered. He wasn't expecting much action for the next few hours; maybe he should get some sleep. Jan had got a bit of sleep, so maybe she could stay up. There was no one else to relieve him with Patti gone. "Can you stay awake for sure?" he asked.

"Yes. I haven't been able to sleep a wink."

"Okay if the phone rings, before anything else, you must push this 'record' button here on the recorder. No matter where you are in the house, get back here and start the recorder. You should get a light like this. Then you yell for me. If the phone has not rung four times wait till it does. Then answer it, but be sure I'm awake, no matter what. In any case, don't let me sleep more than an hour and a half. Okay?" Gary asked.

"Okay."

Gary walked into the bedroom, sat down on the bed, and then sank back, asleep before he got his shoes off.

He awoke thinking he had heard the phone ring. It was strong daylight, and it shouldn't have been. He shot out of the bedroom. Jan was curled up in the living room easy chair and

Operation Phoenix

was talking on the phone. Gary bolted for the office. "Who is it?" he asked urgently. He mashed down the "record" button on the recorder.

Back at the office door he repeated, "Who is it?"

Jan made shushing motions at him.

"Is it the kidnappers?" Gary demanded.

Jan ignored him, and hung up saying, "Okay, we will do that."

"Was that the kidnappers?"

"Yes." Jan answered.

"Oh Jesus. What did you tell them?"

"That we would drop the $10 million in a dumpster behind the Orion Company."

"When?" Gary demanded.

"Right away I guess," Jan shrugged.

"And where is the Orion Company?"

"I don't know. We'll have to look it up." Jan shrugged again.

"What about Heidi? Is she okay?"

"What about Heidi? Once they have the money, they have to let her go."

"Once they have the money, they are free to kill their principal witness. I will have to get Wayne to debrief you. Why didn't you wake me up?"

Jan slowly unwound herself from the chair, obviously stiff from having slept in it. "I fell asleep. I'm going to shower."

"We have to brief Wayne first,"

"Leave me alone. I'm feeling grumpy," Jan said. "I'm going to shower."

"Jan," Gary said, stepping in front of her. "Heidi's life is at stake. We are going to talk to Wayne first."

"I just arranged to have her freed. Besides, you already

Operation Phoenix

know where Heidi is. All you have to do is go and pick her up," Jan said, obstinately stepping around him.

"If it were that easy or sure, why are we paying $10 million ransom? Why have people been worrying and working day and night to rescue Heidi? Why didn't you record the conversation like I asked? Why did you agree right away to do what the kidnappers asked? We have to delay. And we must know that Heidi is alive and well. Right now every second counts if we are to rescue Heidi. Kidnappers often kill hostages because the hostage can identify them. Please come and talk to Wayne now," Gary begged.

"No, I'm going to shower," Jan said stubbornly. "It'll only take a minute."

Gary glared at Jan for nearly thirty seconds, and finally said, "I hope Heidi doesn't have many more good friends like you." He stalked off to the office. He was in a bind. Now that Jan was a core member, they couldn't afford to antagonize her because she had too much dangerous information, but he was so angry he was certainly ready to dump her as a potential wife.

He dialled Wayne.

"Wayne, I or we, have a major problem. After Patti left, there was nobody to relieve me. When Jan woke up and refused to go back to sleep, I decided to get an hour's sleep. She was supposed to wake me but fell asleep too. I woke up to find her talking to the kidnappers, and giving away the farm. I think I managed to get a wee bit of the conversation on tape, but just the last few words. Apparently we are to deliver ten million at an unknown time, to quote Jan 'right away I guess', to an Orion Company dumpster, address unknown. I don't even have any assurance Heidi is okay," Gary summarized.

Wayne was silent for a minute. "We're fairly sure it is Heidi in that house. We also think she knows one of the

Operation Phoenix

kidnappers personally, probably quite well, although judging from what we hear she is indeed a hostage. How well do you know her?"

"Not well at all. It's Jan I don't understand. She's hurting her friend, herself, and us, all for sheer bloody mindedness as far as I can tell. Maybe she gets an impulsive stubborn streak when she's tired, or in the wrong, I don't know," Gary lamented.

"Patti is on the scene at the house. We have the house wired for sound. I have five SEALs in full gear and Eric on their way. If some kidnappers leave we will pick them off piecemeal. One, obviously the telephone caller has just come back. He's the one with Heidi's cell phone. We traced him when he when he was making the call, although we didn't know what he was doing, because we can't do anything but get a location. We believe there are five males plus one female and Heidi in the house. Where is the Orion Company?"

Gary looked up the address. "The only one I see is at 36 Lombard. That's over by the Woodland cemetery, near State Street. It's a built up area, not deserted."

"The kidnappers should be putting a lookout near the dumpster soon. We will check whether one or more leave. In the meantime pack the car. You don't actually need the $10 million but you do need a lot of cash," Wayne said. "In the meantime I'll detach one SEAL and send him there."

"I had been planning on offering $2½ million. I pretty well filled five large gym bags with small bills, total weight about 400 pounds," Gary informed him.

"Sounds right to me," Wayne said. "I doubt they'll have time to count it anyway."

Gary played the tape he had and his original premise was correct. There was little information of value.

Jan came in looking more refreshed, and said, "See, that

Operation Phoenix

didn't take long."

Gary scowled at her, thinking, *Yes, but consciously or not, you have had time to embellish your story so you look better. We needed the truth, no matter how good or bad, not the embellished story.* Aloud he said, "Wayne, Jan has just come in from showering. I'll let you debrief her." He handed over the phone, and left in disgust for the bathroom.

Almost before he finished showering Chris Habel and Roy Bryant showed up at the door. Gary dressed quickly and joined them. Chris handed over the previous day's receipts. He said sales were slowing because fuel was now over $75 a gallon. Gary asked that Chris devote all of his free time to purchasing things for the community and personal packing. He also asked both of them to try to complete all purchases today if possible. Packing and loading of containers was to take place as soon as possible, preferably tomorrow. They were to hire whatever help they needed. Both agreed.

Roy Bryant knew pretty much what he wanted and just came for the money in order to get on with the job. Gary gave a half a million to each and urged them to pick up any spare parts they could get their hands on. Chris and Roy left.

Lynn came up and Jan served breakfast which Gary gulped. He gave them $800,000 to finalize their hospital deal and begin purchasing pharmaceuticals. Delivery was to be immediate. Gary called Wolfgang on his cell and asked him to come over and pick up some money that was now owed to him. Wolfgang said he would come immediately since he was on his way to work.

Gary showed Lynn where the remaining money was, and asked her to leave a note saying how much she had taken if she needed any. He also told her that Wolfgang would be in, and to give him $100,000, and Gary would explain later.

Operation Phoenix

That instruction turned out to be very prophetic. Wayne called and said at least one person had left the house after discussions of picking up the ransom. He urged Gary to get underway soonest and said the SEAL would be in position before Gary got to the dumpster. The person would be allowed to see the cash, and hopefully ask for help moving the large bags, but would not be allowed to take the cash back to the house. Gary said he would be out the door and underway within 120 seconds.

Gary drove over, found Lombard Street, and then number 36. Local roads were developing some pretty significant potholes. Since no repairs were being done driving slowly was absolutely necessary. He checked closely that it was the Orion Company and went around back. Sure enough, a tall dumpster. He started pulling the bags out of the car, and found he could not get the heavy bags over the top. He tried to open the end gates of the dumpster but could not. Finally he moved the car over to the dumpster and piled the bags on the hood. By standing on the hood of the car himself, with one foot on the dumpster rail, he was able to heave the bags into the almost empty dumpster. All the while he was covertly looking for the SEAL. He could not locate him. This was both reassuring and frightening. If the SEAL was not in place it was frightening.

With the difficulty he was having getting the bags into the dumpster, the kidnappers would have even more problem getting them out. One person would not be able to. There was nothing much to stand on inside the dumpster except the moneybags themselves.

Gary immediately drove away. He passed a car on the street whose driver seemed to watch him closely. Gary drove on for quite some distance until he was sure he was out of sight and he had no tail, before doubling back. He parked about four

Operation Phoenix

blocks away, and called Wayne to report. The phone was busy. Eventually he got Wayne, who said, "It's working like a charm. The guy in the dumpster thinks he is stuck in the dumpster and wants help. The SEAL on site can hear him trying to get out and crying. He has verified that there's cash in the bags. They are sending two men to help him. Stay where you are," and Wayne hung up. Gary settled in to wait.

Gary awoke to the phone ringing. "Yes," he said.

"Okay it's all over. Heidi is safe. You can go and get the money. The SEAL is there. His name is Matt," Wayne said.

"Thank you Wayne. The SEALs have been awesome," Gary said simply. "Absolutely awesome. There is no other word."

Gary called Lynn, and passed the news on to her and Jan. He then called Claude, Bruce, Chris and Roy for the same reason. He left for the dumpster. Tall, gangly Matt was sitting with his back against the dumpster, watching the new arrival alertly. Discounting his perfectly clipped moustache and army cut hair, he looked more like an accountant than a SEAL.

"Hi Matt. I am Gary Alden. I presume Wayne said to expect me."

Matt relaxed infinitesimally and said, "Yep. Let's get that money and get out of here. I don't want no neighbours investigating."

Gary drove the car up beside the dumpster, and then noticed a body lying by the corner. As he got out of the car, staring at the body, Matt said, "They have a ladder. I'll get it," and he went around the dumpster and reappeared with an aluminium ladder. He put the ladder up beside the dumpster, and sitting on the edge of the dumpster, swung the ladder over and placed it inside the dumpster. Gary climbed up on the hood of the car and peered into the dumpster. At one end, two male

Operation Phoenix

bodies lay, dead. Matt was ignoring them just getting the moneybags into position to bring up. He glanced up, saw that he was in the right position and started up the ladder to hoist one bag over to Gary. Gary set it down on the hood and the other bags followed in succession.

Sitting on the top of the dumpster Matt swung the ladder back out. Gary started getting the moneybags back in the car. Matt took the ladder around to the end of the dumpster where the body lay, and set it up. Struggling, he got the body on his shoulder, slowly mounted the ladder, and dumped the body into the dumpster. Gary watched horrified. Matt climbed down, and said, "Ready to go?"

Gary went over and repositioned the ladder at the side of the dumpster, and climbed up. Swinging the ladder over he climbed down. Since rigor mortise had not yet set in he was able to straighten out the bodies and close their eyes and mouths. Then he climbed out. Matt, who had climbed the side of the dumpster to look, shook his head, climbed down and said. "They're dead. They don't care anymore."

Gary got in the car and said, "Follow me back to the house," and sadly drove away.

Operation Phoenix

Chapter 34

The atmosphere at the house became euphoric when Heidi, the SEALs and Eric came in. Jan and Lynn both hugged Heidi. Lynn was crying tears of guilty relief. Jan smiled but appeared distant and largely unemotional. *Does she not understand the ramifications of her actions, or is she feeling guilty, or is she simply not affected?* Claude arrived and even he was moved. Everybody but Gary was grinning like Cheshire cats.

Gary was still angry about Jan's actions on the phone. She was supposed to be smart. Surely she would have at least asked how the exchange was to be made or gotten the Orion address. It had been the blindest good fortune that they had been able to rescue Heidi.

Gary gave Heidi a big hug and a smile and, when she started to thank him, told her that it was all the fault of the SEALs, Eric, Wayne, and that Patti in particular had played a big part in her release. He turned to Patti and said, "As soon as you are ready take the blanket down to Lynn's bed and crash. You have been up for far too long. I'm concerned about you."

Patti said, "Okay but I'm still on a high. Later."

Heidi started with her story. "I got grabbed by these guys and couldn't do anything. They lifted me up and ran to the car. I was terrified. We started driving and one guy wanted to rape me. Then I realized I knew one of the guys. His name was Chuck and he was on my list of computer geeks to consider recruiting. I guess he realized about the same time as I did

Operation Phoenix

because he wouldn't let the other guy touch me. At first I was terribly relieved."

"I talked to Chuck and he seemed friendly so I poured on the charm. I asked him if they had a plan, and he said, not really, they just wanted to get some money to get some guns to protect themselves. I said that they had to make a plan and that Gary had lots of money. I told Chuck I was your girlfriend Gary, so he would believe you would pay ransom. Then I made a mistake and mentioned ten million and their goals went from getting enough money to get guns to pure greed. I realized then that I might get killed as a witness. But they did try to keep me alive and well and the talk of rape stopped," Heidi said.

"Smart thinking" Gary said

Heidi continued, "After they got my cell phone they decided to use it to call you to demand the money. I expected it to be a slow process but Chuck came back all excited. They were going to get the money right away. Chuck left to pick up the money, and a guy named Bill, who I was afraid of, started guarding me. He was looking at me in a really creepy way. Then we got a call from Chuck. He had bags and bags of money but was trapped in the dumpster. He was worried that they had so much that even if they got it out of the dumpster they wouldn't be able to handle it.

"Bill was obviously of the opinion that I should be killed because he started making rape first comments. They huddled, and the guy who first wanted to rape me, and Bill decided to go to the dumpster and get Chuck and the money. About half an hour later there were these huge explosions, the doors burst open, and there was shooting and dead bodies everywhere. I was so stunned I just sat there. Guys running all over yelling 'clear' and then it all stopped. Patti came up to me and said 'It's all over. You can come home now'. I cried like a baby. I couldn't even stand up. I kept asking, 'How did you find me, How did you find me?' I still haven't found out. How did you find me?"

Patti said, "When Eric bought your cell phone, he thought that something they call assisted GPS, or assisted Global Positioning System, which allows the cell phone to be queried as to its location, would be a good thing to have in case of hostage taking. He had it installed on every phone he bought. It took us a while to get organized but once Eric told us about the assisted GPS we were able to locate your cell phone within minutes. That did not necessarily mean you were where your cell phone was, so just before dawn, we attached microphones to the windows to hear what was going on."

Gary interrupted, "Just before dawn, with no sleep for days, Patti installed listening devices."

Patti flashed Gary an embarrassed look and continued. "Once we knew you were there it was just a matter of timing to separate as many of them from you as possible so you wouldn't get harmed. A relatively easy operation against amateurs."

Heidi walked over to Patti and hugged her. "Thank you so much. I'll never be able to repay you." Then she walked over to Eric and grabbed him by the ears, and kissed him full on the lips. "You are one smart guy," she said. Eric looked stunned. Then she went around to each of the SEALs in turn hugging them and thanking them.

Gary pulled some frozen dishes out of the fridge and started defrosting them. He asked, "Anybody hungry?"

The SEALs, almost in unison declared they were starved, and Heidi said, "Yes, they didn't have any food. Thank you so much." She took a breath and declared, "After going through this I'll never be frightened of anything or anyone ever again."

There was a general stampede toward the kitchen. Gary eventually drifted off toward the office because he didn't feel

Operation Phoenix

like eating. Claude came over and said, "That was wonderful rescue yet you don't look happy?"

Gary heaved a big sigh. "Well, I'm pissed off with Jan for starters. I know that's why we wanted them in the first place but these SEALs scare me. They kill but not for pleasure. They seem totally emotionless about it. The guy killing animals in a slaughterhouse comes to mind. It is a job and nothing to get excited about one way or another. Once the target is killed they have no emotion about what remains either. If it's in the way they move it in the most efficient way possible. We wanted this but I wonder if we should have thought more about what we were wishing for. I think we got it. Now that we have it I'm not sure that was a good wish, despite the fact that they will raise the probability of success for the community."

"You've never seen somebody killed before?" Claude queried.

"Well I've never been part of somebody being murdered before anyway."

"They have different world, a world that whole country is gravitating towards. We thank our lucky stars we have them. You're having common reaction to violent death. It's shock to system," Claude said.

"It wasn't the death. I admit, I wondered if all these deaths were necessary, but I wasn't going to try to second-guess the guy on the spot. The two bodies in the dumpster did not bother me, nor the one outside. Then Matt picked up the one outside and just dumped it into the dumpster. The way he did it got to me. It was just a piece of garbage that had to be thrown out. I thought it should have a bit more dignity associated with it," Gary said despondently. "I don't know what I wanted him to do, but if he'd even said 'Sorry old bean' before he dumped the body it would have been okay."

Operation Phoenix

"I think you are suffering from shock from the killings. Give yourself some time." Claude shrugged. "In any case we have 743 containers aboard ship. That's near maximum load. I have eye on two other ships, a 24,000 ton and a 17,000 ton."

"That's fantastic. You are awesome Claude," Gary exclaimed. "So what kind of deals are they looking for?"

"They are both owned by two canny brothers," Claude replied. "They want two million per ship plus 5,000 ounces of silver each. They seem to know there aren't many empty, quality ships available here."

"I take it the silver is under the table?"

"Yes, they seem to know the value of the US dollar. I think dollars are so they can straighten out books, and silver's for the boys. Pay off everything so they can't be sued or charged and then take profits outside system."

"That 10,000 ounces is worth about a million seven Euros, or $7 billion US. That's not a discount. Are the ships fuelled?" Gary asked. "We have to get Bruce Nott out of US waters but we have also got to make sure we have transport for the people. That was the primary purpose in the first place. I never expected to have a shipload of products crowding out the people."

"Not much fuel I think. Thousand miles at best."

"Do you have any ideas? How many buyers are out there anyway? I would imagine we could get fuel if we have to. They probably could too."

"I thought you might have silver. I didn't know how much or whether you would part with it," Claude said. "I doubt there are other buyers for ships, particularly in US."

"I have both silver and gold available. It's still way too early to part with it except for very high priority things. I have parted with some because Wayne spent his own money on the SEALs that aided you in Singapore. Actually he doesn't have it

Operation Phoenix

yet. I just brought it here. Which brings to mind, what do I owe you?" Gary asked.

"I did have few things. I had tests to run on cargo, supplies and fuel, and they don't take dollars. I never thought of it when I left. I spent various currencies, Singapore dollars, Hong Kong dollars, Euros, Probably 100,000 Euros total."

"How do you want to be paid? I do have some currencies in Switzerland. I may have to go there as soon, after this kidnap thing is over, one way or another. Or, I can pay you in silver or gold. We have a recent quote from Switzerland that I used for Wayne," Gary said

"I think Wayne's idea is good. Silver."

"Okay, as of Monday, silver was selling on the open market at 171 Euros per ounce," and Gary dug out his calculator. "100,000 divided by 171 equals 585 ounces, say 700 ounces for good faith. I will dig it out of what I have here later today. I suppose if we were really desperate, I could go along with four million, and 10,000 ounces of silver, providing the ships were fuelled and ready to go. But, I think they are in a bind too, because it is unlikely there are any other buyers, and that price is way high."

"I think so too. Do you have any objection to that type of negotiation?"

"No it seems to be a good method, but I would put the price of the ships more in the order of two million cash and maybe up to one thousand ounces of silver total. Before the crash, I calculated that, based on the prices everything was selling at then, an ounce of silver should have a purchasing power of $1-2,000. I'm not very interested in trading much silver for less." Gary shrugged.

Lynn walked by the office door and Gary called out to her. "Did Wolfgang pick up his cash?"

"Yes, and I said you would call him."

Gary turned back to Claude. "I have been thinking about a shipping broker I know for membership, named Wolfgang Perl," Gary said still tired, forgetting that Wolfgang had recommended Claude in the first place.

"Oh, I've known him for years. Strange story. He was farm boy. Then got into the air force. He trained in woodcraft to repair the old airplanes, just as they were being phased out. The old WW II fighters even used spruce wood for spars in wings. Somehow he became one of those guys that, if you wanted something you went to him. In couple of days it would magically appear. When he got out of the air force, he bummed around for a while. He wound up in Argentina handling sheep and then buying wool for one of the British houses. Eventually, he tired of that and landed here in New York. He got job with a shipping broker. One day he got into argument and started his own company."

"What do you think of him? Would he make a good community member?" Gary asked.

"I'd say so. He's versatile, along with the flip side of that. He likes new mental challenges. Too long at one thing and he get bored. He's really smart. But sometimes you wouldn't think so. Doesn't seem to have initiative to start things. He needs somebody to push him in a direction before he will act. When he does take on something he's very good at it."

"So if we were to say to him we need 'X', go out and find it, he would likely do a good job at finding 'X'?" Gary asked.

"Look at his Air Force record. That's what he was famous for."

"Maybe we ought to have him looking for your ship's fuel then."

"That's good idea. Especially if he was community

member." Claude said reflectively.

"How about Bruce's crew? Are they all recommended for membership?"

"Yes, I selected them with that in mind."

"Okay let's get a meeting going for Saturday or Sunday at the apartment hotel to view candidates. I will include Wolfgang too," Gary said. "At the same time could you contact your kids and get their nominees lined up?"

"Okay."

"The meeting for Sunday afternoon about two sound good?" Gary asked.

"Good as any other," Claude responded. "If you have Wolfgang's number I think I'll call him about fuel too."

"I have to call him too. Let's go do that now."

"Okay, let's make it fast. I have to go see canny brothers."

"I think it's about time you had a bodyguard too. How about Jim?" Gary asked as he pulled up Wolfgang's number.

"Sounds good to me."

Gary called Wolfgang, "Wolfgang, I was calling about the payment you picked up."

"What's wrong, Gary?"

"Nothing except it may not be enough. We got unbelievable amounts of merchandise for one million and I'm not sure that payment is fair. It was the magic of the number a million dollars that confused them."

"We agreed on two percent as the finders fee. One hundred thousand is ten percent of one million. I owe you $80,000,"

"If you knew how many containers we got you wouldn't be saying that," Gary said. "Okay I'll want you to understand by knowing what we got before we settle this one way or another. I also wanted to talk to you about a couple of other things. First

Operation Phoenix

we expect the US dollars you are holding to drop dramatically in value so spend anything you can for real goods as quickly as possible. Okay?"

"I certainly have lots of places to spend money," Wolfgang laughed.

"Okay today or tomorrow is best. Next, I was hoping we might get you to do some other things with us, and toward that end, I'm calling a meeting on Sunday at two PM at an apartment hotel we are taking over for security purposes. We want everybody to briefly meet everybody else in the gang. We'll be explaining more in the meeting but the idea is to meet as many new people as you can to see whether you would feel comfortable working closely with them over a long period," Gary said.

"Should I bring my wife?"

"By all means. Do you have children?"

"Yes I got started late in life and I have two teens."

"I suppose we could find somewhere for them. Is there any TV still running?" Gary asked. "I haven't had time to notice if even newspapers are coming out."

"Yes there are a couple stations."

"Good they can watch that then. The last thing I wanted to talk about was part of the type of work we see you doing with us. I suppose your usual business is down to near zero."

"You're bloody right about that, Mon. What were you thinking of having me do?"

"Well your first assignment should you choose to accept it," Gary grinned, "is to spend some money quickly for some ships fuel to be delivered here in New York, hopefully tomorrow. Latest Saturday. I'll likely be out of the country Sunday, so I'm turning this all over to Claude D'Antonio who I'm turning you over to next. Ships are his area anyway so he's in charge."

"Oh I have known Claude for years."

"Okay I would like you to think how you might be compensated for successful completion and let me know," Gary turned over the phone to Claude and left to see whether Patti was still up.

He found Patti in animated conversation with Jan and Lynn. He was still disgusted and angry with Jan but he was also afraid to antagonize her in the present circumstances lest she be vindictive. He was keeping as much distance from her as possible because he didn't want to accidentally burst out in anger. He said, "After this morning, neither of you are going anywhere without a body-guard. Period. Patti, do you think Wayne might still be awake?"

"Yes, I just talked to him."

"Good, I'll call him right away. Would you bring Heidi and come into the office please?" Given Jan's actions Gary had decided to keep as many details from her as possible. He turned to Jan and Lynn. "Lynn did you get your hospital deal done?"

"Yes, it's done and paid for. The doctors are supervising the packing. We sent some containers over there." Lynn responded

"Fantastic. We really needed that hospital," Gary said. "Have Chris store the full containers at the hangar and the same with any pharmaceuticals you have lined up. Get Roy Bryant on the business of helping dismantle the equipment. Get everything paid for and delivered by the weekend. Okay?"

"Yes and we may have the second hospital tomorrow."

"Even more fantastic. You two are awesome. Do you feel more comfortable with these kind of deals now?" Gary asked.

"Yes but I like having Jan along. She's great in negotiations"

Operation Phoenix

"You and Jan work that out. We are having another 'meet the prospective new members' meeting Sunday at the apartment hotel. Two PM. They are coming on thick and fast as we get more people recruiting. Starting in about an hour I'll be sleeping. I suggest everybody get a good night's sleep too," Gary said as he headed for the office. Patti followed. Gary called Wayne, and then Eric to conference him in, and put them on the speakerphone.

"Wayne, it is Gary. I have Claude, Lynn, Eric, and Patti here for a conference. I am presuming you will need money especially since we want to get it spent by the weekend. That means that someone trusted has to bring it down starting in a few hours. Claude's about to go out negotiating, and I think maybe Jim or someone should accompany him. Eric has no big need as far as I know. While I have us all together and awake what does everybody have to say?"

Wayne asked, "How much money can you let me have?"

"Four million, plus or minus. We recovered all the money this morning."

"I'm going to need the four million. I have an opportunity to pick up a fully armed and functional missile destroyer for a million, and a tender loaded with ships fuel, plus some other goodies; shoulder mounted surface to air missiles, Harpoon, Javelin, and AT4 missiles, a huge bunch of rocket propelled grenades, armour piercing sniper rifles and ammo, night vision goggles, artillery, and a bunch more."

"Jesus, how many people are you thinking of recruiting?" Gary burst out. "Those destroyers carry hundreds of people."

"A modern missile destroyer usually has a compliment of four people to stand watch. They can even fight her until the ammo loaded in place runs out. I promised we would let the six people I bribed off at Cuba. Five of the guys are getting

Operation Phoenix

$100,000 each, and the other half a mil. Even $100,000 goes a long way in Cuba. Eric how are your operations going?" Wayne asked.

"Pretty good," Eric said. "Your plan to offer the tenants of the apartment hotel $1,000 cash to move quickly, plus free transport within a forty mile radius is working like gangbusters. We have the third floor cleared, most of the second, and a couple gone from the first. The chain link fence and gates are all installed. We're not getting much resistance. I don't need three SEALs."

"Good we have five there, plus Patti, and I have recruited five, so that's about our quota," Wayne said. "You might as well detach Jim to guard Claude, and Matt could start to Langley with cash"

Gary said, "How about fuel? Does Matt need to bring fuel?"

"Not really. He might bring an extra jerry can or two if there is room but I think I can get whatever I need. No pay for the soldier boys has them selling their frigging mothers if the price is right."

"Wayne that was a superb job by you, Eric, and the SEALs. Thank you. Matt should arrive tomorrow morning. See if you can spend four million in a day." Gary said and hung up. "Patti, do you know if Jim is reasonably rested?"

"About the same as everybody else. He'll be good for a few more hours."

"Make sure he is volunteering for this, brief him, and get him over here so Claude can get going," Gary said "Send somebody else in I have a short side trip for them." Turning to Claude, he said, "How are we going to crew these extra ships that Wayne seems to be buying?"

"I'll work on that," Claude said wearily. "I already have to

Operation Phoenix

crew our two new ships."

"Well, they're navy SEALs after all. There should be some relief there. Wayne seems to have had this in the works, so he may already have thought of a solution."

Gary spent a few minutes of frustration till he got through to a security guard at the IRS, about the only one to answer his phone. Even in government, few employees were at work. He got directions as to how he could get a signature for documentation delivered, photocopied everything and had a SEAL run over with the bank drafts he had obtained in Toronto.

Satisfied with another of his super-cautious preparations, he went with Matt to fuel Matt's car and get him underway. Claude shooed everybody out of the office and began phoning, recruiting crew and looking for fuel.

Gary asked Lynn if she or Jan could phone around and try to find some mattresses, beds, and linens because of the sleeping situation. He showered and crashed.

Chapter 35
Thursday night, March 9th —Day 24

Gary awoke at 8PM, still stiff, but thinking about the crewing of the various ships. Jan was asleep beside him. He slipped on a robe and padded out to the living room. Patti was sleeping in Eric's old room. Lynn must have found some beds. He noticed that the lights in the house next door were ablaze and some sort of meeting or party was going on at the Gibson's. *Unusual.*

Gary had chatted with Brian Gibson and his wife Ana of course, but they were a quiet couple that tended to keep to themselves. Brian was some kind of librarian and looked the part, heavy glasses and slightly balding. Ana was a simple oriental beauty from the Philippines but looked as if there might be some Chinese in her background. She was a horticulturist teaching at the university. Gary often wondered how Brian had managed to snare such a good-looking woman. Maybe because Brian's hobby was breeding unusual plants, and their yard both front and back, was always a marvel. They had two attractive but shy daughters in their mid teens.

In his office the answering machine blinked at him. Claude had left a message to call as soon as he was awake. Gary didn't like calling with everyone so tired but decided that Claude must have thought it important. Claude sounded a bit out of breath and Gary could hear sounds in the background. "Hi Claude. You packing?"

"Yeah. Got crew in. I wanted to tell you we sign for ships

Operation Phoenix

tomorrow. Two million dollars plus 1,000 ounces of silver. We'll have enough fuel to move the ships, load them, and then get into international waters in case Wolfgang doesn't come up with some fuel. We wait for Wayne's fuel tender there."

"Well, it sure looks as if that military stuff could be useful."

Claude hmmmed. "I'm not sure destroyer was best idea. It chews through fuel at rate only government could afford. At cruising speed, the Queen Elizabeth liner gets about 12 feet per gallon. If that destroyer is at battle speed, won't get more than 14 or 15 feet per gallon, despite being much smaller. It uses brute force for that additional speed. Hull design doesn't help fuel consumption after certain point. Loafing along probably will double that," Claude said.

"My god, I had no idea. Feet per gallon?" Gary exclaimed, and paused. "Still if the world reverts to what I think it might, somewhere along the line we will have to fight for our lives. It would be nice to have the tools to do so. Every coin has two sides," he grimaced. "Anyway it sounds as if we may have got her for $1,500 Canadian so we can scuttle her without great cost. She does make good protection for the rest of the fleet. Another negative is that the navy might get somewhat upset with their destroyer floating off without authorization and shoot back first."

"Wayne doesn't seem to think that will be problem. He's there. I assume he knows."

"Aside from fuel considerations do you see any other negatives?"

"I see one," Claude said reflectively. "If guy has gun he tends to think of solutions to problems in terms of guns. If two guys with guns facing each other the possibility of solving problem in imaginative other ways goes down very much."

"True enough, but without minimizing that aspect, I do think we have to add, 'in normal times'. I doubt that most of the population is now completely rational. If the other guy doesn't have a gun it's not likely that any amount of rational thinking will save him," Gary countered.

"You asked me for negative. I think I gave you valid one. The SEALs have been trained that any problem they are handed is solved using force either defensive or offensive. That was case in our world till recently. They were never handed problem unless other avenues were not productive. They were trained specialists in application of force. Part of training will have to be undone or controlled. They must become more generalist. They must apply force if that is the only alternative."

"You have just put into words some of the things I have been feeling. These guys make me uneasy. I doubt there was another way but they killed everyone in the kidnapper organization as a matter of course. That was an assumed conclusion. I didn't help by saying 'anyone who messes with the community will regret it.' We'll definitely have to institute some controls and redirecting of goals, or they will be a great danger to the community. Imaginative thinking will have to take first place." Gary grimaced.

"In fact we have the same problem throughout the community. Our age is one of specialists. We have been getting as many skills as possible, but really, we have little room for 'one shot' specialists. The whole community must be generalists each of which has one or more special skills. We are too small to be otherwise. This will take some serious thinking and I'd like to talk to you later on this subject." Gary paused. "Getting back to our more immediate problems can I be of assistance to you in recruiting ship's crews? Do you have a list of people you would like to get but have not reached yet?"

Operation Phoenix

"Yes I do." Claude read his lists which Gary copied so he could prepare. Claude offered the information that he was moving into the hotel Saturday and some of his children were moving in tomorrow. His own packing was nearly done. The stripping of the Hospital was coming along well since a large crew recommended by Roy Bryant had been hired to pack.

"Are most of Bruce Nott's crew moving their families on to the ship between now and Saturday too?" Gary asked.

"As far as I know."

"What about supplies for the two new ships?"

"We get whatever is there but won't be much," Claude responded. "We may be able to rob a bit from Bruce's ship."

"Do I need to get more money down for Bruce or whoever the captain of the next ship will be?"

"No for the first hours I will be captain of new ships. I'll take some money for ship's safe. We'll have about 150 containers to load at the container facility. I have minimum crew for one ship and captain and a couple of crew for other. Captain is one of the guys on your original list. I can get him to do recruiting if he joins community."

"I was wondering if we could get supplies in Canada," Gary mused. "I have some cash in Zurich. I could either deposit it there or try to bring some back. Would they take a bank draft drawn on a Swiss bank or maybe they have an account there that we could deposit to?"

"Canada might be great idea. I'll check right away."

Gary went in to dress and when he came out the phone was ringing. It was Claude. "We can get whatever we want in Canada including fuel. All we have to do is get to Halifax. They have account in Zurich. You'll be able to deposit directly to it. What did you do with Wayne's silver?"

"It's here in the office. He hasn't been in the city to take delivery," Gary replied. "However Eric has picked up two or three safes from clunker cars we were using to hide things in. We'll give you one of those. So I have to go to Zurich eh? I'll do that Sunday."

"Leave my silver where it is. I won't have place to keep it at hotel anyway."

He separated Claude's two million dollars and 1,000 ounces of silver out into bags. Lastly he made preparation to head hunt for Claude the following morning.

That night despite the tension in the air he still couldn't keep his hands off Jan. It is remarkable how a few days abstinence stimulates the libido and calms anger.

Friday March 10th And Saturday March 11th

Friday and Saturday till he and Patti left for Canada, were a round of small emergencies. Wolfgang was as good as his reputation, and came up with some fuel. The head hunting went relatively well. Gary was able to arrange five appointments between seamen and Claude at the original ship in the container loading facility. The smaller of the two ships was dispatched with Claude commanding, to pick up the balance of containers from Jack Sopper. Jack was a happy puppy because when the last acceptable container was loaded from the list, a review of the remaining list produced enough containers to fill the smaller ship to capacity, and Jack wound up with somewhat more than his desired one million dollars.

The larger of the two new ships was dispatched to New Haven to receive containers of hospital equipment, machine shops and machine tools, electrical generating equipment, woodworking shops, goods stored at the hangars, and the growing number of containers from the families relocating to the hotel.

The tenseness was high for Gary and Patti, constantly

Operation Phoenix

transporting cash thither and yon doling out money to everyone who was busily spending money. The community seemed to have reached critical mass and things were moving along swiftly. They had to keep to the back roads to avoid the masses of humanity streaming from the city because there were invariably some who, despite the general lethargy of starving people, were desperate enough to risk death to loot anything that might give them an advantage. Generally the walking people were dirty and bedraggled. Personal hygiene was becoming a thing of the past leaving a huge vector for disease. Aside from a car with fuel being a huge advantage, the people driving that car were undoubtedly rich, and who knew what the car contained? Already three side windows sported star shaped breaks from thrown rocks.

Aside from human predators, feral dogs and starving abandoned pets made any exit from protective walls such as the car a danger. Largely they were feeding on the stinking, rotting uncollected garbage lining the streets, smelling because of the warmer weather. Like the human population they seemed slightly insane, and a pack of them were not above attacking a human. Gary had shot several of them. Guns they seemed to understand although that did not always deter them, or the human predators.

It was rare to take a drive anywhere without encountering roadblock tolls. Gary had taken to driving the car because he knew the area better than Patti. Patti sat there demurely, a weak female. So few businesses were open that it was difficult to find the goods he needed. They were up north near Groton, the naval base, when a four-man roadblock, two armed with sub-machine guns, stopped them. The two carrying machine guns approached each side of the car. Unlike other roadblocks that simply demanded their toll the two ordered them out of the car. Gary was fairly quick to comply. Patti was acting the frightened female and moving slowly.

"Come on get your cunt out here so I can see whether it is worth pissing on." the sailor leered at her. The third man who had accompanied Gary's machine gun man roughly disarmed him. The fourth man hung back.

"Okay, Okay. Take the money in the trunk but leave her alone," Gary said loudly, and he reached down and popped the trunk. There was about $300,000 in a bag, which Gary had not even bothered to zip up at the last stop.

The fourth sailor came running, and went round to the trunk. "Jackpot" he yelled, holding up packets of bills in each hand.

Gary's two men started around toward the trunk. Even Patti's gunman was distracted. Patti's wicked little knife made short and silent work of his heart. Before he even collapsed Patti had grabbed his machine gun. Then she screamed. Gary hit the deck. Patti stitched new bullet holes in the trunk lid and three stupid sailor heads that popped up from behind the trunk to see what was going on.

"Jesus you are some woman," Gary said shakily.

Patti nudged a blood-spattered packet of bills lying on the ground with the toe of her boot and said, "Sorry, it looks like I got blood and brains all over the money." She grinned and held up her hand for a high five.

"It will wash," and Gary gave her the high five weakly but reverently. Something Gary had been afraid of was already happening. As Claude had said 'We are on a very slippery slope.' Here was murder again and Wayne was very involved in stealing. *It's not ALL our fault. Society is moving that way fast. We have to do something, but what?*

The sun was shining brightly and some hints of green were

Operation Phoenix

evident, heralding a coming spring.

When Gary arrived home Jan was there and her house guard was chatting with Gary's guards. Wayne stopped at the house at about the same time as Gary arrived home. Matt, and Kirk another new seal, who arrived back with Wayne, had gone on with Lynn to the hotel. Jan said that the pharmaceuticals were done and were being loaded. Two SEALs were aboard each of the warships that Wayne had purchased for a bribe of one million dollars each. Wayne told Gary that what little space was available on the deck and below deck was stacked with machine guns, heavier guns, missiles, ammo, and other military equipment that Wayne had been offered. The destroyer and the fuel tender were on their way out of US waters to rendezvous with Bruce's ship.

Gary went into the back yard to do a couple of quick chores. His next-door neighbour hurried out and accosted him. "Gary, Could spare me a moment?" Brian called over the stone wall.

Gary looked around for an escape route still in high-tension mode, and then decided reluctantly that civility was a necessary part of life. "Surely, but I'm in a bit of a hurry. What's your problem?" Gary said, walking over to the wall separating them.

"I hate to bother you with this but I don't know where to turn. I've tried everything and I can't think of anything else. You always seemed to be resourceful and I thought I'd ask you," Brian rambled on. "The world has gone absolutely crazy."

"And what did you want to ask?" Gary said patiently and gently.

"As you know, I'm a librarian at the university library."

"Yes."

"Actually I am the head librarian," Brian said distractedly.

Operation Phoenix

"No, you never mentioned that. Go on."

"They're burning the books," Brian blurted out.

"Who is burning what books?" Gary asked still gently and patiently.

"Some ruffians broke into the library. As you know the university was closed," Brian said, still rambling. "They're making a bonfire to keep warm. They have a gun."

Ah, the Alexandrian Librarians, Gary thought. He considered for a few moments.

Some people work for the love of knowledge and for the value of preserving that knowledge, not for money or fame. Over a thousand years ago, in Alexandria, there existed the greatest repository of learning and literature the world had ever known. It was sacked and burned by an invading army. A couple of current authors had raised and addressed the question of; 'what happened to the Alexandrian Librarians? Had they died defending that knowledge?' The conclusion seemed to be that the librarians perished in an attempt to save the library's contents. Some people love knowledge so much that they have dedicated their lives to it and are quite likely to put the survival of that knowledge ahead of their own survival.

This could be a tremendous opportunity for the community. While they had been trying to pick up skills and while practical skills are absolutely essential, who knew what skills or information they would lack? If they could get that university library they would be half way to developing any skills they needed and didn't have. At least if they had to reinvent the wheel they know it existed, that it is round and moves things more easily. They had a picture of it.

Not only that, but *here is someone trained to manage information, but also with horticultural skills something we are sadly in need of. I should have thought of them as potential*

Operation Phoenix

community members before, Gary thought. *In fact I think I have a little Alexandrian librarian in me because I personally would hate to see humanity lose this information. The way things are going humanity is going to get knocked back several hundred years. There were many things that had to be reinvented in the 1500s, after being lost in the time of the dark ages, starting about 1,000 AD.* Aloud Gary said, "But if you chase them out isn't there a great danger that they will simply come back?"

"Yes that has already happened. Now they have a gun and we have run out of food. I don't know how long we can last."

"If we could find a way to pack up most of those books and move them to somewhere safer would you be willing to help?" Gary asked carefully.

"Oh yes everybody at the university would."

"Well maybe we can arrange something. You say that you are out of food. How long has this been going on?" Gary asked.

"We absolutely ran out of food on Thursday but we had very little before that."

"Why don't you and your wife come over for a minute? I'm sure we could spare a little food. Bring the kids too." Gary suggested.

"Oh thank you. We'll be right over."

Gary went back into the house. "Jan, that roast of beef we had last night? I want four of the thickest sandwiches you ever saw, rice, and milk or coffee. The people next door are starving and they are coming over for a bit of food. Wayne could you please stay I think there is a job here. I should have thought of them as potential community members before. They've not eaten in days."

No sooner had he spoken than there was a timid knock on the door. Gary wheeled and opened the door. "Come on in and meet the gang." Four rather haggard, hungry looking specimens

Operation Phoenix

struggled in.

"Everybody, I'd like you to meet Brian and Ana Gibson and their daughters. Brian is chief librarian at the university and Ana is a horticulturist. They both conspire to have one of the most beautiful and exotic yards in the city. Brian's hobby is genetics and breeding of unusual plants," Gary announced, in order to give those present some background. He introduced everyone in the room by name.

Jan was by now busy cutting huge slabs off the roast beef and preparing the thick, dark heavy bread slices with margarine and just a touch of mustard. Four sets of eyes watched with an unbelievable and undivided intensity, matched only by a dog waiting anxiously for a treat from the dinner table.

"We have some rice pilaf. I'll heat it in the microwave," Jan spooned a bit of gravy over the meat and stuck the sandwiches in the microwave to heat for a few seconds.

"Won't you sit down here at the table?" Gary asked.

Four automatons moved over to the table without once ever losing sight of the food.

Jan served the sandwiches on plates, and stuck the rice into the microwave to heat. Four pairs of hands exercised great restraint and decorum while they carefully, delicately picked up the sandwiches. The sandwiches made it all the way to their mouths before the wolfing began. Gary poured four glasses of milk while Jan divided the rice, and they served the second course. It disappeared in instants too.

Then the Gibson's just sat there, slightly slumped forward, breathing deeply, waiting as their stomachs converted the food to energy, and feeling the strength flow back into their limbs.

Finally, Brian straightened up and said simply, "I don't believe I have ever tasted anything so good. Thank you." Murmured 'thank yous' echoed around the table.

Operation Phoenix

Gary said, "We have a bit of frozen stuff we can give you before you go home but in the meantime I would like to talk to Wayne about your problem."

"Oh please do," Brian said.

"Wayne, there have been some kids who invaded the University library who have been making bonfires with the books to keep themselves warm. I'd hate to see all that knowledge lost to mankind. I foresee that this particular thing will likely happen over and over again around the world. If we can chase out the kids, at least one of whom has a gun, then I thought maybe we could get these books into containers and haul them to somewhere safer. Besides I think that having this information available to us would be invaluable. Do you see a way of removing these kids without causing a whole lot of blood to be spilled?" Gary asked. "Brian assures me that the whole university would pitch in to help pack the books."

Wayne frowned elaborately. "On the face of it I think we could probably do that. I'd have to look at the situation to have a firm opinion but I think it could be done." Wayne then began to question Brian about the people involved, their arms, their numbers and ages, etc., and the layout of the building. He ended again with an opinion that it was probably doable but he would have to see first.

Gary went downstairs and got a roast of beef, a pork roast, a few tins of peas and corn, some rice, and a few loaves of bread and bags of milk. He struggled up the stairs and dumped the boxes at the front door. He then went back into the living room and queried the community present with his eyebrows as to their reaction to the Gibson's. Receiving affirmative nods he addressed the Gibson's. "We are having a meeting tomorrow afternoon at two. This meeting is for those people that are working with us and for all the members to get to know one

Operation Phoenix

another. I suppose you have no fuel so I will ask Jan to pick you up and bring you back. I'll be out of the city. As yet it is secret so only your present family is invited or even to know about the meeting. No one else under any circumstances is to know, do you understand?" he asked the girls. "No telling your friends in confidence please."

They nodded.

Addressing Brian and Ana, he said, "Would you like to attend?"

"Of course. Do you foresee further work together?" Brian asked.

"I certainly hope so. Someone will have to manage this information. In the meantime it is imperative that we act quickly to get those books to a safe place. We need a bit of time together to plan. Is your phone still working?" Gary asked Brian.

"Just my cell," answered Ana.

"Okay give us half an hour and we'll call you with the next steps." Gary said.

Gary saw them to their own door with the frozen food he had dropped near his door. As he returned he went over to the guard outside. "I'm pulling a guard from elsewhere to help here. I want you to keep an eye on the house and the people next door. They are to receive protection too please."

Gary went back into the house. Wayne said, "That library could be a life saver. I'd hate to see that knowledge lost to us. It'll be invaluable in training. I wish I had thought of that while I was in Langley. I picked up all sorts of special equipment but I would have picked up texts too."

"I think we have to get those books on board the ship as soon as possible, starting tonight. Jan would you get as many pot roasts as possible started cooking, please. We will have to feed the workers as part of their pay. Say we pay them $10 per hour, with a meal at the start and the finish of each six-hour shift. They could take a sandwich home to the family. Better get lots of rice started too. Can you organize some of the people at the hotel to get a food preparation and distribution line going? Do you see any problems Wayne?"

"No we can probably wipe them out easily." Wayne shrugged.

"Now, there's something I don't want to happen. In the previous world you guys always got problems when there was nothing left but force. Now your job is much larger. Not only are you going to be our enforcement arm, you're also part of our diplomatic arm. No killing unless you are directly threatened or the community is aware, and approves ahead of time that killing is contemplated, and the reasons for it. I concur that sometimes killing is necessary but it's not the first resort, it's the last resort. In this case if you kill anyone that does not have a gun and is threatening to use it the whole university workforce will turn against us." Gary said. "No short notice killing unless you or someone in the community is threatened. Okay?"

"Yes, I suppose you're right. We don't have what might be termed a diplomatic arm. Okay an expanded mandate as a diplomatic arm."

"Exactly. Patti, I'm going to be up for a while, so I'll want to sleep on the way to Canada and I'd like you to drive. Can you get some sleep now please?" Gary asked.

"Yes Sir," she responded, and left for the shower and bedroom.

"You seem to have been elevated in her mind," Wayne observed. "I've never heard her bestow the honour of 'Sir' on a civvy yet."

"Presuming we can get those kids out of the library I guess we need containers and a lot of pallets to stack the books on.

Operation Phoenix

And some cling wrap plastic to hold the pallet loads together. We need somebody to take those racks apart. We'll need the racks later. How difficult would you expect the job of getting the kids out to be?" Gary asked.

"The job of getting the kids out should be easy. The hard part will be inspecting the library to insure no one else is left there." Wayne said. "Two SEALs would probably be enough to get the kids out but we'll require a lot of time to detail inspect."

"Okay more work for our already overworked SEALs. Would you look to the SEALs and I will contact Chris Habel about the rest of it."

Operation Phoenix

Chapter 36

Gary dialled Chris. "Hi, it's Gary. How are things going?"

"Pretty good. Sales are down now that fuel is over $100 per gallon but our profit remains about the same."

"I have good news and bad news. We've located a university library which we think is invaluable for the knowledge it contains. We want to get those books aboard the ship as soon as possible. Yesterday would be best," Gary said. "I'm hoping to have a good number of people working at putting books on pallets and wrapping them in plastic. But we need containers in a rather continuous flow. We have the 'full container' lift truck at the docks in New Haven so we can get the containers off the trailers but I still have to buy some containers. We'll need at least three tractors, and hopefully a lot more to yank the trailers around. Hopefully it will be a 24 hour operation."

"The drivers will not be so happy going back to driving seeing the money they are getting for selling fuel. They have been bitching about hauling people's stuff from and to the hotel already."

"Pay them whatever they are getting from selling fuel from the money you have for me from fuel sales," Gary decided quickly. "I'll also need at least one, and preferably two forklift drivers and fork lifts, and a number of manual pallet lifters for the library. Do you know where we can get those rolls of cling wrap plastic to hold the pallet loads together?"

"I have a couple of cases. I think I know where I can put

Operation Phoenix

my hands on several more cases quickly. I can bring two forklifts with the first container and a half a dozen pallet lifters. Are you going to need pallets?"

"Oh, God yes. Whatever you can round up that are in half decent shape. I'll try to get some more. This is a seven-story building so I expect to get several hundred containers of books, with about 48 pallets average if pallets can be stacked two high in a container. We won't be able to take all the books of course, but I want to get as much as possible." Gary said. "We still have to get the family containers loaded on top at the ship and containers for the animals."

"Okay."

Gary continued his rapid-fire delivery "One other thing we will need is some food from the hangars. Can you or Eric get a pickup truck over there to pick up a few sacks of rice, and some pork and beef roasts from the reefers? We'll have to feed these workers as part of their pay. I hope to get the operation started by midnight so hopefully we'll have some pallets there before that so the workers can start loading them right away. I'll be gone by then but someone can take over. Would you do that?"

"Yeah, I'll be in it up to my neck anyway. Might as well."

"I'll try and get somebody else looking for pallets and containers too. We'll need about fifty of the empty containers stacked aside at the docks for families to live in for a few days while we travel plus how ever many containers you need to transport the animals. By the way buy food for the animals for at least a couple of months, preferably six or more months."

"Okay."

"I'll get Eric to locate some other stuff I want to put in the Trambull office container before we take it over to the ship. He'll need a small truck," Gary said. "You work it out with him. Anything else you need?"

Operation Phoenix

"Not that I can think of."

Gary called Wolfgang. "Wolfgang it's Gary. What are you doing in the office?"

"Just sitting here crying or rather thinking bleak thoughts," he said. "I came to pack some of the files."

"Well, packing seems reasonable but I called because I have another rush job."

"More fuel?" asked Wolfgang.

"No. I need at least 500 weather tight, ocean-going containers. You might try Containerhaus in Jersey. You should be able to get them for less than $750 cash each, maybe as little as $300. As well, tonight I urgently need about a thousand wooden pallets or any type of similar sized pallet with a flat top. Ultimately we will need enough pallets to fill those containers. What is it, 48 pallets per container, comes to 25,000 pallets, probably by tomorrow. We're packing books on them so I don't need new ones just good working ones. We also need a large quantity of cling wrap plastic to wrap around pallet loads of goods to keep them stable. Do you think you could find some this afternoon?"

"I could try Mon. That's awfully short notice," Wolfgang said.

"One more thing, absolutely necessary but not as urgent although we would like to pay for it today, is two or more good liquid food truck tanks. I need it for water for human consumption," Gary said, suddenly realizing that fresh water need. The ship would have some water storage but it wasn't designed for that many people and animals. "The containers and pallets are top priority. I want them starting to be used by midnight. Contact Chris Habel at this number," and Gary gave him the number. "Tell Chris to pick up the money to pay for everything at my house. Coordinate everything with him. I'll be

Operation Phoenix

gone for a few days. Anything else you need? I'm in a terrible rush."

"No, I don't think so. " Wolfgang said dubiously. "At least 500 containers, pallets to fill them and cling wrap to stabilize the loads."

"Okay I gotta hop. Please try to be at the meeting tomorrow even if someone has to pick you up."

Gary called Eric and brought him up to speed, asked that he bring the others at the hotel up to speed, particularly Lynn, who he wanted to coordinate the people working in the library and getting meat and rice from the hangars. Then he was to arrange for changed guard assignments at the house. Eric said Wayne had already been in touch with him and the SEALs there. Gary asked Eric if he could spell Wayne on the organizing of the packing.

Next he called Brian Gibson back. "Hi it's Gary Alden next door."

"Oh yes Gary. I'm afraid your food overwhelmed us and we didn't thank you adequately when we left. I think we were in a bit of a state of shock." Brian started.

"Think nothing of it. We try to look after those who are working with us. I have an answer regarding the library. We'd like to go ahead and try," Gary said to get the subject on what he wanted to discuss.

"Oh that's wonderful. How soon can we start? Do we have to wait for Monday to get those ruffians out?" Brian gushed.

"We were thinking more like the kids being out in three hours and beginning to work at midnight packing books on a 24 hour basis. The guy you were talking to, Wayne, is a SEAL. They'll move those kids out quickly. We need you to let us in. If you have any home numbers of people who might be willing to work and Ana can phone them, please have her do it. We want

Operation Phoenix

to get at least 50 to 75 people there by midnight, ready to work. We want hard workers only. This is not a place and time to philosophize and discuss. Once we secure the place I'll want you on the phone recruiting workers. Anybody not working will be immediately let go." Gary emphasized.

"How can we let people go who are volunteering?"

Gary was mildly put off by Brian's hesitance. "Oh they'll be paid. Cash and food like you got. We don't know how many containers of books the library has but we can take several hundred containers but that's all. So we will prioritize what we take. The important thing is to recruit workers to start working at midnight tonight, so your job will be to start phoning people as soon as we get the premises secure. We'll pay $10 per hour in cash and the workers get a sandwich and rice like you had at the start of a six-hour shift, and at the end of that shift. If the workers want to work 12 hours then they get four sandwiches. They can bring a bag to take some home to their families if they want. Not extra but if they want to save some of what we pay they can eat it there or take it home. If Ana can start phoning too it would help a lot. In fact Jan might be able to help too. We have to move really, really fast on this because the ship that the books will go on may have to leave at any minute. Okay?"

Brian paused as if he had blinked at the speed with which events were moving, and said, "Yes I understand. May I tell Ana what is happening?"

"Of course. She can hardly recruit workers without both her and the workers knowing what is going on. One moment," and Gary placed the mouthpiece of his phone against his belly, and shouted, "Wayne how long till we will want Brian Gibson to let us in to the library?"

"Half an hour plus travel time," Wayne shouted back.

"Brian, we will be ready to pick you up in half an hour to

Operation Phoenix

let us into the library. Can you be ready?"

"Uh, yes. This is very fast isn't it?"

"Every minute that we delay more books are burned. Do you want that?" Gary demanded.

"No."

"Is there a problem with doing this?"

"Well, no, but it's very fast. I'll get ready."

"You said I was resourceful. The biggest part of being resourceful is actually doing something not agonizing over it. We have a complete plan now and circumstances demand we act quickly. We're doing so. Nobody will get hurt unless they threaten us. If they threaten us then it's okay for us to defend ourselves and we will. You don't have to face them, just open the door for us so we can do what needs to be done," Gary said.

"I'll get ready."

Gary hung up and said to Wayne. "He's getting cold feet. Not a good person to rely on in an emergency but he's a worker when he's left alone. I guess we can't all be chiefs, there has to be some Indians. Maybe he'll learn with a bit of exposure to the real world that once you have a goal, focus on it totally."

Gary, Wayne, and the others finished their preparations, picked up Brian and left for the library. It was a gray building, probably a formed concrete building with few windows above the first floor. It was clear that the alarms ringing were fire and smoke alarms. Eric arrived with a couple of SEALs. Brian showed them the window that had been smashed, boarded up, and then the boarding had been ripped off to regain entry. He then let them in through the main doors.

The SEALs fanned out, first investigating the immediate surroundings so they were not subject to surprise attack, then heading for the section of the main floor where the noise was coming from, the camping ground of the squatters. The section

Operation Phoenix was located between the current popular fiction section, the telephone book reference section, and the official government publications section, in a comfortable reading area with soft couches.

A small bonfire because the weather was warm, obviously the source of the smoke alarms, was burning cheerfully. Amazingly the sprinkler system had not gone off nor had the fire spread, probably because the fire was small and the ground floor ceilings quite high.

Gary, who had been following Wayne came out from between aisles of bookshelves. Further down a SEAL appeared, and finally, diagonally about one third of the way around the circle, another SEAL.

At first nothing happened. The squatters did not notice the SEALs. Then someone did and consternation erupted. A young man jumped up into a crouch, pulled a gun and shot without aiming. Two machine pistols burped three round bursts and the young man fell back, riddled. The SEALs had aimed, accurately. A young woman screamed and began to run towards their 'secret' exit.

Gary shot a round into the ceiling, and yelled, "Hold it. Take your friend, and your junk with you but don't go near that gun. Anybody that touches that gun is dead." The young man was still twitching his death throes and many of the squatters watched him in fascinated horror. The rest watched the SEALs in shocked horror.

"Fucking move it," bellowed Wayne in parade square volumes.

A tall young man with a scraggly beard eventually stood up, shouldered his backpack and grabbed one of the gunman's hands. Come on he motioned to another. Once started the crowd had a direction and they all moved mindlessly to gather their

Operation Phoenix

stuff, grab a piece of the dead mans clothes or a leg, and help carry him out. Gary and Wayne wedged the plywood on the window back into place and then the SEALs began a slow, detailed search of the building. Shortly after two, and then another pair of lovers who wanted to be alone, appeared shepherded by a SEAL. They were escorted out.

One of the SEALs found a fire extinguisher and doused the flames. Brian was escorted in and Gary asked him, "Can you bypass that alarm system? It's driving me nuts. I don't know how those kids stood it."

Brian did as requested and the silence was awesome. The air conditioning system laboured to clear the air of smoke.

"How many freight elevators have you got?" Gary asked Brian.

"Two, but all eight of the passenger elevators are heavy duty because we are always transporting heavy loads of books between floors."

"Okay. We're going to want all the card catalogues, technical and reference books first, our official government publications last. Fiction next to last." Gary said. "It's time for you to get started on getting workers down here. We're extremely short of time. We want work to begin sharp at midnight so you have a lot of work to do fast. A guy named Chris Habel will back a couple of containers up to your loading docks. How many docks do you have?"

"Six."

"Good. Chris and Wayne will be in charge of getting things actually moving. My daughter Lynn will coordinate the people stacking books on pallets," Gary said. "Can you get 75 workers into here by midnight? We have to arrange to feed them. We want double that working by tomorrow. If you know someone who is persuasive get him or her in to help you recruit,

Operation Phoenix

although we may not be able to feed them till we get the food down here." Gary said, hoping for at least 50 to 100 workers the following day.

"Yes, I know just the person, in fact I know several. But you don't seem interested in the great literature of our history?" Brian asked.

"Good, get them down to help recruit. Get card catalogues and technological stuff including maps and other geographical stuff first, which will allow us to protect ourselves and disseminate the information. Any CD's you have, library programs, or other computer-based information is important. We need people to strip down and move the computers themselves. I'll get Heidi, a woman I know to help recruit computer people but you get university staff because they know the system. Do you have any libraries besides this one?"

"Yes," answered Brian. "There is the engineering library and pretty well every department has a small group of often used texts and other useful data."

"Those are probably the most useful books of all. We want that whole engineering library as a top priority after the card catalogues and computers. I want you to get a crew to go to every department and every professor's office and strip out any books on any subject you find. Get technical books then any history, followed by the great thinkers. I am less interested in general fiction but it does have a very vital place. Great, or imaginative thinkers are very valuable no matter what the field. Artists and creative people who think like that are the most valuable thinking one can have. Conditions will get worse before they get better; so we need to have a central repository of knowledge to enable mankind to rebuild quickly. Okay?"

"Yes, I think so."

Gary continued to instruct in great detail lest Brian began

Operation Phoenix

agonizing over some new question. "We'll place pallets in the aisle between rows of bookshelves. Workers will carry books and load the pallets as level and as tightly as possible to about 40 inches of books in height. Try and get the pallets as close to the same height as possible, but don't stack them too high. We have to stack one pallet on top of another inside the containers. No stacking of books outside the edges of the pallet. They'll get damaged. A second person or crew will come along and plastic wrap the load tightly so it won't slide around. A third crew will take the pallets to the dock. A fourth crew will disassemble shelves because we are going to need those shelves later.

"We'll throw shelf parts on top of the pallets of books in every container. Keep the small parts like nuts and bolts in buckets or wastebaskets. We want the job complete by Sunday afternoon. Any questions?" Gary asked.

"Sunday! The whole library?" Brian looked at Gary as if he were crazy.

"Yes. We are going to have some problems soon that might stop us from getting more books. So the longer you dilly-dally around getting workers down here the fewer books we can take. Any questions?" Gary repeated.

"No. In view of the rush, which I don't quite understand, you plans make sense," Brian admitted.

"Okay, Wayne and I are going to leave soon, as will the currently in place SEALs. A few new SEALs will take their place. Their job is simply to guard, nothing else. For food we will require access to the cafeteria. The people staffing the cafeteria will only deal with the food and the proper distribution of it, along with the cash payments. I'll be out of the country for a few days. Hopefully, we will have 300 to 400 containers loaded by tomorrow night but that's pushing it. Any other questions?" Gary asked.

Operation Phoenix

"No. I guess I had better get on the phone."

"Get your people who can recruit first. It's vital you multiply your efforts as fast as possible," Gary said. He conferred with Wayne, and left. On the way home he called Roy Bryant to see if he knew of anyone who would like to work disassembling racks at these rates. Roy thought he did and said he'd send them with enough tools to do the job.

Gary got back home and immediately began to take the necessities for the Canada trip into the garage. His overnight bag and things he would need such as his notes regarding what was stored at the various warehouses, and all the available Canadian cash.

Following his nose he checked the oven where roasts were cooking. He checked and basted them. He tiptoed into the bedroom where Jan appeared to be getting some sleep in preparation for a long night. Checking the clock radio he found it set to go off in an hour which suited him just fine because he had planned to get about an hour and a half sleep himself. He climbed into bed and snuggled up to Jan. Sliding his hand toward her breast, she "ummm'ed," moved back towards him and raised her arm slightly to give him access, all apparently without waking up. Despite how upset he was with her kidnap actions, Gary felt a rush of tenderness toward her. *Men in love are truly irrational beings* he thought. *We sure have not evolved far from the animals.*

When Gary awoke to the alarm he was still feeling tender so he leaned over and clicked off the radio, and started kissing her shoulder and neck. "Hi sweetie." When she rolled over to kiss him back she discovered he was not only feeling tender he was also feeling horny.

"Oh HO, Don't move. I'll be right back," and she slipped on a robe and padded off to the kitchen to check her roasts.

Operation Phoenix

When she returned, she closed the bedroom door carefully and crawled over the foot of the bed not even taking off her robe, but merely undoing the belt so it fell open. Crawling, straddling his body until she reached a level that she could get her toes under the covers and slide back down onto him, she rode him to what is known in the trade as a quickie.

Gary showered and discussed with Jan a quick and easy way of controlling the pays and food give away at the library. Jan informed him that a number of the women at the hotel were pitching in on shifts and that SEALs would be chauffeuring them back and forth.

He and Patti ate a quick meal and packed two sandwiches each for the trip. Gary's prepaid ticket and Patti's Canadian citizenship should forestall most questions at customs. They packed most of the available Canadian, Swiss, and Euro cash, as well as a bit of US cash for roadblocks and bribes, if necessary. The pile of US cash had certainly been depleting, with six million for Claude and Wayne alone gone and another 1.5 million immediately accounted for.

Gary and Patti left early, deciding that roadblocks and deteriorating roads would slow them considerably. During the first two hours they discussed Patti's assignment of recruiting farmers in Canada and keeping an eye open for specific products that might be useful. If Gary was delayed beyond a Tuesday return, and it were possible, she was to fly to Halifax and try to pick up one or two containers of dried potato flakes. They could be picked up in Halifax while the two new ships were taking on supplies. Gary doubted she had enough money for even that.

Gary put his seat back and went to sleep. At customs there was the usual delay but no problems and they drove to Toronto. Patti drove Gary to the airport to drop him before making her final dash to her parents home. In due course Gary boarded his

Operation Phoenix

plane and flew off to Zurich, studying, thinking about his plans and sleeping along the way.

Chapter 37
Sunday March 12th -- Day 27

At the Zurich airport Gary paused, looking around and trying to get a feel for the crime situation. There seemed to be slightly more cops around than he remembered from the previous trip. He stopped one cop and asked him.

"The crime situation has not changed appreciably. Just the usual dunderheads, but things are getting tense and we are on higher alert."

"Is unemployment up and are businesses operating normally?" Gary asked.

"Well unemployment is up, especially in the export sector because of the currency problems. We can still trade in Euros, but things are pretty uncertain and seem to becoming more so. We are alert but are waiting to get a better idea of circumstances before acting."

This was about what Gary had expected. Usually anyone who saw trouble ahead were either the 'survivalists' who essentially prepared for nuclear war in their bunker, or the gold bugs who were going to become wealthy instantly by owning precious metals and thought their wealth could buy them a normal life in today's terms, but made no preparations for the guaranteed ripple effects. In the US because of the oil crisis, the whole plastics industry was shut down. Every heavy user of energy such as steel mills, glass factories, or paper mills was shut down. Every electrical plant that used hydrocarbons to generate electricity was shut down.

Operation Phoenix

Gary knew of one small city of 120,000 people. A small steel mill employing less than 200, alone consumed fully one quarter of the electrical power used by all of the city and over one third of the natural gas. Thankfully, with all the big industrial users shut down the hydro generated electricity could largely keep up with the reduced demand but each of these, in turn, affected other downstream entities. If you didn't now have a steel butcher knife, a nail, a razor blade, or a car or car part, you weren't going to get one anytime soon.

Gary checked in to the hotel and rented a car. He showered to try to combat jet lag, and as he was showering he thought, *One thing that I am going to miss is long hot showers when we start rebuilding from scratch. The small things that made life so good. In the '30s, with wood or coal heating, there were no showers, and women used to wash their hair once a month. Personal hygiene in New York is already going to hell in a hurry.*

He called his Zurich lawyer at home and discussed the possibility of buying a dormant private Swiss bank license. The lawyer thought it would be easy and under the current conditions possibly even inexpensive to get one. Gary left him with instructions to investigate further. As usual, Gary was thinking of events far in the future, part of his hoped for trade network.

Gary dialled Claude, New York being six hours behind Swiss time.

"Claude, it's Gary. Everything under control?"

"Yes for me anyway. They're just finishing loading smaller new ship at the container storage docks. I'll be taking that ship to international waters shortly. Bigger one is at New Haven taking on books. I don't know much about books. Last I heard they were having normal start-up problems. They were

Operation Phoenix

getting out container about every twelve minutes but Chris hoped to have that cut down to one every four minutes within the hour. He hopes he can cut to one every three minutes eventually. By now he should be down to that. It was early this morning I talked to him."

"He has to be tired by now. Has anybody arranged to relieve him?" Gary asked.

"Yes, he's sleeping where he is. Roy Bryant and Eric have taken over."

"Good. How many families can you pack aboard the ships now at the docks without keeping them in containers?" Gary asked.

"We could probably get most of them in if we bunk them in the galley ways and such. Maybe we should call Bruce back so we can get few more people on his ship. We have quite a few people but not nearly 300. Maybe 100."

"As you think best," Gary shrugged. "I think it could be a good idea but there are dangers. The reason I called is because I need to know how much to deposit tomorrow morning, and where."

"The chandlers bank is Union Bank of Switzerland at main office in Zurich", and he gave Gary the account information. "Now we have fuel I expect supplies to run to 100,000 Euros. I was thinking of taking extra because of uncertainties," Claude said.

"I certainly agree with that. I've been trying to find some dried potato flakes, dried eggs and freeze dried foods at least. One of the big potato farm areas in Canada is near Halifax. Did you know that I asked Wolfgang to round up a couple of truck tankers capable of carrying potable water?" Gary asked.

"Good idea. If I call Bruce back I'll get Wolfgang to get more for him."

Operation Phoenix

"I think you should run the bill at the chandlers up to 150,000 Euros, unless you find a few containers of some food product that has a long shelf life, in which case call me right away and I'll deposit enough to cover. I'll deposit 150,000 euros tomorrow morning. That is currently about half a million dollars Canadian. I'm planning on flying out tomorrow night late, but if I'm still here I'll happily stay over to deposit more later," Gary said. "By the way, in addition to the containers for the animals, empty flatbed trailers and tankers of fuel have to go on the top of the load. You should get Chris Habel to select say three, but preferably all of his tractors and trailers along with spares to be loaded. We'll probably need them at the far end."

Gary didn't go to bed but immediately took the car and belted off to Rapperswill. He stripped all the available cash out of Lynn's boxed safe except one packet of Swiss francs, just in case. He was back at the hotel in bed in three hours.

Monday March 13th Day 28

The next morning he was up and doing early and arrived at the *Storhaus* warehouse that he was using for his boxed safe before 8 am. He was just locking up when the guard that patrolled the site came round and asked him for his ID to check he belonged to that locker. Gary was happy to comply with this house rule. It was true, one needed a magnetic passkey and pin number to access the site, but after all once through the gate, anyone could visit anyone else's locker even if they had not climbed over the high page-wire fences topped with barbed wire to start with. The only thing to stop them entering your locker was your lock, and a bolt-cutter would make short work of that.

Once outside with his cash, he noticed the office was now occupied so he decided to go in and chat up the girl to get a better reading on local conditions. "Hi there. My name is Gary

Operation Phoenix

Alden, and I have a locker here." He said producing his company issued ID. "I have a locker in the US where the storage company has closed its doors, and I am having a terrible time getting my stuff out. I wondered what would happen here in a similar circumstance."

"Oh, we have quite strict laws here. If you are paid up, by law you can get access during normal business hours at a minimum. We allow 24 hour access though."

"What about if your company goes bankrupt or something?" Gary persisted.

"Not much danger of that." She laughed. "Our company is an old conservative company who has very small mortgages on their properties that they could probably pay off instantly."

"Well, seeing what is going on in the US it is a concern for me. Is unemployment suddenly rising here?"

"Yes," she said slowly. "My fiancé got laid off Friday, and he is very well educated. We thought his job was very secure. At least my job is secure. Aside from the security guards and maintenance people I am the only administrator. Holidays are always a problem for me."

"I wonder if I could ask you a favour. I would hate to have the same problems I have in the US happen here where I might not be able to notice it as quickly. If you get laid off, or if there is the slightest hint that the company is having difficulty keeping its doors open would you phone me immediately?" Gary pulled out a business card and wrote his satellite phone number on the back. " I would prefer you call me collect, but if that is not possible here is 50 francs to prepay a short call. As soon as I can get over here, I will pay you 500 francs cash for that information. We can't send money orders in foreign currency out of the US. If you do get laid off or something, 500 francs could be useful to you. Would that be okay?"

Operation Phoenix

"Oh, you don't have to pay me. I would be happy to do that for you."

"Well, advance notice would be worth it to me so the offer stands."

Gary went immediately to Eric's storage space, pulled cash out and 20 ounces of gold but leaving one packet of Swiss francs. He then had a virtually identical conversation with the administrator there. He called a coin dealer he had noticed in the hotel lobby and enquired about gold and silver prices. He was quoted 4840 euros to buy one ounce of gold, and 220 to buy silver.

His next stop was at the Union Bank at 10 am where he started his chandler banking. Gary enquired about the bid/ask of gold and silver in euros.

"Gold bid 5,117, ask 6,117. Silver bid 285, ask 350 Euros."

God, thought Gary. *They really don't want to sell gold, with a 1000 Euro spread. I'll bet the black market is way over 6,000. To bad I have to deposit this money now for food for the gang. Later would be so much better. Oh, well, I have no time left.*

Six thousand Euros times $4,380 US dollars per Euro equalled a selling price per ounce of gold of $26,280,000 US.

Gary enquired about cash next. At first look, spreads were astounding. It looked as if all currencies were floundering. The bank was bidding half the rate for most currencies they would deal in, principally the European currencies such as the pound, and offering to sell at one and a half times the rate. That meant that while there was a risk, all they had to do was buy one lot of a currency, and sell that same lot, usually the same day, and everything thereafter was pure profit. Sure, they might eventually lose the initial investment, but they would rack up

Operation Phoenix

good profits even if the situation only lasted for a few days.

The bank refused to touch US dollars. They would accept Japanese yen, but strangely, would not accept Australian, Hong Kong, or Singapore dollars. With the exception of an extra packet of Swiss francs, Gary unloaded everything else he could at horrendous losses for Euros. Finally, to make up the balance of the 150,000 Euro deposit, he sold five ounces of gold. He waited until the bank gave him a copy of the fax to the chandlers confirming the deposit.

Left with some gold and currencies, he again drove down beside the long beautiful lake to Rapperswill, put the balance of the cash and gold in Lynn's safe and had the same conversation with the company clerk.

Back in Zurich, while still in the car, he decided it was late enough in New York he could call Eric and check up on progress. Eric was a fount of information.

"Last night, the US declared a state of emergency, and is enforcing the Patriot act. They have announced a new currency, the Amero, a digital only currency, lopping two zeros off the old one, and only minimal amounts of the old cash currency are convertible to the new currency. After June first it is an act of treason to use anything but the Amero in settling debts. They are busy fighting crime, or at least those were the reasons given. You must have the card to do any transaction, and it is going to be one of these new cards with imbedded biometric information. We're covered, just don't ask with what. Ya gotta love the smell of bullshit in the morning. As well, Texas and Vermont have declared independence."

"Good God," Gary exclaimed. "That really tears it. I was expecting some extreme reactions. Certainly the Patriot act and the new currency were things I thought might happen, but I didn't think of digital currency. Marry that up with whatever

Operation Phoenix

files exist on you and they control every individual in the US. They can monitor your spending habits, suddenly impose taxes taken automatically, decide you are an enemy of the state and shut down all your resources in less than one second. I also thought the US and a number of countries might break up, especially Canada, what's left of Russia, and the European union, but not this fast. The combination of currency and Patriot shows these guys are panicking and fighting to save their treasury at any cost. If they're showing it's that grim, it's probably much grimmer. Texas probably means civil war. That giant popping sound you hear is just another step along the way in the ongoing, seismic readjustment that is taking place in the global social, economic and political order."

"Yeah, the Patriot act suspends all civil rights including the right of habeas corpus, as well all other law including the constitution. No court can order you to appear before it. Merely on a whim, you can now be 'disappeared' in the US. There's no proof or hearing required to hold you or any other action. Just like under Hitler, the Homeland Security officers don't answer to any higher law, or to any court. Just like under Hitler, the emergency will last as long as the president decides it should. You can't believe how much pressure that put on us," Eric exclaimed.

"I can believe it. How far along are you?"

"We got most of the books we wanted, although Brian is threatening to stay and guard the rest. We probably could have gotten another 30 or so containers, but we shut that operation down as quickly as we could. We cleaned out the Engineering library completely. Last night we decided that while it was risky, there was no better time to take the risk than in the confusion when the Patriot act was just declared so we ordered Bruce back with his ship to cram as many people as possible on

Operation Phoenix

board. He should be back to New Haven any time now," Eric said. "Hopefully he'll only be here a couple of hours, and then back to sea."

"Sounds good. Tell Claude I deposited 150,000 Euros to the chandlers account, and it was confirmed by fax. How about the new inductees to the community? Are they all packing fast?" Gary asked.

"Yes, they claim they are, but not nearly fast enough for me. Which brings to mind that you are one of our worst offenders in that regard."

"I'll get onto Jan next. Not much else I can do from here I'd say your rush to get offshore is the smartest thing we can do. Anything we are missing we will probably be able to pick up in Canada."

"That's good. Chris is dithering that he hasn't been able to pick up many animals," Eric said.

"Never mind. I'll be in Canada tomorrow if I don't miss the plane. What I will do depends on the situation. In the worst case I can probably find some things in Canada, but exactly what I will use to pay for it is another question. Chris must have been going steady for days now with no sleep."

"Yeah, I think he's sleeping now."

"He might like it if we donated the rest of those two fuel tankers to his drivers. I think you are headed in the right direction. Get as many people and containers offshore as fast as possible. I'd like Lynn to go on the smaller new ship if possible. We'll just finish the loading of the last ship with laggard people, their belongings, and some empty containers. We don't want all our senior people at risk at the same time, in the same place. There's less risk from government if you are offshore."

Eric laughed. "Wayne managed to spend some more of the old dollars, and got some more armament. He got everything from missiles to machine guns, and deflatable speedboats. I think he was even going after a diesel, battery powered attack sub."

"We can't have many dollars left now. I think you guys are doing better without me than with me. Mind you, I think a sub is a bit much. I'll get onto Jan now. Good luck and pass on my plaudits to everyone," Gary said. "You're all doing an amazing job. I'll contact you before I get on the plane."

He dialled Jan. "Hi sweetie, how's it going?"

"This place is a disaster," she exploded. "Everyone ran out leaving their mess."

Oh, oh, she's got another bee in her bonnet, he thought. Aloud he said, "That's because we're now all fleeing, almost for our lives. When did you last get some sleep?"

"Yesterday," she replied crossly. "Everyone is running around yelling, and I can't get anyone to cooperate."

"Well, the situation is serious enough that I've been thinking of just abandoning everything we have, and getting you on the next boat out."

"Is this another one of your crazy ideas? Abandon all my things?" she exploded. "No way Jose. I'm going to take my stuff and go up to my folks place till things return to normal. I'm sick and fed up with your crazy ideas. Things will return to normal soon enough. I'm not going to some jerkwater place to have babies. I want flush toilets."

Gary lowered his face on to the steering wheel and curled one hand over the top of his head. He felt himself getting dizzy. He tried to breath deeply until it passed. Despite her personal quirks that had proved very dangerous during Heidi's kidnap he still loved her, warts and all. "Are you saying you don't want to get married?"

"Damned straight. I'm going to find a sane husband not a

Operation Phoenix

crazy one."

"Jan, I love you. I want you by my side for the rest of my life. I can't, and won't even try to stop you if that is what you really want. I want your happiness above all else. I think that is what love is all about, putting the interests of your loved one before your own. If you're sure this will give you more happiness, then I'll try to help you get your stuff up to your Dad's place." Gary felt chest pain, thought he was having a heart attack, and realized he didn't care. "But please think about this. Please? I love you."

"No, my mind's made up. I'll wait till I can get my old job back."

"Where is your container? Have they picked it up yet?" Gary asked.

"No, it's in the yard. I haven't finished packing. I'm going to take what I have packed and put it back in the house, and drive with my clothes up to the Adirondacks to my family. I don't want your help," she stormed. "Stay out of my life."

"Jan, you're tired. Please get some sleep. If you change your mind, call me. I love you and I'll understand."

"I won't be calling. Stay out of my life." And she hung up.

Gary spent a few minutes grieving and then realized it was near checkout time, and he would rather be back home where it might be possible to do something. He didn't know what exactly he wanted to do. Logically, Jan was pure poison. Emotionally, it would be hard to live without her. He went into the hotel and asked that his bill be prepared. The clerk looked at him sympathetically and asked "Are you okay sir? You look to be a bit under the weather."

"No, I just had a personal jolt, but I'll live I suppose. Not many people die of broken hearts I'm told." He forced a twisted grin trying for some graveyard humour. Now he simply wanted to find a hole and pull it in after himself. He felt he was doing something like what one would do at a funeral. You lost a loved one but it was essential that you hurry and make arrangements of various kinds, notify the relatives, and so on, thus distracting yourself.

At the airport he found that there was no earlier flight than the one he had booked, so he busied himself as much as possible. Gary called Patti to let her know he was expecting to be back on schedule but was uncertain where they would go from there. Patti reported that she felt her farmer brother and a neighbour might be willing to join them, but her parents were unlikely to give up what they had and start over. Gary frowned because there was no way to have the community vote on them, and then suddenly had an idea. He asked Patti if she could get at least a couple of hundred tobacco plant seeds. She thought she could, despite tight government control on them. Gary asked her to keep her eyes open for any equipment and supplies that would make starting a new tobacco farm easier. Mankind loves its vices.

He called Eric and learned that they were indeed the possessors of a fully fuelled and armed modern diesel electric submarine. All the US cash was gone. They'd tried to bundle Jan aboard Bruce's ship and had learned the hard way that Gary and Jan were no longer an item. While waiting for people they'd got the remaining road tankers of fuel from the hangars atop the containers and lashed down. Eric was of the opinion that Bruce had already left or was leaving now. They expected the smaller of the two new ships to leave within the hour. A good number of ships crew's families, and some of Claude's family were aboard Bruce's ship. Eric thought that it totalled more than a quarter of the community population. Bruce's ship, and the two warships that he had rendezvoused with previously

Operation Phoenix

were now to rendezvous near Cuba to conserve fuel and supplies while they awaited the other ships.

Claude, acting as captain, and the rest of his family, Lynn, Roy Bryant and family, Heidi, and about another quarter of the community population would be aboard the second ship to leave.

Eric felt he wouldn't be able to catch the second ship as he had too much of a critical nature yet to do. Gary was not happy with this. It left too many members of the family at risk, still available to the authorities. There was little he could do about it. Gary asked if they could get a few people aboard the submarine, which Eric thought to be a good idea. All told, Gary estimated they had about one third, or a bit more of the community population to get aboard the larger of the two new ships. He was not exactly sure what the population numbered now, just that it was not as large as they had hoped.

. Gary was becoming increasingly concerned about Wayne and his need for the diesel electric submarine. Wayne's enthusiasm was great, but it scared Gary as being out of control. Wayne was a man who had discovered a new religion, or a hoary new truth, and he was pursuing it with unreasonable fervour. His excessive zeal would have to be controlled without killing his enthusiasm. Claude was right. Nothing less than a rich government could handle the care and feeding of such an armada.

Operation Phoenix

Chapter 38

Gary's flight back to Canada was uneventful, as was clearing customs. Gary slept fitfully, if at all, unable to get Jan out of his mind. As he and Patti cleared the airport and headed southwest Gary was considering what was still needed for the community, and whether they could purchase it in Canada. The question boiled down to how they would pay for it now that they were out of cash. Precious metals had not achieved recognisability as a medium of exchange. Moreover their fortune was tied up in Switzerland and in the containers now at sea. More concerning was predicting what Jan would do. Would she simply go to her parents, or would she vindictively spill her guts?

Tuesday March 14th -- Day 29

Once Gary and Patti had been underway for half an hour he decided that a stop for a bite to eat, with some time off to think would be smart. Once in the diner he asked Patti if she had spent any of the money she had been given.

"No," she replied. "Dad gave me two varieties of tobacco seeds, totalling about a pound. I didn't know, but five hundred grams of tobacco product is legal for an individual in Canada. He has some old tobacco equipment sitting around he's willing to give me. Most important are a lot of UV resistant plastic sheets for greenhouses. I've just bought fuel for the car and a couple of small things like that. We only got here Sunday morning you know."

Operation Phoenix

"Sorry, I have a lot on my plate right now. I don't suppose you know, but Jan has scuttled our marriage plans and who knows how vindictive she will be. She seems to have gone off the deep end. Stay out of my life she said," Gary said morosely.

"I'm so sorry," Patti said, reaching over and covering his hand with hers. "I know you loved her."

"Everybody is acting a little strange these days. As long as I keep my mind on the community work I'm not too bad. Speaking of which, that tobacco stuff is invaluable. Tell your Dad thanks. I was just stewing out loud about how to purchase some things we need. Wayne has just spent our last US cash buying a submarine not that the dollars are worth anything. The only cash we have left is what you and I are carrying at the moment. About $20,000 US plus bits of other currencies. All our other resources are either on a ship at sea or in Switzerland. We have good opportunities to get what we need in Canada, if we can just figure out some way of paying for it."

Patti withdrew her hand, and said, "What do you have left in the States?"

"How do you mean? Personally not much, just what I have in my house." He paused. "Hey, wait a minute. Patti, I could kiss you. I do have some precious metals there," and Gary immediately dialled Eric.

Eric answered the phone groggily.

"Sorry to wake you Eric," Gary apologized. "Did you collect the precious metals I had at home in my safe for inclusion in the container on the boat?"

"No, I don't have the combination,"

"Fantastic. I'm in Toronto, and headed south. Go back to sleep. Sorry to have waked you," and Gary hung up the phone.

"Patti, How do you feel about doing a bit of smuggling?"

"Same as we did last time?" Patti frowned.

Operation Phoenix

"Probably, but from the US into Canada and I won't be with you. Someone else will be. Probably Wolfgang Perl if I can get him. Have you ever met him? No, you couldn't have. He was at the induction meeting Sunday," Gary was all excited. "Wolfgang has a gift for sourcing things. I have least one million Canadian at home in gold, about 50 ounces, plus a few hundred ounces of silver if we need it. If we can get his abilities up here we can probably have most of what we need, ready to be loaded aboard the ship in Halifax when she docks."

"I wouldn't be guarding you?" Patti sounded disappointed. "Wayne said I was to stick to you like glue and not let you out of my sight."

"Yeah, but I will have Wayne and a whole bunch of SEALs there to look after me. Besides, you have become more of a partner in crime, than a bodyguard. I need your skills, brain, and experience in Canada to help get the rest of the things we need. With the banks now closed in Canada cash and things like that are going to be extremely valuable. We should be able to pick up things for pennies on the dollar just like we did in the US when the banks were closed. We can use our experience in the US to be more effective when we live it all over again in Canada."

"Maybe we should drop off some, or almost all of the Canadian cash with your family so they can get containers and get things underway for Halifax?" Gary continued. "That way we don't have to smuggle the cash back and forth over the border."

"Okay."

"You drive to your parents, and then the border, and I'll try to sleep. Then I'll take over the driving, and you sleep. It's going to be a long day for you."

"And I thought they were pushing us hard in boot camp,"

Operation Phoenix

Patti laughed. "Those drill sergeants were patsies along side of you. I'd complain but I know you'll be pushing yourself even harder."

"Thank you. Well, let's get going."

Back in Stamford, Gary was appalled to find definite evidence of just how shook up he was about Jan. His thinking was totally out to lunch. There sitting beside the house was his container with two boxed safes inside, containing thousands of ounces of gold. He had forgotten about it entirely in his quest for assets to buy things in Canada. If Jan got vindictive nearly half of his US gold stash was sitting in plain sight for authorities to grab if they searched at all, as they surely would.

Gary immediately asked Patti "Could I get you to do something for me?"

"Yes."

"You're supposed to say 'what?' not 'yes'," Gary grinned at her. "Could you go around to about four houses in every direction till you find half a dozen strong adults that could help me pack and load a container? I will pay $50 per hour old dollars, plus sandwiches before and after, starting as soon as possible, for about six hours tonight and probably some tomorrow. Then I'd like you to go down again and try to get some sleep. You might want to shower too, because you will have a long day."

"I'd like to get some washing done too."

"Good idea," said Gary. "Throw your stuff in the washer, and I'll change it to the dryer when it's done. In the meantime I'll get to work on arranging for the Canada purchases." Gary called Chris for a rush pickup of the container in the front yard. The best Chris could do was have a driver over in about three to four hours. He would drop a new container and pick up the old one.

Operation Phoenix

Gary contacted Wolfgang. "How's the packing going?" he asked.

"It's been pretty frantic around here, but we're about finished packing."

"Great. I'm just back but I have another job for you, if I can talk you in to it. It's in Canada this time. Can you get your packing finished ASAP and get your family over to the hotel for protection?" Gary asked.

"And?"

"I have a SEAL I've been working with as an assistant and bodyguard. She's one of the smartest, best looking, and deadliest women I have ever met. She's a Canadian. I was hoping to have both of you drive to Canada. The first objective is to smuggle a bit of gold or silver across the border. She'll show you how. Once there I'm hoping you can dispose of it a bit at a time, and buy the list of stuff I'm going to make up shortly. I don't want to dispose of any more gold than I absolutely have to but we need the goods even more. A lot of the list is foodstuffs and animals, so you will probably source it near Halifax to reduce shipping time. For most of the other things you should be able to get them for pennies on the dollar cash, just like we did in the US when the banks were closed. For the food, you'll likely have to pay top dollar. Would you be willing to try? You could meet the ship in Halifax," Gary asked.

"Sounds like a challenge," Wolfgang paused. "Why not? We're about done here."

"Wonderful. Thank you very much, and by the way, those pallets and containers were an unbelievable job. See what you get for being good at something? I'll have Patti meet you at the hotel in five hours with the list. You can fuel up at the hotel. I'll be at home packing if anything comes up. We have still a few loose ends to wrap up here."

Operation Phoenix

Gary got a roast in the oven and started some rice. He called Eric, and there was no answer. Puzzled and worried, he called Wayne who was packing. "Wayne, I have just been trying to get Eric and there's no answer. Do you know where he is?"

"I'm not surprised. I persuaded him to take a berth on the submarine so he's surrounded by metal."

"Oh, good. How about your girlfriend, Mona?"

"Her son was killed and I wasn't there to help. I'm in her bad books but I persuaded her to go on the basis of safety. She's packing now," Wayne said.

"I have Wolfgang going to Canada to source some things, primarily foodstuffs. I wondered if you had anything that I should add to the list?" Gary asked. Wayne gave him half a dozen items, and they hung up.

Gary got busy on his list. Patti came back and reported success in her search for helpers, and went off to shower and to bed. Gary finished his list, changed Patti's laundry to the dryer, and began to prepare for the packing of the house. The neighbours began to straggle in. Gary cut finished cooking bits off the outside of the roast, and made sandwiches. He also served some rice to start the workers off.

He fuelled the car and backed it out of the garage. He started three workers to work packing the garage. A second crew of three began packing the living room. Full boxes, furniture, etc., were moved to the container and packed. Gary noticed one particular gentleman appeared to be growing fatter by the minute. He waited until Patti was up, and called him out on it. After some blustering and threats, he began to empty his pockets of an astonishing variety of things he had found to steal. After patting him down and finding another couple of valuables, Gary paid him the hours worked and fired him. The thief had the audacity to demand his second sandwich. Gary announced that everyone would be searched before they left.

The books, bookcases, and ornaments from the office were next. So far Gary had not allowed anyone to touch his desk, safe, files, or to go downstairs where they might view the food or wake Patti. Gary was pleased to see that while the container was only about half full, it was packed tightly over the entire floor space so it would likely ride safely. The Habel driver arrived with an empty container, spotted it and hooked up to the loaded container to drop it at the New Haven docks. He said Bruce Nott's ship had come and gone, and that the second, smaller ship had just left.

A combination of jet lag and general fatigue forced Gary to call a halt after five hours. He prepared the sandwiches, and as a gesture, cut the remaining roast in five equal pieces, wrapped it and with the remaining rice, handed it to the workers with their pay. After checking for theft, he offered them more work the following morning and was accepted gratefully.

Ushering them out and calling Wayne for a SEAL guard tomorrow, he put another roast on to slow cook, alarmed the house, and crashed.

Operation Phoenix

Chapter 39
Wednesday March 15th --Day 30

At 6AM he was up and doing, mightily refreshed. He still felt fatigued but put it down to jet lag or depression about Jan. Sometime during the night his subconscious had dragged up another 'stash' of gold. In the rush and confusion of the moment he had thrown the fifteen ounces of gold that he had purchased from the 'bright kid' at Premet, into the top drawer of his desk and it was still there. He checked his freezer for frozen spaghetti sauce containing bags of gold. There was none there. Obviously Eric had efficiently collected it. He packed his desk, moved the contents of the now somewhat empty basement freezers together into one freezer, and closed the pantry door.

The workers of last night began to show up at the door, in addition to three times their number of hopeful workers who turned into hopeful beggars when Gary didn't need them. He did hire one who claimed he had electrical experience. Gary immediately put him to work salvaging as much of his security system as possible. Kirk, a SEAL showed up and Gary briefed him.

The day was cool but sunny with a few puffy clouds, about 40 degrees. The breeze had freshened just slightly, possibly indicating a coming storm front.

He got a couple of workers going cleaning up and packing the main floor, and the other three he took downstairs to start packing everything but the freezers and the pantry.

The doorbell rang. Gary peeked out through his peephole, and saw a single man, well dressed. He opened the door with the chain still in place. "Yes?"

"Are you Gary Alden?"

"Yes," Gary admitted shamelessly.

"I'm with the treasury department. You purchased some gold last month and I'm here to secure it."

"I did?" Gary asked to gain time and information. His worst nightmare was coming true.

"Yes, nine ounces. It's illegal for citizens to own gold," the agent said Obviously this inspection was not motivated by Jan. If it had been, they would be looking for more than nine ounces. The government was simply following paper trails of gold purchases, and Gary had forgotten the credit card purchase he had made from the bright kid that first day. It was his own damned fault that he had come to the attention of government. He had left a paper trail.

"Oh, that," Gary said. " I've been so busy trying to stay alive, I forgot. It's okay. I'm a goldsmith and I'm exempt. It's inventory"

"What do you mean?" the treasury man said in shock.

"I am a goldsmith and goldsmiths are permitted to own gold. Wait, I'll show you," and Gary went to his office. He pulled out a file marked 'defence-Armageddon' and extracted a couple of documents. Returning to the door he thrust the papers through. "See, my government tax licenses and my membership in the American Society of Goldsmiths which I have been a member of for ten years. I bought that gold as inventory because the price was going up. Goldsmiths are permitted to own gold," Gary repeated.

"Oh. I didn't know that." The man seemed confused but he handed Gary's papers back. "Okay, thanks," and he turned to leave.

Gary called Wayne. "Wayne, I have just been visited by

Operation Phoenix

treasury department authorities wanting precious metals. I got out of this one cheap but we're on their radar and they'll be back. We have to move soonest. Please contact everyone. Are you packing too?"

"Yes I'm packing. I'll alert the SEALs and start a chain going. You start a chain with Chris. Bye."

Gary dialled Chris and gave him the message. Chris said that under the circumstances he would send a bobtail tractor over soonest, and the truck driver would remain at Gary's house while the container was loaded. He also said drivers would be dispatched to every container being loaded for pick up right away.

The doorbell rang again.

Gary peeked out and the treasury man was back. Gary opened the door with the chain lock still on. "Yes," he said.

"I've just been talking to my boss and he says we are seizing it under the patriot act." The treasury guy looked distinctly uncomfortable.

Gary exploded. "What the hell, that's not fair. There isn't enough starvation and unemployment around now? You want to take my livelihood and what is properly mine away too?" Gary appeared to calm down and appeared to be mulling things over in his mind. There was no doubt he would hand over the gold to them just to get them off his back, but he had to appear to be objecting.

He finally said reluctantly, "Okay, but I want an official receipt. I'm going to get this back. You can't take my livelihood away from me," letting his jacket fall back so the shoulder holster was visible.

The man said, "I'll get a receipt from the car." Gary went in and got the nine ounces that he had purchased from the bright kid at the bank as well as a pen and some paper. They arrived

Operation Phoenix

back at the door at about the same time.

Gary opened his hand and said, "See, nine one ounce bars. May I have my receipt and your identification please?"

The man passed over his identification, and Gary copied down the pertinent details while the man filled out his receipt. Gary handed over his gold and the identification, and the man handed over the receipt. "Sorry, just doing my job," the man said as he left. Gary watched him drive off.

He called both Wayne and Chris saying; "I got rid of them but they forgot to search the house. Not that they would find much but they'll want to open every box. It's just a matter of time till this gets out of hand. Get everybody moving to grab whatever they can and abandon the rest."

Gary raced downstairs. "Finish packing whatever boxes you're working on. Here's your pay for four hours. If we get out of here without incident there will be more and some food as well. I want it to be really fast. Get all the packed boxes and that freezer," pointing to the empty one, "outside to the container right away. The other freezer is full. I want to distribute what is in it later because most of it will likely spoil. Next pick up all the boxes in the pantry and get them upstairs into the container."

He grabbed an envelope, stuffed it with cash and sealed it. He ran outside to the commercial guards on duty and handed it over saying it was for the company owner. Miraculously, the Habel driver pulled in. "I was close by and Chris redirected me."

"Fantastic," Gary was overwhelmed. "Hook up and then I would like to ask a favour. Do you have any experience packing household goods?"

"Sure," said the driver.

"Can I persuade you to do the packing in this container while you wait?" Gary asked. "There's a lot of stuff in there. I'll

Operation Phoenix

pay you an additional $50 per hour, old dollars."

"You don't have to pay me anything. Chris told us you have given us the tankers of fuel."

"Well I'll pay you anyway. By the way if anybody asks, you think the container is going to Wyoming with a truck convoy that was organized. Maybe Medicine Bow Wyoming," a place Gary had once visited.

"Gotcha," the driver grinned.

Gary ran next door where a container was backed up to Brian, the librarian's house. He did not see any loading being done. Brian answered the door.

"Oh, hi Gary. Won't you come in?"

"There's no time. How close are you to being packed and ready to go?" Gary demanded.

"We are packing carefully because it's a long trip."

"Well, did Chris not call you and ask you to be ready in an hour?" Gary asked.

"We can't pack in an hour." Brian said.

"Well," Gary said, taking a deep breath and looking down in frustration for an instant, "If you want to go you'll have to be ready. Do you have any helpers?"

"A couple, but we spend so much time overseeing them we might as well do it ourselves."

"Forget overseeing them and grab whatever you can," Gary almost screamed. "This has become a matter of do it now, or die. The ship will be leaving in about two hours. Do you want to stay here and watch your family die? That is your choice but I would hate to see that happen. I'll try to get a couple of more hands over here. Just point at a room and say, 'Get that room out into the container, I don't care how.' If anybody asks including your helpers, say you are going by truck convoy to Medicine Bow Wyoming."

Operation Phoenix

Ana Gibson and the girls came to the door to stand beside Brian.

"But we're not." Brian sounded puzzled.

"Just do it. If someone asks you're going by truck convoy to Medicine Bow, Wyoming. There's less people there and there's food there. In the meantime, I'll be gone in about an hour. If you want to come you should be gone too."

"Well, we do want to come but we want to bring our stuff. We're already giving up our house."

"On the way back yesterday I saw a dog eating on a dead human. Disease is starting to spread in epidemic proportions There's no food. Do you want to stay for that or do you want to go?" Gary demanded.

"We want to go of course."

"Well, what's more important, your house, your stuff, or your life and the lives of your children? You have very little time left maybe only an hour," Gary cried in frustration. "Get them loading stuff into the container packed or not. Furniture first, tight at the front because it is heavy. Okay? I'll try to get some hands over here."

"Okay," Brian said bewilderedly.

"We will be ready," Ana said firmly. It appeared the velvet glove had a rarely displayed iron fist in it.

"Good, I'll see if those guys that are guarding us will lend a hand," and Gary ran back to the guards. "Guarding is your first job but would you guys be willing to lend a hand helping to get the container next door packed? I'll pay an extra $50 per hour old dollars extra plus some food. We're now in a terrible rush."

The mention of food obviously worked its magic. They both grinned and said, "Yes."

"I'll pay a minimum of three hours if you are done in an hour and a half. Don't let anyone distract you from keeping an

Operation Phoenix

eye open as guards, or in getting stuff aboard that container. He likes to philosophize so don't let him do it to you or the other two helpers. Just get in there and start grabbing stuff, boxed or not, and hauling it out to the container. Pack it as tightly as possible, heavy stuff on the bottom. It has to travel to Wyoming. Since time is so short if we want to join the truck convoy, I'd appreciate it if you could start right now. But remember, your first job is as guards."

"Okay," and they got out of their cars and started over.

Gary ran back to his house past Kirk his new SEAL guard, who was trailing along but never quite catching up. Aside from his military quarter inch haircut, Kirk didn't look like a fast moving SEAL. He was a square block, a bit shorter than Wayne. If there was a brick wall ahead he was a bulldozer who would pause for a second, snort once, and then march right through it.

In the office Gary gathered up the stuff he had packed from his desk. He handed Kirk his keys and said, "Would you put these into the trunk of my car please? While you are there there's a small tool kit in the trunk. Bring it please."

Kirk came in with the toolbox and the keys. Gary opened the toolkit and said. "See this safe. It's screwed down. You should be able to unscrew it with this wrench. Could I get you to make it movable please? By the way, your first job is as a guard but if you can help otherwise I'd appreciate it. If anybody asks we're trying to catch a truck convoy to Wyoming. You're not sure where. You're just a dumb guard. Okay?"

Gary went downstairs and started packing the shelves of his pantry. He was nearly finished when Kirk yelled down, "you have visitors Mr. Alden." Gary went upstairs and noticed the two guards from next-door walking over. Two men with briefcases stood outside the door. *Oh, SHIT* thought Gary. *They're coming back to search for gold. Damn.*

Operation Phoenix

"Gareth McTier Alden?" Gary immediately thought *that's why children are given middle names. They can easily know when moms are really mad, or officials are being really official and serious.*

"Yes."

Kirk walked up to stand by his side. The two guards stopped a pace short of the foot of the porch.

"We're from the IRS, and we're here to collect taxes on a windfall profit you made in the stock market. You made approximately 58 million dollars I believe."

"I paid an instalment. Don't you guys ever look at your records?" Gary said in disgust. "First of all it wasn't a windfall profit, it was long term since I had been using that vehicle for some long time."

"How much did you pay on your instalment, Mr. Alden?"

"$20 million and change, and another $5 million on something that's not turning out to be so damned profitable at all. So, a total of over $25 million," Gary said. "I expect to be demanding money back."

"Can you show us how you paid it, an endorsed check perhaps?"

"It was bank drafts drawn on American Citybank. I have photocopies in the car. Come with me," and Gary led the way to the car trunk. As the two gentlemen turned around their shock at seeing two more armed guards was almost humorous to see. It was easy to see one check out Kirk and discover he was armed too. The bulge under Gary's armpit was noticed. Then the extra heavy body armours both he and Kirk were wearing came under scrutiny. The realization that they were outgunned was now the law. He who had the power made the rules, which always included, 'I win.'

Gary dug into a box and pulled open his defence file,

Operation Phoenix

without pulling it out of the box. He selected the photocopy of the bank drafts, and the signature, time stamped, by the IRS. Holding the paper up, he said, "Feel free to make note of any details you may find pertinent. As you see, I paid $20 million, 357.23, and another $5 million as an estimate. I'm not trying to avoid paying tax. Lord knows the country needs the money. But recently I've been losing my shirt. With the food situation who knows even if one is going to live? This is the signature for the drafts, date and time stamped."

"May I have them please?"

"I'd rather not. They're my only copy," Gary said.

"We're empowered to seize them you know?"

"Yes, and I'm entitled to have a copy and a receipt. Unless you have a photocopier with you I'm afraid I must refuse," Gary said adamantly.

Looking at the armed guards lined up beside Gary, with four against two, apparently the gentlemen decided that prudence was in order and began making notes.

"You seem to be moving Mr. Alden. May I enquire where to?"

"Wyoming I expect." Gary said shortly. He noticed that loading the container was proceeding apace.

"Do you have a forwarding address?"

"No. The urgent question is to get away from the huge population, the lack of food, and the death and disease, to somewhere where there are fewer people and more potential food. I think Medicine Bow Wyoming would fit that bill but I have to determine whether I can find somewhere to settle there," Gary said.

The gentlemen exchanged significant glances and one said, "It's apparent that you are making some effort to meet your tax obligations so we'll accept that for the moment. Kindly

Operation Phoenix

forward your new address when you settle. Here is my card. Do you have one by chance?"

"Yes, but I can't see what good that will do. I'm moving and probably won't be back," and Gary dug in his wallet and handed one over.

"Thank you and have a good trip." The gentlemen left.

Gary stared after them in puzzlement. *Somehow I have the feeling they put one over on us, but I can't think what. That was a bit too easy.* Turning to the two guards he said, "Thank you for showing up. That was beautiful, the way you did it and the timing. Now let's get back to packing. I'm afraid they may be back and it might not be so pleasant. I don't want to be here if they do come back."

On the way over to his container Gary said, "Thanks Kirk that was exactly the right attitude. Walk softly and carry a big stick."

At the container he spoke to the driver. "Did they talk to you at all?"

"Yep, all sorts of questions," the driver grinned. "Where you were going and all. I told them Wyoming, maybe Medicine Bow but I couldn't remember specifically."

"Fantastic. That was what that exchange of looks was about. They thought I was confirming what you said. Wonderful. I owe you a big one. How are we doing?" Gary asked. As he spoke, the guys were manoeuvred the empty freezer out of the house. Before they tried to get it in the container, Gary said, "Put it down, I have more boxes. Have you moved all of boxes in the kitchen?"

"Yes, the whole main floor is clean except for your desk, the safe, the fridge and the stove."

Gary started for the house, and went into the basement. "I'll finish packing these shelves, but in the meantime can four

Operation Phoenix

of you try to get that safe out of the office and onto the truck. After you're finished I would appreciate it if you would move next door and get them loaded too. Okay?"

"We're getting pretty tired."

"I'll bet. I can't believe how fast you have worked. We'll take a break before we move the fridge in the kitchen, and empty the fridge into our stomachs. Okay?" Gary asked.

The atmosphere brightened immediately. In short order, the boxes and sacks from the pantry were moved. Gary called a halt. He beckoned the driver and his worker assistant in. They closed the container doors and came in. Gary started cutting the roast and had a couple of guys buttering bread. After sixteen sandwiches were made, he put eight aside, and handed out cold pop. He ran next door and asked everyone to come over. He handed out the other sandwiches and more pop. Then he spoke privately with the Gibson's. "I want these workers to feel good about us. There'll be more food for you later. Keep an eye on the containers and move some boxes. I want to finish here."

"Come on back downstairs," he said to everyone else after the Gibson's left. "I want everybody to have a box to put your stuff in and line up over there, everybody including the guards. Kirk keep a lookout upstairs please."

"This is all frozen goods and we can only use so much of it," Gary explained. "I'm going to try to divide this up as equally as possible. I am going to take two portions for our group. The driver will take two, one for himself, and one for all the other Habel drivers who are also working hard. He must have a minimum of seven pieces of meat for all seven Habel drivers if we don't have seven rounds. I want each of you to take one piece of meat. You have to be able to see it and once you point it out, it is yours regardless of whether it was what you thought it was or not."

Operation Phoenix

Gary drew out two pieces of meat, and said. "I also want everyone to take a loaf of bread on this first round so we can empty the freezer faster." So saying, he took out 2 loaves of bread and added them to his box.

The line wound around and Gary estimated what was left. To the driver he said. "I want you to take seven pieces of meat this time, one for you and six for the other drivers."

The line wound around and there were two pieces of meat left over. Gary added them to the community box. They did one more round of bread, one of desserts, and a round of milk. Gary added leftovers to the community box.

Once they had done that Gary ordered the two steel shelving units that were in the pantry into the container, and divided up the remaining food in the fridge. The two guards and the two Gibson workers went back to their duties.

Gary's crew finished up with just enough room to include the desk, the last item. After locking the container Gary asked the driver to be sure he wasn't followed and if he thought he might be to call right away and not go to the dock. It was just going on to noon, and another driver pulled in to pick up the Gibson container. He got his pick of meat out of the driver box. Gary paid the first driver his extra money.

Gary sent all his workers and their boxes of food over to the Gibson's and then called the guard company. "I've given Jake an envelope of cash that should more than cover our bill. As of tonight we have no more work. We're headed out to the wide-open spaces. If you want to contact me I'll try to keep my website open." he said.

"I'm sorry to hear that. It's your cash that has been keeping us alive. But I wish you all the best."

Gary then locked the house. He went over to the Gibson's, paid everyone lavishly, noticed that there was very little more

Operation Phoenix

work to be done, and spoke to the driver, Brian and Ana privately. "With the visits of the authorities this morning I expect problems soon. I want you out of here in half an hour. If you think you are being followed don't go to the docks. Call me and we'll set something up. Somebody is sure to want what we have. If anyone questions you remember we are going to Medicine Bow, Wyoming. Any questions?"

"No."

"Okay, see you later."

Chapter 40

When he got back outside his container was gone. Gary and Kirk drove to New Haven, putting a few twists in their path to check if they were being followed. They got to the ship where a tense but happy atmosphere awaited. Gary's container was being loaded aboard. Gary asked Wayne "Who's still missing?"

"Just Chris Habel, the Gibson's, and the McClouds."

"Who are the McClouds?" Gary asked.

"They're a Roy Bryant recommend. Millwright and general all round super machinist I gather. They were at the meeting Sunday. He's being delayed because he has a lot of machinery to pack. I gather it's essential stuff," Wayne said.

The captain came up and introduced himself as Captain Julius Struckless. That was one of the names on Gary's original list. The accent was obviously from Newfoundland Canada, as was his use of 'boy' the way Wolfgang used 'mon', except he pronounced it more like 'bye'. About Wayne's height, he was slim and dressed neatly in jeans and a plaid shirt. Gary said, "I'm so glad to finally meet you. I'd heard of you even before Claude sang your praises." Gary shook his hand warmly. "Do we have an estimated time before lift-off?" Gary grinned.

"Wayne, do you have anything new bye? My last information was about an hour and a half before we had everybody aboard." The captain said. "Give us half an hour to get the containers aboard, so two hours."

Wayne said. "I was talking to Chris, and the McClouds, and they are pretty much finished. Mostly it's travel time. How

Operation Phoenix

about the Gibson's?"

"If we got him stopped philosophizing they were ordered to leave within a half an hour of our leaving my house or risk getting left behind," Gary said. "I think Ana at least believes I mean it. So they should be underway now."

"I've had a number of enquiries. Do you want to load the cars bye?"

"Can you take them without danger?" Gary asked.

"I think so. I can swing some empty containers down. We can probably get three cars into a container."

"Well, I think that even if they are not useful as cars, their motors might be useful," Gary said. "If we have empty containers I don't see why not."

"I'll get that organized right away. The natives are getting restless with nothing to do but get nervous," the captain said.

"I have some frozen food to get out of my car. Where do you want me to spot my car?" Gary asked.

"The containers will be coming down over there. Park directly across the dock from there bye."

As Gary made his way toward the gangway a red headed man he did not know approached him. "Mr. Alden? I gathered we were waiting for you. Why are we not getting underway?"

"We have three other families we are waiting on." Gary said shortly.

"Can't we just leave them and let them catch up with us?"

"This is a community," Gary began in revulsion. "We look out after each other at all times. One of the families is the guy who neglected his own family to get you down here on time. Unless something like shooting starts we're not about to leave him under any circumstances. That's why we formed a group, to look out after each other. Absolutely not."

"So you think there will be shooting?"

Operation Phoenix

"In the past month, have you seen gunplay? Anybody that decides we have something they want is likely to try to use guns to get it. Anything is possible. We're preparing for the worst and hoping for the best. Now if you will excuse me," and Gary turned away in disgust.

"It's my right to know when we are going to leave."

The words 'my right,' along with the tension caused Gary to snap. He whirled and began to rant. "Listen you dumb fuck, one of the reasons we are in this mess is that everyone has rights and no one has responsibilities. Here it is different. You have no rights till you earn them by being a good community member. You will automatically get those rights when you earn respect. So far you haven't earned any rights at all. Now get out of my face. I am busy trying to save lives including your sorry ass. You will know when we are leaving as soon as I do. We will cast off the lines."

"Do you know who I am?"

"I neither know nor care. What matters is what kind of a man you are. If you're not that kind of man, now is the time to get off the ship." Gary again turned away and followed by Kirk, made his way down the gangway.

Gary and Kirk parked their cars as directed leaving the keys in, and gathered up the food out of the back. A line was forming at the head of the gangway for car owners to park their cars. The first empty container was coming over the side. A crew was headed down the gangway to tie down the cars in their containers.

Wayne walked Gary and Kirk to the galley with their boxes of food, and directed them to a freezer and a fridge.

Outside, Wayne's radio squawked. "Single car coming in. A blue Chevy with four people in."

"Sounds like the Gibson's," Gary said.

Operation Phoenix

"Right, expected," Wayne said into his radio. To Gary he said, "I have a guard posted over at those administration buildings over there. There's a single road leading to here so he can come up behind any trouble. I also have two machine guns posted on the high points on the ship."

"Sometimes I wonder whether I should worship you or be scared as hell of you," Gary laughed. "You think of everything. Sounds good to me."

Nine Habel trailers pulled in, followed by four McCloud containers, and the families in their vehicles. Gary asked the captain, "We had planned on taking a few tractors and empty trailers if possible for the far end. That container lifter too. Is it possible to lash that equipment on the top of containers?"

"Yes, I suppose so bye."

"Good, lets do it and get the hell out of here. I'm getting antsy," Gary said, leaving for a better view of the loading near the stern. Wayne joined him. Gary said, "We have to discuss destination soon."

"I thought we would do that in Cuba when we get all the ships rendezvoused. Then we can get everyone together at one time."

"Makes sense. I always wanted everyone in the community to have a voice in where we went." Gary said then pointed up. "My god, look at that. A jet contrail. I haven't seen one in nearly a month. They used to be all over the place."

"Looks like a South American flight to Canada. They sure don't have any Av fuel here. Even the air force has none. Somebody's awaiting court martial for selling the entire supply. He got too greedy. He should've left enough to keep the air force flying while he made his get away. That's why I have not been so worried once we get to sea. They're not likely to have enough fuel to send planes after us or they'll have to send them from somewhere else," Wayne said, "and we do have missiles to shoot back with."

"Wow, That's the best news I have heard in ages. Well I guess we'll be underway soon. That's the last tractor going up now. "

Wayne spoke to the captain by radio. "How long till we cast off? I have a guard to bring in."

"About ten minutes. I have steam up, but we still have to get a few things lashed down bye. Bring him in."

Wayne spoke into his radio. "Peter, come on in. We're about to get underway." A minute or so later what was obviously Peter, jogged around the corner carrying a sub-machine gun. As he went up the gangway a crewmember went down and cast off the bowline from the dock.

One of the machine gunners yelled down from his vantage point, "Convoy coming sir. Looks like one army truck and a couple of cars."

Wayne said into his radio, "Looks like trouble. Army convoy coming. Get that stern line cast off and the people below decks."

The convoy rounded the corner and the army truck spewed out soldiers, who spread out, most carrying sub machine guns. The crewmember passing near the gangway decided that he wasn't going to make the stern line in time and shot up the gangway.

An official with a bullhorn yelled, "Gary Alden, you are under arrest. This ship is detained for inspection." The bow of the ship, which had been slightly moving, swung away and the gangway hung on its hooks for a moment before falling into the water. Gary watched in horror as the stern line tightened. He spotted a fire axe and grabbed it. He ran to where the line went over the rail. He swung at the line, making a nice cut, but not severing it. He swung again. Still not severed. He swung a third time, and the taut line lashed as it separated.

He remembered no more.

He awoke to the thrum of engines. Wayne was dozing in a chair next to him. It looked like he was in a hallway, on a stretcher. His chest and left arm felt like they had been run over by a truck. A few feet down, the Gibson's dozed. A lady he did not recognize came up and noticed he was awake. "So, you are back with us are you?" she said in a professional way.

"You have to be Wayne's girlfriend, Mona. What happened?" Gary asked.

She smiled, "And alert too." She shook Wayne's shoulder slightly, and like Patti, he was instantly awake. "Your friend is awake and alert."

"What happened?" Gary repeated.

"That was a fucking good job you did, cutting that line. In any case you got hit by a three bullet burst, one in the solar plexus which is the one that we think knocked you out, one over your left breast and one through the left shoulder. Your vest stopped the first two bullets. We think the third caused only a flesh wound. Mona patched you up, but you'll have to wait until we get to Halifax to see a doctor while we pick up Claude's supplies. You've been out for about three hours,"

Wayne continued. "The SEALs manning the machine guns above us returned fire killing the guy who shot you, and one of his buddies. Suddenly the guys on the ground realized how exposed they were and how little they had to shoot at. So they threw down their arms and surrendered. We just sailed off. We're being followed by our submarine which I had waiting outside the harbour. Eric and everybody knows you are alive. I have to let him know you are awake and lucid."

"How did the authorities know where to go? Where we

would be? I am sure nobody followed us," Gary asked plaintively. "Maybe they followed one of the trucks?"

Wayne drew a deep breath. "I think they followed your cell phone. That assisted GPS we used to find Heidi is not an added feature. It is a part of every cell phone and you simply pay for it to be activated as additional revenue for the phone company. The system was originally conceived as a locator device for the emergency services to locate a cell phone in an emergency. They simply used that to follow you."

"Oh shit, and I gave it to them on a platter. They asked for my business card. It has my number on it."

It was a beautiful day, sunny with few clouds and a light breeze. The seas were quite calm. Now that they had "gotten away", grief for Jan came. He again became conscious of the fact that he was a poor judge of people and their emotions, not only with Jan but he badly misjudged people like the frightened red haired man who merely sought confidence by asking him when they were leaving. His assumed that once facts became known the logical actions to be taken were clear but that did not take into consideration emotions. *Maybe that is why I am such a great head-hunter. I found a way to cut my own thinking and emotions out of the process. I am just a master of technical details and their ramifications.*

His train of thought continued to the successes they had accomplished. Lives saved, and building blocks for the future obtained. Now it remained to set up a functioning community and then to make it work on a continuing basis. *This correcting of imbalances can't be avoided. Millions will die. History does not repeat exactly but by studying what happened in the past, we gained a good insight as to what could happen now. We were damned lucky to find the right analog to compare against. While we cannot avoid the fall, we may now have a parachute that*

Operation Phoenix

gives us a softer landing. Gary brightened, anticipating life's new escapades and smiled. *In any case, the adventure has just begun. There are sure to be many unusual incidents and experiences ahead of us as we learn to cope in this new world. We will have to adapt to weather, disease, whatever comes, or our Phoenix will never arise from the ashes. Life is a continuing adventure, and so far I haven't died from adventure even once.*
END